AN ANSWER FOR EVERY QUESTION

Q: What could I call a bouncy dog who loves everyone?
A: Aquarius is a suitable name with an astrological touch.

Q: What's an unusual name for a Scottish Terrier?
A: Bixby was one of the developers of the American standards for this breed.

Q: What about a name with a color in it?
A: Black Pearl (the name of Jack Sparrow's ship) could be a great name for a black dog.

Q: What's a name from a famous novel?
A: Candy was the sheepdog in Steinbeck's *Of Mice and Men.*

Q: Can I find a name that would make people laugh?
A: Captain Woof was a Muppet dog.

Q: What would be a special name that would show how much I already love my rescue dog?
A: The final line of **Casablanca** is "I think this is the beginning of a beautiful friendship."

Q: How can I express how much my dog means to me?
A: Haruki (which means "shining brightly" in Japanese) would be lovely.

Q: Can I find a name that is pretty much guaranteed to be unique?
A: Hecuba of Trojan legend was punished by the gods by being turned into a dog.

Q: What could I call my Chihuahua other than Tiny?
A: Pixel would be a more original name with a modern twist.

THE GIANT BOOK OF DOG NAMES

THE
GIANT BOOK
OF
D🐾G NAMES

LAURIE BOGART MORROW

G
GALLERY BOOKS

NEW YORK   LONDON   TORONTO   SYDNEY   NEW DELHI

G

Gallery Books
A Division of Simon & Schuster, Inc.
1230 Avenue of the Americas
New York, NY 10020

First Gallery Books trade paperback edition October 2012

GALLERY BOOKS and colophon are registered
trademarks of Simon & Schuster, Inc.

For information about special discounts for bulk purchases,
please contact Simon & Schuster Special Sales at
1-866-506-1949 or business@simonandschuster.com.

The Simon & Schuster Speakers Bureau can bring authors to your live event. For
more information or to book an event contact the Simon & Schuster Speakers
Bureau at 1-866-248-3049 or visit our website at www.simonspeakers.com.

Designed by Ruth Lee-Mui

Manufactured in the United States of America

10 9 8 7 6 5 4 3 2 1

Library of Congress Cataloging-in-Publication Data

Morrow, Laurie.
   The giant book of dog names / Laurie Bogart Morrow.
      p.   cm.
   1. Dogs—Names   I. Title.
SF422.3.M67   2012
636.7—dc23   2012006823

ISBN 978-1-4516-6690-8
ISBN 978-1-4516-6691-5 (ebook)

Dedication

The bell had stopped, and he closed his eyes and looked across the stream. The other side was basked in gold bright sunshine, and he could see the road rising steeply through the clearing in the woods, and the apple tree in a corner of the stone wall. Cider was standing motionless, the white fan of his tail lifted a little, his neck craned forward, one foreleg cocked. The whites of his eyes showed as he looked back, waiting for him.

"Steady," he called, "steady, boy." He started across the bridge. "I'm coming."

—Corey Ford, "The Road to Tinkhamtown" (1965)

For Teal, Frost, Abe, Bess, and Tessie—

Beloved dogs waiting for me, I pray, across the stream

—L. B. M.

CONTENTS

Introduction   XI

PART I
GOOD NAMES FOR DOGS AND THEIR MEANINGS   1

PART II
DOG NAMES BY CATEGORY   425
   COLOR   427
   BREED   429
   LANGUAGE   437
   DESCRIPTIVE WORDS   450
   HISTORY   453
   MYTHS AND LEGENDS   457
   LITERATURE   460
   THE ARTS   467
   HOLLYWOOD   469
   SPORTS   476
   THE NATURAL WORLD   478

Afterword   485

INTRODUCTION:
HOW TO NAME YOUR DOG

No matter how you look it, this is a very sobering thought. The fact that you are reading this book suggests that you are already owned, or plan to be owned, by a dog. Conversely, if you bought this book to give as a gift, it suggests you are in favor of the notion.

This matter settled, let's move on to the next important question: What shall you name your dog? Obviously, that's why you are thumbing through these pages—and precisely why I wrote them. Here you'll find more than 5,000 names to choose from. That's a lot of names, I know—though perhaps not so many when you consider fifty million dogs are owned in the United States alone (and that's not counting strays or shelter dogs). But let me assure you that somewhere in these pages there's a name that's just right for your dog. You need not go through each and every name in Part One, which is an alphabetical listing full of descriptions. Part Two offers names organized in a variety of categories—literature, film, music and art, ancient and modern history, mythology and legend, sports, names by color, by breed, and more. Each was selected with a purpose. And there isn't one I wouldn't name a dog o'mine.

First, I made it my priority to find actual names of dogs living and dead, fictitious and real, and then found names that are purely associated with dogs. A book of people names for dogs was never my intent—though naturally, there are quite a few in these pages. After all, there will always be a dog named Susie, but it's unlikely there will ever be a woman named Fido. After that, I looked to some of my favorite books for inspiration, such as *Gone with the Wind*, *Pride and Prejudice*, *Lord of the Rings*, the works of Charles Dickens, Jane Austen, Rudyard Kipling, and others; then books that were the delight of my childhood, such as *The Wonderful Wizard of Oz* and *Alice's Adventures in Wonderland*. Next I went to the movies and found inspiration in Hitchcock and Spielberg, and in film legends such as Dietrich and Chaplin. Then off I went to the ball field and found Babe (Ruth) and Joe (DiMaggio) and other baseball greats; I followed the Olympics from the first modern games held in 1896 and applauded some gold medalists.

Now, let's discuss the biggest challenge of all: how to teach your dog his name. In the beginning, most dogs believe their name is Kommere, Sitanstay, Nooooo, or Gooddogbaddog. This should come as no surprise to you. Let's say, for example, your dog's name is Spot. Spot runs off. You call out, "Come here, Spot!" The first words Spot hears are "Come here." Since he cannot spell, he quite plainly interprets his name to be "Kommere," or perhaps "Kommerespot." The same can be said when you command him to sit and stay or praise or admonish him with "good dog," "bad dog." Of course, if he doesn't do what you tell him to do—common behavior, by the way, in all puppies—then you may, despite your better judgment, blurt out, "Darn it, Spot!" Don't berate yourself. You have no idea how many puppies believe their name is Darnit.

In closing, here are a few tips to help you choose the right name for your dog:

- Choose a name that suits the physical aspects of your dog. For example, if she is white, name her Snowball. Ebony or Black Beauty will not be nearly as effective.
- If you have a small dog, shy away from names such as Brutus or Zeus, both of which are fitting for a Great Dane. This said, President Franklin Delano Roosevelt had a Great Dane named Tiny. Amusing, but a name that's so at odds with a dog's physical attributes may

result in an inferiority complex. (For you, not the dog. Only a four-term president could get away with it.)

- If you have a sporting dog, such as a Labrador Retriever, or a working dog, such as an Australian Sheepdog, choose a short, sharp name that gets his attention so you can easily call him back. "Rufus of Glencoe King of the Highlands and Lower Dales III" doesn't exactly slip off the tongue and is not conducive to getting your dog's attention as he's running into the next field.

- Select a name that makes you feel good when you say it. Because if it does, it will make your dog feel good to hear it.

Now you are off on your great adventure—and believe me, it *is* a great adventure. Just as much as you are bringing a dog into your life, he is taking you into his. As much attention as you give him, your dog will return tenfold in companionship. As much joy that you give him, he will return tenfold in happiness. As much care that you give him, he will return a hundredfold in devotion. There's only one instance where the rule does not apply, and that is love. For the love of a dog for his master is unconditional and knows no bounds; once the heartstring is tied, it is unbreakable. And no distance, no man, not even Time itself can sever the bond between you.

Go, now, and give your dog his name.

—LAURIE BOGART MORROW
Freedom, New Hampshire

THE GIANT BOOK OF DOG NAMES

Gentlemen of the Jury: The best friend a man has in this world may turn against him and become his enemy. His son or daughter that he has reared with loving care may prove ungrateful. Those who are nearest and dearest to us, those whom we trust with our happiness and our good name, may become traitors to their faith. The money that a man has, he may lose. It flies away from him, perhaps when he needs it the most. A man's reputation may be sacrificed in a moment of ill-considered action. The people who are prone to fall on their knees to do us honor when success is with us may be the first to throw the stone of malice when failure settles its cloud upon our heads. The one absolutely unselfish friend that a man can have in this selfish world, the one that never deserts him and the one that never proves ungrateful or treacherous is his dog.

Gentlemen of the Jury, a man's dog stands by him in prosperity and in poverty, in health and in sickness. He will sleep on the cold ground, where the wintry winds blow and the snow drive fiercely, if only he may be near his master's side. He will kiss the hand that has no food to offer, he will lick the wounds and sores that come in encounters with the roughness of the world. He guards the sleep of his pauper master as if he were a prince. When all other friends desert he remains. When riches take wings and reputation falls to pieces, he is constant to his love as the sun in its journey through the heavens. If fortune drives the master forth an outcast in the world, friendless and homeless, the faithful dog asks no higher privilege than that of accompanying him to guard against danger, to fight his enemies, and when the last scene of all comes, and death takes the master in his embrace and his body is laid away in the cold ground, there by his graveside will the noble dog be found, his head between his paws, his eyes sad but open in alert watchfulness, faithful and true even to death.

—SENATOR GEORGE GRAHAM VEST, 1870

Inscription on a monument to Old Drum, a coonhound, at Warrensburg, Missouri. The dog was killed by a neighbor and the inscription records Vest's statement to the court which considered the offense.

PART I

GOOD NAMES FOR
DOGS AND THEIR MEANINGS

A

AARON Mountain of strength (Hebrew). Good name for a stout and sturdy dog, such as a Mastiff, Great Dane, or Boxer.

ABAYOMI One who brings much joy (Nigerian). A dog that is loved and cared for properly always brings much joy to his master. Good name for your happy puppy.

ABELARD Peter Abelard (1079–1142), important twelfth-century theologian, poet, composer, and, according to medieval lore, Heloise's tragic lover. Romantic names for a male dog and his female mate.

ABELIE Honeysuckle (Italian).

ABERCROMBIE Old Scottish surname, wonderful for a Scottish Deerhound or a Scottish Terrier.

ABERFORTH Younger brother of Albus Dumbledore, headmaster of Hogwarts School of Witchcraft and Wizardry, who doesn't come into the picture until J. K. Rowling's seventh and final book in the Harry Potter series, *Harry Potter and the Deathly Hallows*.

ABETI Like the ears of a dog (Yorùbá). *Abeti-aja* is a triangular hat traditionally worn by the Yorùbá people, a large and ancient ethnic group that predominantly inhabits West Africa.

ABIGAIL Resourceful woman (Hebrew). One of the thirty most popular names for female dogs. Also **Abbie, Abby**.

ABILITY Skillful, capable of doing a job. Good name for a herding or working breed dog, such as a Border Collie, Shetland Sheepdog or Siberian Husky.

ABIOLA One who is born in wealth and honor (African).

ABLE Capable, intelligent, possessing considerable ability.

ABRA Abra of Poitiers (AD 343–360), daughter of Saint Hilary of Poitiers, a French bishop. Born prior to her father's conversion to Catholicism and ordination, Abra, at her father's behest, took the vow of virginity and became a nun. Adored by the people of Poitiers for her good works, she died young, at the age of eighteen. She and Saint Hilary of Poitiers are the only father and daughter to be canonized by the early church. Saint Abra's feast day is celebrated on December 12.

ABRAHAM Father of many (Hebrew). **Abriana** is the feminine form, **Abe** is the diminutive, and **Abram** is an alternative spelling.

ABRUZZI Prince Luigi Amedeo Giuseppe Maria Ferdinando Francescodi Savoia-Aosta (1873–1933), Duke of the Abruzzi, commander in chief of Italy's Adriatic naval fleet throughout most of World War One. An important Arctic explorer and mountaineer, he was elected as an honorary member of the famed Explorers Club in 1912. The Abruzzese Mastiff was named after his dukedom, a region west of Rome on the Adriatic Sea. Wonderful name for any Italian dog breed, such as the Maltese, Italian Greyhound, and Spinone Italiano. *See* Dog Names by Category: History.

ABSALOM Rebellious third son of King David of Israel. "There was not a man so highly praised for his handsome appearance as Absalom" (2 Samuel 14:25). Good name for a handsome puppy with attitude.

ABSO The Tibetan name for the Lhasa Apso is *Abso Seng Kye*, which means "Bark, sentinel lion dog!"

ACACIA "Secret love" in the language of flowers.

ACADIA A colony of New France in the seventeenth and early eighteenth centuries. Spanning northeastern Canada and northern Maine, this vast territory was the battleground of six colonial wars fought between the French, the Wabanaki Confederacy, the British, and American colonists. Henry Wadsworth Longfellow wrote his epic poem *Evangeline, a Tale of Acadie*, after fellow Bowdoin College classmate, Nathaniel Hawthorne, regaled him with stories of Acadia.

ACAPULCO Famous resort and historic seaport on Mexico's Pacific coast. Elvis Presley had *Fun in Acapulco* (1963). Good name for a dog of Mexican origin, such as the Chihuahua or Mexican Hairless.

GERMAN SHEPHERD MOTHER AND HER PUPPY

ACCLAIM *See* Dog Names by Category: Breed; Westminster.

ACE Ace the Bat-Hound, Batman and Robin's canine crime-fighting partner, who first appeared in 1955 in *Batman* comic #92; Ace the Wonder Dog, German Shepherd Dog canine actor and rival of Rin Tin Tin, who appeared in fifteen films between 1938 and 1946, most notably as Rusty in *The Adventures of Rusty*, the first of eight "Rusty" films produced by Columbia Pictures; Ace and Little Man, hunting hounds in the 2002 movie adaptation of *Gentle Ben*, based on the 1965 children's novel by Walt Morey; Ace Hart Private canine detective and star of *Dog City*, a Jim Henson Productions animated TV series. Ace Hart fights crime together with Surelick Bones, Rosie O'Gravy, and Sam Spayed.

ACER Sharp (Latin). Tall, leafy, deciduous tree commonly known as the maple.

ACHERON River that runs through Hades in Greek mythology.

ACHILLES Hero of the Trojan War and strongest of all warriors in Greek mythology. Achilles was killed by a poisonous arrow, which struck the only vulnerable part of his body—his heel.

ADA Ada Byron, Countess of Lovelace (1815–1852), founder of scientific computing, and regarded to be the "world's first computer programmer." She was the only legitimate child of tortured English Romantic poet Lord Byron, who died when she was a child.

ADAM The first mortal man. Fitting name for the firstborn male puppy in a litter.

ADAMO Earth (Italian).

ADAMS John Adams (1735–1826), champion of American independence, second president of the United States, and relentless advocate of the Declaration of Independence. Thomas Jefferson served under Adams as vice president but vanquished Adams's bid for reelection when he won the popular vote in the election of 1800 to become the third president of the United States. The bitter schism between the two former political colleagues healed with old age, when they resumed a fervent correspondence that sustained them intellectually the last fourteen years of their lives. In a profound twist of fate, Jefferson predeceased Adams by five hours on July 4, 1826—the fiftieth anniversary of the signing of the Declaration of Independence. *See Dog Names by Category: History.*

ADDIE ADDIE model, a theoretical parameter applied to achieving a result through Analysis, Design, Development, Implementation, and Evaluation. Adrian "Addie" Joss (1880–1911), legendary Major League Baseball pitcher for the Cleveland Broncos.

ADDISON The dog that was fascinated by the movies of British actor George Sanders in Thomas Pynchon's 2009 novel *Inherent Vice*.

ADE Royal (Nigerian).

ADEBAYO Born in the time of happiness (Nigerian).

ADEBEN The twelfth born (Ghanaian). Good name for the twelfth dog in a litter.

ADEEN Little fire (Nigerian). Good name for an Irish Setter puppy or any dog with a red coat.

ADELAIDE Noble, kind. The popular, German-born, much younger wife of King William IV of England. The royal couple had five children, none of whom survived. The king's niece, a petite and timid girl, assumed the throne upon her uncle's death in 1837. As Queen Victoria, she was destined to rule over "this vast empire on which the sun never sets, and whose bounds nature has not yet ascertained" (George Macartney, 1773), until her death in 1901. She was Great Britain's longest-reigning monarch thus far.

ADELE William the Conqueror's youngest daughter; Rosalinde's maid in the endlessly popular operetta *Die Fledermaus* by Johann Strauss II, which was first performed in 1874 in Vienna.

ADELINA Little noble (Italian).

ADIRA Strong, noble, powerful (Hebrew).

ADJUTANT Long-lived Labrador Retriever who died at the age of twenty-seven; an officer who serves a senior officer.

ADMIRAL United States naval commander Admiral Frederick Sherman risked his life to rescue his black Cocker Spaniel, Admiral Wags, who was with him when the Japanese attacked and sank the aircraft carrier USS *Lexington* in World War Two during the Battle of the Coral Sea.

ADOBE Ancient Arabic word for a hut or building made of sun-dried earthen bricks. Good name for a dog with a yellowish brown coat.

ADOLFO Noble wolf (Italian). A name befitting a regal dog, such as an Irish Wolfhound or a Borzoi (also known as a Russian Wolfhound).

ADONA Good (Italian). From the Biblical name **Adonijah**, which means "my lord is God."

ADONIS Handsome youth beloved by Aphrodite in Greek mythology.

ADRIAN Six popes bore this name, including Pope Adrian IV of England and Pope Adrian VI of Holland, the only English and Dutch popes in the history of the Roman Catholic Church. **Adriana** is the feminine form and the nickname is **Ade**.

AEGEAN Arm of the Mediterranean Sea delineated by the coastlines of Greece and Turkey.

AELIAN *See* Claudius.

AESIR Collective name for the principal race of gods in Norse mythology.

AESOP (620–564 BC) Ancient Greek writer of hundreds of fables such as "The Tortoise and the Hare" and "The Wolf in Sheep's Clothing."

AFFINITY Empathy, attraction, closeness.

AFFONSO Noble and ready (Italian).

AFRICA World's second largest, second most populated continent. Good name for a Basenji.

AGAPETO Beloved (Italian).

AGARIC Large-capped fungus.

AGATHA Impeccable virtue (Greek). Agatha Christie (1890–1976), English crime novelist and the best-selling author of all time, whose most beloved characters, Miss Marple and Hercule Poirot, individually solved some of her greatest mysteries—but not her greatest. In 1926, Christie disappeared for eleven days after discovering her husband was romantically involved with another woman.

AGED P Affectionate name that John Wemmick calls his deaf, dotty, "aged parent," the cheerful old father in Charles Dickens's classic novel *Great Expectations*. What better name for an older dog?

AGENT 11 Crime-fighting Bull Mastiff in the comedy film *See Spot Run*, starring David Arquette.

AGILAZ Legendary archer in Germanic mythology.

AGNES Holy, pure, chaste (Greek). Third most popular name in the English-speaking world for four hundred years, up until the twentieth century.

AGNI God of fire in Hindu mythology.

AGOSTINA Venerable (Italian). **Agostino** is the men's version.

AH CUM Ah Cum, Boxer, and Mimosa were Pekingese dogs celebrated as "pillars of the Stud Book" in Victorian England.

AI Love (Japanese).

AIBE A twelfth-century Irish manuscript tells of a noble Irish Wolf-hound named Aibe, owned by Mesrodia, King of Leinsternien and coveted by the King of Ulster and the King of Connacht. Each offered six thousand cows for the wondrous beast. Alas, the fate of the dog or, for that matter, the kings and cows was never revealed.

AIDA Visitor (Arabic). Grand opera by Italian composer Giuseppe Verdi set in ancient Egypt. This lavish production has been a mainstay of opera houses around the world since 1871 and usually includes at least one camel in the cast.

AIKIDO Japanese martial art.

AIKO Little loved one (Japanese). Sweet name for an Akita or Japanese Spitz puppy.

AILEEN Scottish form of Eileen. Lovely name for a female Scottish Terrier.

AILSA Ailsa Craig, an island off the west coast of Scotland.

AIM Point, target. Smart name for a sporting breed dog trained to hunt wild game birds.

AIMEE Beloved (Old French). Adorable name for a Papillon, Bichon Frise, French Bulldog, or Havanese.

AINSLEY *See* Phoebe.

AIRBORNE Flying, carried by the wind. A wonderful name for a Greyhound, the fastest breed in the world and one of the oldest.

AJANI He who wins the struggle (African).

AJAX Warrior-hero of the Trojan War, second only to Achilles in courage and strength, described by Homer in *The Iliad* as the tallest and strongest of all the Achaeans.

AKABA *See* Jebel.

AKAIKA Powerful (Hawaiian).

AKAMA Smart (Hawaiian).

AKELA Single, solitary (Hindi). Akela was the cunning leader of the Seeonee pack of wolves in Rudyard Kipling's *The Jungle Book*.

AKINORI Akinori Iwamura, Japanese Major League infielder formerly with the Tampa Bay Rays and currently playing with the Rakutan Golden Eagles of the Japanese Pacific League.

AKIO Intelligent boy (Japanese). Great name for a Japanese Chin.

AL Al Capone (1899–1947), Italian American bootlegger, gangster, and murderer whose Chicago-based crime syndicate was finally crushed when Capone was convicted on federal charges of tax evasion. Diminutive of **Albert**, **Alphonse**, **Alfred**, and **Alan**.

ALADÁR Aladár Gerevich of Hungary won ten Olympic medals in fencing between 1932 and 1960.

ALADDIN Nobility of faith (Arabic). Hero in the Middle Eastern folktale *The Arabian Nights: Tales from a Thousand and One Nights.*

ALAN Fox, deer or other animal with reddish-brown fur (Brittonic).

ALANS *See* Alaunt.

ALANI Orange (Hawaiian).

ALANO Handsome, noble. The Alano Español is a Spanish breed of Mastiff.

ALARIC Noble ruler. Alaric I, King of the Visigoths from AD 395 to 410, was the first Germanic leader to conquer the city of Rome.

ALASHAK Vast country (Russian). Early name for Alaska and a terrific name for an Alaskan Malamute.

ALASTAIR Scottish version of Alexander.

ALASTOR Alastor "Mad-Eye" Moody, one of the leaders of the Order of the Phoenix and Defense Against the Dark Arts professor at the Hogwarts School of Witchcraft and Wizardry in the Harry Potter series.

ALAUNT In 1400, Chaucer wrote about an extinct breed of dog known as the Alaunt: "About his char ther wenten white alauns, Twenty and mo, as gret as any stere, to hunten at the leon or the dere." The modern Caucasian Shepherd Dog and the Mastiff are believed to resemble the Alaunt, a working dog known to have originated with a fourth-century tribe of warriors and horsemen called the Alans.

ALBANIA Ancient, historically rich country in southeastern Europe.

ALBEMARLE George Monck, First Duke of Albemarle (1608–1670), English soldier, and Royalist who played a decisive role in restoring King Charles II to the British throne after the death of Cromwell.

ALBERT Albert Einstein (1879–1955), German-born American physicist who developed the theory of general relativity. "The father of modern physics" was awarded the 1921 Nobel Prize in Physics.

ALBERTA Intelligent, well-known, upright (Germanic, Italian). **Alberto** is the male version.

ALBINA Soviet space dog. *See* Dog Names by Category: History.

ALBRECHT Albrecht Dürer (1471–1528), German painter, printmaker, mathematician, and theorist. Appropriate name for a Dachshund, German Shepherd Dog, or other breed of German origin.

ALBUS Albus Percival Wulfric Brian Dumbledore (1881–1997), daunting headmaster of the Hogwarts School of Witchcraft and Wizardry in the Harry Potter series.

ALCHEMY Medieval protoscience that attempted to change iron and other base metals into gold.

ALDA Noble (Italian).

ALDEN Old friend (Old English). Delightful name for the dog you hope you'll grow old with.

ALDO Wise one (Italian).

ALDRICH Old (Gaelic). Terrific name for an Old English Sheepdog.

ALDROVANUS Ulisse Aldrovandi, aka Aldrovanus (1522–1605), an Italian naturalist who wrote about a Maltese that sold for a sum of money equivalent to five figures today.

ALDYS Battle-seasoned (Old English).

ALEC Alec Baldwin (b. 1958), Long Island–born, award-winning American film, stage, and television actor. Good name for a personable dog like a Labrador Retriever.

ALEJANDRO Alexander (Spanish).

ALEMANA Warrior (Hawaiian).

ALEN Scandinavian unit of measure for distance. Good name for a Norwegian Elkhound.

ALEXANDER Alexander the Great (356–323 BC), King of Macedonia who, by the age of thirty, had amassed one of the greatest empires in ancient history. **Alexandra** is the feminine form. Queen Alexandra of England owned Samoyeds.

ALEXEI Alexei Nemov of Russia won twelve medals in gymnastics during the 1996 and 2000 Olympic Games.

ALEXIS Greek comic poet (394–275 BC).

ALFALFA A forage crop used to feed cattle and horses.

ALFIE British film from 1966 starring Michael Caine as a cocky young Englishman. Great name for an English Cocker Spaniel.

ALFONSE Ready for battle (German, French).

ALFRED Magical counsel, elf (Gaelic). Alfred, Lord Tennyson (1809–1892), poet laureate of Great Britain during the reign of Queen Victoria. His 1854 popular narrative poem "The Charge of the Light Brigade" immortalized the British cavalry's charge against the Russians in the Crimean War at the Battle of Balaclava.

ALFREDO Italian version of Alfred. Popular Italian pasta dish created by Chef Alfredo di Lelio and named for his famous Rome restaurant, Alfredo alla Scrofa. Delicious name for an Italian Greyhound.

ALGEBRA Mathematics using letters and symbols instead of numbers.

ALGERNON With mustaches (Norman French). Perfect name for a Scottish Terrier or Wirehaired Pointing Griffon.

ALHAJA Jewel, treasure, precious object (Spanish).

ALI High, exalted (Arabic).

ALICE Heroine of *Alice's Adventures in Wonderland*, written in 1865 by English author Charles Lutwidge Dodgson, known to the world as Lewis Carroll. Alice has followed the White Rabbit down the rabbit hole to otherworldly places populated by anthropomorphic creatures in over a dozen film adaptations and countless live theater performances.

ALIDA Small, winged creature (Latin).

ALIDUKE Sir Aliduke, a noble knight of King Arthur's legendary Round Table.

ALIIKAI Queen of the sea (Hawaiian).

ALIKI Noble (Hawaiian).

ALISANDE *See* Yankee.

ALLAIRE Old Breton surname, perfect for a Griffon Fauve de Bretagne puppy.

ALLEGRA Cheerful, lively (Spanish, Italian). **Allegro** is the male version.

ALLEN Precious (Gaelic).

ALLESANDRA Defender of mankind (Italian).

ALLISON Grand, dignified (French).

ALLISTER All Scottish Terriers are descended from English Ch. Allister, who was whelped in 1885.

ALMIRA Almira Gulch, aka the Wicked Witch of the West in *The Wizard of Oz*, was played in the classic 1939 film adaptation by American character actress Margaret Hamilton. Miss Hamilton was severely burned when a trap door failed to open as she disappeared from Munchkinland in a cloud of green smoke. She spent six weeks recuperating before she was able to return to the set.

ALMONDINE The dog that belongs to Edgar, the mute boy in David Wroblewski's novel *The Story of Edgar Sawtelle* (2008).

ALNWICK *See* Phoebe.

ALOYSIUS Famous warrior (Latin).

ALPHA Dominant, chief, important; the dominant dog in a litter.

ALPHONSE Alphonse Mucha (1860–1939), Czech painter of the Art Nouveau style.

ALPIN *Cindeda meic Ailpín* was a Scottish clan from the ninth century. Beautiful name for a Golden Retriever or Rough Collie, hearty breeds that hail from Scotland.

ALPINE High, pine-covered mountains carpeted with wildflowers in the spring and summer.

ALRUNA Wife of the great archer Agilaz in Germanic mythology.

ALSGAARD Thomas Alsgaard of Norway won six Olympic medals for cross-country skiing in games held between 1994 and 2002.

ALVIN Friend (Old English). Good name for a devoted dog.

ALYESKA Great land (Eskimo-Aleut). Fitting name for an Alaskan Malamute.

AMABLE Kind, amiable (Spanish).

AMALA Hope (Arabic).

AMANDA Lovable, deserving of love (Latin).

AMARANTH Unfading flower (Greek). A genus of approximately sixty species of herbs.

AMARETTO Sweet, almond-flavored Italian liqueur. Great name for a dog with a dark golden coat.

AMARI Endowed with great strength (Swahili).

AMARYLLIS "Full of pride" in the language of flowers.

AMATO Beloved (Italian).

AMAYA Night rain (Japanese).

AMAZON Legendary nation of female warriors in Greek mythology.

AMBASSADOR Highest-ranking diplomat to represent his country to a foreign land.

AMBER Fossilized tree resin of a deep golden color. Consider this name for a Golden Retriever puppy.

AMBRIEL Angel associated with the Gemini, the sun sign of the zodiac. Wonderful name if your puppy was born in May.

AMBROSE Immortal (Greek).

AMBROSIA Food of the gods in Greek mythology.

AMEDEA Love of god (Italian).

AMES Friend (French). How about this name for a French breed, such as a Löwchen or Brittany?

AMETHYST Ancient Greeks believed that amethyst, a variety of purple quartz, when worn as jewelry will protect the wearer from drunkenness.

AMIABLE Cordial, congenial.

AMIGA Girlfriend (Spanish).

AMIGO Boyfriend (Spanish).

AMĪR Commander, general, prince (Arabic).

AMIRA Princess (Arabic).

AMOKA Strong (Hawaiian).

AMORE Love (Italian).

AMOS Born of God (Hebrew).

AMTEN The earliest known depiction of the Greyhound was four thousand years ago in the tomb of Egyptian pharaoh Amten in the Valley of the Kings.

ANACLETO To invoke (Italian).

ANAIS Favored, grace (Hebrew).

ANASTASIA Resurrection (Greek). On July 17, 1918, Tsar Nicholas II of Russia, his wife, Alexandra, and their five children were executed by a Bolshevik firing squad. The Tsar's youngest daughter, Anastasia, was rumored to have escaped, but this was finally disproved in 2008 by a team of forensic scientists.

ANATOLIA *See* Sahara.

ANATOLIO Sun rising in the east (Italian).

ANDALUSIA Autonomous community in the southern Iberian Peninsula where the Spanish Alano, a relative of the Boxer, originated.

ANDERSON Warrior, son of Anders (Scandinavian). Dame Judith Anderson (1897–1992), Australian-born actress best known for her role as Mrs. Danvers in Alfred Hitchcock's psychological suspense film *Rebecca*, which won the Oscar for Best Picture in 1940.

ANDRÉ Major John André (1750–1780), dashing British adjutant-general and head of intelligence under General William Howe, commander-in-chief of the British forces during the American Revolutionary War. He was captured near West Point, New York, after facilitating the defection of American turncoat Benedict Arnold to the enemy camp. Tried and found guilty, André was hanged by order of General George Washington, purportedly as reparation for the hanging of American spy Nathan Hale by the British at the beginning of the Revolution.

ANDREA Warrior (Italian).

ANDREAS Manly, masculine (Welsh).

ANDRETTI Mario Andretti (b. 1940), Italian American world racing car champion.

ANDREW Warrior (Greek). Saint Andrew is the patron saint of Scotland. The Banks family's dog in the 1964 Walt Disney film *Mary Poppins*, based on the P. L. Travers books about a magical London nanny who teaches the parents—not the children—the priceless lesson that money can't buy happiness.

ANDROMEDA Princess in Greek mythology who is rescued by Perseus after the gods chained her naked to a rock as a sacrifice to a sea monster.

ANDY Faithful Saint Bernard in *Mark Trail*, a popular syndicated comic strip created by cartoonist Ed Dodd in 1946. Andy was finally neutered in 2000.

ANEKO Older sister (Japanese).

ANELA Hawaiian version of Angela.

ANEMONE "Undiminished love" in the language of flowers.

ANEUENUE Rainbow (Hawaiian).

ANGEL Messengers of God in the Bible, the Tanakh, and the Quran. Derived from the Greek word *aggelos*.

ANGUS One choice (Celtic). A breed of cattle native to Aberdeenshire, Scotland.

ANIMAL Drummer in the Muppets' rock band, Dr. Teeth and the Electric Mayhem.

ANISE *Pimpinella anisum*, a flowering plant.

ANJING Dog (Malay).

ANNA She who God has favored (Hebrew).

ANNABELLE Whippet in the 1989 animated film *All Dogs Go to Heaven*.

ANNALISA Favor, grace (Italian).

ANNIE Among the thirty most popular names for a female dog.

ANNUNZIATA To announce (Italian).

ANORAK Parka or warm waterproof coat. Swell name for an Alaskan Malamute or a Siberian Husky.

ANSCOMBE Gertrude Elizabeth Margaret Anscombe (1919–2001), British analytic philosopher.

ANSELMO Divine helmet (Italian).

ANSWER Response, reply.

ANTHEM Chorale, song of praise.

ANTIS Alsatian war dog that served in the French Air in North Africa during World War Two. Antis was awarded the Dickin Medal in 1949.

ANTONIA Invaluable, precious, irreplaceable (Italian).

ANTONY Mark Antony (83–30 BC), Roman general under Julius Caesar and tempestuous lover of Cleopatra after Caesar's death. Also **Antoine** (French), **Antonio** (Italian), **Anton** (Russian), **Anthony** (English), and as a nickname, **Tony**.

ANUBIS Ancient Egyptian god represented in art with a man's body and a dog's head.

ANYA Russian variation of Anna.

APACHE Southwest nation of Native Americans.

APALA Apple (Hawaiian).

APHRODITE Daughter of Zeus and goddess of love, lust, and beauty in Greek mythology.

APOGEE Apex, summit, peak.

APOLDA City in Thuringen, Germany where the Doberman Pinscher was first recognized as a breed in 1890.

APOLLO Greek God of music, medicine, health, fitness, light, and truth. Apollo 13, seventh manned mission in the Apollo space program, crewed by American astronauts Jim Lovell, Jack Swigert, and Fred Haise. The command module suffered extensive damage after an oxygen tank explosion on the outbound leg of the mission. Although the mission failed to meet its goals, its success must be measured by the courage and combined efforts of the astronauts and Mission Control to get the men back home safely. This was surely NASA's finest hour. Apollo and Zeus, pair of Doberman Pinschers on the popular television series *Magnum, P.I.* (1980–1988), starring Tom Selleck as private investigator Thomas Magnum.

APPLE Sweet, firm, round fruit that turned things rotten for Adam and Eve.

APPOLLO (1992–2006), German Shepherd Dog in the K-9 unit of the New York Police Department. Appollo and 350 other SAR (search and rescue) dogs braved fire and falling debris to locate victims of the September 11 terrorist attacks on the World Trade Center. Appollo was awarded the coveted Dickin Medal for courage.

APRICOT Sweet fruit with a fuzzy, golden-orange skin. Delightful name for a Basenji or other dog with an apricot-colored coat.

APRIL Fourth month of the year in the Gregorian calendar. Pretty name for a puppy born in April.

AQUARIUS Individuals born under the eleventh sign of the zodiac have an extroverted, positive character. Is your dog an Aquarius?

ARABELLA Prayerful (Latin). Arabella Churchill (1648–1730), royal mistress of King James II of England and mother of four of his children; Arabella Allen eventually marries Mr. Winkle in Charles Dickens's humorous novel *Pickwick Papers*.

ARABESQUE Pattern of interlacing scrolls and foliage in Islam art; Stanley Donen's 1966 suspense thriller starring Gregory Peck and Sophia Loren.

ARAGORN Called Strider by the hobbits in J. R. R. Tolkien's legendarium. In the end, when the great battle is finally won, he is crowned King Elessar Telcontar.

ARAPAHO Native American tribe that populated the eastern plains of Colorado and Wyoming.

ARBUTUS "Devoted love" in the language of flowers.

ARCHER Bowman (Old English). Robin Hood was a legendary archer.

ARCHÈRE Bowman (French). Good name for dog of French origin, such as a Dogue de Bordeaux or a Brittany.

ARCHIBALD Brave, courageous, valiant (French). Archibald Dunan and his brother Lord Colonsay successfully restored the Scottish Deerhound to its original standard in 1825.

ARCHIE Stray Welsh Terrier played by canine actor Corky in the film *Behave Yourself*, starring Shelley Winters and Farley Granger.

ARCHIMEDES (287–212 BC), Greek scientist, mathematician, inventor, and astronomer.

AREND Eagle (Dutch).

ARES Most violent god in Greek mythology. Son of Zeus and lover of Aphrodite, he represents war.

ARETHA Aretha Franklin (b. 1942), "the Queen of Soul." The first female recording artist to be inducted into the Rock and Roll Hall of Fame, she began her recording career in 1960 at the age of eighteen. However, it was her 1967 recording of the ballad "I Never Loved a Man (the Way I Love You)" that catapulted her to fame.

ARFARA A village in southern Greece.

ARGENT White or silver on a family coat of arms. Good name for a dog with a white coat.

ARGOS Dog that belonged to Odysseus, the legendary Greek King of Ithaca, whose eventful journey home after fighting the Trojan War inspired Homer's epic poems, the *Iliad* and the *Odyssey*.

ARGUS Springer Spaniel belonging to the Worthington family in the 2008 film *Familiar Strangers*.

ARGYLE The West Highland Terrier originates from Argyllshire, Scotland.

ARI Lion, eagle (Greek). Nickname for **Aristides**, **Aristotle**, and **Arius**.

ARIANNA Unblemished, pure (Italian).

ARIEL Shakespeare's mischievous spirit who serves Prospero in *The Tempest*.

ARIES First sign of the zodiac. Good name for a puppy with a positive, dynamic disposition.

ARISTIDES Just, fair (Greek).

ARISTOCRAT Grand, noble, lordly.

ARISTOTLE (384–322 BC), Greek philosopher and teacher of Alexander the Great.

ARIUS Immortal (Greek).

ARIZONA Admitted in 1912 as the forty-eighth and last state in the contiguous United States.

ARLENE Vow, promise (Gaelic).

ARLETTE Mistress of Robert, Duke of Normandy, whose son she bore became William the Conqueror.

ARLO Charles (Italian); beloved Irish Setter of the late American humorist Erma Bombeck, who satirized the plight of the suburban housewife in fifteen best-selling books and 4,000 newspaper columns. About dogs she wrote, "When you leave them in the morning, they stick their nose in the door crack and stand there like a portrait until you turn the key eight hours later."

ARMANDO Soldier (Italian).

ARMANI Famous Italian couture fashion house founded in 1976 by the late Giorgio Armani.

ARMSTRONG Scottish clan established in 1237 in the border country between Scotland and England.

ARNOLD Eagle, powerful (German).

ARRIAN (AD 86–160) Roman historian, philosopher and military commander who mentions a dog similar to the Irish Wolfhound in his account of the sacking of Delphi.

ARROW Oblio's dog in American singer-songwriter Harry Nilsson's allegorical musical *The Point!* Micky Dolenz, drummer in the wildly popular 1960s TV sitcom *The Monkees*, played the part of Oblio in a London stage production in 1977, which also featured his former band member and longtime friend, the late Davy Jones.

ARTEMIS Twin sister of Apollo and the goddess of hunting. Artemis is represented by a bow, dogs and a deer. Good name for a sporting dog.

ARTEN *See* Balderoff.

ARTFUL DODGER Street name of Jack Dawkins, the leader of Fagin's band of pickpockets in Charles Dickens's classic novel *Oliver Twist*.

ARTHUR Known as Arthur Pendragon before he pulled the sword from the stone and was proclaimed King of Britain. He defended his people against Saxon invaders in the fifth century—and the feats of King Arthur and the Knights of the Round Table thereafter became legend.

ARUBA Island of the Lesser Antilles in the southern Caribbean.

ARUM "Intense love" in the language of flowers.

ARWEN Arwen Undómiel, a Half-elven who lived during the Third Age in *The Lord of the Rings* by J. R. R. Tolkien. At the age of twenty-seven hundred years, she married twenty-year-old King Aragorn, thus giving hope to older women the world over.

ASCOT Eastern cottage (Anglo-Saxon). Style of men's neckwear. Thoroughbred racecourse in Berkshire, England. The Royal Meeting, attended every June by Queen Elizabeth and the Royal Family, is the centerpiece of the British summer social calendar. Here Eliza Doolittle fictitiously encouraged the racehorse she'd bet on to win when, to the horror of the assembled aristocrats, she shrieked, "Move yer bloomin' arse!"

ASERA Lucky (Hawaiian).

ASGARD Dwelling place of the Aesirin gods of Norse legend. Superb name for a Norwegian Elkhound.

ASH Spear (Old English). Species of tree. A shade of grey. Perfect name for a Weimaraner, whose nickname is "the grey ghost" because of the color of his coat.

ASHLEY Meadow (Old English). Whippet acknowledged as the first Frisbee dog and three-time winner of the Canine Frisbee Disc World Championship in the seventies.

ASHTON Ash tree town (Old English).

ASIA Sunrise (Greek). Earth's largest and most populated continent.

ASIMA Protector (Arabic).

ÁSLEIKR Old Norse name from which the Hebrew name Abshalom, was derived.

ASO Dog (Filipino).

ASPEN Deciduous tree native to northern regions. Come fall, its leaves turn a shimmering gold.

ASQUITH Herbert Henry Asquith, First Earl of Oxford and Asquith (1852–1928), Liberal Prime Minister of England from 1908 to 1916 and longest continuously serving prime minister in the twentieth century until Margaret Thatcher, "the Iron Lady," who held Great Britain's highest office from 1979 to 1990.

ASTA *See* Skippy.

ASTAIRE Fred Astaire (1899–1987), American dancer, choreographer, actor, singer, and film legend. Gene Kelly said of his friend and sometime dance partner, "The history of dance on film begins with Astaire." The great twentieth-century humorist Robert Benchley wrote, "I don't think that I will plunge the nation into war by stating that Fred is the greatest tap-dancer in the world." And yet the man who ranks fifth on the American Film Institute's 100 Greatest Movie Stars of All Time received this criticism on his first screen test for RKO Radio Pictures: "Can't sing. Can't act. Balding. Can dance a little." Can't sing? Astaire recorded more hit songs in the thirties than any other singer, including his *Holiday Inn* co-star, Bing Crosby. His film partnership with Ginger Rogers is the stuff of which Hollywood legends are made. This modest, gifted gentleman died of pneumonia at the age of eighty-eight. His last request was to thank his fans for their years of support. Astaire will continue to enthrall new audiences whenever and wherever his films are shown.

ASTER "Love and delicacy" in the language of flowers.

ASTRO Star, heavenly body. Silly, gibberish-talking Great Dane in the 1962 Hanna-Barbera animated children's television series *The Jetsons*.

ATHENA Daughter of Zeus and sister of Ares, Athena is the Greek goddess of war.

ATHERTON Town by the spring (Old English).

ATLANTIS Mentioned first by Plato in 360 BC, when the legendary island sank into the sea "in a single day and night of misfortune."

ATLAS A collection of maps. In Greek mythology, Atlas was tricked by Heracles and forced to carry the heavens upon his shoulders.

ATOM Smallest part of an element. Clever name for a dog in the toy group, such as a Miniature Poodle.

ATTICUS Ancient Roman philosopher; Archbishop of Constantinople and Christian martyr. Atticus Finch, fair-minded Alabama lawyer in Harper Lee's Pulitzer Prize–winning novel *To Kill a Mockingbird*. It is the only book Lee has ever published.

ATTILA Attila the Hun, warring ruler of the Hunnic Empire from AD 434–453, who mercilessly plundered, murdered, and conquered a vast swath of Europe, the Roman Empire, and Constantinople.

AUBREY Magical being, power (Old German). Sir C. Aubrey Smith (1863–1948), aristocratic English actor whose gentlemanly demeanor added class to such films as *Little Lord Fauntleroy*, *The Prisoner of Zenda*, *Kidnapped*, *And Then There Were None*, *The Four Feathers*, and notably, in the 1940 Hitchcock thriller *Rebecca* as Colonel Julyan. An avid cricketer, "Round the Corner" Smith bowled for Cambridge University from 1882 to 1885. In 1932 he founded the Hollywood Cricket Club, whose members included fellow actors David Niven, Boris Karloff, Leslie Howard, Laurence Olivier, and Nigel Bruce. His mustache, chiseled features and military deportment were recognized by filmgoers the world over, and yet there is a marvelous story that took place years after Smith's cricket days were behind him: Two men were watching a cricket game at Lord's Cricket Ground in London when one thought he recognized the actor seated at the Pavilion. "That man over there seems familiar," he said. His companion glanced over and replied, "Chap called Smith. Used to play for Sussex."

AUBURN Fitting name for a Welsh or English Springer Spaniel with auburn markings.

AUDACITY *See* Dog Names by Category: Breed; Hounds.

AUDLEY A village in Staffordshire, England.

AUGOT Augot Clariette, early Wirehaired Pointing Griffon out of Mouche, the breed's foundation bitch. *See* Mouche.

AUGUST Eighth month in the year in the Julian and Gregorian calendars.

AUGUSTINE Saint Augustine of Hippo (AD 354–430), theologian whose writings were influential in the development of Western Christianity.

AUGUSTUS (63 BC–AD 14), first emperor of the Roman Empire.

AULD "The immortal six" Dandie Dinmont Terriers that established the breed. Raised by farmer James Davidson, they were Auld Mustard, Young Mustard, Little Mustard, Auld Pepper, Young Pepper, and Little Pepper; Ch. Hobergays Fineus Fogg, a Dandie Dinmont Terrier affectionately known as Harry, took first place in the Terrier Group at the 2007 Westminster Kennel Club Show. He was co-owned by Dr. William H. Cosby, Jr., popularly known as Bill Cosby.

AUNTIE EM Dorothy's aunt, wife of Uncle Henry, a hardworking hardscrabble Kansas farmer in *The Wonderful Wizard of Oz* (1900) by American author L. Frank Baum.

AURA A subtle, distinctive quality emanating from an individual, sometimes perceived as a golden glow.

AURELIUS *See* Quintus.

AURORA Roman goddess of the dawn.

AUSSIE Mutt with an Australian accent in the heartwarming 2009 family film *Aussie and Ted's Great Adventure*.

AUSTEN Jane Austen (1775–1817), English novelist among whose timeless classics include *Pride and Prejudice*, *Sense and Sensibility*, and *Emma*, source of inspiration for innumerable film adaptations, and a modern cult movement of hopeless romantics. Her formula? Take one high-spirited, well-bred, marriageable young woman upon whom age is fast encroaching, throw her feverishly into a physically repressed relationship with a handsome, marginally arrogant aristocrat, and wait patiently while they blissfully

AUSTRALIAN SHEPHERD PUPPY

succumb to marriage. Sadly, Jane's real-life story had a tragic ending. She died a spinster at the age of forty-one and is buried in Winchester Cathedral.

AUSTIN State capital of Texas.

AUTOBAHN Germany's nationally coordinated motorway system on which cars are driven incredibly fast-and-furious. The construction of the first segment of the autobahn, a fourteen-mile expressway connecting Frankfurt and Darmstadt, was ordered by Adolf Hitler in 1933 when he became chancellor of the Third Reich. By the end of 1941, 2,400 miles had been constructed and an additional 1,550 miles were under way. Hitler wanted a small, efficient "people's car" made available to the masses to drive on his motorway and ordered Austrian-

German automotive engineer Dr. Ferdinand Porsche to build such a car. It was named the Volkswagen.

AUTUMN The season of the year that begins with the September equinox and ends with the December solstice. This is a beautiful name for a Springer or Field Cocker Spaniel, English or Irish Setter, Brittany, or other upland dog.

AVA From the Latin *avis*, meaning "bird." Ava Gardner (1922–1990), American actress and one of the most beautiful women in the world. Her films include *The Snows of Kilimanjaro*, *The Barefoot Contessa*, and *The Night of the Iguana*. But it was her superb portrayal of Julie La-Verne in the 1951 Kern and Hammerstein musical *Showboat*, based on the Edna Ferber novel that is arguably her most memorable. Among Gardner's many husbands were Mickey Rooney, bandleader Artie Shaw, and Frank Sinatra, with whom she remained emotionally tied until her final release at the age of sixty-seven from a long, grueling illness.

AVALANCHE The sudden falling of a large mass of snow and ice.

AVALON From the Welsh *afal* for "apple." According to Arthurian legend, King Arthur's sword Excalibur was forged on the isle of Avalon— and there Arthur died after sustaining fatal wounds at the Battle of Camlann.

AVANTI Ancient Aryan kingdom that flourished in India from 600 to 400 BC.

AVENGER Servant boy that Pip hires to give him the air of a gentleman in *Great Expectations* by Charles Dickens.

AVERILL Ferocious fighter (Old English).

AVERY Elf (Old English).

AVON Stratford-upon-Avon, market town in Warwickshire, England, and birthplace of William Shakespeare.

AXEL Father of peace (Hebrew).

AYAME Iris (Japanese).

AYO Happiness (Nigerian).

AZALEA "Passion" in the language of flowers.

AZIBO Youth (Nigerian).

AZIZI Precious (Egyptian). Regal name for a Saluki, the royal dog of Egypt.

AZOR Italian Greyhound belonging to Prussian-born General Friedrich Wilhelm von Steuben (1730–1794). Von Steuben was the architect of the United States military drill manual, which transformed General George Washington's Continental Army from a motley band into the effective fighting machine that won the American Revolutionary War.

AZTEC People of the Empire of Tenochtitlan and original breeders of the Mexican Hairless.

AZURA Clear blue sky (Spanish).

B

B. B. Riley B. "B. B." King (b. 1925), legendary Mississippi-born blues guitarist, singer, and songwriter who influenced Jimi Hendrix, John Mayer, and Eric Clapton, with whom he made the album, *Riding with the King*. While on tour in 2006, he was asked if this would be his farewell tour. King replied, "One of my favorite actors is a man from Scotland, Sean Connery. Most of you know him as James Bond, Agent 007. He made a movie called *Never Say Never Again*." Long live the King. Great name for a dog who rocks.

B. DAWG Golden Retriever in the 2009 film *Snow Buddies*.

BABA Old woman (Polish).

Babe George Herman Ruth Jr. (1895–1948), aka "the Bambino" and "the Sultan of Swat." American Major League baseball player from 1914 to 1935, who began his professional career as a starting pitcher for the Boston Red Sox, then as a right fielder for the New York Yankees. He led the Yankees to win seven pennants and four World Series titles and retired after a short stint with the Boston Braves. Babe Ruth was one of the first five players elected to the Baseball Hall of Fame.

Babette Foreign (French).

Babs Affectionate name for Barbara.

Baby Infant or newborn.

Baby Cinnamon Canine friend of *Hello Kitty*.

Baby Doll Doll made to resembles a baby; term of endearment.

Baby Face Nelson Canine criminal who, along with five other Doberman Pinchers, attempts a bank heist in the 1972 film *The Doberman Gang*.

Babycakes A Pomeranian that stirs things up with Hollywood's trouble-prone Saint Bernard, Beethoven, in the family film *Beethoven's 5th*.

Baccarat Game of cards where the player bets against the bank.

Bacchus Roman name for the good-time, jubilant semidivine god of wine in Greek mythology.

Bach Johann Sebastian Bach (1685–1750), masterful German composer whose work defines the Baroque period.

Bachelor A man who is unmarried. The parson's helpful friend in Charles Dickens's *The Old Curiosity Shop*.

Bachelorette Young woman who has yet to marry but would sure like to.

BACI Kisses (Italian). Daughter of Petals, American actress Sigourney Weaver's Italian Greyhound.

BACKSLASH Oblique stroke used in computer operating systems.

BACON Francis Bacon (1561–1626), Viscount St. Albans, English essayist, philosopher, statesman.

BADGER Dachshund are ground dogs that ferret out badgers, a furred animal and member of the weasel family; from the French word *bêcheur*, which means "digger."

BAEKGU Korean Jindo Dog forced to be sold by his owner due to financial hardship, only to find his way home after seven months—a journey of two hundred miles.

BAFFIN The largest island in Canada, where transportation is by sled dog.

BAGHEER Black panther in *The Jungle Book*, by Rudyard Kipling.

BAGMAN The One-eyed Bagman is the storyteller in Charles Dickens's first novel *The Posthumous Papers of the Pickwick Club*, also known as *The Pickwick Papers*. If you have a Siberian Husky with one blue eye and one brown eye, call him Bagman!

BAGSTOCK Major Joseph Bagstock, Miss Tox's neighbor, who describes himself as, "Tough, sir, tough, and de-vilish sly!" in Charles Dickens's *Dombey and Son*.

BAGUETTE Long, thin loaf of French bread, soft inside and crusty out.

BAHAMAS The Bahamas is a commonwealth nation made up of three thousand tropical and subtropical islands and cays in the Atlantic Ocean between Cuba and Florida. If you love the surf and sun, name your dog Bahamas.

BAILEY Defensive wall surrounding a castle (Old English). Adorable Golden Retriever puppy star of the 2010 family movie *The Adventures of Bailey: The Lost Pup*.

BAILIFF Chief magistrate. Overseer of a manor.

BAILIWICK Territory under the jurisdiction of a bailiff as authorized by the British Crown.

BAKARI Promising (Swahili).

BAKER Dr. Baker reveals Rebecca's awful secret, but not before it is too late in *Rebecca*, by Daphne du Maurier.

BALACLAVA Type of helmet or hat; Ukrainian seaport on the Baltic Sea.

BALBOA Vasco Núñez de Balboa (1475–1519), Spanish conquistador who became the first European to successfully lead an expedition to the Pacific Ocean.

BALDEROFF Woronzova Kennels, owned by Arten Balderoff, and Perchina Kennels, owned by Grand Duke Nicholas of Romanoff, were the two most prestigious breeders of Russian Wolfhounds in the nineteenth century.

BALDOVINO Brave friend (Italian).

BALDUR Strong ruler (Old Norse). Norse god of beauty.

BALDWIN Brave friend (Germanic).

BALDY Common nickname for bald people and a humorous name for a Mexican Hairless or Chinese Crested dog.

BALEIA The boy's dog in the Brazilian *cinema nôvo* film adaptation of *Vidas Secas*, by Gracilianos Ramos.

BALI Common surname in India; "Bali Ha'i" from Rodgers and Hammerstein's musical *South Pacific* was inspired by the real island of Vanuatu in the South Pacific.

BALKAN Vast mountain chain that spans Bosnia and Herzegovina, Croatia, Macedonia, Montenegro, Serbia, Slovenia, Romania, Bulgaria, Kosovo, Albania, Greece, and the European part of Turkey. Herding, working, and hunting breeds such as the Croatian Sheepdog, Karst

Shepherd Dog, Bosnian Coarse-Haired Hound, Serbian Tricolour, Montenegrin Mountain Hound, Serbian Hound, Dalmatian, Yugoslavian Tricolor Hound, and the Yugoslavian Shepherd Dog originate from this region.

BALL A "curt-tailed cur" in "Dancing Dog," a poem by Michael Drayton, an English poet of the Elizabethan era.

BALLERINA Female ballet dancer.

BALM "Compassion" in the language of flowers.

BALMORAL Royal estate in Scotland belonging to the British Royal Family and beloved residence of Queen Victoria and Prince Albert, who purchased the estate in 1856. It was at Balmoral that Queen Victoria first admired the Rough Collie and added the breed to her canine family.

BALOO The "sleepy brown bear" in Rudyard Kipling's *The Jungle Book*.

BALSAM "Fervent love" in the language of flowers.

BALTHAZAR One of the three Magi who, along with Gaspar and Melchior, followed the star to the manger with gifts of gold, frankincense, and myrrh for the newborn Christ.

BALTO (1919–1933), Siberian Husky that led Norwegian musher Gunnar Kaasen's sled dog team in 1925 under hazardous conditions to transport lifesaving diphtheria antitoxin from Nenana to Nome over a distance of 674 miles. This feat has been commemorated annually since 1967 by the Iditarod Trail Sled Dog Race. There is a statue of brave Balto in Central Park in New York City.

BAM BAM Canine friend of Randolph, the poetry-loving Labrador Retriever with a nose for murder in J. F. Englert's *A Dog About Town* and other detective dog books

BAMBI The 1942 animated Walt Disney film about the adventures of an orphaned whitetail deer. Based on the book by Austrian author Felix Salten.

BAMBINA Female child (Italian).

BAMBINO Male child (Italian).

BAMBOULA Tribal drum made of giant bamboo and stretched hide brought by African slaves to New Orleans, possibly as early as 1706, when chattel slavery was introduced by the French colonists in Louisiana. Character from the Land of Oz who appears in L. Frank Baum's sequels to *The Wonderful Wizard of Oz.*

BAMSE Beloved Saint Bernard war dog that was a symbol of the Free Norwegian Forces in World War Two.

BAN Bandogge, predecessor of the Mastiff and Medieval guard dog whose origins in thirteenth-century England were documented in Abraham Fleming's 1576 translation from the Latin of Johannes Caius's 1570 book, *Of Englishe Dogges,* in which the breed was described as a "vast, stubborn, eager dog of heavy body."

BANANA Amusing name for a yellow Labrador Retriever or any dog with a yellow coat.

BANCHORY Blessed place (Scottish Gaelic).

BANCO Early Wirehaired Pointing Griffons whelped by Mouche, the breed's foundation bitch.

BANDANNA Derived from the Hindu *bandhana,* a colorful kerchief tied around the head or neck.

BANDAR-LOG A tribe of monkeys in *The Jungle Book,* by Rudyard Kipling.

BANDERSNATCH Fictional character in Lewis Carroll's *Through the Looking Glass* (1872), sequel to *Alice's Adventures in Wonderland,* and in his 1874 narrative poem "The Hunting of the Snark."

BANDIT Outlaw, highwayman. The Ingall family's black-and-white Scottish Border Collie in the popular television series, *Little House on the Prairie* (1974–1983), was played by canine actor Jeff the Dog. Johnny's dog in the 1964 Hanna-Barbera cartoon series *Johnny Quest*.

BANG Westminster Kennel Club champion. *See* Dog Names by Category; Breed: Westminster.

BANGA Pontius Pilate's dog in Mikhail Bulgakov's novel *The Master and Margarita*.

BANGALORE Capital of "the garden city" of Karnataka in India.

BANGLE Windholme's Bangle, first fifteen-inch Beagle to win an All-Breed show, in 1901, at the Ladies Kennel Association of America.

BANJO Musical instrument with five strings that mind-blowingly multitalented American Renaissance man Steve Martin strums so well. Steve was owned by a yellow Labrador Retriever named Wally.

BANKER *See* Dog Names by Category; Breed: Crufts.

BANKS Jaded, erudite anthropomorphic dog in the online comic strip *Barkeater Lake*, by Corey Pandolph.

BANDUM Flag or heraldic banner (Latin).

BARBARIAN Savage, uncivilized, warlike people.

BARBARY Barbary lions were pitted against gladiators in Rome's Coliseum to fight to the death. The largest, heaviest, and most majestic lion subspecies became extinct in 1922. If you have a lionlike dog such as a Pekingese or a Chow Chow, what finer name than Barbary?

BÄRBEL Bärbel Wöckel of East Germany won four gold medals in track and field in the 1976 and 1980 Olympic Games.

BARBIE Mattel's iconic fashion doll and culture icon, created in 1959 by Ruth Handler, based on a German doll named Bild Lili. Barbie's perpetual life partner is Ken.

BARBRA Barbra Streisand (b. 1942), Brooklyn-born, multi-award-winning, iconic American singer, actress, film producer, and director. According to the Recording Industry Association of America, in a career that spans five decades, Streisand has released fifty-one gold albums, thirty platinum albums and thirteen multi-platinum albums, of which thirty-two hold the top-ten selling albums of any female recording artist. Her voice pours like liquid velvet; her lungs have the power of Vesuvius.

BARD Court poet engaged by a nobleman or monarch. William Shakespeare is commonly called "The Bard."

BAREE Part wolf and part dog, Baree the Wolfdog was separated from his litter and befriended by a trapper in James Oliver Curwoods's 1917 novel *Baree, Son of Kazan*.

BARFY The Thel family's Labrador Retriever in one of the most widely syndicated comic strips in the world, *Family Circus*, first published in 1960. Cartoonist Bil Keane modeled the comic strip after his own family. Barfy was joined in 1970 by a shaggy-haired mutt named Sam.

BARGE American humorist James Thurber's beloved, beer-drinking dog.

BARGHEST Legendary, monstrous, ghostly black dog believed to roam the Yorkshire dales in the north of England, and Dartmoor in Devenshire in *The Hound of the Baskervilles*, Sir Arthur Conan Doyle's most famous Sherlock Holmes mystery. The unnamed hound is thought to be a barghest—until the world's greatest detective solves the age-old mystery for once and for all. Sirius Black, an Animagus, transforms himself at will into a barghest in the Harry Potter series. And a barghest figures in Roald Dahl's 1983 children's book, *The Witches*.

BARING Exposing, revealing. A name to consider for a Poodle or Chinese Crested.

BÄRKE Court district in Sweden. Saucy spelling for "bark."

BARKERVILLE One of the American toy company Tonka's Pound Puppies.

BARKIS Quiet yet persistent cart driver who finally gets Peggotty to accept his proposal of marriage in *David Copperfield*, by Charles Dickens.

BARKLEY Linda's large, friendly dog, originally named "Woof Woof," on the long-running PBS children's television series, *Sesame Street*.

BARNACLE "Barnacle Bill the Sailor," a traditional American folk song, became Bluto's theme song in the very first *Popeye the Sailor* cartoon, in 1933.

BARNEY There's Barney Rubble in *The Flintstones*, Barney Gumble in *The Simpsons*, and that purple dinosaur on children's television, but the best Barney of all was Barney Fife, the inept deputy sheriff played by Don Knotts in the beloved television series *The Andy Griffith Show*.

BARNUM P. T. Barnum (1810–1891), founder of Ringling Bros. and Barnum & Bailey Circus, "the greatest show on earth." Ideal name for a puppy that likes to clown around.

BARON Title of nobility (Old French). The name of the dog in the 1953 film *Back to God's Country*, starring Hugh O'Brian and Rock Hudson.

BARONESS Helen Violet Bonham Carter, Baroness Asquith of Yarnbury, DBE (1887–1969), daughter of H. H. Asquith, diarist, Sir Winston Churchill's closest female friend and grandmother of British actress Helena Bonham Carter (b. 1966), who you love to hate as the evil Bellatrix Lestrange in the Harry Potter movies—and love to admire as Queen Elizabeth in the Academy Award–winning *The King's Speech*.

BAROQUE Type of pearl. Decorative, ornate period of music, art, and architecture in Europe in the seventeenth century.

BARREGES *See* Dauphin.

BARRETT Strong as a bear (English).

BARRIE J. M. Barrie (1860–1937), Scottish writer and author of *Peter Pan; or, The Boy Who Wouldn't Grow Up*.

BARRINGTON Irish surname and title in the peerage of Ireland.

BARRY Barry der Menschenretter (1800–1814), a mountain rescue dog at Great Saint Bernard Hospice in Switzerland, from which the Saint Bernard breed took its name. Barry saved more than forty lives.

BARRYMORE American acting dynasty whose founder, Maurice, (1849–1905) fathered actors Lionel, Ethel, and John; Drew Barrymore is his great-granddaughter.

BARS Soviet space dog. *See* Dog Names by Category: History.

BART Anatolian Shepherd in the 2001 romantic comedy *Kate & Leopold*, starring Meg Ryan and Hugh Jackman.

BARTHOLOMEW Abounding in furrows (Hebrew). One of the Twelve Apostles of Jesus, also called Nathanael.

BARTON Lands of the manor (Old English).

BARTY Bartemius "Barty" Crouch Senior, director of the Department of Magical Law Enforcement during the First Wizarding War in the Harry Potter series. His evil son, Barty Crouch Junior, joined Lord Voldemort to become a Death Eater.

BASCOM The dog in *Hollywood or Bust* (1956), Dean Martin and Jerry Lewis's last film together.

BASHFUL Shy, timid. Good name for a Basset Hound or other bashful dog.

BASIE Count Basie (1904–1984), American jazz bandleader, composer, and pianist best known for his songs "One O'Clock Jump" and "April in Paris." Frank Sinatra, Tony Bennett, Ella Fitzgerald, Billie Holiday, and other greats have sung with Basie. Though he played many times with Louis Armstrong, to their mutual regret, the two legends never recorded together.

BASIL Basil Rathbone (1892–1967), English actor best known as Sherlock Holmes on radio and in films in the forties.

British actor Basil Rathbone, best known as Sherlock Holmes, at home with his black German Shepherd dog

BASILIO King (Italian).

BASKERVILLE Baskerville the Hound, canine Sherlock Holmes who
frequently stops by *The Muppet Show*. The murderous hound purported to seek out and kill every lord of Baskerville Hall since the curse
descended upon Sir Hugh Baskerville in the seventeenth century. Will
the young Canadian heir meet a "bloody and mysterious death," or
will Sherlock Holmes come to the rescue? If, by some remote chance,
you do not know the answer to this cliffhanger, read Sir Arthur Conan
Doyle's *The Hound of the Baskervilles*. *See* Barghest.

BASQUE Nineteenth-century Basque fishermen are said to have
brought large working dogs with them across the Atlantic when they

established a fishing colony on the coast of Newfoundland, Canada—thus, the origin of the Newfoundland breed.

BASS Most popular sport fish in America. If you're a bass fisherman and you plan on taking your puppy fishing, why not name him Bass?

BASSET *See* Galway.

BASTINDA Wicked Witch of the West in *The Wizard of the Emerald City*, Russian writer Alexander Melentyevich Volkov's interpretation of L. Frank Baum's *The Wonderful Wizard of Oz*.

BATMAN Superhero that first appeared in 1939 and has kept Metropolis safe from evil fiends ever since, thank goodness.

BATTINA *See* Fay Ray.

BATTLESHIP Terrific name for a tough dog like the Bulldog.

BATZ *See* D'Artagnan.

BAUDWIN Sir Baudwin, knight of King Arthur's legendary Round Table.

BAVARIA The Schnauzer breed of dog originated in Bavaria.

BAXTER Baker (English). Chow-Labrador mix who died at the age of nineteen after a career of easing the pain and grief of critically ill children and adults at a San Diego hospice. The "little gentleman" played by canine actor Peanut in the 2004 comedy *Anchorman*, starring Will Ferrell.

BAY Perfect name for a Chesapeake Bay Retriever, a bay-colored water dog.

BAYOU Land surrounding a marshy lake or wetland.

BIRDSHOT Pretty good name for a sporting breed that hunts upland birds.

BEACHCOMBER Someone who "combs" the beach looking for shells, driftwood, or other washed-up treasure; crashing wave rolling in from the ocean onto the shore. If you're going to take long walks on the beach with your puppy, here's his name.

BEAMER Type of pitch in the British game of cricket.

BEAMISH Radiantly, beamingly happy, possibly an Old English word and used by Lewis Carroll in *Alice's Adventures in Wonderland*.

BEAN Charles "Pete" Conrad, Richard Gordon, and Alan Bean, the crew of Apollo 12, which made the first precision landing on the moon on the Ocean of Storms, a vast lunar mare on the western edge of the near-side of the moon. One of Sir Ector's hunting dogs in T. H. White's *The Once and Future King* (1958).

BEANIE Brightly colored knitted cap worn by children and Ivy League college undergraduates in bygone days.

BEANS Edible seed or pod of a plant, derived from the Middle English word *bene*.

BEAR Mammal from the family Ursidae.

BEARDSLEY Aubrey Beardsley (1872–1898), English illustrator of the Aesthetic period celebrated for his stylized pen and ink drawings.

BEASLEY Drooling Dogue de Bordeaux in the 1989 comedy *Turner & Hooch*.

BEATER Tool used in weaving.

BEATRICE Mary Beatrice d'Easte of Modena, Italian consort of King James II, owned many Italian Greyhounds.

BEATRIX Beatrix Potter (1866–1943), children's author and illustrator who created Peter Rabbit, Tom Kitten, Jemima Puddle-Duck, and other beloved anthropomorphic characters that have delighted children across the years.

BEAU Handsome (French).

BEAUFORT Beaufort, an American Bench and Field Trial Champion sired by Bow, was one of the first Pointers imported from England to the United States.

BEAUMONT Gordon Setter sold by Mr. Parsons of Taunton, England, to Mr. Morris of New York in 1883 to help establish the breed in the United States.

BEAUREGARD Beautiful view (English). Beauregard "Hound Dog" Bugleboy, the bloodhound in Walt Kelly's long-running syndicated comic strip *Pogo*.

BEAUTIFUL JOE Abused Airedale-Terrier mixed breed dog that was rescued from a brutal master, inspiring Canadian author Margaret Marshall Saunders to write *Beautiful Joe*, published in 1893, one of the first books to bring wide attention to animal cruelty.

BEAUTY My beloved "British Setter" (my made-up name: her dam is my English Setter, Bogie, and her sire, my Irish Setter, Flame). She is a lovely black dog with a white chest who I named after *Black Beauty* by Anna Sewell. Wire Fox Terrier that rescued sixty-three animals buried in the rubble during the London Blitz in World War Two. She was awarded the Dickin Medal in 1945.

BEAVER Fine name for a Beagle with brown saddle-back markings.

BEBE Baby (French).

BEDIVERE Sir Bedivere, a knight of King Arthur's legendary Round Table. He cast the sword Excalibur into the water in *Le Morte d'Arthur* by Sir Thomas Malory, first published in 1485.

BEDLAM Confusion, chaos. Good name an active puppy that gets into things . . . which pretty much means any puppy.

BEDOUIN Nomadic desert people (Arabic).

BEECHGROVE *See* Avendale.

BEEFEATER Ceremonial guard at London's Tower of London, officially known as "Yeomen Warder of Her Majesty's Royal Palace and Fortress the Tower of London, and Member of the Sovereign's Body Guard of the Yeomen of the Guard Extraordinary."

BEEJAY The first German Shepherd Dog to play Rex on the European television series *Inspector Rex*, originally filmed in Vienna and later in Rome.

BEER The most popular alcoholic beverage in the world since 500 BC.

BEETHOVEN (1770–1827) Ludwig von Beethoven, the great German Romantic composer. Though his hearing began to deteriorate in his early twenties, he continued to compose, conduct, and perform his music until his death. Saint Bernard star of the *Beethoven* series of films.

BEGGAR Suitable name for most any dog with a healthy appetite.

BEGONIA "Cautious" in the language of flowers.

BEIJING Also known as Peking, the capital of China and birthplace of the Pekingese breed.

BELA Bela Lugosi (1882–1956), born Béla Ferenc Dezső Blaskó, Hungarian actor best known as Hollywood's Count Dracula, the greatest Dracula of them all. Impoverished and forgotten at the end of his life, he was resurrected by quirky B-movie director Ed Wood. Frank Sinatra learned of Lugosi's deteriorating health and, though he did not know him, contributed anonymously toward Lugosi's hospital expenses.

BELINDA Beautiful (Spanish).

BELLA Dog belonging to the young Thomas Cromwell, later First Earl of Essex in the court of Henry VIII, in Hilary Mantel's acclaimed book *Wolf Hall*, set in sixteenth-century England.

BELLADONNA Beautiful woman (Italian).

BELLATRIX Female warrior (Latin); Bellatrix Lestrange, first female Death Eater in the Harry Potter series and one of Voldemort's devoted inner circle of evil witches.

BELLE Beauty (French). Snoopy's only sister in Charles Schulz's *Peanuts* family. Pyrenean Mountain dog owned by six-year-old Sébastien in *Belle et Sébastien*, a French novel by Cécile Aubry. Yorkville Belle, a famous Bull Terrier in England in 1901. Belle Watling, Rhett Butler's intimate and trustworthy friend in *Gone with the Wind*.

BELLS *See* Dog Names by Category; Breed: Crufts.

BELL-SNICKLE Villain that looks like a buckwheat cake in *The Scalawagons of Oz*, a sequel of *The Wonderful Wizard of Oz*, by L. Frank Baum. Swell name for a Wheaten Terrier.

BELTON Predominantly white Setter with flecks of black ("Blue Belton Setter") or golden brown ("Orange Belton Setter") in its coat.

BELUGA Marine mammal familiarly known as the "white whale." Beluga caviar, the most expensive caviar in the world (about $5,000 a pound), comes from sturgeon in the Caspian Sea, the world's largest saltwater lake.

BELVEDERE The Colonel's Bulldog in Merrie Melodies's animated 1950 short "Dog Gone South."

BELVOIR *See* Cuthbert.

BEN British Royal Family's Black Cocker Spaniel. Golden Retriever actor that played Shadow in *The Incredible Journey Homeward Bound*, William in *Maybe Baby*, Rusty in *Purely Belter*, and Messenger in *Made in Hong Kong*.

BENDICÒ Great Dane belonging to Don Fabrizio Corbera, Prince of Salina, in Giuseppe Tomasi di Lampedusa's novel *Il Gattopardo (The Leopard)*, published posthumously in 1958 after being rejected by Italy's leading publishing houses during the author's lifetime. *Il Gattopardo* is the best-selling novel in Italian history and one of the most important novels in modern Italian literature. The novel was adapted in 1963 into an award-winning film starring Burt Lancaster and Claudia Cardinale.

BENGAL Northeast section of India and one of the most densely populated. The Bengal Tiger, native to this region, is on the International Union for Conservation of Nature endangered species list. Less than 2,500 are believed to exist—and that number is rapidly dwindling.

BENIGNO Kind (Italian).

BENJAMIN Son of my right hand (English).

BENJI Star of a series of movies and television specials created, written, and produced by director Joe Camp. The original Benji was a shelter dog named Higgins; over the twenty-five years that *Benji* movies were made, Higgins's offspring followed in the pawprints of their forebearer.

BENNET The Bennet family, in which the second of five daughters, Elizabeth, is the prideful protagonist in Jane Austen's classic novel of love won, temporarily lost, and won back again in *Pride and Prejudice*, first published in 1813. *See* Austen.

BENNY Oliver's dog in the 1989 black comedy *The War of the Roses*, starring Michael Douglas and Kathleen Turner.

BENNY GOODMAN (1909–1986), bandleader, virtuoso clarinetist, and "King of Swing." Goodman's 1938 Carnegie Hall concert was lauded as "the single most important jazz or popular music concert in history: jazz's 'coming out' party to the world of 'respectable' music." His was the first racially integrated band and one of the most successful of the thirties and forties. The son of Russian Jewish immigrants, Goodman had a love affair with classical music that began early in life and influenced his work. Swingin' name for a dog.

BENTLEY Clearing covered with bent grass (Old English). The white blaze on the forehead of many Australian Cattle Dogs. Bentley Motors, Ltd., a British automobile manufacturer founded in 1919 responsible for producing some of the most elegant and efficient cars in automotive history.

BEPPE God shall bestow another son (Italian).

BERET Round, flat, knitted or wool felt hat traditionally worn by Frenchmen and Basque shepherds and considered the official headgear of British commandos in World War Two, the special ops arm of the French Navy and the United States Army Special Forces, particularly known as the "Green Berets."

BERGER *See* Chien.

BERMUDA British overseas territory discovered in 1505 by Juan de Bermúdez, who claimed the island, which then was inhabited by pigs. Bermuda has since evolved into a prized vacation destination, though surely some pigs must still remain.

BERNADETTE Basset Hound canine actor that played Cleo in the television series *The People's Choice,* starring Jackie Cooper.

BERNARD Brave, hearty (Germanic). *See* Shaw, George Bernard.

BERNARDINO As bold as a bear (Italian).

BERRY Small, succulent, edible fruit such as blueberries, strawberries and blackberries. Affectionate name for Shadowberry, the black German Shepherd that played Padfoot, canine alter ego of Sirius Black in the Harry Potter movies. Sadly, Padfoot and his mate, Porridge, a white German Shepherd/Lab mix, were put up for adoption at German Shepherd Rescue in Great Britain because their owner was no longer able to care for them. Happily, they were adopted by an immensely loving family. Alas, Porridge died of liver cancer in December 2011. Berry continues to thrive in his adoptive home. Supporting dog rescue organizations such as this (http://germanshepherdrescue.co.uk/) through donations is a solid expression of your love of dogs.

BERT Ernie's best friend on *Sesame Street*. Bertie, family name of King George VI of England. Diminutive of **Albert**.

BERTHA Bright, famous (Germanic).

BESS Along with Porgy, one of Jude Law's dogs. Bessie, President Calvin Coolidge's Rough Collie. *See* Dog Names by Category: Hollywood.

BESSIE Bessie Smith (1894–1937), one of the most influential jazz vocalists in history and the most popular American female blues singer of the twenties and thirties. Her life was cut short by a fatal car accident, but her voice will live forever in recordings such as "Nobody Knows When You're Down and Out."

BETA Second letter of the Greek alphabet.

BETH Diminutive of **Elizabeth**.

BETSEY Dog in the 1999 Frank Oz cult comedy film *Bowfinger*, starring Eddie Murphy and Steve Martin.

BETSY BOBBIN A year older than Dorothy, she appears in *Tik-Tok of Oz*, a sequel of *The Wonderful Wizard of Oz*, by L. Frank Baum.

BETTINA Blessed (Italian).

BETTY BOOP Animated Max Fleischer character that first appeared in 1930. Betty was the star of her own cartoon series until 1939 but made a comeback in the partly animated live-action feature film *Who Framed Roger Rabbit* (1988) without having gained a single ounce of celluloid on her hourglass figure.

BEULAH Married (Hebrew).

BEVERLY Beaver dam or stream (Old English).

BEWICK Thomas Bewick, nineteenth-century artist that first depicted the Rough Collie in his woodcut prints.

BEWLEY Largest supplier of coffee in Ireland since 1840.

BEYONCÉ Beyoncé Giselle Knowles (b. 1981), multi-award-winning American singer, songwriter, and actress who catapulted to fame in the Nineties as the lead singer of one of the most popular girl groups ever, Destiny's Child. She and her husband, Jay-Z, have a daughter named Blue Ivy.

BHISTI Native Muslim water carrier in northern India. Here's a name for a Labrador Retriever or Chesapeake Bay Retriever—indeed, any water dog. *See* Gunga Din.

BIAGGIO Talks with a lisp (Italian).

BIANCA White (Italian). Italian feminine for Blanche.

BIBIANA Alive (Italian).

BICHE Another name for the Mexican Hairless breed.

BIDDY Joe Gargery's housekeeper after Joe is widowed by Pip's awful sister. Biddy marries good old Joe after an acceptable period of mourning in Charles Dickens's classic novel *Great Expectations*.

BIFF Biff Barker is a Pound Puppy.

BIG BEN President Herbert Hoover's Fox Terrier. *See* Dog Names by Category; History.

BIG BIRD A little over eight foot tall, Big Bird is the tallest bird known to mankind and the first Muppet on *Sesame Street*.

BIG MAMA Big Mama Thornton (1926–1984), best-selling American rhythm and blues singer and songwriter who, in 1952, first recorded "Hound Dog," a song Elvis Presley would make his own two years later.

BIG MO Golden Retriever in the Alpo dog food commercials.

BIG RED Irish Setter in Jim Kjelgaard's novel *Big Red*, adapted by Walt Disney in 1962 into a wonderful film starring one of Hollywood's most gentlemanly actors, Walter Pidgeon.

BIG SAM In *Gone with the Wind*, the slave in charge of the field workers at Tara and, after the Civil War, Scarlett O'Hara's heroic rescuer.

BIJOU Jewel (French). **Bijoux** is the plural form.

BILBO BAGGINS Protagonist in *The Hobbit* and a pivotal character in *The Lord of the Rings*, by J. R. R. Tolkien.

BILKA Common name for German Shepherd Dogs and Siberian Huskies.

BILL, BILLY Cocker Spaniel in *Boule et Bill*, the popular 1959 Belgian comic about a seven-year-old boy and his dog.

BILLIE Billie Holiday (1915–1959), also known as "Lady Day," American jazz singer whose unsurpassed renditions of "God Bless the Child" and "Lady Sings the Blues" are singular not only because of her delivery, but also because she cowrote the songs. Her sultry vocal delivery as a woman scorned in love was mirrored in real life. Her career took off in 1937 with Count Basie and then Artie Shaw, with songs such as "I Must Have That Man" and "I Can't Get Started." Perhaps the most devoted man in her life was her Mastiff, Mister. Troubled and tormented, she poured her body and soul into her music, dying of liver and heart disease at the tragically young age of forty-four—but leaving behind an unmatched musical legacy.

BILLINA Dorothy's talking pet hen and matriarch of a large family of chickens in *Ozma of Oz*, a sequel to *The Wonderful Wizard of Oz*, by L. Frank Baum.

BING Alsatian attached to the US 13th Battalion Airborne Division that parachuted into Normandy on D-Day; Harry Lillis "Bing" Crosby (1903–1977), one of the most popular singers and performers of his, or any, day. Born in Tacoma, Washington, in a house his father built, he was the fourth of seven children and a direct descendant of William Brewster, the Pilgrim minister who came to America on the *Mayflower*. His rich, baritone-bass voice and unruffled delivery influenced singers from Frank Sinatra and Perry Como to Michael Bublé.

Irving Berlin's "White Christmas" was first sung in 1942 by Crosby in the classic holiday film *Holiday Inn*, in which he starred with Fred Astaire. It would become the greatest hit of his career—and the greatest holiday song of all time. Crosby won the Academy Award for Best Actor in 1944 for his role as Father Chuck O'Malley in *Going My Way*. His film partnership and personal friendship with Bob Hope were immortalized in seven "Road" comedy films (*Road to Zanzibar*, *Road to Bali*, *Road to Rio*, et cetera), which also starred Dorothy Lamour. An avid golfer, he died in Madrid, Spain, shortly after finishing eighteen holes of golf despite his doctor's order to play no more than nine. He and his partner won. His last words supposedly were, "That was a great game of golf, fellas."

BINGLEY Charles Bingley, handsome, congenial, wealthy single young gentleman who leases Netherfield Park near the home of Mr. and Mrs. Bennet and falls in love with the eldest of their five marriageable daughters in Jane Austen's *Pride and Prejudice*, first published in 1813.

BINGO Dog on the Cracker Jack snack box. Runaway circus dog that saves a young boy's life in the endearing 1991 TriStar Pictures film *Bingo*.

BINKY Binky Barnes, Bulldog on the PBS animated children's educational television series *Arthur*.

BINX Character in the kingdom of Oz in L. Frank Baum's sequels to *The Wonderful Wizard of Oz*. Alien from the planet Naboo in the *Star Wars* saga.

BIRDSONG *See* Rosseau. Popular novel by Sebastian Faulks.

BISCUIT Made with flour, water, salt, and baking soda, baked to a golden yellow, and served warm with butter . . . delicious! Great name for a Golden Retriever.

BISHOP Supervisor, protector (Greek).

BISMARCK German noble family descended from Herebord von Bismarck in the thirteenth century. Among its members are many important politicians and diplomats, notably Otto "Blood and Iron" von Bismarck (1815–1898), who designed the German Empire and, in 1871, became its first chancellor. Great name for any German breed of dog. *See* Dog Names by Category: History.

BISQUE Unglazed porcelain used in making doll heads and decorative items; a creamy color, this is a good name for a Pembroke Welsh Corgi or Chinese Shar-Pei.

BISTRE Dark brown pigment made from soot; good name for an Irish Water Spaniel.

BITON Born after a long wait (African). Kleobis and Biton were two human brothers in Greek mythology.

BITSY Good name for a toy breed, such as a Chihuahua.

BITTERSWEET "To be true" in the language of flowers.

BITZER The farmer's long-suffering sheepdog in *Shaun the Sheep*, the 2007 BBC stop-motion animated television series created by six-time Academy Award–nominated animator Nick Park, creator of *Wallace and Gromit*.

BIXBY Messrs. Cadwalder, Megargee, and Bixby sat on the committee that adopted American standards for the Scottish Terrier breed in 1925. Edwin Megargee was a famous twentieth-century American dog artist.

BIZET Georges Bizet (1838–1875) French composer of the Romantic period best known for one of the world's most beloved operas, *Carmen*, which Bizet did not live to see performed. He died at the age of thirty-six of heart failure.

BJ Actor Matthew McConaughey's mixed-breed dog.

BJØRN Wolf (Old Norse). Bjørn Dæhlie, Norwegian skier who holds the record for the most Olympic gold medals—eight—in cross-country skiing.

BLACK BOB Border Collie in the world's third longest running comic, *The Dandy*, published since 1937 in the UK. Black Bob was featured between 1944 and 1982. That's some old dog!

BLACK KNIGHT Usually the evil knight in medieval stories—none more hilariously than in *Monty Python and the Holy Grail* (1975). *See* Dog Names by Category: Breed; Westminster.

BLACK PEARL Captain Jack Sparrow's ship in the Walt Disney's *Pirates of the Caribbean* series of films. Good name for a Doberman Pinscher.

BLACK SHUCK Demonic black dog with glowing, saucer-sized eyes that roams the eastern coast of England, according to legend. Black Shuck was Sir Arthur Conan Doyle's inspiration for the murderous hound in *The Hound of the Baskervilles.*

BLACK TOOTH "The biggest and sweetest dog in the USA" and canine star of the 1953 children's television series *The Soupy Sales Show.*

BLACKBEARD Edward Teach (1680–1718), better known as the notorious pirate Blackbeard and so named for his thick black beard. He attacked, pillaged, and plundered ships sailing in the Caribbean and along the eastern coast of North America, dying in battle at the age of thirty-eight, off the coast of North Carolina's Ocracoke Island. His highly romanticized legend has inspired numerous books and movies; however, the most endearing of all was the 1968 Walt Disney film *Blackbeard's Ghost*, starring Dean Jones, Suzanne Pleshette, Elsa Lanchester, and, as the ghost of Blackbeard, the inimitable Peter Ustinov.

BLACKBERRY President Calvin Coolidge's Chow. *See* Dog Names by Category: History.

BLACKCAP Type of songbird. *See* Dog Names by Category: Breed; Crufts.

BLACKIE Eric Clapton's favorite Fender Stratocaster guitar. President John F. Kennedy's puppy, whelped from Pushinka.

BLACKJACK Most popular casino card game in the world, also known as Twenty-one (*Vingt-et-un*, in French).

BLACKSTONE Major H. Blackstone, noted English antiquarian, identified images on tombs in the Valley of the Nile dating to 4,000 BC to be that of the Afghan Hound, known as cynocephalus, which means "monkey-faced hound."

BLACKTOE Commander William Riker's dog in the 1987 television series *Star Trek: The Next Generation*.

BLACKWELL Dweller near the old stream (Old English).

BLADE Toledo Blade, important English Setter painted by German-born American dog painter Edmund Henry Osthaus in 1891.

BLAINE Yellow (Gaelic). Fine old Scottish name for a Golden Retriever, a breed that originated in Scotland.

BLAIR Battlefield (Scottish). A collie acknowledged as the first canine movie actor. Blair starred in the 1905 silent film *Rescued by Rover*.

BLAISE *See* Dog Names by Category: Breed; Crufts.

BLAKE Black (Old English).

BLANCHE White, fair (French). One of Lear's dogs in Shakespeare's tragedy *King Lear*.

BLANDINGS Fictional castle of Clarence Threepwood, Ninth Earl of Emsworth, in P. G. Wodehouse's stories. *Mr. Blandings Builds His Dream House*, a delightful 1948 comedy film starring Cary Grant and Myrna Loy based on the Eric Hodgins best-seller about a husband and wife and their two teenage daughters who flee the congestion of Manhattan for the simplicity of country living—and soon realize that country living ain't all that simple.

BLARNEY Nonsense, flattery, tosh. *See* Dog Names by Category: Breed; Westminster.

BLASÉ Nonchalant, carefree.

BLAZE President Franklin Delano Roosevelt's son Elliot's Mastiff.

BLEMIE Playwright Eugene O'Neil's Dalmatian, of whom he said, "No dog is as well-bred or as well-mannered or as distinguished and handsome."

BLENHEIM Strain of English Toy Spaniel developed by John Churchill, First Duke of Marlborough around 1700.

BLESSING Benediction, miracle.

BLINDE Señor Blinde was an expert on the Mexican Hairless breed of dog.

BLITTER A shade of gray. Cute name for a gray dog such as a Skye Terrier.

BLITZ German aerial attacks over Great Britain (September 1940–May 1941) in which over 40,000 people were killed, half of whom were Londoners.

BLITZEN One of Santa Claus's reindeer—nine in all, counting Rudolf.

BLIZZARD Intense snowstorm. Good name for a white dog.

BLOKE Good chap, a regular gent.

BLONDIE Popular, long-running comic strip by cartoonist Chic Young. Blondi, Adolf Hitler's German Shepherd Dog.

BLOOD Dog played by canine actor Tiger in Harlan Ellison's film *A Boy and His Dog*.

BLOOMSBURY Fashionable residential district in central London that spawned the Bloomsbury Set, a collective of writers, philosophers and artists in the first half of the nineteenth century that included Virginia Woolf (*Mrs. Dalloway*) and E. M. Forster (*Howard's End*, *Passage to India*).

BLOSSOM The first bloom, or budding, of a flower (English).

BLUE Nick Jr.'s popular children's television show *Blue's Clues* stars a blue beagle named Blue. Primary color in the spectrum. Dog that belongs to Dilsey, powerful matriarch of a black servant family in William Faulkner's fourth novel, *The Sound and the Fury*.

BLUEBELL "Gratitude" in the language of flowers.

BLUEY (1910–1939) Australian Cattle Dog from Victoria, Australia, that lived to be almost thirty years old.

BLUFF Steep hill or cliff.

BLUTO Sometimes called Brutus, Popeye's nemesis who first appeared in 1933 in the comic strip by Elzie Crisler Segar. Alas, despite his biceps and blarney, Bluto never beats Popeye—probably because Bluto doesn't eat his spinach.

BLYTHE Cheerful (Old English).

BO To live, from the Norse word *bua*. Bo Diddley (1928–2008), Mississippi-born American R&B singer, songwriter, and guitarist, nicknamed "The Originator" for his role in merging blues with rock and roll. His hard-edged, technically innovative guitar style influenced Eric Clapton, Jimi Hendrix, Buddy Holly, and the Rolling Stones. The "Bo Diddley beat" became his trademark, along with his triangle-shaped guitar. President Obama's family dog.

BOATSWAIN Deck hand on a merchant ship. Favorite dog of Lord Byron and the object of his poem "Epitaph to a Dog."

BOB Dogs that had their tails docked indicated to the authorities that they were working dogs, such as cart dogs, drovers' dogs, or plow dogs, in nineteenth-century Europe and therefore exempt from taxes; also called "Bob-tail" or, affectionately, "Bobs." Hercule Poirot's unwitting canine accomplice in Agatha Christie's riveting mystery *Dumb Witness*. Patrol dog attached to the Sixth Battalion, Queen's Own Royal

West Kent Regiment, Green Hill, North Africa, and awarded a Dickin Medal in 1944 for bravery.

BOB DOG Lived in the Kingdom of Make-Believe in the long-running PBS children's television series *Mister Roger's Neighborhood*, which first aired in 1968 and ended in 2001. Fred Rogers helped generations of mothers raise our children, and when he said his last, "I like you just the way you are," I realized that all those years he not only gave my children self-assurance—but he also gave me a great deal.

BOB THE RAILWAY DOG German Collie cross that loved to travel the South Australian Railways and was made the railroad's mascot.

BOB THE RETRIEVER DOG Dog in *The Tale of Little Pig Robinson*, by Beatrix Potter, published in 1930.

BOBBIE Bobbie the Wonder Dog was accidentally separated from his family during a cross-country trip. He eventually found his way back home—after a journey of over 2,800 miles.

BOBBIN Spindle around which thread is wound.

BOBBY'S GIRL *See* Dog Names by Category: Breed; Westminster.

BOBO One who is born on Tuesday (Ghana).

BODGER Woodworker. *See* Luath.

BODINUS Dr. Bodinus, a Great Dane enthusiast who, in 1880, attempted to change the breed's name to Deutsche Dogge—but obviously did not succeed.

BODKIN Arrowhead used on broadhead arrows from the time of the Vikings through the seventeenth century.

BOGART Orchard (Dutch). Humphrey DeForest Bogart (1899–1957), iconic Hollywood actor whose performances in *Casablanca*, *Key Largo*, *The Big Sleep*, and *The African Queen* are the stuff that great films are made of. His nickname was **Bogie**.

BOGLODORE Character in the kingdom of Oz in L. Frank Baum's sequel to *The Wonderful Wizard of Oz*.

BOHEMIA Region in Central Europe that today occupies a great part of the Czech Republic. Called *Boihaemum* by the Romans.

BOJANGLES Bill "Bojangles" Robinson (1878–1949), Black American tap dancer and actor who made seventeen movies, including *Stormy Weather* with Lena Horne, but none so endearing as his four films with child star Shirley Temple, including *Rebecca of Sunnybrook Farm* and *The Little Colonel*. "Mr. Bojangles" was written by Jerry Jeff Walker in 1968 and has since been recorded by many artists, most famously by Bob Dylan.

BOLD Brave, courageous.

BOLERO Sensual Latin dance music accompanied by a guitar.

BOLIK Soviet space dog.

BOLINGBROKE Lord Bolingbroke was an early breeder of Gordon Setters. His champion, Argyle, was described as having "a grand frame, powerful hocks and loin, with neck and shoulders so long, well-poised and muscular that he would have taken high rank anywhere."

BOLIVAR Donald Duck's dog.

BOLO Wildflower; large knife; string tie. *See* Lady Howe.

BOLT White hero dog in the Walt Disney animated feature film of the same name was nominated in 2008 for an Oscar. Bolt is voiced by John Travolta.

BOLTON Ch. Bolton Woods Mixer, an Irish Terrier bought by an Englishman named Mr. Wilson for ten pounds. The dog earned many prizes and commanded enormous stud fees. At one point Mr. Wilson was offered £700 for the dog, which he summarily refused. This was in the 1880s. The equivalent amount today would be about £70,000 to over $110,000.

BOMANI Strong soldier (Malawian).

BONAVENTURE Good fortune (Italian).

BONBON Candy.

BOLDDOGGE Old English name for the Bulldog, dating to the sixteenth century.

BONES Skeleton, framework.

BONFILIA Good daughter (Italian).

BONFIOLIO Good son (Italian).

BONFIRE Large, controlled outdoor fire lit for a celebration.

BONGO One of the largest of the African species of antelope, known for its distinctive white-striped chestnut coat. A percussion drum.

BONNET Cap, hat.

BONNIE One of six Doberman Pinschers that attempt a bank heist in the 1972 film *The Doberman Gang*.

BONNIE BELLE First Scottish Terrier bitch imported to America.

BONO Stage name of Paul David Hewson (b. 1960), lead vocalist for the Dublin rock bank U2, humanitarian, and social activist.

BONSAI Japanese miniature trees grown in containers.

BOO RADLEY Silent hero in *To Kill a Mockingbird*, by Harper Lee. Puggle (Pug-Beagle cross) owned by actor Jake Gyllenhaal. "Boo is a joy to have around and makes me smile every time I see him," Gyllenhaal said of his canine companion.

BOODLES Boodles Gin, a brand of gin named after the exclusive gentlemen's club in London, founded in 1762. Boodles is the second oldest club of its kind in the world.

BOOKER Maker of books (English).

BOOMER Jasmine and Steve's dog in the sci-fi adventure film *Independence Day*, starring Will Smith.

BOONE Daniel Boone (1734–1820), a militia officer during the American Revolutionary War and, most notably, a legendary pioneer and frontiersman.

BOOS Exclamation of surprise or discontentment. *See* Mons Lane.

BOOT Old English Sheepdog that believes he is a reincarnated eighteenth-century English lord and lives with Wellington, the boy in the British comic strip *The Perishers*, which ran in London's *Daily Mirror* from 1959 to 2005. Canine narrator of Rudyard Kipling's short story "Thy Servant a Dog."

BOOTLEGGER *See* Dog Names by Category: Breed; Westminster.

BOOTS British pharmacy chain. *See* Dog Names by Category: Breed; Crufts.

BOQ The Munchkin that offers Dorothy shelter in *The Wonderful Wizard of Oz*, by American author L. Frank Baum; short name for a short dog.

BORDEAUX Dogue de Bordeaux is the French relative of the Boxer. Wine from the Bordeaux region of France.

BORDER *See* Cheviot.

BOREAS God of the North Wind in Greek mythology.

BORIS William Henry Pratt (1887–1969), English actor who never changed his legal name to his stage name, which became synonymous with Frankenstein—Boris Karloff. He was a gentle, kind man who did much for children's charities. And it was he who captured the hearts of children everywhere as the narrator of the animated version of Dr. Seuss's holiday classic, *How the Grinch Stole Christmas*.

BOROGROVE "An extinct kind of parrot," according to Lewis Carroll in *Alice's Adventures in Wonderland*.

Bosco Chocolate syrup stirred in milk to make a delicious chocolaty drink. Bosco was invented in 1928.

Boss Chief, manager, the person who cuts your paycheck.

Bossa Nova Brazilian dance music with a strong beat.

Bossy Domineering, bossy. *See* Dog Names by Category: Breed; Crufts.

Boston Beans President Calvin Coolidge's Bulldog.

Boston Blackie Fictional film detective. *See* Strongheart.

Boswell James Boswell, Ninth Laird of Auchinleck (1740–1795), lawyer, diarist, and author born in Edinburgh, Scotland, best known for his biography of the great English literary figure Dr. Samuel Johnson.

Botticelli Alessandro di Mariano di Vanni Filipepi, known as Botticelli (1445–1510), early Florentine Renaissance painter.

Boucher François Boucher (1703–1770), French Rococo painter. *See* Rubens.

Boughley *See* Mop.

Bouldogue *See* Mida.

Bounce Another dog in Sir Ector's kennels in T. H. White's Arthurian book *The Once and Future King*.

Bouncer One of "the hounds that were singing" in Frederick Watson's 1932 book *In the Pink*. Big burly guy standing at the door of nightclubs. Good name for a Bulldog.

Bouquet A bunch of cut flowers.

Bourbon An American whiskey. Royal dynasty of France and Spain. Historic street in the French Quarter of New Orleans.

BOURDET Monsieur Bourdet, fifteenth-century historian who chronicled the Great Pyrenees breed in his writings.

BOURNE Winterbourne, stream (Old English).

BOW WOW Shad Gregory Moss (b.1987), American rapper known as Bow Wow whose first album, released when he was thirteen years old, was called *Beware of Dog* (2000), followed by *Doggy Bag* (2001), and *Unleashed* (2003). Too obvious a name for a dog, but you had to know.

BOWSER The hound in the stories of prolific Massachusetts writer Thornton Burgess (1874–1965), author of 170 books.

BOXER Ah Cum, foundation dog that established the Boxer breed in England, obtained by Major Gwynne during the Boxer Rebellion in 1900.

BOXWOOD Shrub. *See* Dog Names by Category: Breed; Westminster.

BOY Another of Sir Ector's dogs in *The Once and Future King*, by T. H. White. Male child that grows up to became a man.

BOYD Forensic anthropologist Temperance Brennan's dog in Kathy Reich's forensic thrillers.

BOYE Prince Rupert of the Rhine's dog that always accompanied him into battle in the seventeenth century.

BOYER Charles Boyer (1899–1978), debonair French actor (*Algiers, Gaslight, Around the World in Eighty Days*), nominated four times for a Best Actor Oscar. Boyer owned a Scottish Terrier. Good name for a Bichon Frise or any other breed that originates from France.

BOZO Famous clown that first came onto the scene in 1946, on Capitol Records' *Bozo at the Circus*, the first read-along, story-telling record and book set. Soon he was on television, launching one of the first children's series that blossomed into an enormous franchise.

BRABANCON Petite Brabançon, Dutch toy breed with a smooth coat.

BRACKEN Wild-growing fern.

BRAD Thin, tapered nail used in building.

BRADFORD Broad ford or crossing (Old English).

BRADLEY *See* Cuthbert.

BRAEBURN "Chance seedling" or unintentional variety of apple inadvertently discovered by a New Zealand farmer in 1952.

BRAGI Norse god of eloquence.

BRAIN Inspector Gadget's dog in the 1983 animated cartoon series of the same name.

BRAMBLE Border Collie in the UK that lived to be more than twenty-seven years old.

BRAMSHAW *See* Dog Names by Category: Breed; Crufts.

BRAMWELL Bramwell Brontë (1817–1848), troubled painter, poet, and brother of writers Charlotte, Emily, and Anne.

BRAN Mythical hunter Fionn mac Cumhaill's Irish hound.

BRANDO Marlon Brando (1924–2004), acclaimed American actor whose performances as Stanley Kowalski in Tennessee Williams's *A Streetcar Named Desire* (1951), Terry Malloy in *On the Waterfront* (1954), Vito Corleone in Francis Ford Coppola's *The Godfather* (1972), and Colonel Kurtz in Coppola's 1979 film *Apocalypse Now* are considered among Hollywood's finest.

BRANDON Hill covered with broom (Old English); Punkey Brewster's Labrador Retriever in the 1984 NBC television series.

BRANDY Aged, distilled wine containing more than 35 percent alcohol. Derived from the Dutch word *brandewijn*, meaning burnt wine. Animated children's television series *Brandy and Mr. Whiskers*, about Brandy Harrington's mixed-breed dog Brandy and Mr. Whiskers, a hyperactive rabbit.

BRASS Alloy metal composed of copper and zinc.

BRASSY A French municipality. Harsh, high-pitched noise and good name for a little dog with a shrill bark.

BRAVA Ovation after a noteworthy performance by a female vocalist.

BRAVO Ovation after an excellent performance by a male performer, ensemble, orchestra, or theatrical cast.

BRAVEHEART Courage under fire. Excellent name for a guard dog such as a German Shepherd Dog or a Doberman Pinscher.

BRAWNY Strapping, muscular.

BRAYTON Baronetcy in Great Britain; English surname.

BREEZE A cool, gentle wind.

BREEZY One of three canine actors that interchangeably played Porthos in *Star Trek: Enterprise*.

BRENDA STARR Comic strip created in 1940 by Dale Messick about a daring, gorgeous, redhaired reporter who always gets the scoop.

BREUNOR Sir Breunor le Noir, knight of King Arthur's legendary Round Table. Breunor's nickname was "La Cote Mal Taillée" ("of the badly-fitting coat") because of his ill-fitting armor, which had been his father's and didn't quite fit. He received his knighthood after saving Guinevere from an attack by a rampant lion. Terrific name for a Chinese Shar-Pei, Bulldog, or other dog that doesn't quiet seem to fit in his skin.

BREWER Someone who makes beer.

BRIAN BORU Irish Wolfhound mascot of the Royal Irish Regiment. The dog was actually named after Brian Bóruma mac Cennétig (c. 941–1014), the Irish king who crowned himself King of Munster and founded the O'Brien dynasty.

BRIAN GRIFFIN Cynical talking dog in the animated television series, *Family Guy*.

BRIANNA Hill (Irish).

BRIAR Thicket of thorny plants, mostly associated with roses. Ch. Master Briar (1897–1906), patriarch of the Airedale Terrier breed.

BRICE Speckled (Old English).

BRIDGET Irish for *brighid*, meaning "exalted one."

BRIE Soft, double-cream French cheese best served at room temperature and eaten when you're not on a diet.

BRIGADIER Senior officer in command of a brigade. *See* Sable.

BRIGAND Robber, thief. *See* Clee.

BRIGARE To Fight (Italian). Name that might suit a Pit Bull.

BRIGHTON English seaside resort where the foundation dog of the Golden Retriever breed was inadvertently acquired. *See* Dudley.

BRIGITTA From the Scandinavian word *brighid*, which means "exalted one."

BRILLIG Possibly an Old English word for "boil" and used by Lewis Carroll in *Alice's Adventures in Wonderland*.

BRINDLE If your dog's fur is several shades of brown with some white, his coat is called brindle—and that's a good name for him.

BRINK Where the water runs deep (Old English).

BRINKLEY David Brinkley (1920–2003), American newscaster—the kind they don't make anymore—professionally partnered with Chet Huntley on *The Huntley-Brinkley Report* (1956–1971), NBC's evening news show.

BRINSLEY Village in Yorkshire, England.

BRIONY To swell, surge (Greek).

BRISK Rapid, zesty, sharply cold.

BRISTLE Quill, stiff hair, feather.

BRITA Diminutive of Brigitta (Scandinavian).

BRITCHES Knickers or knee-length pants; also called breeches.

BRITON Celtic people living in the British Isles during the early Middle Ages.

BRITTANY Large peninsula in northwest France rich in early Celtic history. The Brittany, a sporting dog bred to point upland birds, originated in Brittany. In the past, the breed was called Brittany Spaniel or French Brittany. Today it is simply called Brittany.

BROADWATER *See* Dog Names by Category: Breed; Crufts.

BROADWAY Heart of New York City, center of the American theater; known as the Wickquasgeck Trail to the Native Americans who inhabited Manhattan before the Dutch christened the island Nieuw Amsterdam.

BRODIE Ditch, channel (Gaelic).

BRON Source, origin.

BRONANT Stronghold of the early Celts, established in 1282 in mid-Wales. Once known as Cardiganshire, today the county is the constituency of Ceredigion, represented in the British House of Commons. Place of origin of the Cardigan Welsh Corgi.

BRONCO Wild mustangs; untrained horse that bucks.

BRONSON Lithuanian-born American actor Charles Bronson (1921–2003), who played the tough guy with the steel gaze in numerous films, notably *The Dirty Dozen* and *The Great Escape*.

BRONTË Family name of an Irish-born Church of England minister, whose daughters were writers Charlotte (*Jane Eyre*), Emily (*Wuthering Heights*), and Anne (*Agnes Grey*). *See* Bramwell.

BRONWEN White breast (Welsh). Good name for a dog with a white chest.

BROOKE Robert Brooke sailed for the Crown Colony in America in 1650, bringing with him his cherished pack of hunting hounds.

BROOKLYN "The greatest city in the greatest city in the world" lies across the East River from Manhattan. The first European settlers were the Dutch who, in 1624, gave Brooklyn its official motto: *Eendraght Maeckt Maght*, meaning "Unity Makes Strength."

BROONZY Big Bill Broonzy (1903–1958), prolific African American blues singer, songwriter, and guitarist who copyrighted more than three hundred songs in his brief lifetime. A pioneer of the Chicago blues style, he famously led the American folk music revival in the sixties along with folk greats such as Pete Seeger and Peter, Paul and Mary. One of seventeen children of a poor Mississippi family, he died too young of throat cancer. Ron Wood of the Rolling Stones said Broonzy's "Guitar Shuffle" was his favorite acoustic guitar music. Eric Clapton recorded Broonzy's "Hey Hey" on his *Unplugged* album. Just a great name.

BROWNIE Rich, chocolate, sinfully delicious cake and good name for a chocolate Lab.

BROWNING English Victorian poet Elizabeth Barrett Browning (1806–1861) owned a much-loved spaniel named Flush. In 1845, at the age of thirty-nine, she married poet Robert Browning. Theirs was a magnificent romance that served as the inspiration for their works. Fragile in health, she died in her husband's arms, "smilingly, happily, and with a face like a girl's. Her last word was 'beautiful.' "

BRIOC Sixth-century Welsh-born saint and first Abbot of Saint-Brieuc in Brittany. Therefore, a righteous name for a Welsh Springer Spaniel or a Brittany Spaniel.

BRUCE "Willowlands" (Scottish). Bruce of Falkirk, Scotland was the first modern breeder of the Italian Greyhound. **Brucie**, *See* Dog Names by Category: Breed; Westminster.

BRUISER Chihuahua in the 2001 comedy film *Legally Blonde*, starring Reese Witherspoon and Luke Wilson.

BRÚN Brown (Old English). *See* Dog Names by Category: Color.

BRUNHILDA Warrior woman (German). Brunhilda, AD 543–613, powerful, warring Visigoth princess; the Norse version is **Brynhildr**. Excellent name for a female Bouvier des Flandres, Belgian Sheepdog, or Belgian Malinois, all important war dogs in France and Belgium in the First World War.

BRUNI Brown (Old Norse).

BRUNO Brown (German). Bloodhound in Walt Disney's classic animated film *Cinderella*; Basset Hound in *The Triplets of Belleville*.

BRÛNOZ Brown (Germanic), also **Brûnâ**. Great name for a Leonberger or other brown dog of German origin.

BRUTON Town in Somerset, England listed in the *Domesday Book*, From the Old English, *briuuetone*, meaning "vigorously flowing river."

BRUTUS Marcus Junius Brutus (85–42 BC), Roman senator who famously struck the first blow in the assassination of Julius Caesar. Popeye's nemesis.

BUBBLES Fizzy, effervescent. "Bubbly" is slang for champagne.

BUCCANEER Pirate that attacked Spanish galleons laden with riches in the Caribbean in the seventeenth century.

BUCCLEUCH Duke of Buccleuch, early enthusiast of the Labrador Retriever. The Duke's stud book helped establish the pedigrees of the two dogs most responsible for setting the modern standard of the breed— Peter of Faskally, owned by Mr. A. C. Butter, and Flapper, owned by Major Portal. Their pedigrees were recorded in 1878.

BUCHANAN James Buchanan, fifteenth president of the United States.

BUCK Dog on the television sitcom, *Married with Children*. Saint Bernard–German Shepherd Dog cross sled dog in Jack London's novel of the Klondike gold rush, *The Call of the Wild*. Bluetick Coonhound in the 1947 Academy Award–winning film for Best Short Subject, *A Boy and His Dog*.

BUCKAROO Cowboy good at handling horses. From *vaquero*, the Spanish word for "cowboy."

BUCKEYE North American T-2 Buckeye, the US Navy's intermediate training aircraft.

BUCKINGHAM Buckingham Palace, London residence of the British Royal Family.

BUCKLES Anthropomorphic dog in the 1996 King Features comic strip by David Gilbert. Buckles is "more of an only child with canine instincts than he is the family pet." Bet your puppy is, too.

BUCKLEY Hound in the 2001 drama-comedy film *The Royal Tenenbaums*.

BUCKSHOT Hound dog in the 1997 Sundance Film Festival's "Centerpiece Premier" film *Ulee's Gold*, starring Peter Fonda. Popular name for a sporting dog, although buckshot is used for hunting large game, such as whitetail deer, which cannot be legally hunted with dogs in most states.

BUDAPEST Largest city in Hungary and an early Celtic settlement. Good name for a Komodor, Kuvasz, or Viszla, breeds that originated in Hungary.

BUDDY Buddy Holly (1936–1959), Texas-born American pioneer of rock and roll music, called "the single most influential creative force in early rock and roll" and ranked among the Fifty Greatest Artists of All Time by *Rolling Stone* magazine. He signed his first contract in 1956 with Decca Records and recorded "That'll be the Day," "Peggy

Sue," and "Oh Boy" and garnered national attention on the *Ed Sullivan Show* the following year. He was killed in a plane crash, dying at twenty-two years of age. Buddy is a common name for a dog, but a dog named after Buddy Holly knows how to rock.

BUDDY Partner, mate. Female German Shepherd Dog that was the first trained Seeing Eye dog in the United States. Buddy was owned by Morris Frank, founder of The Seeing Eye, America's first guide dog school. Golden Retriever canine actor that played Comet in the American sitcom *Full House*, which ran from 1987 to 1995; Bloodhound in *Cats & Dogs*.

BUFF Childhood nickname of Elizabeth Bowes-Lyon (1900–2002), Queen consort of King George VI of England. She became Queen Elizabeth the Queen Mother in 1952, when her daughter became Queen Elizabeth II upon the death of her father the king. Indeed, the long line of Corgis famously associated with the Royal Family was started by King George VI and his queen. During the Blitz, the queen was urged by the king's advisors to send her two daughters, Elizabeth and Margaret, to Canada for safety. Her famous reply was "The children won't go without me. I won't leave the king. And the king will never leave." Fine name for a dog with a buff-colored coat like the queen's Pembrokeshire Corgis.

BUFFON Georges-Louis Leclerc, Comte de Buffon (1707–1788), naturalist who wrote thirty-six volumes on nature and the animal kingdom, in which he claimed the Irish Wolfhound was the principal ancestor of the Great Dane.

BUGLE ANN *The Voice of Bugle Ann*, a 1936 film starring Lionel Barrymore and Maureen O'Sullivan, loosely based on a Foxhound named Old Drum.

Bugs Bunny Animated Looney Tunes rabbit supposedly born in a warren under Ebbets Field in Brooklyn, voiced by Mel "the Man of a Thousand Voices" Blanc, who blessed Bugs with an accent between the Bronx and Brooklyn.

Bugsy Bugsy Siegel (1906–1947), American gangster and driving force behind the development of Las Vegas. Bugsy pronounced actress-comedienne Rose Marie "the Queen of Vegas" when she headlined the first opening night in Vegas history, at Bugsy's Flamingo Hotel. "It was one street in the middle of a lot of sand," Rosie later recalled.

Buick Founded in 1899 as the Buick Auto-Vim and Power Company, Buick today is a luxury brand of General Motors.

Builder Craftsman or contractor that builds houses.

Bull English Bulldog in Walt Disney's 1955 animated motion picture *Lady and the Tramp*.

Bull's-Eye Bill Sikes's abused Bull Terrier in Charles Dickens's *Oliver Twist*.

Bullet Bullet the Wonder Dog was a black and silver German Shepherd Dog belonging to Roy Rogers and Dale Evans. He appeared regularly with his master and mistress on *The Roy Rogers Show*, which aired on television from 1951 to 1957.

Bullwinkle Bullwinkle J. Moose, Rocky the Flying Squirrel's sidekick in the long-running animated cartoon series *Rocky and Bullwinkle*.

Bully Nickname for a Bull Terrier. Explosive expression coined by Theodore Roosevelt that became a part of his oratorical rhetoric, meaning "well done" or "fantastic." The English Bulldog is the mascot of Mississippi State University.

Bummer One of two stray dogs, the other called Lazarus, who roamed the streets of San Francisco killing rats in the early 1860s, gaining local notoriety and lots of appreciation from the city's residents.

Bumpkin A country person with unsophisticated manners and ways.

BUNGEE An elastic cord. Bungee jumping is an adventure sport that requires an elastic cord, a tall bridge, and a lunatic willing to jump off an insanely high place.

BUNGEY Another of the dogs in Sir Ector's kennels in *The Once and Future King*, by T. H. White. Sir John Harington's dog in "Letter to Prince Henry" (1608).

BUNGLE Clumsy, blundering. Character in one of the sequels to *The Wonderful Wizard of Oz*, by L. Frank Baum.

BUNNY Small, adorable, furry, long-eared mammals, some wild and some cuddly domestic pets.

BUNTING Warm, snug sleeping bag for an infant.

BUNYAN Giant mythological lumberjack.

BURBLE Mixture of the three verbs: *bleat*, *murmur*, and *warble*. The word was invented by Lewis Carroll.

BURDETT *See* Phineas.

BURGUNDY Deep red color. Region of France where red wine is made from pressed, fermented Pinot Noir grapes.

BURKE Fortress (Old English).

BURMA Country in Southeast Asia where rare, blood-red Mogok rubies are mined.

BURNET A shade of brown. Good name for a Dachshund.

BURNETT *See* Gyp.

BURNISH Handsome name for a dog with dark brown markings, such as a Belgian Turveran.

BURTON Richard Burton (1926–1984), Welsh stage and screen actor nominated for seven Academy Awards and winner of none, famously married to Elizabeth Taylor—twice. Mr. W. Burton of Thorneywood Kennels, famous breeder of Bull-Mastiffs in Victorian England.

"Little Buster" was a gift to silent film great Anita Page from her costar, Hollywood icon Buster Keaton on the first day of shooting *Sidewalks of New York*.

BUSHIDO *See* Samurai.

BUSHY Shaggy, abundant hair. Fitting name for an Old English Sheepdog.

BUSTER Andy's pet Dachshund in all three *Toy Story* films. Dog on the television series *The Wonder Years*. Frederick Algernon Trotteville's Scottish Terrier in *The Five Find-Outers*, by Enid Blyton, a series of children's mystery novels, published between 1943 and 1961. Springer Spaniel that served with the Duke of Wellington's regiment and located a weapons arsenal in Safwan, Iraq, in March 2003. Buster Keaton (1895–1966), "the great stone face," lauded as the greatest physical comedian of all time and most famously known for *The General*, a 1926 American silent film in which he both starred and

PAPILLON MOTHER AND HER PUPPY

co-directed. American actor-director Orson Welles considered *The General*, "the greatest comedy ever made, the greatest Civil War film ever made, and perhaps the greatest film ever made."

BUTCH Anatolian Shepherd in *Cats & Dogs*. Butch is played by three canine actors—Noah, Moses, and Cain. Bulldog in the *Tom and Jerry* cartoons. American actress Laraine Day's Scottish Terrier.

BUTLER Great Dane belonging to Captain James T. Kirk, played by William Shatner, in *Star Trek: Generations*. The name of the dog in the script was Nexus, but it was changed to Butler, after William Shatner's own dog, who died before filming.

BUTTER Dairy product made from churned cream used in cooking, spread on bread, melted on corn on the cob . . . *mmmm!* Name a deliciously yellow dog Butter!

BUTTERBALL Roly-poly, plump. Cunning name for a Chow Chow.

BUTTERCUP "Wealth" in the language of flowers. Pick a buttercup and hold it under a friend's chin. If the buttercup glows, then your friend is telling the truth; if not, get a new friend.

BUTTERFLY Papillon, a member of the Toy Group, means "butterfly" in French, reflecting the breed's long, feathered tail and ears. President John F. Kennedy's dog, offspring of Pushkinar, along with White Tips, Blackies, and Streaker.

BUTTERMILK American actress Ashley Judd's Cockapoo, a mix between a Cocker Spaniel and a Poodle. Milky liquid produced from churned butter.

BUTTERSCOTCH Tasty hard candy, a sinful sauce over ice cream sundaes, and a delectable treacle pudding, made from brown sugar, corn syrup, cream, and vanilla and a pinch of salt.

BUTTON Small closure sewn on clothing since 2000 BC and generally made from bone, plastic, shells, porcelain, glass, or fabric. Dick Button, Olympic Men's Figure Skating gold medalist at the 1948 and 1952 games and one of the most outstanding commentators of the sport in television broadcasting history.

BUTTON-BRIGHT Little boy whose parents say "is bright as a button." He first appeared in the 1909 sequel to *The Wonderful Wizard of Oz*, *The Road to Oz*, by L. Frank Baum.

BUZZ Neil Armstrong, Michael Collins, Edwin E. "Buzz" Aldrin, the crew of Apollo 11, which took off on July 16, 1969, and made the first lunar landing near the Sea of Tranquility, a lunar mare that sits within the Tranquillitatis basin on the moon. The astronauts had to overcome navigation errors and computer alarms to land the first humans on the Moon, Armstrong and Aldrin. **Buzzy,** Thomas Jefferson's Briard.

BYRD Rear Admiral Richard Byrd Jr., United States Navy (1888–1957), pioneer aviator, and arctic explorer of both the North and South poles.

BYRON Lord George Gordon Noel, Sixth Baron Byron (1788–1824), British Romantic poet described by Lady Caroline Lamb as "mad, bad and dangerous to know."

C

C.J. Canine actor in the 2001 family film *Cats & Dogs*, starring Jeff Goldblum and Elizabeth Perkins.

CAACIE President Dwight D. Eisenhower's Scottish Terrier.

CAB Cab Calloway (1907–1994), New York–born bandleader and jazz singer whose personal history is entwined in the Cotton Club in Harlem, a legendary jazz venue. Composer of "Minnie the Moocher," which he wrote in 1931, he was instantly recognizable for the famous zoot suits he wore during his performances.

CABARET Nightclub that features entertainment. The first cabaret opened in Paris in 1881 and was immortalized by the brush of French artist Toulouse-Lautrec. The Tony Award–winning Broadway play, and later in 1972 Bob Fosse musical film starring the remarkable American singer-actress Liza Minnelli as Sally Bowles and a compelling Joel Grey as the Emcee of the Kit Kat Klub, was set in tumultuous Berlin of 1931.

CABERNET Cabernet Sauvignon, a red Bordeaux varietal wine.

CABOOSE Last car coupled at the rear of a train. Last pup in a litter.

CABOT One of the prestigious "first families of Boston" whose remarkable members includes Henry Cabot Lodge and his son, Henry Cabot Lodge Jr., both US senators. H. C. L. Jr. was Richard Nixon's running mate in the 1960 presidential election.

CADBURY British confectionary company that has made some of the finest candies in the world since 1824.

CADDY Fellow who lugs a player's clubs around a golf course; however, a professional caddy is something more: he gives valuable suggestions and moral support to the player for whom he cuddies.

CADENCE Rhythm or harmonic closure to a musical phrase.

CADET Military student, trainee. Cadet is a shade of grey; good name for a Bouvier des Flandres, a particularly heroic breed, used as a war dog in the First World War.

CADILLAC Luxury car first produced in 1902 by Henry Leland and owned today by General Motors. The word has come to mean best in quality, top-of-the-line, in all things.

CADWALDER *See* Bixby.

CÁEL Slender (Irish). Superb name for an Irish Greyhound.

CAESAR Imperial Roman title.

CAFALL Dog belonging to the legendary King Arthur, sometimes called **Cabal.**

CAFÉ AU LAIT Hot, milky coffee. Good name for dog with a light brown coat and perfect name for a French Bulldog.

CAGNEY James Cagney (1899–1986), American actor branded by tough-guy roles early in his career in movies such as *Angels with Dirty Faces* and *The Public Enemy*, in which he famously thrust half a grapefruit in Mae Clarke's face. One of the first independent actors to defy the studio contract system, he was a very private man who preferred the life of a country farmer at Verney Farm, his working farm in Dutchess County, New York, where he died on Easter Sunday 1986 at the age of eighty-six.

CAIN Canine actor in the family comedy film *Cats & Dogs*.

CAIRO Vanquisher, conqueror (Egyptian). Capital of Egypt. Joel Cairo, played by Austrian-born American character actor Peter Lorre, who coveted *The Maltese Falcon* (1941), along with Humphrey Bogart, Mary Astor, and Sidney Greenstreet.

CAITLAND *See* Dog Names by Category: Breed; Crufts.

CAITLÍN Irish for Katherine.

CAIUS Dr. John Caius (1510–1573), master of Gonville and Caius College, Cambridge, and court physician to Queen Elizabeth I, was the first to write a book entirely devoted to the Skye Terrier breed.

CAJUN French ethnic group living in Louisiana and known for their distinctive, spicy cuisine.

CAL Diminutive of Calvin.

CALADIUM "Immense delight and joy" in the language of flowers.

CALAIS French city and the closest in continental Europe to England.

CALAMITY JANE President Calvin Coolidge's Shetland Sheepdog.

CALANDRA Beautiful singer (Italian).

CALCUTTA Indian bloodhound that could not smell in the British comic strip *The Perishers*.

CALDWELL *See* Laird.

CALEDFWLCH Welsh name for the King Arthur's legendary sword Excalibur.

CALEDONIA Ancient Roman name for Scotland. Regal name for a Scottish Deerhound.

CALGARY Ch. Calgary Grizzle, British Captain C. A. Monson's champion Curly-Coated Retriever and winner of the Ashburton Cup.

CALIBER Quality, high standard. Internal diameter of a gun barrel.

CALICO A worsted cotton fabric with a printed design.

CALIFORNIA The thirty-first state to enter the United States.

CALLA "Pig's ear" (Afrikaans). Good name for a Saluki. "The calla lilies are in bloom again," Katharine Hepburn's oft-quoted line in the 1937 film *Stage Door*.

CALLAGHAN *See* Dog Names by Category: Breed; Crufts.

CALLAHAN Bright-headed, from the Irish surname, *Ó Ceallacháin*.

CALLIE Affectionate for Caroline.

CALLISTO The most handsome (Italian).

CALLOWAY Cab Calloway (1907–1994) Singer, bandleader whose big-beat rhythm was a force to be reckoned with in American jazz.

CALOGERA Beautiful elder (Italian).

CALVERT Seventeenth-century Canadian settlement that today comprises the provinces of Newfoundland and Labrador. Splendid name for a Newfoundland or Labrador Retriever.

CALVIN *Calvin and Hobbes*, Bill Watterson's syndicated comic strip about a six-year-old boy named Calvin and his toy tiger, Hobbes. Calvin Coolidge, thirtieth president of the United States.

CALVINA Little bald one (Italian). Wonderful name for a female Mexican Hairless or Chinese Crested. (**Calvino** for a male puppy.)

CALYPSO Sea nymph in Greek mythology. Trinidadian folk music with steel drums and a strong beat.

CAMDEN Enclosed valley (Old English).

CAMEL Good name for a Pharaoh Hound, a breed of Eygptian origin; a warm, medium yellow color.

CAMELLIA Lovely, fragrant flower. Good name for a dog with a white coat, such as a Beddlington Terrier.

CAMELOT Twelfth-century castle fortress of King Arthur that may have stood where the haunting ruins that buttress the sea at Tintagel, in Cornwall, England, still stand today.

CAMEMBERT Soft, age-ripened cheese from Normandy, France. Authentic Camembert has a pungent smell, utterly divine taste, and should always be served at room temperature.

CAMEO Brooch of carved shell or ivory, usually a bas-relief of a woman's face. Brief appearance by an actor in a performance, often uncredited.

CAMERON "Crooked nose" (Gaelic).

CAMILLO Attendant, guard (Italian).

CAMUS Spanish surname from the Basque country of Northern Spain.

CAN Dog (Galician).

CANDY Sheepdog belonging to Candy, the emotionally and physically scarred ranch worker in American writer John Steinbeck's classic book of the Great Depression, *Of Mice and Men*.

CANE Dog (Italian).

CANICHE Poodle (French).

CANIGOU CAMBRAI *See* Dog Names by Category: Breed; Crufts.

CANIS MAJOR Larger dog (Latin). Large constellation represented as the large dog that follows the constellation Orion (The Hunter) in ancient astronomer Ptolemy's constellation of forty-eight constellations.

CANIS MINOR Smaller dog (Latin). Small constellation represented as the small dog that follows the constellation Orion in ancient astronomer Ptolemy's forty-eight constellations.

CANTON *See* Sailor.

CANUTE CNUT (AD 985–1035), King of Denmark, England, Norway, and parts of Sweden. Rule thirty-one of the Canute Laws, which was enacted in the British Parliament at Winchester in AD 1016, states: "No meane person may keepe any greihounds, but freemen may keepe greihounds . . ." which appears to fine the owners of Greyhounds that approach within ten miles of the King's forests.

CÃO Dog (Portuguese, Romanian).

CAP'N BILL Peg-legged, retired sea captain in *Scarecrow of Oz*, a sequel to *The Wonderful Wizard of Oz*, by L. Frank Baum.

CAPER Frolic, cavort gambol.

CAPERS Deciduous plant used for medicine, makeup, and a piquant of flavors to salads, pasta, and fish.

CAPPUCCINO Small cap (Italian). Hot espresso coffee drink "capped" with steamed milk, created by the Capuchin friars in Vienna, Austria in the seventeenth century.

CAPRICE Impulsive, on a whim, from the Italian word *capriccio*.

CAPRICORN Tenth astrological sign of the zodiac, ruled by Saturn and represented by a goat with a fish tail. Those born under Capricorn, an earth sign, are introspective and reserved by nature.

CAPTAIN WOOF A Muppet dog.

CAPTAIN Naval officer or the person in charge of a boat; from the Greek word *katepánō*, meaning "the one placed at the top."

CARAWAY Anise-flavored seeds of a biennial plant used to flavor liquors and as a seasoning for foods.

CARDOS King Cardos of Scotland, knight of the Round Table, came with five hundred knights to the great feast of Pentecost after the coronation of King Arthur at the "citie of Carlion" in Wales, according to *La Mort d'Arthur: King Arthur and his Noble Knights of the Round Table*, compiled by English writer Sir Thomas Malory in the fifteenth century.

CARBON Black organic compound and swell name for a black dog.

CARCASSONE Fortified medieval town in the former French province of Languedoc where early bas-reliefs depict the Great Pyrenees breed of dog.

CARDIGAN Knitted sweater without a collar. Cardigan Welsh Corgi is older than the Pembroke Welsh Corgi and the one with the tail. A herding dog that came with the Celts to Cardiganshire on the western coast of Wales in 1200 BC. A favored breed of Queen Elizabeth II of England.

CARFACE CARRUTHERS Villainous American Pit Bull in the 1989 animated film *All Dogs Go to Heaven*.

CARGO Great name for a dog that carries a doggy backpack.

CARIBOU North American reindeer. Good name for an Alaskan Malamute.

CARL German form of **Charles**, **Carlo** in Italian, **Carlos** in Spanish. *Good Dog, Carl*, one in a series of illustrated children's books by Alexandra Day about a Rottweiler named Carl and a little girl named Madeleine.

CARLA Italian feminine of **Carlos**. Also **Carlita**, **Carlotta**—good names for a female Italian Greyhound or Spinone Italiano.

CARLYLE Thomas Carlyle (1795–1881), Scottish satirist, social commenter, and historian who called economics "the dismal science." The Carlyle, a five-star Manhattan hotel, was named after this celebrated Scotsman.

CARMELO Garden (Hebrew).

CARMEN Song (Latin). Popular opera by George Bizet that takes place in the nineteenth century in Seville, Spain. The seductress Carmen is one of the most coveted mezzosoprano roles in opera.

CARMICHAEL *See* Dog Names by Category: Breed; Westminster.

CARNARVON George Edward Stanhope Molyneux Herbert, Fifth Earl of Carnarvon (1866–1923). English aristocrat and financier of the expedition that discovered King Tutankhamen's tomb in the Valley of the Kings. The Earl of Carnarvon passed away shortly after the discovery from "the curse of King Tut" though in actuality he died from septicemia as the result of an infected mosquito bite.

CARNATION Cut flower commonly used in floral arrangements. Legend says pink carnations fell in the wake of Mother Mary's tears as she followed her son Jesus as he carried the cross to Golgotha, where he was crucified. Pink carnations symbolize a mother's undying love.

CARNEGIE Andrew Carnegie (1835–1919), poor Scottish immigrant who became one of the richest men in America. A great philanthropist, by the time of his death he had given away virtually his entire fortune. Part of his fortune was used to build over 3,500 Carnegie-endowed libraries in the United States.

CAROB Beans from the carob tree. Carob can be used as a substitute for chocolate in cooking.

CAROL Song, hymn.

CAROLINA North and South Carolina, the seventh and eighth states admitted into United States.

CAROLUS Charles (Latin).

CAROLYN Female form of **Charles**. **Carol** is the diminutive form.

CARRAWAY Nick Carraway is the narrator of *The Great Gatsby* by F. Scott Fitzgerald.

CARROT Cute name for a Chow Chow or other dog with an orange-ish coat.

CARRUTHERS Scottish surname, great for a Scottish Terrier or Scottish Wolfhound.

CARSON Unknown (Gaelic). Charles Carson, the butler of *Downton Abbey* played by English actor Jim Carter. Downton simply could not run without Carson, nor could the series be as compelling without Jim Carter. He is married to one of England's most accomplished actresses,

Imelda Staunton, who we all loved to loathe as Dolores Umbridge in the Harry Potter movies.

CARTER Individual that drives or pushes a cart (English).

CARTIER Famous jewelers founded by Louis-François Cartier in Paris in 1847.

CARTWRIGHT Repairer and maker of carts. Good name for a Bernese Mountain Dog, a breed historically used as a draft dog to pull carts.

CARUSO President William Howard Taft's daughter, Helen's, dog, given to her by the greater tenor, Enrico Caruso.

CARY Derived from the Irish word *ciar*, which means black. Cary Grant (1904–1986), English actor born Archibald Leach in Bristol, England, Hollywood's most charismatic leading man, known for his comedic abilities and charm. The depth he brought to his dramatic roles was widely underestimated.

CASABLANCA White house (Spanish). Hollywood film, perhaps the greatest wartime romance ever, in 1942, starring my relative Humphrey Bogart with Ingrid Bergman, Sydney Greenstreet, Peter Lorre, and the great Claude Rains, to whom Bogie directs the final line of the movie: "Louis, I think this is the beginning of a beautiful friendship."

CASANOVA Giacomo Girolamo Casanova de Seingalt (1725–1798), legendary womanizer whose name is synonymous with seduction.

CASBAH Walled cities in North Africa.

CASEY Vigilant (English). Casey Jones (1863–1900), American railroad engineer who tried to stop his steam-driven train, the Cannonball Express, before it collided with an oncoming passenger train, saving every life except his own. His self-sacrifice was immortalized by his friend, Wallace Saunders, who wrote the popular American ballad.

CASHMERE Soft, luxurious, light, warm wool shorn from the Cashmere goat, a breed found on the Alashan Terrace of Mongolia.

CASIMIRO Commands peace (Italian).

CASINO A place where gambling takes place. Martin Scorsese's 1995 film based on *Casino*, a book by Nicholas Pileggi about the Mob in Las Vegas in the seventies.

CASPAR One of the three Magi who followed the star to present gifts to the infant Jesus Christ, "born King of the Jews," according to the Gospel of Matthew. Interestingly, the Magi, or kings, are not named in the Bible.

CASPER Casper the Friendly Ghost first appeared in Paramount's Noveltoon animated cartoons in 1945 and has happily haunted us in comic strips, on television, and in movies ever since.

CASPIAN The rightful King of Narnia in C. S. Lewis's *Chronicles of Narnia*.

CASSANDRA Shining upon man (English). Trojan princess given the gift of prophesy in Greek mythology.

CASSELL According to the nineteenth-century work *Cassell's Popular Natural History*, the Great Dane breed dates back to Egyptian times, ca. 3000 BC, as proven by ancient hieroglyphics discovered on monument walls.

CASSIDY Curly-haired (Gaelic).

CASSIE Diminutive of **Cassandra**.

CASTAWAY Person who is shipwrecked on a tropical island, such as Robinson Crusoe, and in *Swiss Family Robinson*.

CASTLE Castle Kennels, belonging to the Duke of Gordon, was one of a half dozen eighteenth-century Scottish breeders of Gordon Setters. Though the breed was named after the Duke, it did not actually originate at his kennels.

CASTOR From the word *castory*, which describes the shade of brown of a beaver's pelts. Good name for a Chesapeake Bay Retriever. The Harrier breed of dog was favored by the Greek demigod Castor.

CATALINA Spanish feminine for Katherine. Island off the coast of Southern California.

CATERINA Pure (Italian).

CATO A Newfoundland dog painted in 1870 by English artist George Earl, a member of the British Royal Academy of Art and an early member of the Kennel Club of Great Britain. Earl's portrait of Cato is in the collection of the American Kennel Club.

CATULLA *See* Issa.

CAVALIER "The White Cavalier," early nickname of the Bull Terrier.

CAVALL Yet another dog in Sir Ector's kennels in T. H. White's Arthurian fantasy novel *The Once and Future King*.

CAVIAR Harvested eggs of wild sturgeon, a great delicacy; *see* Beluga. Great name for a black Poodle.

CAYENNE Hot red chili pepper used for seasoning. Great name for a red-hot hunting dog.

CAYKE Cayke the Cookie Cook bakes her delicious cookies in gold, diamond-studded cookie pans in *The Lost Princess of Oz*, the 1917 annual sequel to *The Wonderful Wizard of Oz* by L. Frank Baum. Hey, don't we all.

CECIL Derived from *Sextus*, a Latin name given to the sixth child. Artist Andy Warhol's Great Dane.

CECILIA Blind, from the Latin word, *caecus*. Patron saint of musicians.

CEDRIC Founder of the Kingdom of Wessex in the sixth century; character in the 1819 novel *Ivanhoe*, by Sir Walter Scott.

CEFFYL DŴR *See* Kelpie.

CELESTE Of the sky, heavenly (Roman). Celeste Holm (1917–2012), American-Norwegian actress who won the 1947 Best Actress Academy Award for *Gentlemen's Agreement*, was nominated for a Best Supporting Actress Oscar for her role as a nun in *Come to the Stable* in 1949 and nominated the following year as Best Supporting Actress for her role as Karen Richards in *All About Eve*. An accomplished stage and screen star, she is perhaps best known for her role as Liz Imbrie in the 1956 musical film *High Society*, which starred Bing Crosby, Grace Kelly, and Frank Sinatra, with whom she sang "Who Wants to Be a Millionaire?" You'd be naming your dog after a warm and classy lady if you choose Celeste.

CELIA Heaven (Italian). Rosalind's cousin in Shakespeare's *As You Like It*.

CELLO Bowed string instrument in the violin family.

CELSO Upright, noble (Italian).

CELT Early breeders of the Cardigan Corgi. Iron Age society from 800 BC.

CERBERUS With Orthus, one of the pair of hounds of Hades in Greek mythology. The Greyhound in the 2004 Irish comedy *Man About Dog*.

CERIL Hellhound that haunts the Castle Carra, Scotland, in the 1987 children's book *The Haunting of Hira*, by Eva Ibbotson.

CERISE Cherry (French).

CESARE Severed (Italian). Good name for a dog with a docked tail.

CESARIO Shipwrecked, Viola, disguised as a boy in Shakespeare's *Twelfth Night*, assumes this name.

C'EST MOI "It is I!" (French).

CETSHWAYO *See* Zulu.

CHABLIS Northern region of Burgundy where Chardonnay grapes have been grown for wine-making since Roman times.

CHACHA Strong (Zimbabwe).

CHAD Battle (Welsh).

CHAGALL Marc Chagall (1887–1985), Russian French Jewish modern artist celebrated for his use of color and combination of elements of Cubist, Fauvist, and Symbolist art.

CHAIRO Brown (Japanese). Good name for an Akita Inu.

CHALET Cottage indigenous to the Alpine region of Switzerland.

CHALK White sedimentary rock used for blackboard chalk and in toothpaste, as well as a wide variety of other uses. Great name for a white dog.

CHALKY Jack Russell Terrier (1989–2007) owned by English chef Rick Stein. Chalky's Bite and Chalky's Bark, two beers brewed by Sharps, were named after this dog. So popular was the little dog that his death was announced on the floor of Great Britain's Parliament.

CHALLENGER NASA's second Space Shuttle orbiter to be put into service tragically blew up seventy-three seconds after launch on January 28, 1986. On board was New Hampshire schoolteacher and mother, Christa McAuliffe.

CHALULU Character in the *The Purple Prince of Oz*, sequel to *The Wonderful Wizard of Oz*, by L. Frank Baum (1900).

CHAMBRAY A light cotton or linen fabric used to make clothing.

CHAMOIS Shy, graceful species of wild goat native to the Carpathian Mountains and the Alps in northern Europe.

CHAMP Short for "champion."

CHAMPAGNE Sparkling white wine from the Champagne region of France that's brought out to toast special occasions. Fine name for a French Bulldog.

CHAMPION General Henry Champion, Connecticut-born Federalist and first acting general of the First Battalion Light Brigade under General George Washington during the American Revolutionary War.

CHANCE The American Bulldog in the best-selling novel *Homeward Bound: The Incredible Journey*, by Sheila Burnford, which spawned several films. Chance was voiced by American actor Michael J. Fox.

CHANDLER *See* Dake.

CHANEL Twentieth-century French couture designer Coco Chanel. *See* Coco Chanel.

CHANG Chinese general during the Ming Dynasty (1368–1644). Great name for a Chinese breed, such as a Pekingese, Pug, Shar Pei, Shih Tzu, or Chow Chow.

CHANG WANG WOE Emperor in *The Royal Book of Oz*, by Ruth Plumly Thompson, L. Frank Baum's official successor as "Royal Historian of Oz."

CHANGBAI Mountains between the border of China and Korea.

CHANNING Carol Elaine Channing (b. 1921) American singer, actress, and comedienne whose career spans seven decades. Her trademark portrayal of blond bombshell Lorelei Lee in *Gentlemen Prefer Blonde*s and Dolly Gallagher Levi in *Hello, Dolly!* is Broadway legend.

CHANTILLY Fine handmade lace from Chantilly in the Bayeux region of France dating from the seventeenth century.

CHAPLIN Sir Charles Spencer "Charlie" Chaplin, KBE (1889–1977). "The only genius to come out of the movie industry," said George Bernard Shaw. Chaplin branded silent films with his immortal, mustachioed, cane-twirling character, The Tramp, during the Great Depression, when American needed a good laugh. Composer of one of the loveliest and surely the most bittersweet songs of all time, "Smile," Chaplin also wrote, "This Is My Song," which Michael Jackson said was his favorite song of all.

CHARADE Stanley Donen's 1963 suspense motion picture starring Cary Grant and Audrey Hepburn. Popular parlor game.

CHARCOAL Organic, dark grey form of carbon. Great name for a dog with a dark grey coat, such as a Kerry Blue Terrier.

CHARDON Thistle (French).

CHARDONNAY A full-bodied, citrusy white wine . . . with, perhaps, a hint of vanilla?

CHARISMA Personable, charming.

CHARITY Compassion, generosity, goodwill to those who are less fortunate than ourselves.

CHARKIE Steve and Betsy's disobedient black Cocker Spaniel in the PBS animated children's TV series *Curious George*, based on the books by Hans Augusto Rey and Margret Rey.

CHARLEMAGNE (742–814) King of the Franks, Emperor of the Romans, ruler of all Europe, and founding father, biologically speaking, of the French and German monarchies. Good name for an active dog with an alpha personality.

CHARLENE Rufus's girlfriend in the 2006 computer animated film *Open Season 2*.

CHARLES Army, warrior (Germanic). Given name of many English kings and princes; the Italian Greyhound has been a favorite of European royalty since King Charles I.

CHARLEY John Steinbeck's French Standard Poodle and traveling companion during a 1960 cross-country road trip that he chronicled in *Travels with Charley*.

CHARLIE B. BARKIN Roguish German Shepherd Dog in the 1989 animated film *All Dogs Go to Heaven*. President John F. Kennedy's Welsh Terrier.

CHARLIE BROWN Ageless little boy and perennial loser beloved by millions, created in 1950 in the comic strip *Peanuts* by Charles M. Schulz. His dog, of course, is Snoopy.

CHARLIE DOG Mel Blanc–voiced animated Looney Tunes dog that boasted of his pedigree that he was "Fifty percent Collie! Fifty percent setter, Irish Setter! Fifty Percent Boxer! Fifty percent Doberman Pinscher! Fifty percent Pointer—there it is! But, mostly, I'm all Labrador Retriever!"

CHARLOTTE Female diminutive of **Charles**. Charlotte Brontë (1816–1855), English author and eldest Brontë sister whose celebrated romantic novel *Jane Eyre* has been adapted umpteen times in films and on television none more perfectly than Joan Fontaine.

CHARMER Someone who is charming, an enchanter, a Lothario.

CHARMING Prince Charming, handsome, brave nobleman who wins the heart of *Sleeping Beauty, Cinderella, Snow White* but not Princess Fiona in *Shrek*.

CHARON Boat pilot who ferries dead souls across the river Styx to Hades in Greek mythology.

CHASE Fitting name for a dog that doesn't come when he's called and is therefore a good candidate for obedience school and/or an electronic dog training collar.

CHASEN Renowned Hollywood restaurant opened in 1936 by vaudevillian Dave Chasen. Regulars included Humphrey Bogart, Marilyn Monroe, James Stewart, Shirley Temple, Cary Grant, Joe DiMaggio, Corey Ford, Jack Benny, Jackie Gleason, W. C. Fields, James Cagney, Clark Gable—a veritable Who's Who of Hollywood.

CHASSE To hunt (French).

Carole Lombard, comedienne and wife of Clark Gable, with a Dachshund puppy and a black Cocker Spaniel puppy.

CHATSWORTH *See* Devonshire.

CHAUCER Geoffrey Chaucer (1343–1400), father of English literature and one of the greatest poets of the Middle Ages, his epic *The Canterbury Tales* secured him an eternal resting place in Poet's Corner at Westminster Abbey.

CHAUFFER Heat, warm up (French).

CHAUFFEUR Individual hired to drive a luxury motor car around for people who can afford it.

CHAUNCEY Chauncey Gardiner, who actually is Chance the gardener, played poignantly by the great, complex comic actor Peter Sellers in his last film, *Being There* (1979), adapted from the Jerzy Kozinski novella.

CHAUVE Pronounced *show-va*, it is the French word for "bald." An elegant name for a Mexican Hairless dog or a Chinese Crested dog.

CHECKERS American board game played by two opposing players, each starting out with twelve round playing pieces called checkers, and one player ultimately ending up with none; called "draughts" in England. President Richard M. Nixon's family's famous Cocker Spaniel.

CHECKMATE "The king is ambushed" (Middle English). Victor who makes the decisive move in a game of chess.

CHEDDAR Hard, yellow, sharp-tasting cheese that originated in the town of Cheddar in Somerset, England. Absolutely delightful name for a yellow Labrador Retriever.

CHEEKY Saucy, insolent, a bit of a smart aleck.

CHEERIO Informal British greeting.

CHEERS Slang for see you later, thanks, or a salute after a toast.

CHEESECAKE Sinful dessert that goes straight to my hips. *Et vous?*

CHEETAH Large, spotted wild African animal from the feline family. The cheetah is the fastest mammal on earth, can run up to seventy-five miles per hour, and has been clocked to accelerate to sixty-two miles per hour in three seconds. Perfect name for a Greyhound.

CHEKHOV Anton Pavlovich Chekhov (1860–1904). Playwright (*Uncle Vanya*, *The Cherry Orchard*) and one of the greatest writers of short stories in world literature. Chekov was also a physician. "Medicine is my lawful wife and literature is my mistress," he wrote. An extremely handsome man who enjoyed the company of women, he married late in life, living largely apart from Olga, his wife of only three years, before he died of tuberculosis at the age of forty-four. One of his most famous short stories is "The Lady with the Dog."

CHELSEA Landing place for chalk (English). Swank district in London. Only relatively recently a popular girl's name.

CHEN Dog (Haitian Creole).

CHEQUERS Sixteenth-century estate situated in Buckinghamshire that has served as the official country residence of Britain's prime ministers since 1921. Although Winston Churchill is associated with the English Bulldog, he never owned one; he owned two Poodles, one named Chequers, named after the estate, and the other named Rufus.

CHÈRE Dear, cherished, expensive (French). Also, **Chéri**.

CHERNUSHKA *See* Dog Names by Category: History;.

CHEROKEE Sidney Prescott's Golden Retriever in the 2000 Wes Craven film *Scream 3*.

CHERRY Black Labrador Retriever belonging to American actress Julianne Moore and her husband Bart Freundlich.

CHERUB Second highest order of angels, according to the Bible.

CHESS Tactical two-player board game invented in southern Europe in the twelfth century, based on the ancient Indian game of Shatraj and refined in 1475 to the modern game; François-André Danican Philidor, eighteenth-century musician, was a French chess grand master.

CHESSY Nickname of the Chesapeake Bay Retriever. Diminutive of **Francesca**.

CHESTER Fortified place (Latin). Small, happy, yellow Terrier and Spike's foil in the *Looney Tunes* and *Merrie Melodies* animated cartoons of the fifties.

CHESTNUT From the Ancient Greek *kastaneia*, a genus of eight species of nut-bearing trees. The shell of a chestnut is dark brown; if that's the color of your dog's coat, that's a name for him. Great Dane in the 2004 film *Chestnut: Hero of Central Park*.

CHESTY English Bulldog mascot of the United States Marine Corps.

CHET First month in the Nanakshahi calendar, coinciding with March and April in the Gregorian and Julian calendars.

CHEVALIER Maurice Chevalier (1888–1972), French actor and singer who personified *Sprechgesang*, part singing and part speaking the words of a song. One of the most debonair actors of his time, his best-known role was Honoré Lachaille in director Vincente Minnelli's classic 1958 musical motion picture *Gigi*, starring Leslie Caron, Louis Jourdan, and that marvelous English actress Hermione Gingold, who sang that enchantingly wistful song, "I Remember It Well" with Chevalier. Here's the name for a French Poodle, a Bichon Frise, or a Papillion.

CHEVIOT Cheviot Hills, which forms the border between England and Scotland, is the home of the Border Terrier, the oldest strain of Terrier in the United Kingdom.

CHEWBACCA Han Solo's big, hairy, unintelligible (unless you speak Wookiee) first mate on the beat-up galaxy cruiser, the *Millennium Falcon*, in George Lucas's *Star Wars* saga.

CHEYENNE Native American Plains tribe belonging to the Algonquin nation.

CHI *See* Spirit.

CHI CHI Nickname for the Chihuahua. Chi Chi Rodriguez is American actress Reese Witherspoon's Chihuahua.

CHIANTI Full-bodied Italian red wine produced in Tuscany.

CHIC Fashionable, in vogue. Good name for a well-coiffed Poodle.

CHICA "Little girl" (Spanish); Chico is masculine for "little boy."

CHICLET Young chicken or bird.

CHICORY Woody, herbaceous plant used instead of, or in addition to, coffee.

CHIDI God exists (Nigerian).

CHIDLEY *See* Dog Names by Category: Breed; Westminster.

CHIEF Old hunting dog voiced by American actor Pat Buttram in the 1981 Walt Disney animated feature film *The Fox and the Hound*.

CHIEFTAIN Highland chieftains in Scotland hunted with Scottish Deerhounds.

CHIEN Dog (French). Chien Berger de Brie ("Sheepdog of Brie") is a very old breed of herding dog that originated in Brie, the region of France best known for the production of Brie cheese.

CHIFFON Cloth (Old French). Sheer silk cloth used in dressmaking. Pretty name for the silky-coated Lhasa Apso or an Australian Silky Terrier.

CHIK *See* Dog Names by Category: Breed; Westminster.

CHIKA Near (Japanese).

CHIKE Power of God (Nigerian).

CHILD Julia Child (1912–2004), "the French Chef," America's most famous television cooking show personality and award-winning American cookbook writer. *Mastering the Art of French Cooking*, which she co-authored, was published when Child was fifty years old. Her memoir, *My Life in France*, was a bestseller. She was the subject of the 2009 film *Julie & Julia*, starring Meryl Streep and Amy Adams, based on Julie Powell's book of the same name, which Child refused to endorse. Judith Jones, Child's friend and longtime editor at Knopf, commented on Child's reaction to the book and its author in *Publishers Weekly*. "She didn't suffer fools, if you know what I mean," she observed.

CHILI Spicy Mexican dish traditionally made with ground beef and beans.

CHILLA Long-lived Australian Cattle Dog–Labrador Retriever mix that died at the age of thirty-two.

CHIMALSI Young, proud (Nigerian).

CHINA Most populated country in the world and the second largest in land mass. Great name for a Chow Chow, Chinese Crested Dog, Lhasa Apso, Pekingese, Pug, Shar Pei, or Shih Tzu, all Chinese breeds.

CHIN-CHIN Ceremonial toast in England, Portugal, and Argentina. Chinese three-string banjo.

CHING Chinese dynasty from 1644 to 1911.

CHINOOK Official state dog of New Hampshire. First bred by Arthur Treadwell Walden of Wonalancet, New Hampshire, in 1917, a Chinook was Walden's lead sled dog in the Byrd Antarctic Expedition of 1928. Siberian Husky that leads the Canadian Mounted Police in the 1951 movie *Yukon Manhunt*.

CHINWENDU "God owns life" (Igbo).

CHIP Piece, token. "Chip off the old block" means a son who is like his father.

CHIPMUNK Small, striped relative of the squirrel. Three of them are known to sing pretty well—Alvin, Theodore, and Simon.

CHIPS Most decorated canine war dog of World War Two. *Goodbye, Mr. Chips*, by James Hilton, was adapted into the 1939 motion picture starring Robert Donat, who beat out Clark Gable in *Gone with the Wind* for the Best Actor Academy Award that year. Mr. Chipping, affectionately known as Chips, was a devoted professor at Brookfield, a private boys' school England during the years spanning the two world wars. His tragic early life was compensated by a long and fulfilling one as a beacon to hundreds of Brookfield boys over three generations.

CHIQUITA "Little girl" (Spanish). **Chiquito** is "little boy."

CHISS Four-legged, porcupine-like character in *The Patchwork Girl of Oz*, an Oz sequel by L. Frank Baum. Swell name for a dog with a rough coat, such as a Wirehaired Pointing Griffon or a Wire Fox Terrier.

CHISULO "Very strong, like steel" (Nigerian).

CHIVAS Blended Scotch whiskey distilled in Aberdeen, Scotland, since 1801.

CHLOE Green shoot (Greek). Chihuahua voiced by American actress Drew Barrymore in the 2008 Disney film *Beverly Hills Chihuahua*.

CHO CHANG Ravenclaw student at Hogwarts School of Witchcraft and Wizardry who gave Harry Potter his first kiss.

CHO CHO Talking Briard voiced by American comedic actor Chevy Chase in the 2004 movie *The Karate Dog*,

CHÓ Dog (Vietnamese).

CHOCOLATE Beans from the Theobroma cacao tree, the basic ingredient in hot chocolate, chocolate cake, brownies, and other sinful delights. Great name for a chocolate Labrador Retriever.

CHOLULA Pyramids of Cholula, home of the Toltecs, the Mesoamerican predecessors of the Aztecs.

CHOO-CHOO Royal Family of England's Tibetan Lion Dog. The family tradition of owning this breed of dog began with Queen Victoria.

CHOO-TAI *See* Dog Names by Category: Breed; Crufts.

CHOPIN Frédéric François Chopin (1810–1849), Polish composer and virtuoso pianist who, in his short lifetime, was a major figure in the development of nineteenth-century Romantic music. He had a decade-long love affair with Amantine Lucile Aurore Dupin, later Baroness Dudevant (1804–1876), which ended with his death. A writer, she is known in the world of literature by her nom de plume George Sand.

CHOPPER The protective white Bulldog that befriends Yakky Doodle on the animated children's TV series *The Yogi Bear Show*.

CHOPS Jowls, jaw.

CHOPSTICKS Eating utensils used in Far Eastern countries, believed to have originated in Ancient China.

CHORTLE Chuckle plus snort equals "chortle," a distinctive type of laugh.

CHOW MEIN Chinese dish with stir-fried noodles.

CHOWDER Dog in *The Expedition of Humphrey Clinker*, by Tobias Smollett.

CHRIS The family dog in *The Searchers*, by Edward Buscombe.

CHRISTIAN A follower of Christ.

CHRISTINE Feminine form of **Christian**, from *Christianus*, Latin for "follower of Christ."

CHRISTMAS *A Dog Named Christmas*, heartwarming 2009 CBS Hallmark Hall of Fame movie about a yellow Labrador Retriever, based on the book by Greg Kincaid. The Christmas Rose means "calm and peaceful" in the language of flowers.

CHU CHIN CHOW Long-running 1916 musical comedy on the London stage, inspired by the story of Ali Baba and the Forty Thieves.

CHUCHO Great Dane in the 2008 Disney film *Beverly Hills Chihuahua*.

CHUCHUNDRA Muskrat in *The Jungle Book*, by Rudyard Kipling.

CHUCKLES *See* Dog Names by Category: Breed; Crufts.

CHUM Buddy, pal, mate.

CHUN Chun Lee-Kyung of South Korea, short-track speed skater who won five medals in the 1994 and 1998 Olympic Games.

CHUNDO *See* Fay Ray.

CHURCHILL Sir Winston Leonard Spencer-Churchill (1874–1965), the greatest British statesmen of the twentieth century. He stoically led his country through World War Two, ending his magnificent political career at the age of eighty-one, in 1955. In a rare gesture, he was given a state funeral by royal decree of Queen Elizabeth II, the first and certainly most esteemed of her thirteen prime ministers to date.

CHUTNEY Spicy condiment used in South Asian cuisines. One such is called Major Grey's Chutney, believed to have been created by a British officer in British Colonial India of that name and rank.

CHUTZPAH Yiddish word for brazen self-confidence.

CHZI GOU *See* Foo.

CI Dog (Welsh).

CIABURRI Great Dane enthusiast who published an article in an Italian publication in 1929 stating the Great Dane was bred in China in 1121 BC.

CIAO Italian greeting for hello or good-bye, depending upon whether you are coming or going.

CIARÁN Black (Gaelic). Lovely name for a black Labrador Retriever, black Cocker Spaniel, or a Gordon Setter, all breeds that originated in Great Britain.

CIDER Beloved English Setter of Corey Ford, immortalized in "The Road to Tinkhamtown" (1965), widely considered the greatest American outdoor short story ever written.

CIMARRON Acclaimed 1929 novel by Edna Ferber about the Oklahoma land rush of 1882, inspiring two highly acclaimed film adaptations.

BLACK LABRADOR RETRIEVER AND HER LITTER

CINDER Remains of something burnt, from the Old English word *sinder*.

CINDERELLA French folktale more famously adapted into the classic animated movie by Walt Disney in 1950—the thirteenth motion picture adaptation of the story in film history. The first, incredibly, was made a half century earlier in 1899, produced by pioneering French filmmaker Georges Mèliés, recently venerated by Martin Scorsese in his Academy Award–winning film *Hugo*, produced by Johnny Depp.

CINDY Greyhound in *The Guinness Book of World Records* that cleared a five-and-a-half-foot hurdle, the highest jump ever achieved by a dog.

CINNAMON Spice from the bark of the cinnamon tree used in baking and mulled cider. Canine friend in the Japanese cartoon *Hello Kitty*. The reddish brown color of cinnamon makes this a clever name for a Rhodesian Ridgeback or an Irish Setter.

CINNAR *See* Dog Names by Category: Breed; Westminster.

CINZIA Woman from Kynthos (Latin).

CIPHER Transmitting a coded message using an algorithm.

CIPRIANA From Cyrus (Italian).

CIRO Like the sun (Italian).

CISCO Character in O. Henry's 1907 short story "The Caballero's Way."

CITRON Edible, fragrant, lime-colored citrus fruit also called "Persian apple." It keeps moths away from clothes.

CITRUS Genus of edible fruit that includes oranges, lemons, grapefruit, and tangerines.

CLAPTON Eric Clapton (b. 1945), British singer, songwriter, and guitarist who is considered one of the greatest guitarists of all time. Clapton is the only three-time inductee to the Rock and Roll Hall of Fame. A member of the Yardbirds and then John Mayall's Bluesbreakers before he formed Cream and subsequently became a solo artist, his songs speak from his soul; indeed, "Layla," "Wonderful Tonight," and "Tears in Heaven" are bathed in deep-seated personal experience. There's no point going on about Clapton—there's simply too much to say. Name a dog that rocks Clapton.

CLARA Clear, bright, famous, from the Latin *clarus*.

CLARANCE King Clarance of Northumberland, knight of King Arthur's legendary Round Table.

CLARENCE Kind-hearted, well-intentioned angel that steers James Stewart back on track in Frank Capra's holiday classic *It's a Wonderful Life*, made immediately after World War Two in 1946. Clarence the angel delivers the true meaning of Christmas at the end of the movie: It's Christmas Eve. George (James Stewart) is surrounded by his wife (Donna Reed) and loving friends and family that have just presented him with a basket brimming with sorely needed cash. Resting atop the heap is a copy of Mark Twain's *Tom Sawyer*, which George recognizes as Clarence's most treasured earthly possession. He gently opens the book. Inscribed on the frontispiece are these words: "No man is a failure who has friends." Words to cherish not just at Christmas but the whole year long.

CLAS Clas Thunberg of Finland won seven medals in speed skating in the 1924 and 1928 Olympic Games.

CLAUDE Claude Lacombe, a French government scientist, played by François Truffaut in Steven Spielberg's *Close Encounters of the Third Kind*. **Claudia** is the feminine form.

CLAUDIUS Caesar Augustus Germanicus (AD 37–68), the last emperor in the Julio-Claudian dynasty. Male German Shepherd K9 police dog from Oakland, California that attacked an assailant who shot his handler five times before reinforcements arrived—and saved his master's life. Roman writer Claudius Aelianus (Aelian) wrote about the Bloodhound in the third century in *Historia Animalium*, claiming the dog was unrivaled in its scenting powers and determination to trail his quarry.

CLAVELL James Clavell (1924–1994), Australian-born British novelist who wrote *The Great Escape, Tai-Pan, To Sir with Love*, among others.

CLAYTON Clay settlement (Old English).

CLEARWATER Taken from the name of Credence Clearwater Revival, American rock band from the sixties that was inducted into the Rock and Roll Hall of Fame in 1993.

CLEE Ch. Clee Courtier and Clee Brigand, noted champion Airedale Terriers (1928–1935).

CLEMENTE Gentle, understanding (Italian).

CLEMENTINE Variety of mandarin orange. "Oh My Darling Clementine," nineteenth-century American Western folk ballad.

CLEOPATRA Glory of the father (Latin). Cleopatra VII Philopator (69–30 BC), last pharaoh of Egypt who consummated her love of Julius Caesar to strengthen her political power. Believed to have been one of the world's great beauties, she committed suicide, dying from the poisonous venom of an asp. However, a recent theory suggests she drank a mixture of hemlock, wolfsbane, and opium; and yet another theory is that Caesar Augustus, the first emperor of the Roman Empire, had her murdered.

CLETO To call back (Italian).

CLEVELAND Hilly land (Old English).

CLICKETT Mr. Macawber's jolly servant girl in *David Copperfield*, by Charles Dickens.

CLIFFORD PBS children's television series *Clifford the Big Red Dog*, based on the children's book series by American author Norman Bridwell.

CLIFTON Settlement by the cliff (Old English).

CLINTON Settlement on the summit (Old English).

CLIPPER Fast-sailing, three-mast, square-rigged ship. President John F. Kennedy's German Shepherd.

CLITHEROE *See* Lomax.

CLIVE Cliff (Old English).

CLONMEL Ch. Clonmel Monarch, son of Ch. Master Briar, patriarch of the Airedale Terrier breed.

CLOROX Liquid laundry bleach invented in 1913. Good name for a white dog, but don't *ever* wash him with the stuff.

CLOUD Good name for a dog with a white coat, such as a Great Pyrenees or a Kuvasz.

CLOVE Aromatic dried buds of the clove tree that, when grated, make a lovely spice added to a variety of baked goods.

CLOVEN Bonded or deeply connected (Gothic).

CLOVER "Marriage proposal" in the language of flowers. Genus of over three hundred species of wildflower that includes white clover and shamrocks. Clover would be a beautiful name for a white miniature poodle or any dog with a white coat, for that matter.

CLUE Evidence, sign; crime fiction board game created in 1949 in England by Waddingtons and known there as Cluedo.

CLUMSY One more of the dogs in Sir Ector's kennels in T. H. White's *Once and Future King* (1958).

CLYDE One of six Doberman Pinschers that attempt a bank heist in the 1972 film *The Doberman Gang*; famous river in Scotland.

CNUT *See* Canute.

COACH English nicknames for the Dalmatian include the English Coach Dog, the Carriage Dog, Plum Pudding Dog, the Fire House Dog, and Spotted Dick.

COASTER A small trivet to rest a glass or mug.

COB Term used to gauge the standard of sturdiness of build in dogs.

COBYCO Crufts champion. *See* Breed; Crafts.

COCKSPUR Barbados's leading golden rum, produced since 1884 by Hanschell Inniss Ltd.; Crufts champion.

COCO Dorothy Lamour did not have a dog until the death of her second husband, William Howard Ross III, in 1978. Lamour got a Scottish Terrier to fill the void and wrote to a friend, "I've shocked friends when I told them I have a new boyfriend and then bring out a photo of that little dog."

COCO CHANEL (1883–1971), French couture designer who defined elegant simplicity in fashion; actress Reese Witherspoon's French Bulldog.

COCOA Another name for hot chocolate. Chocolate is made from the cocoa (or cacao) bean. Great name for a Chocolate Lab.

COCONUT Large round hard-shelled nut of the coconut palm tree that, when split open, reveals a white pulpy fruit.

COCOPUFF Chocolatey-tasting puffed grain cereal "that kids love," first made by General Mills in 1958.

CODGER British informal name for a good fellow or chap.

CODY William "Buffalo Bill" Cody (1846–1917). The enormously popular Buffalo Bill's Wild West Show toured the country and Europe, playing to commoners and kings. One of his star performers was Annie Oakley. It is little known that William Cody was awarded the Medal of Honor—the highest military decoration bestowed by the United States government—in 1872 for his heroic service as a US Army scout; Cody was the name of the adopted three-legged dog in the 2004 black comedy *The Life Aquatic with Steve Zissou.*

COFFEE Brewed beverage from the ground coffee beans that most of us cannot start the day without. Name to consider for a coffee-colored Miniature Pinscher.

COG Component of a wheel.

COGER To pick, harvest from the Latin word *colligere.*

COGNAC Brandy made in Cognac, France.

COLA Carbonated beverage flavored by the cola nut.

COLE Cole Porter (1891–1964), American Broadway musical composer and songwriter whose enormous body of work includes *Kiss Me, Kate*, *The Gay Divorcee*, and the film *High Society*, which included the great duet sung by Grace Kelly and Bing Crosby, "True Love." The list of Broadway and Hollywood stars who have sung Cole Porter's songs is seemingly endless, topped by Fred Astaire, Frank Sinatra, Gene Kelly, Ethel Merman, and Ella Fitzgerald. A horseback riding accident, after many unsuccessful operations, cost him a leg. After the amputation, he became a recluse—never to write another song again.

COLERIDGE Samuel Taylor Coleridge (1772–1834) English poet, who, together with his friend and fellow poet William Wordsworth founded the Romantic movement.

COLLARBONE *See* Dog Names by Category: Breeds; Crufts.

COLLE Another one of the dogs in Sir Ector's kennels in T. H. White's *Once and Future King* (1958).

COLLEEN Colleen Barke, heroine of *Dog City* and Muppet girlfriend of Ace Yu.

COLLEY Original spelling of the Collie breed of dog.

COLNE The rivers Colne, Calder, Warfe, and Aire in the Yorkshire Valley fostered the development of the Pembroke Welsh Corgi, a great companion dog of farmers and hunters across the Yorkshire dales.

COLOMBINA Dove (Italian). Pretty name for a female Neapolitan Mastiff or Giant Schnauzer—any dog with a soft gray coat.

COLONEL CRINKLE Character in the kingdom of *The Wonderful Wizard of Oz*, of which there were thirteen sequels written by L. Frank Baum. Good name for a Bulldog.

COLONEL ROCK Bulldog mascot of Western Illinois University.

COLONEL Officer rank in the United States military.

COLONSAY *See* Archibald.

COLPACH Legendary Irish water horse. Perfect name for an Irish Water Spaniel, which originally was bred as a waterfowl dog.

COLT Foal, offspring of a horse; Samuel Colt (1814–1862), founder of Colt's Patent Fire Arms Manufacturing Company in Hartford, Connecticut, premier American maker of handguns to this day.

COLTER Author Rick Bass wrote about hunting with his German Shorthaired Pointer in Montana in *Colter: The True Story of the Best Dog I Ever Had.*

COLUMBIA Patriotic personification of the USA, graphically portrayed on posters in the first half of the twentieth century by a woman draped in a US flag.

COLUMBUS Christopher Columbus (1451–1506), Italian explorer credited with the discovery of America (though Norse explorer Leif Erikson established Vinland—today known as Newfoundland—five hundred years before). Columbus was an admirer of the Mexican Techichi dog, forebear of the Chihuahua.

COMELY Hounds that "were singing" according to Englishman Frederick Watson in 1932 in his book on hunting entitled *In the Pink, or The Little Muchley Run.*

COMET Phenomenon of the solar system that travels the heavens, usually with a white fiery tail. The great American writer Mark Twain was born as Halley's Comet crossed the night sky and died seventy-five years later, when it next returned.

COMFORTER Affectionate name given the English Toy Spaniel by Dr. Johannes Caius, celebrated professor and physician to Queen Elizabeth I. He called the breed as "Spaniell Gentle."

COMMAND Westminster Kennel Club champion.

COMMANDER Leader, chief; *see* MacMillan.

COMMODORE Commodore Perry steamed into Harbor of Wraga in 1853 and opened trade with Japan to the world. As a token of welcome, Perry was presented with several Japanese Chin dogs and he, in turn, gave a pair to Queen Victoria, who immediately fell in love with the breed.

COMTE *See* Galway.

CONAN Little wolf (Gaelic).

CONCETTA Conception (Italian).

CONDOR Vulture; large, soaring birds with an enormous wingspan.

CONFECTION Candy or a sweet concoction, usually for dessert or snacks.

CONFETTI Tiny pieces of colored paper thrown into the air to herald a celebration such as a wedding.

CONFUCIUS (551–479 BC), Chinese philosopher who championed family loyalty and whose wisdom has been handed down through the ages.

CONFUSION Canine actor in *Cats & Dogs*.

CONGO State in central Africa formerly known as Zaire.

CONNACHT *See* Aibe.

CONQUEROR *See* Dog Names by Category: Breeds; Westminster.

CONRAD Brave counsel (Germanic).

CONSOLATA Consolation (Italian).

CONSTABLE A British police officer today, but in Norman England, at the time of Robin Hood, a constable was responsible for supervising and maintaining the king's armaments.

CONTEALX Comte Le Contealx, one of the largest breeders of Basset Hounds in France.

CONWAY Holy water (Welsh).

COO-EE-OH Queen Coo-ee-oh was Queen of the Skeezers in *Glinda of Oz*, a sequel of *The Wonderful Wizard of Oz* by L. Frank Baum (1900). Wouldn't this make a wonderful name for a Coonhound, Foxhound, or Beagle!

COOKIE Delicious, delectable, bite-sized dessert; Cookie Monster just *loves* cookies on Sesame Street.

COOLER One of the Pound Puppies.

COOPER Gary Cooper (1901–1960), surely one of Hollywood's most versatile, endearing, and popular actors, he made an indelible mark as Lieutenant Henry in the film adaptation of Hemingway's *A Farewell to Arms* (1932), Longfellow Deeds in Frank Capra's 1936 poignant comedy *Mr. Deeds Goes to Town*, and Capra's more serious 1941 movie masterpiece *Meet John Doe*. He also starred in numerous Westerns; *Cloak and Dagger* (1946), a semiautobiographical story of an OSS agent in World War II by the tremendous but largely forgotten writer Corey Ford; *The Fountainhead*, where his affair with costar Patricia Neal incited the scrutiny of a merciless public eye. But no movie tops his Academy Award–winning performances in *Sergeant York* and *High Noon*. In fact, few performances in the history of motion pictures ever could.

COORS American beer brewed in Golden, Colorado.

COPERNICUS Nicolaus Copernicus (1473–1543), Polish Renaissance astronomer whose findings displaced the Earth as the center of the universe; Dr. Emmett "Doc" Brown's dog in *Back to the Future*.

COPPER The Coonhound puppy (voiced by actor Corey Feldman) that struggles to maintain his friendship with a red fox named Tod in the 1981 Walt Disney animated feature *The Fox and the Hound*.

COPPERFIELD David Copperfield, who opens his life story with, "I am born." Of all his characters, it is said that Dickens modeled David after himself. If you haven't read this book, then shame on you.

COQUETTE French word for a flirtatious woman. Terrific name for a Toy Poodle or a Bichon Frisé.

CORA The Right Honourable Cora, Countess of Grantham.

CORAL A nice name to consider for a female Airedale Terrier, in *Downton Abbey*.

CORAZON Heart (Spanish).

CORBETT Jim Corbett (1875–1955), British dangerous game hunter who spared the lives of countless people in India from the very real threat of man-eating tigers and leopards. A hunting dog can proudly wear this name. *See* Robin Hood.

CORDIAL Pleasant, amiable; an after-dinner drink.

CORDOVAN Deep, brownish-burgundy color associated with fine leather. This could be just the name for an Ibizan Hound.

COREY Ravine, from the Old Norse word *Kori*.

CORKY Child star Shirley Temple's Scottish Terrier. Dog in the *Superman* comics that knew that Clark Kent and Superman were one and the same.

CORNEIL *Corneil et Bernie*, French-English animated series (called *Watch My Chops* in England) about the antics of a rich, highly intelligent dog that can read and write.

CORNFLAKE Kind of a cute name, perhaps, but if your dog is the color of cornflakes, it might just work.

CORNFLOWER "Refinement" in the language of flowers.

CORNSILK The silken threads of a fresh ear of corn. Good name for a dog with a white, silky coat.

CORNWALL *See* Devon.

CORONA Crown (Latin).

CORPORAL Noncommissioned military rank.

CORRIN *See* Gerwn.

CORSHE *See* Nic.

CORSICA Mountainous Mediterranean island where Napoleon Bonaparte was born.

CORTEZ Hernán Cortés (1485–1547), conquistador who led the expedition that discovered and then destroyed the Aztec Empire of central Mexico and opened Spanish colonization in the New World.

COSIMA Order, beauty (Italian).

COSMO The Second Duke of Gordon, an eighteenth-century Scottish nobleman, named his first son and heir in honor of his Italian friend Cosimo III de' Medici, Grand Duke of Tuscany, whose fifty-three-year reign is the longest in Tuscan history.

COSTANZO Steadfast, loyal (Italian).

COSTELLO From the Irish surname *Oisdealbhach*, meaning "resembling a deer"; Lou Costello (1906–1959), hilarious half of comedy team Abbott and Costello. Their classic radio routine "Who's on First?" was a masterpiece of comic timing. Fate dealt Lou a lousy hand; he suffered tragic personal loss and left the world too soon.

COSY One of the hounds that "were singing" in Frederick Watson's *In the Pink* (1932).

COUNT NOBLE More than any other English Setter, Count Noble set the American standard for field trial Setters.

COUNT Tally, compute; also, titled European nobleman; **countess,** a titled European noblewoman.

COURAGE *Courage the Cowardly Dog*, the children's animated television series first broadcast in 1999 on Cartoon Network.

COURTIER *See* Clee.

COURTNEY Short nose (Old English).

COURVOISIER Brand of cognac preferred by Napoleon Bonaparte. Its rich golden color might match the coat of your Golden Retriever puppy.

COUSCOUS Savory North African dish made from semolina.

COUSTEAU Jacques-Yves Cousteau (1910–1997), French naval officer, underwater explorer, leading ecologist, documentary filmmaker, photographer, and author, inventor of the aqualung.

COWBOY Western rancher that herds cattle and horses; **cowgirl** is a female ranch hand.

CRAB Launce's dog in act II, scene 3 of Shakespeare's *Two Gentlemen of Verona* who laments, "I think Crab, my dog, be the sourest-natured dog that lives."

CRACKERDOG Crazy, bonkers. Mrs. Pumphrey's dog Tricky-Woo distressed his mistress whenever he went crackerdog, in *All Creatures Great and Small*.

CRACKERJACK Outstanding, extremely skillful.

CRACKERS Unleavened biscuits.

CRAKNOR *See* Dog Names by Category: Breed; Crufts.

CRANACH *See* Lucas.

CRANBERRY Burgundy colored; edible berry of a bush that thrives in bogs. Cranberries are boiled with sugar and water to make cranberry sauce.

CRANE Large, long-legged member of the Gruidae family of birds that lives everywhere in the world except Antarctica and South America.

CRANFORD Novel by the nineteenth-century writer Elizabeth Gaskell, who based her novels on the eccentricities of life in an English country village. It was originally serialized in 1851. Gaskell's first editor was Charles Dickens.

CRANKY Oscar the Grouch's pet dog on *Sesame Street*.

CRASH Smash! Bang! Thump!

CRATCHIT Bob Cratchit, Scrooge's underpaid, underappreciated clerk—until the Three Ghosts come to visit in Charles Dickens's immortal *A Christmas Carol*. After that, everything changes.

CRAWFORD Crow's ford (Old English); surname derived from the name of a town.

CRAWLEY Frank Crawley, estate manager at Manderley and the best friend Maxim de Winter ever could have had in the romantic thriller *Rebecca*, by Daphne du Maurier.

CRAWLEY Matthew Crawley, third cousin of Lord Grantham and heir to *Downton Abbey*. He's such a likable fellow and so handsomely portrayed by terribly talented British actor Dan Stevens (oh, those blue eyes!).

CREAM Good on or in just about every dish you cook and a great name for a dog with a creamy white coat.

CRÈME Crème caramel, custard dessert with a caramel topping and a good dog name for a West Highland Terrier.

CRESCENT Semicircular, half-moon. If your dog has a half-moon-shaped marking, call him Crescent.

CRESS Small white plant, a member of the mustard family. Good name for a dog with a white coat.

CREST Dog Names by Category: Breeds; Westminster.

CRIB Crib and Rosa, English Bulldogs painted by Abraham Cooper in 1817, important in the development of the breed.

CRICKET Exceedingly popular British outdoor bat-and-ball game.

CRIMPLE David Crimple, aka Crimp, pawnbroker and partner in the Anglo-Bengalee Disinterested Loan and Life Assurance Company in Charles Dickens's *Martin Chuzzlewit* (1843).

CRIMSON Deep cherry color.

CRINOLINE Stiff fabric used to shape an underskirt from the late sixteenth century through Victorian times. A Farthingale was the earlier version of a hooped skirt or stiffened petticoat.

CRISCO Solid white vegetable shortening used in baked goods since 1911. Sis May, an elderly, portly Southern lady with a wrinkle-free, peaches-and-cream complexion, used to say, "Honey, did you ever see a wrinkle in a can of Crisco?" Great name for a pure white Bull Terrier.

CRISPARKLE "Mr. Crisparkle, Minor Canon, early riser, musical, classical, cheerful, kind, good-natured, social, contented, and boy-like" of Cloisterham Cathedral in Charles Dickens's *The Mystery of Edwin Drood* (1870). This was Dickens's last novel, and it was unfinished at his death.

CRISPIN Patron saint of shoemakers (Roman).

CRISPINO Curly-headed (Italian).

CRISTIANA Believer (Italian).

CRITTER Endearing name for a dog. Cousin Kate had a dog named Critter. Ugliest dog you ever saw and, oh, how she loved him!

CROCKETT Davy Crockett (1786–1836), real-life frontiersman and American folk hero that inspired Disney and Fess Parker to immortalize on film. Colonel, politician, congressman from Tennessee; he was killed in the Battle of the Alamo.

CROCUS Bright little flower that peaks through the snow, heralding the start of spring. Crocus means "good cheer" in the language of flowers.

CROISSANT Buttery, flaky French breakfast pastry.

CROMPTON Ch. Crompton Marvel, son of Ch. Master Briar, an Airedale Terrier that set the standard for the breed.

CROMWELL Oliver Cromwell (1599–1658), English military commander who led the English Civil War in which King Charles I was beheaded. Cromwell then proclaimed himself Lord Protector of Great Britain and Ireland and ruled like a despot. Cromwell died of septicemia not too long after that, and then Charles II was crowned king.

CROOKY *See* Fay Ray.

CROSBY *See* Bing.

CROUTON Cube of herbed dried bread used as garnish in soups and salads.

CRUISER Small ship, yacht; also refers to a police car.

CRUMB Morsel, scrap, a tidbit.

CRUMMLES Mr. and Mrs. Vincent Crummles, whose traveling dramatic troupe embraces Nicholas Nickleby and gives him sanctuary in Charles Dickens's 1838 novel.

CRUMPET A traditional toasted English tea cake, sort of like a chewy English muffin, served with jam and clotted cream usually at teatime.

CRUNCHER Munching food noisily.

CRUSADER One who fought in the Crusades, a long series of religious-military campaigns between 1095 and 1291 seeking the Holy Land.

CRUSHER Traditional soft felt hat worn by a hearty breed of native northern New Englanders known as Yankees. L.L.Bean sells crushers.

CRUSOE Daniel Defoe's classic 1719 novel about the adventures of a castaway who spends twenty-eight years on a remote tropical island. Don't you wish . . .

CRYSTAL From the Ancient Greek *krustallos*, meaning "clear," "ice," "transparent."

CUBA The Toy Poodle was called the White Cuban in the eighteenth century, even though the breed originated in England, evolving from a cross between a white French Poodle and a Maltese.

CUBBY An original Disney Mouseketeer; one of Peter Pan's Lost Boys; Albert "Cubby" Broccoli (1909–1996), producer of the James Bond movies. Cute name for any dog.

CUBITUS Fat, round white dog in the eponymous Belgian comic by Dupa.

CUCARACHA Cockroach (Spanish); "La Cucaracha" was a Spanish folksong that became popular during the Mexican Revolution.

CUCINA Kitchen, cooking (Italian).

CUCKOO The call that announces the hour on Swiss-made cuckoo clocks is meant to suggest the call of the cuckoo bird.

CUCUMBER A gourd that grows on a creeping vine, originally from India. When peeled, the flesh of a cucumber is almost white. A delightful name for a dog with a white coat.

CUDDLES Wonderful name for a soft, precious, cuddly dog, big or small.

CUERVO Raven, vulture (Spanish). Famous brand of tequila since the eighteenth century.

CUJO The rabid Saint Bernard dog in the Stephen King novel. In his autobiography, *On Writing*, King states he "barely remembers writing (Cujo) at all," as it came about during a particularly dark period in his life. (Now that you've read this bit, maybe you'd rather just move on to another name, like Cupcake, that's a bit more jolly.)

CULLODEN After the Battle of Culloden in 1745, the Scottish Deerhound as a breed diminished sharply in numbers.

CULVERTON English surname.

CUMBERLAND Cumberland County, England, place of origin of the Lakeland Terrier.

CUMMINGS e. e. cummings (1894–1962), preeminent American poet who had an aversion to capital letters.

CUPCAKE Individual round iced cake—very yummy.

CUPID God of love in Roman mythology.

CURIOUS Good name for a nosey, inquisitive little dog.

CURLY A swell name for a Curly-Coated Retriever or a Poodle.

CURRY Spice from India used to season zesty dishes. Yellow in color, this could be a nice name for a yellow Lab puppy.

CUTHBERT Cuthbert Bradley describes Belvoir Gambler in 1885 as one of the greatest Foxhounds ever bred. This dog set the standard for the breed.

CUTIE Obvious name for a cute dog.

CUVIER (1769–1832) Anatomist who found evidence that the Old English Mastiff was bred from the Irish Wolfhound.

CYBER Virtual, computer generated.

CYCLAMEN "Resignation" in the language of flowers.

CYCLONE Tempest, tornado, whirlwind.

CYCLOPS The giant in Greek mythology with one eye that sees all. Proper name for an attentive dog with only one good eye.

CYNEBURGA Royal fortress (Old English).

CYNTHIA Basset Hound belonging to Oliver Wendell Douglas (Eddie Albert) and his wife, Lisa (Eva Gabor), on the 1965 CBS sitcom *Green Acres*; woman of Kynthos in Greek mythology.

CYPRESS Large family of conifer trees. From the Ancient Greek name Cyparissus, a mythological boy beloved by Apollo.

CYRANO Hercule-Savinien de Cyrano de Bergerac (1619–1655). French dramatist and duelist whose nose was pretty big but not as big as portrayed in the play *Cyrano de Bergerac*, written by Edmond Rostand in 1897—or anywhere near as big as Steve Martin's was in the 1987 film *Roxanne*.

CYRIL Lord (Greek); Cyril, the dog in Connie Willis's 1997 futuristic novel *To Say Nothing of the Dog*.

CYRUS Cyrus the Great, founder of the Persian Empire, was given a Mastiff as a gift from the king of Albania in 550 BC.

CZAR Derived from the Latin *Caesar*, designation of a Russian hereditary emperor or king.

CZARINA Wife of the Czar of Russia.

D

D.J. Siberian Husky that played Demon in the family films *Snow Dogs* and *Eight Below*.

D'ARTAGNAN The Irish Terrier has been called the "D'artagnan of the Show Ring" by purebred enthusiasts. Charles Ogier de Batz de Castelmore, Comte d'Artagnan (1611–1673), was the real-life captain of the Musketeers of the Guard who served Louis XIV. French author Alexandre Dumas immortalized him in *The Three Musketeers* (1844), set in seventeenth-century France.

DA VINCI Leonardo da Vinci (1452–1519), Italian Renaissance painter, inventor, scientist, mathematician, engineer, geologist, and botanist, best known for his painting *Mona Lisa*, which hangs in the Louvre in Paris. His mural of the Last Supper at the Convent of Sta. Maria delle

Grazie, in Milan, Italy, was painted in egg tempera and as a result has disintegrated badly over the centuries despite fervent restoration measures. Mystery enshrouded Leonardo long before the *Da Vinci Code* and even in the Rennaisance man's lifetime.

DABBLE To putter around, try something out for the fun of it.

DACHSIE Short name for a short dog, the Dachshund.

DADDY Affectionate name for father.

DAFFODIL "Sunshine" in the language of flowers. Cheerful, early-blooming flower that heralds the beginning of spring and a good name for a yellow dog with a sunny disposition.

DAFFY Duck. Loud-mouthed duck created in 1937 by Tex Avery and voiced by the inimitable voice actor Mel Blanc.

DAGMAR Day maid (Old Norse).

DAGONET Sir Dagonet, knight of King Arthur's legendary Round Table, was actually a coward under all that armor.

DAGWOOD Dagwood Bumstead, protagonist in the long-running Chic Young comic strip *Blondie* since 1933.

DAHLIA "Forever thine" in the language of flowers. Colorful flower native to Central America and Mexico, used to make pipe stems by the Aztecs.

DAIQUIRI One of the six staples of bartending, it is a rum cocktail with sugar and lime juice, first concocted in Cuba in 1900.

DAISY "Freshness, modesty and simple beauty" in the language of flowers. Pretty name for a dog with a white coat. Dagwood Bumstead's Weimaraner in *Blondie*. Clint Eastwood's yellow Lab in *Grand Torino*. Humorist Dorothy Parker's Scottish Terrier. Facing blacklisting when questioned by the House Un-American Activities

Committee as to whether she was a communist, Parker responded: "Listen. I can't even get my dog to stay down. Do I look to you like someone who could overthrow the government?"

DAKARAI Happiness (Swahili).

DAKE First Scottish Terrier registered in America, a brindle bred by O. P. Chandler of Kokomo, Indiana, and whelped in 1884.

DAKOTA Friend (Dakota-Lakota). Search and Rescue dog credited with one hundred search missions, including the futile search for the astronauts in the tragic Space Shuttle Columbia disaster.

DALAI Historically, the Dalai Lama periodically sends Lhasa Apsos as gifts to the rulers of China.

DALE Lives near or in a valley (English).

DALÍ Salvador Dalí (1904–1989), flamboyant Spanish Surrealist painter best known for his rather disturbing 1931 masterpiece *The Persistence of Memory*.

DALLAS Third largest city in Texas and third largest financial center in the United States.

DALMATIA Province of Austria credited with being the original home of the Dalmatian, an ancient breed.

DALTON Valley town (Old English).

DAMIANO To tame (Italian).

DAMKA *See*, Dog Names by Category: Legendary.

DAMOCLES Ever-present danger or threat. "Heavy hangs the head that wears the crown," comes from the Greek legend about a courtier to Dionysius II of Syracuse, who trades places with the king only to realize that a sword suspended by a single hair from a horse's tail hangs over his throne.

DAMSEL "Damsel in distress" is an age-old image of a beautiful maiden caught between a rock and a hard place—sometimes quite literally. One of "the hounds that were singing" in Frederick Watson's book on English fox hunting, *In the Pink* (1932).

DAN Important early stud dog out of the Laverack line of English Setters. Compson's hound in American author William Faulkner's fourth novel, *The Sound and the Fury*, published in 1929.

DANA Surname referring to a native of Denmark.

DANCER Performer who expresses art through dance, usually to music.

DANDELION Lion's tooth (French). Wildflower with multiple yellow petals that turn to milky white, fluffy seeds that disperse in the wind. Cute name for a Pomeranian.

DANDY Cultivated, well-dressed, rather pompous gentleman who puts on airs. Bertie Wooster, P. G. Wodehouse's fictitious fop, was a dandy, a swell—but the word can also mean swell, as in "terrific" or "really neat."

DANFORTH Traditional English surname.

DANICA Venus, the morning star (Slavic).

DANIEL God is my judge (Hebrew). The Book of Daniel in the Bible depicts a series of royal dreams and interpretations of visions. Daniel lived from 605 to 562 BC during the reign of Nebuchadnezzar.

DANNY Affectionate for Daniel.

DANTE Durante degli Alighieri (1265–1321), known as Dante, Italian poet whose epic poem *The Divine Comedy* is a literary masterpiece deemed the greatest work ever written in the Italian language.

DANU The Water Goddess in Irish mythology.

DANUBE Second longest river in Europe and inspiration behind Johann Strauss II's famous waltz "The Blue Danube."

DAPHNE Laurel (English). Nymph that was turned into a laurel tree to avoid pursuit by an amorous Apollo in Greek mythology.

DARA Name that means many things in many languages—"star" in Cambodian, "leader" in Turkish, "wealthy" in Persian, "beautiful one" in Swahili, "virgin" in Indonesian, "second" in Gaelic, "dragon killer" in Scottish, as well as Biblical and other religious connotations.

DARBY Deer town (Norse).

DARCY In Jane Austen's *Pride and Prejudice*, the arrogant, prejudiced aristocrat who meets his match in Elizabeth Bennet: she tears down his defensive prejudices, and he breaks down her foolish pride—after which they live happily ever after.

DAREDEVIL Fearless, reckless risk taker.

DARE-DEVIL Nickname of the Irish Terrier because it reflects his temperament.

DAREN Born at night (Nigerian).

DARIN Bobby Darin (1936–1973), cool, suave, popular singer-songwriter and actor whose marriage to Sandra "Gidget" Dee made them America's sweethearts. Tragically, a congenital heart defect cut Darin's life short at the age of thirty-seven.

DARIO Wealthy (Italian).

DARLENE Dearling, darling (English).

DARLEY Darley Matheson, nineteenth-century writer of books on the Terrier breeds.

DARLING Wendy, John, and Michael Darling, the children in J. M. Barrie's 1911 classic *Peter Pan*—originally published as *Peter and Wendy* and based on Barrie's 1904 stage play *Peter Pan; or, the Boy Who Wouldn't Grow Up.*

DARLINGTON Dog show held in England where, in 1870, the Rough and Smooth Collies were first divided into separate classes for show purposes.

DARO *See* Dog Names by Category: Breed; Westminster.

DARTH Darth Vader, who in his younger days was the Jedi Knight Anakin Skywalker, father of Luke Skywalker and Princess Leia. He succumbed to the Dark Side in the *Star Wars* saga. Voiced by one of America's greatest actors, the incomparable James Earl Jones.

DARWIN Charles Darwin (1809–1882), eminent English geologist and naturalist whose theory of evolution, first published in 1859 as *On the Origin of Species*, was in large part the result of research he collected from his five-year, trans-world voyage on the HMS *Beagle*. It is little known that Darwin was a great dog lover who owned many Terriers, among them **Nina**, **Spark**, **Sheila**, and **Polly**; a Retriever named **Bob**, a Pomeranian named **Snow** and a kennel of hunting dogs, including a Scottish Deerhound named **Bran**.

DARZEE A tailorbird in *The Jungle Book*. *See* Kipling.

DASH King Charles Spaniel owned by Queen Victoria. Outdoor television host Dez Young's Llewellyn Setter. President Benjamin Harrison's Rough Collie.

DASHER Santa Claus's lead reindeer when Rudolf is off-duty on a foggy Christmas Eve.

DASHIELL Dashiell Hammett (1894–1961), American author of detective novels (*The Thin Man*, *The Maltese Falcon*) in which his heroes Nick Charles and Sam Spade are street-smart and tough as flint. His thirty-year affair with writer Lillian Hellman ended with his death. A broken man, Hammett was convicted, blacklisted, and jailed for contempt of Congress House Un-American Activities Committee as a result of the "witch trials."

DATA Lieutenant Commander Data, sentient android and Chief Operations Officer aboard *Star Trek's* USS *Enterprise*.

DAUPHIN The Dauphin of France fell in love with the Great Pyrenees in 1675 while visiting Barreges with Mme. De Maintenon and assumedly fell in love with Mme. De Maintenon, too.

DAVE President Woodrow Wilson's Airedale Terrier.

DAVIDE Beloved (Italian).

DAVU The beginning (Nigerian).

DAVY Shade of grey. Good name for any dog with grey in his coat, such as an Affenpinscher. Davy Jones's Locker, watery resting place at the bottom of the ocean of people drowned at sea. Davy Jones (1945–2012), English actor and recording artist, heartthrob member of the Monkees, a rock group fabricated for a popular television series. Initially not taken seriously by the music industry, the group actually sold more records one year than the Beatles and the Rolling Stones combined.

DAWG THE DOG Muppet dog on PBS's *Sesame Street*.

DAWN The end of night and the break of day. Olympic swimmer Dawn Fraser of Australia won four gold and four silver medals in the games that were held between 1956 and 1964.

DAYLILY "Coquetry" in the language of flowers.

DAZZLER Sparkling, attention-grabbing, like the Taylor-Burton diamond.

DEAREST The most beautiful word anyone could be called.

DEBORA Bee (Italian).

DEBOUNAIR *See* Dog Names by Category: Breed; Crufts.

DEBUTANTE Young woman introduced, or debuted, into society for the first time.

D'ECURIE "Griffons D'Ecurie," French term for the Brussels Griffon breed.

DE-DOP-DE-DIDDLY-DOG BOP A Muppet dog that first appeared in *The Tale of the Bunny Picnic*. Long name for a long dog, such as a Dachshund.

DEGAS Edgar Degas (1834–1917), French artist categorized as an Impressionist even though he identified with the Realist movement. Degas is best known for his paintings and sculptures of ballerinas.

DÉJÀ VU An unsettling feeling that something that just happened actually happened before.

DELFINA Woman from Delphi (Italian).

DELGADO German Shepherd Dog voiced by Andy Garcia in the 2008 Disney film *Beverly Hills Chihuahua*.

DELILAH Delicate, weak, languishing. Biblical mistress of Samson who betrayed him to the Philistines.

DELORA Sorrow (Spanish), also **Delores**.

DELPHI *See* Arrian.

DELPHINIUM "Bighearted" in the language of flowers.

DELTA Estuary or channel, mouth of a river. Toy Poodle in the 2008 Walt Disney family film *Beverly Hills Chihuahua*.

DEMETER Goddess of fertility, grain, agriculture, harvest, and sometimes the goddess of creativity in Greek mythology.

DEMON Along with **Nana, Mac, Scooper, Diesel, Ralph, Sniff, Yodel**, and **Duchess**, the Siberian Huskies in the 2002 Walt Disney film *Snow Dogs*, inspired by *Winterdance*, a novel about the the Iditarod, by Gary Paulsen.

DEMPSEY Jack Dempsey, aka "the Manassa Mauler" (1895–1983), American boxer and World Heavyweight champion from 1919 to 1926.

DENG Deng Yaping of China won a total of four gold medals in table tennis in the 1992 and 1996 Olympic Games.

DENHOLM Valley island (Old English). Denholm Elliott (1922–1992), prolific British film actor who played Marcus Brody in Steven Spielberg's first Indiana Jones film *Raiders of the Lost Ark* (1981).

DENIM Rugged cotton twill fabric died indigo in the manufacture of blue jeans.

DENVER Mining town that rose from the prairie to meet the Rockies in 1858 as a result of the Pike's Peak Gold Rush, to become the largest city in Colorado and the state capital.

DEPUTY Deputy Dawg, deputy sheriff in the Mississippi bayou in the Terrytown's 1962 animated cartoon series.

DERBY The Kentucky Derby, the most prestigious three-year-old thoroughbred race in the world, the proverbial first jewel in the Triple Crown, held at Churchill Downs in Louisville, Kentucky, the first Saturday of May every year.

DEREK Ruler of the people (Germanic).

DERRY *See* Dog Names by Category: Breed; Crufts.

DESCARTES Apollo 16 was the only mission to land on lunar highlands, the Descartes Highlands. Fraught with malfunctions that reduced its length of time in space, the crew of Apollo 16—John W. Young, Ken Mattingly, and Charles Duke—made it safely home. The mission took off on April 16, 1972.

DESDEMONA Ill-fated heroine in Shakespeare's *Othello* who inspired Italian composer Giuseppe Verdi to write a tragic opera, one of his greatest, *Otello*.

DESERT Nice name for a dog with a coat the color of sand.

DESI Longing for something or someone (Italian). *Desiderius* means longing and desire in Latin; also **Desiree**.

DESMOND From the Gaelic, *Deas-Mhumhan*, which means a person that hails from South Munster, Ireland.

DESOTO One of the finest cars to ever hit the road, produced by Chrysler from 1928 until 1960.

DESPERADO Bandit, wanted man.

DESTINY That which awaits you in your future, just you see.

DESTRY Classic American Western film *Destry Rides Again* (1939), starring James Stewart and Marlene Dietrich.

DETONATOR Device that triggers the explosion of a bomb or other explosive device.

DETOUR Diversion, bypass.

DEUCE A tie score of forty-forty in tennis. Softail Deuce, the Harley-Davidson FXSTD/FXSTDI model motorcycle.

DEUTSCHE *Deutsche Dogge*, German name for the Great Dane.

DEVIL The Phantom's dog who lives deep in the jungles of Bangalla with his purple-costumed master in the popular comic strip series created by cartoonist Lee Falk in 1936. Personification of evil, brilliantly portrayed by British actor Rowan Atkinson in his comedy routine, "Welcome to Hell."

DEVON English county where the Old English Sheepdog was first bred, along with the county of Somerset and the Duchy of Cornwall.

DEVONSHIRE The Duke of Devonshire bred English Mastiffs from Lyme Hall bloodlines at his kennels at Chatsworth.

DEWDROP Droplet of water that kisses flowers at dawn.

DEWEY Siberian Husky in the 2006 Walt Disney family adventure film *Eight Below*, set in Antarctica. The other Huskies are **Buck**, **Dewey**, **Max**, **Maya**, **Old Jack**, **Shadow**, **Shorty**, and **Truman**.

DEXTER One who dyes cloth (Old English).

DEZIKN *See* Dog Names by Category: Legendary.

DIA Champion (African).

DIABLO Devil (Spanish).

DIALLO The brave one (African).

DIAMANTE Diamond (Italian).

DIAMOND Gemstone, derived from the Greek word *adámas*, meaning unbreakable, untamed. English astronomer Sir Isaac Newton's favorite dog.

DIAMOND JIM *See* Dog Names by Category: Breed; Westminster.

DIANA Roman goddess of hunting. Princess Diana of Great Britain (1961–1997), "the people's princess," divorced first wife of Prince Charles and beloved mother of Prince William and Prince Harry. Yes, she made a difference.

DICE Small dotted cubes used for the gambling game Craps.

DICK TURPIN Old nickname of the Welsh Terrier breed.

DICKENS Charles Dickens (1812–1870), along with William Shakespeare, one of the greatest English writers of all time. Dickens's vast body of work depicts life and society in Victorian England. Numerous cinematic adaptations of Dickens's novels have been made. The year 2012 marks bicentennial of his birth.

DICKEY One of the dogs on *The Little Rascals* movie shorts produced by Hal Roach, starring Spanky, Alfalfa, and the gang from 1922 through the mid-fifties.

DIDI Feminine of Dieter.

DIDO Dido, Lion, and Nelly belonged to Miss J. J. Hales, a prominent English breeder in the late nineteenth century.

DIEGO From the Greek *didache*, which means to teach; a common Spanish boy's name.

DIETER Warrior of the people (Germanic).

DIETRICH Marlene Dietrich (1901–1992), German actress and singer who rose to stardom before World War Two. Few realize what Dietrich did to elevate the morale of the Allied Forces. She raised War Bonds in America. She performed for soldiers from Algeria to Germany, sometimes within spitting distance of the Front Line. She was an OSS agent and stood against Hitler and decried her native land. But when Marlene sang the emblematic "Lili Marlene," even gunfire ceased. Dietrich was awarded the Medal of Freedom by the United States government and the Légion d'honneur by the French government. A great lady.

DIGBY Golden Retriever on the black comedy television series *Pushing Daisies*; Sheepdog in the 1973 family film *Digby the Biggest Dog in the World*.

DIGGER Good name for a dog that digs up your lawn.

DIGGS German Shepherd Dog in the family movie *Cats and Dogs: The Revenge of Kitty Galore*. Oscar Diggs, whose full name was Oscar Zoroaster Phadrig Issac Norman Henkel Emmannuel Ambroise Diggs, a magician from Omaha, Nebraska, whose initials O.Z.P.I.N.H.E.A.D., were still too long—so he took his first two, *O* and *Z*, and painted them on his hot-air balloon. One day he lost control of the balloon and it sailed off, to a magical kingdom. The people thought he must be a mighty wizard and proclaimed him Supreme Ruler. From that moment on, Oscar Diggs, the carnival magician from Omaha, was known as the Wizard of Oz. And so it is chronicled in *Dorothy and the Wizard of Oz*, a sequel to *The Wonderful Wizard of Oz*, by L. Frank Baum.

DILLARD Annie Dillard (b.1945) Pulitzer Prize–winning American author of *Pilgrim at Tinker Creek*, whose work has been compared to that of Emily Dickinson and Virginia Woolf.

DILLINGER Led a gang of Doberman Pinschers in a bank heist in the 1972 family film *the Doberman Gang*.

DIMPLES Dimples the Dog, a Muppet beagle who first appeared on *Sesame Street* in the seventies.

DIN Great (Congolese).

DINGO The shipwrecked dog that Dick Sand, a boy of fifteen, adopts during a sea voyage to North America in *A Captain at Fifteen*, a little-known novel by Jules Verne (1828–1905), the great French science fiction writer, better known for *Twenty Thousand Leagues Under the Sea*, *Around the World in Eighty Days*, and *Journey to the Center of the Earth*. Published in 1878, it is one of the earliest books to confront the issue of slavery and the African slave trade.

DINGUS Anthropomorphic dog that aspires to be a novelist and writer of "hell-raising op-eds" in *Dingus Dreaming* and *The Canine Condition*, by Alex A. Vardamis.

DINKIE Famous foundation bitch of the Lhassa Apso.

DINO Little sword (Italian). The Flintstones' pet, a doglike dinosaur, in the popular animated cartoon series.

DIOGENES Canine companion of Paul Dombey and his sister Florence in Charles Dickens's *Dombey and Son* (1846). *Alexander and Diogenes*, important painting by the great nineteenth-century painter Sir Edwin Landseer, known for his paintings of dogs and other animals.

DIONYSUS Greek God of wine and merriment, the original party guy, who wears a grape vine and not much else. He's Bacchus to the Romans.

DIP Large, hairy black dog that is the emissary of the Devil in a Catalan myth.

DIPPY DOG Original name for Walt Disney's beloved cartoon dog Goofy.

DIPSTICK One of Walt Disney's *101 Dalmatians*.

DISNEY In making the 1996 live-action version of Walt Disney's 1961 animated classic *101 Dalmatians*, 230 Dalmatian puppies and twenty adult Dalmatians were used. Pongo and Perdita had fifteen puppies of their own before their brood numbered a total of 101. Not all the puppies, however, had names. Those who did were **Lucky, Thunder, Rolly, Patch, Pepper, Dipstick, Penny, Cadpig, Freckles, Wizzer, Jewel, Two-Tone, Fidget,** and **Spotty**. The dogs that helped rescue the puppies were **Jasper, The Colonel, Captain,** and **Sgt. Tibbs**.

DISRAELI Benjamin Disraeli, Earl of Beaconsfield and Viscount Hughenden (1804–1881), four-time British Prime Minister under Queen Victoria and her closest, wisest, and most trusted advisor. An Italian-born Jew, Disraeli converted to the Anglican faith when he came to England.

DITZY Airheaded, scatterbrained.

DIVA Celebrated singer of superior talent.

DIVORCEE A woman whose marriage is legally terminated.

DIXIE Colloquial term for the American South. Up until the end of the Civil War, the North (Union) and the South (Confederacy) were separated by the Mason-Dixon Line.

DIXIE-DOO One of Scooby-Doo's cousins.

DIZZIE Dizzie Gillespie (1917–1993), American jazz trumpet player, bandleader, and songwriter who, with Charlie Parker, is credited for the development of bebop, a form of jazz.

DIZZY Faint, unsteady, shaky.

DOBBY Annoying house-elf of the Malfoy family in the Harry Potter series; his devotion to Harry cost him his life in the movie *Harry Potter and the Deathly Hallows, Part One.*

DOBE *See* Dog Names by Category: Breed; Westminster.

DOBRI City in Hungary; a good name for a Hungarian breed, such as the Vizla, Komodor, Puli, and Kuvasz.

DOC Slang for physician or dentist. John Henry "Doc" Holliday (1851–1887), dentist, gambler, gunfighter in the Old West, best known for the shoot-out at the O.K. Corral alongside the Earp brothers.

DOCKLEAF *See* Orry.

DOCTOR Physician, practitioner.

DODGER The Artful Dodger, skillful pickpocket and leader of Fagan's gang of juvenile criminals in Charles Dickens's *Oliver Twist*, published in 1838. Alec Guinness was Fagin in the 1948 David Lean film classic.

DODIE Diminutive of **Dorothy**.

DODO Bird indigenous to the island of Mauritius in the Indian Ocean, extinct since the seventeenth century. Character in Lewis Carroll's *Alice's Adventures in Wonderland.* Carroll, whose real name was Charles Lutwidge Dodgson, had a stutter and pronounced his surname Do-do-dodgson—hence, his affinity to the Dodo Bird.

DOG Australian Cattle Dog in *Mad Max 2: The Road Warrior* (1981); John Wayne's dog in the 1971 Western *Big Jake,* starring his longtime friend and costar, legendary actress Maureen O'Hara.

DOGBERT Self-confident dog owned by Dilbert in Scott Adams's satirical comic strip, syndicated in 1989.

DOGGE Dog (Old English).

DOGGIE Affectionate name for a dog; also **Pooch**.

DOGGIE DADDY Smooth-talking dog introduced in *Quick Draw McGraw*, the 1959 Hanna-Barbera animated children's television series.

DOGMATIX Canine companion of Obelix in the British version of the French comic book series *Asterix*.

DOGTANIAN *Dogtanian and the Three Muskehounds*, Spanish-Japanese animated series based on Alexandre Dumas's classic tale of d'Artagnan and the Musketeers.

DOGWOOD "Playful" in the language of flowers. The dogwood blossom is white, which makes this a lovely name for a playful dog with a white coat.

DOINA Romanian peasant music. Hungarian composer Béla Bartók integrated peasant songs in his music.

DOLCE Sweet (Italian).

DOLLY Affectionate name for a child's doll.

DOLLY MARTIN Canine actor in *Legally Blonde 2: Red, White & Blonde*.

DOLORES Sorrow (Spanish).

DOLPHUS Noble, majestic wolf (Germanic). Good name for a Wolfhound or Siberian Husky.

DOMBEY Paul Dombey, head of the House of Dombey in Dickens's *Dombey and Son*, published in 1848.

DOMENICA "Belonging to the Lord" (Latin). **Dominic** is the male version. Traditionally given to a child born on Sunday. **Dominique** is the French version.

DOMINO Fats Domino (b. 1928), American R&B and rock and roll pianist, singer, and songwriter best known for "Blueberry Hill," "I'm Walkin'," "Valley of Tears," and "Whole Lotta Loving." Fats and his family were rescued from their home by helicopter during Hurricane Katrina and lost everything. Mathematical game played with tiles numbered with dots.

DON It was said of Don, a Mastiff, that he "possessed of a mild temperament which will bear restraint under provocation and, at the same time, with the courage to defend his master until the death," in *A Breed Apart*, by William Secord.

DON CARLOS Sire of **Don Leon**, foundation dog of the English Bulldog breed, whelped in the 1890s.

DON GIOVANNI Opera in two acts by Wolfgang Amadeus Mozart, based on the life of the fictitious rake Don Juan. First performed in Prague in 1787.

DONAHUE Dark fighter (Irish).

DONALD Ruler of the world (Gaelic).

DONALD DUCK One of Walt Disney's most beloved animated characters, created in 1934.

DONAR Thunder (German).

DONATELLA Given by God (Italian).

DONNA Feminine form of Donald.

DONNER German name for the Norse god Thor.

DONNIE Doberman Pinscher rescue dog featured in *National Geographic* for his ability to arrange stuffed toys in recognizable designs.

DONOVAN Descendant of Donndubhán (Irish).

DOODLE Scribble, sketch.

DOOGIE Affectionate version of **Doggie**.

DOOKIE Pembroke Welsh Terrier belonging to King George VI of England and his family. Dookie arrived in 1933, marking the beginning of the Royal Family's love affair with the breed. The Queen's most beloved Corgi was Susan, who accompanied her while she was still Princess Elizabeth on her honeymoon after her marriage to Prince Philip. All of the Queen's Corgis have since been bred from Susan's line. Others of Her Majesty's dogs have included **Emma, Linnet, Holly, Willow,** and **Monty,** and "Dorgis" **Cider, Berry, Candy,** and **Vulcan,** offspring of Princess Margaret's miniature Dachshund who indiscriminately gave her favors to a Corgi that shall remain nameless. Queen Elizabeth also owns many hunting dogs, which are kenneled at Sandringham.

DOOLEY Mr. Dooley, fictitious, nationally syndicated newspaper character created by political satirist Finley Peter Dunne. His wry humor struck a popular chord regarding the political and social issues of the day, from the late nineteenth century into the first part of the twentieth. A favorite of President Teddy Roosevelt, he would read *Mr. Dooley* out loud each week to his White House Cabinet.

DOOLITTLE Eliza Doolittle, fictitious flower girl who becomes a lady in the George Bernard Shaw play *Pygmalion.*

DOONESBURY Long-running, popular comic strip by Gary Trudeau.

DOONIE Actress Ann Southern's Scottish Terrier that costarred with her in *Maisie Goes to Reno.*

DORA *See* Dog Names by Category: Breed; Crufts.

DORIANS One of the four major tribes of Ancient Greece.

DOROTEA Gift from God (Italian).

DOROTHY Dorothy Gale, immortalized by the great Judy Garland in the 1939 MGM motion picture adaptation of L. Frank Baum's children's classic *The Wizard of Oz.* At the end of the movie, Glinda asks Dorothy what she learned in Oz. Dorothy says, "I suppose, if I ever go looking for my heart's desire again, I won't look any further than my own backyard, because if it isn't there, I never really lost it to begin with." Words to live by.

DOT Diminutive for **Dorothy.** President Rutherford B. Hayes's Cocker Spaniel.

DOUGAL Philosophical Skye Terrier in the 1964 French animated television series *The Magic Roundabout* (*Le Manège Enchanté*); Dougal is also known as **Pollux**.

DOUGHNUT Sweet, deep-fried breakfast food.

DOUGLAS Dark river (Scottish).

DOURON Valley where the town of Pontou, France, is situated, birthplace of the Brittany breed of dog.

DOVE A type of pigeon; the word also means peacemaker, pacifist. Dove is a soft shade of grey. A fine name for an Italian Greyhound with a dove grey coat. *See* Duffield.

DOWNTON *Downton Abbey*, the critically acclaimed Carnival Films British television series, filmed at England's Highclere Castle, a thousand-acre Jacobean estate in Hampshire, England, and home to the Carnarvon family since 1679.

DOYLE Sir Arthur Conan Doyle (1859–1930), Scottish physician, historian, and prolific writer who created the most famous fictional detective of all time, Sherlock Holmes. Doyle found great solace in spiritualism after the deaths of his wife, son, brother, both brothers-in-law, and two nephews, all within a painfully short period of time.

DR. DOPPLER Humanoid canine in Disney's *Treasure Planet*.

DR. PIPT Inventor of the Powder of Life which, when sprinkled on an inanimate object, makes it come to life in *The Patchwork Girl of Oz*, the seventh in L. Frank Baum's series of *Oz* books. Other characters in the series include **Woozy**, **Ojo**, **Uncle Nunkie**, **Shaggy Man**, and the Patchwork Girl herself, **Scraps**. **Patchwork** would be a darling name for a dog with a tricolored coat.

DR. TEETH No rock band plays quite like the Muppet band Dr. Teeth and the Electric Mayhem.

DR. STRANGELOVE Stanley Kubrick's 1964 black comedy, *Dr. Strangelove or: How I Learned to Stop Worrying and Love the Bomb*, starring

Peter Sellers, George C. Scott, and the unforgettable Slim Pickens, who rides the bomb to its target at the end of the flick. Quirky name for a dog, but hey, it may work for yours.

DR. WATSON Sherlock Holmes's loyal, long-suffering friend and chronicler.

DR. WHO The longest-running science fiction television series in history, about an eccentric humanoid alien who travels through the galaxy and bounces around time in his Tardis, "a dimensionally transcendental" London police box, in order to save civilizations and that sort of thing.

DRACO Draco Malfoy, towhead antagonist from Slytherin House at Hogwarts School of Witchcraft and Wizardry who schemes against Harry Potter.

DRAGO Dragon (Italian).

DRAGON Serpent of huge size, water-snake (Greek).

DRAGONORA *See* Dog Names by Category: Breed; Westminster.

DRAMBUIE Rich, brown-colored liqueur sweetened with heather honey.

DREAMER One who dreams great and hopes greater.

DREYFUS Saint Bernard mixed-breed dog on the 1988 NBC sitcom *Empty Nest*.

DROOPY Anthromorphic dog created by Tex Avery in 1943 for the MGM Cartoon Studio troupe of animated characters.

DROVER Early Old English Sheepdog have been drovers's dogs since the beginning of the eighteenth century. They help a drover drive, or herd, his sheep (a drover is a sheep farmer or herder).

DROYA *See* Nic.

DRUD Expensive (Welsh).

DRUMMER Musician who plays the drums.

DRUNKARD George Washington's Black and Tan Coonhound.

DU LAC Sir Lancelot du Lac, King Arthur's most trusted knight of the Round Table, who betrayed his king when he fell in love with Guinevere, Arthur's consort.

DU MAURIER Daphne du Maurier (1907–1989), British author and playwright, best known for Alfred Hitchcock's film adaptations of her suspense novels *Rebecca* and *Jamaica Inn*, and her short story "Don't Look Now," which inspired Hitchcock's thriller *The Birds*.

DUBLIN The Kerry Blue Terrier was first introduced to the show ring at the Dublin Dog Show. Director Alfred Hitchcock, singer Perry Como, and heavyweight boxer Jack Dempsey all owned Kerry Blue Terriers, the little dog that hails from County Kerry in southwest Ireland.

DUBS Alaskan Malamute mascot of the University of Washington.

DUC *See* Dog Names by Category: Breed; Westminster.

DUCHESS Ribby the cat holds a tea party for Duchess the dog during which Duchess believes Ribby swallowed a patty pan (tin pastry cutter) in Beatrix Potter's delightful little book, *The Tale of the Pie and the Patty-Pan*.

DUCHY *See* Devon.

DUCKLING Baby duck.

DUCKY Cockney term of endearment that also can mean "that's fine."

DUDE Guy, man (American English slang), originally meant to describe a wealthy, aristocratic Easterner who travels west to experience the cowboy culture at a "dude ranch." Interestingly, a woman that did the same was called a **Dudette** or **Dudess**.

DUDLEY In 1860, Sir Dudley Marjoribanks, later known as Lord Tweedmouth, saw what he believed to be the immediate ancestor of the Golden Retriever breed at a Russian circus touring in Brighton, England. He made an offer for two of the troupe's dogs but this was refused as the trainer said it would ruin his act. So Lord Tweedmouth purchased the whole pack. These dogs became the foundation stock that established the modern Golden Retriever breed. The dogs were kenneled and bred at Lord Tweedmouth's Scottish seat in the Guisachan deer forest in Invernesshire. **Nous** proved to be the best of the Brighton dogs. By 1935, the Golden Retriever was "Still one of the rare breeds, [but] it is likely that within the next decade [the breed] will make appreciable progress." Today the Golden Retriever is the fifth most popular dog in the United States and Australia, and the eighth most popular in Great Britain.

DUET Twosome, duo, couple.

DUFF Dark (Gaelic).

DUFFIELD Belonging to the dove field (Old English). *See* Dove.

DUFFY Julie Andrews's dog, Ch. Boldmere's Surf's Up, called Duffy. Franklin and Eleanor Roosevelt's first Scottish Terrier, which they acquired in Scotland on their honeymoon.

DUG The talking dog that adopts Mr. Fredricksen in the marvelous, award-winning 2009 Pixar-Disney animated film *Up*.

DUKE Leader (Latin). Nobility, highest rank after the monarchy. Mixed-breed dog in Ruben Santiago-Hudson's autobiographical play *Lackawanna Blues* with a 2005 HBO film adaptation produced by Halle Berry. Bloodhound belonging to the Clampett family in *The Beverly Hillbillies*, the popular CBS television series that ran from 1962 to 1971. Anthromorphic dog in the syndicated Sunday comic strip *Kelly and Duke*, by Jack Moore, which ran from 1972 to 1980. The

Robinson family's dog in the 1960 Disney film *Swiss Family Robinson*. President Rutherford B. Hayes's English Mastiff. Penrod Schofield's Terrier mixed-breed dog in *Penrod: His Complete Story*, by Booth Tarkington. This obviously is a popular dog name . . . but lest we forget, affectionate nickname for the great American actor John "Duke" Wayne.

DUKEY Johnny's dog in the 1995 Canadian-American animated television series, *Johnny Test*.

DULCIE Sweet (Latin).

DUMISANI Give praise (Zulu).

DUMPLING Balls of dough boiled, steamed, fried, or baked; affectionate term for a sweet little child.

DUN Good name for a dog with a dun-colored coat, such as a Brussels Griffon—sort of an oatmeal or wheat color.

DUNCAN Chief, noble (Scottish). King Duncan in Shakespeare's *Macbeth*.

DURAN Natsuki Kuga's dog in the Japanese animated series *My-HiME*.

DURANGO Mountain resort and former nineteeth-century American mining town in Colorado, built in 1881 by the Denver and Rio Grande Railroad to house its workforce; SUV manufactured by Dodge.

DURANTE Enduring (Italian). Jimmy Durante (1893–1990), Brooklyn-born singer, pianist, and comedian and one of the most beloved of all American radio, television, and screen actors; also known as "the Schnoz" for his large nose. His trademark was "Inka Dinka Doo," the opening theme of his act. He would sign off his shows with, "Good night, Mrs. Calabash, wherever you are," a bittersweet nod to his beloved wife of twenty-two years, who died in 1943.

DURBAN Busiest port in South Africa.

DÜRER Albrecht Dürer (1471–1528), German painter who portrayed Schanauzers in his paintings as early as 1492.

DURHAM County in England where Terrier breeds originated.

DUSK Twilight, the time of day when the sun is just setting and the moon is just rising.

DUSKY Dusky D'Orsay, bred by Mr. Francis Redmond in 1915 to improve the standard of the Smooth Fox Terrier breed.

DUSTY Dirty, covered with dust.

DUTCH Dutch chocolate is considered by chocolate epicureans to be among the finest in the world. Dutch is a great name for a chocolate Labrador Retriever. The Pug, a breed native to Holland, is also known as the Dutch Pug.

DUVALL Robert Duvall (b. 1931), Academy Award–winning American actor and director, celebrated for his portrayal of Arthur "Boo" Radley in the 1962 film *To Kill a Mockingbird*, with Gregory Peck, Duvall's first feature film. His role as Frank Burns in the 1970 film *M*A*S*H*, directed by Robert Altman, and Tom Hagen in the *Godfather* saga led an incredible body of work on stage and in film and television.

DWARF Papillons were known as "dwarf spaniels" in the sixteenth century.

DWIGHT Dwight D. Eisenhower, thirty-fourth president of the United States. *See* Dog Names by Category: History.

DYLAN Dylan Thomas (1914–1953), Welshman and one of the preeminent poets of the twentieth century. His poems pour like cream; he knew how to put the right word in the right place, always. But he "liked the taste of whiskey" too well and died too young, at the age of thirty-nine.

DYNAMITE Originally called "Nobel's Blasting Powder." Explosive invented by Alfred Nobel, Swedish scientist and armaments manufacturer. A French newspaper erroneously published Alfred's obituary when his brother, Ludvig, died. It read: "The merchant of death is dead. Dr. Alfred Nobel, who became rich by finding more ways to kill people faster than ever before, died yesterday." In 1895, Nobel signed his last will and testament, bequeathing the bulk of his estate—approximately $250 million—to establish and fund the endowment that bears his name, The Nobel Prizes. Nobel died the following year. First presented in 1901, awards are granted for accomplishments in the fields of physics, chemistry, physiology or medicine, literature, and peace.

DYNAMO Extrovert, go-getter, someone who goes after things in a big way.

E

E.T. Steven Spielberg's 1982 heartwarming science fiction film about an extraterrestrial befriended by some suburban children who help him phone, and go, home.

EAGLE National bird of the United States of America. Founding Father Benjamin Franklin wanted a wild turkey.

EAGLEHURST GILLETTE President Herbert Hoover's Setter.

EARL The Earl of Malmesbury was so impressed with dogs he saw on fishing boats in Newfoundland that he imported several to England in the nineteenth century, thereby establishing the most popular breed in the United States and Great Britain today, the Labrador Retriever.

EBO Born on Tuesday (Nigerian).

EBONY Strong character (Egyptian). Dense black wood and wonderful name for a black Labrador Retriever or any black dog. *See* Dog Names by Category: Color.

ECATERINA Catherine (Russian). Ecaterina Szabo of Romania won five Olympic medals in gymnastics in 1984.

ECHO Natural phenomenon that's a reflection of sound.

ECLIPSE To overshadow, conceal, block out.

ECOSSAIS Scotch (French).

ECRU Off-white color and a good name for a dog whose coat is not quite white.

EDEGA Wealthy (Hawaiian).

EDELMIRA Princess (Arabic).

EDELWEISS "Courage and nobility" in the language of flowers. Small white flower that grows wild in the Alps; beloved song from the Rodgers and Hammerstein musical *The Sound of Music*.

EDGAR Rich, happy, prosperous (Old English). The Pattersons' dog in Lynn Johnston's syndicated Canadian comic strip *For Better or Worse*.

EDISON Thomas Alva Edison (1847–1931), inventor, scientist, holder of 1,093 US patents, and one of the most influential men in modern history. Old English Sheepdog in Disney's 1968 musical motion picture *Chitty Chitty Bang Bang*.

EDMONDA Protector of prosperity (Italian).

EDMUND Rich protector (Old English).

EDNA Kernel (Gaelic). Edna May Oliver (1883–1942), American actress whose long face and distinctive voice branded her many film roles, especially Lady Catherine de Bourgh in the 1940 film adaptation of Jane Austen's *Pride and Prejudice*, starring Greer Garson and Laurence Olivier; *Drums Along the Mohawk* as Mrs. McKlennar; the Red Queen in *Alice in Wonderland* (1933); and Aunt March in *Little Women* (1933).

EDOARDO Guardian of prosperity (Italian).

EDOUARD Edouard Manet (1832–1883), French Impressionist painter who is credited for having launched the modern art movement.

EDRIC Blessed ruler (Old English).

EDSEL Edsel Ford (1893–1943), only son of Clara and Henry Ford, founder of the Ford Motor Company. Edsel was Ford's president until his death, from stomach cancer.

EDVARD Scandinavian version of Edward. Edvard Munch (1863–1944), Norwegian symbolist painter, forerunner of Expressionism, best known for his painting *The Scream*.

EDVIGE Contender in battle (Italian).

EDWARD Rich guard (Old English). American actress Ida Lupino's Scottish Terrier.

EDWIN Edwin Brough, English breeder who introduced Bloodhounds in America in 1888 and established kennels in this country with J. L. Winchell.

EDYTHE Edythe Van Hopper, the rich, loud, nouveau riche American who appears at the beginning of Daphne du Maurier's *Rebecca*—and thankfully goes away soon after that.

EGGSHELL Soft white and a good name for a delicate little dog with a white coat.

EGLANTINE "Poet" in the language of flowers.

EILEEN Irish form of Helen.

EIN Corgi in the 1998 animated series *Cowboy Bebop*.

EINAR One warrior (Norse). Einar Liberg of Norway won seven Olympic medals in shooting in games held between 1908 and 1924.

EINSTEIN Doc Brown's sheepdog in *Back to the Future*. The Golden Retriever in *Watchers*, the 1987 suspense novel by Dean Koontz. Albert

CORGI PUPPY

Einstein (1879–1955), German-born physicist who revolutionized physics with his theory of relativity. American actor, director, film director, screenwriter, eternal "sexiest man alive" George Clooney named his rescue dog Einstein.

EIRA Snow (Welsh). Beautiful name for a Sealyham Terrier, a dog of Welsh origin.

EISENHOWER Dwight D. "Ike" Eisenhower (1890–1969), five-star general in the US Army and Supreme Commander of the Allied Forces in World War Two, first Supreme Commander of NATO, and thirty-fourth president of the United States.

EKON Strong (Nigerian).

EL DIABLO Doberman Pinscher voiced by Edward James Olmos in the 2008 Disney film *Beverly Hills Chihuahua*.

ELARIO Happy, joyful (Italian).

ELBE River that flows through much of Germany.

ELCHO One of the first Irish Setters imported to the United States, in 1875.

ELDA Battle (Italian).

ELDER *See* Dog Names by Category: Breed; Crufts.

ELDRITCH Spiritual, old, experienced (Gaelic).

ELEANOR Eleanor of Aquitaine (1122– or 1124–1204), one of the wealthiest and most influential women of the Middle Ages, she was queen consort of Louis VII, King of France, and after his death married Henry II, King of England. She was the only woman in history to be queen of two countries.

ELECTRA Amber (Greek). Cathy's dog, rescued as a puppy, in the popular syndicated comic strip *Cathy*, by Cathy Guisewite, which ran from 1976 to 2010. Vengeful daughter of King Agamemnon in Greek mythology.

ELENA The bright one (Spanish). Elena Novikova-Belova of the Soviet Union won six medals for Fencing in Olympic Games held between 1968 and 1976.

ELEONORA Foreign (Italian). Short story by Edgar Allan Poe.

ELETTRA Shining, beaming (Italian).

ELEWA Very intelligent (African).

ELF One of a race of divine beings in Germanic mythology. Legolas was an Elf of the Woodland Realm and one of nine members of the Fellowship of the Ring in J. R. R. Tolkien's legendarium, *The Lord of the Rings*.

ELFRIC Elfric, Duke of Mercia, a Saxon chieftain, is illustrated in a ninth-century manuscript with a brace of Greyhounds.

ELGIN The Elgin Marbles are classical bas-relief tablets that were part of the Parthenon and Acropolis of Athens from ancient Greek times and removed around 1800 by the Seventh Earl of Elgin, then British ambassador to the Ottoman Empire, and shipped to the British Museum, where their display is a point of controversy to this day.

ELI Ascension (Hebrew).

ELIAS My god is Yahweh (Hebrew). Sir Elias de Midhope established the Penistone Harriers, a famous pack of thirteenth-century hunting dogs.

ELIMU Knowledge (African).

ELISABETTA God is my oath (Italian). Elisabeta Lipă of Romania won eight Olympic medals in rowing in games held from 1984 to 2000.

ELIZA Eliza Doolittle, fictitious flower girl turned lady in George Bernard Shaw's 1912 *Pygmalion*, from which the musical *My Fair Lady* was famously adapted.

ELIZABETH My god is abundant (Hebrew). Mother of John the Baptist. Elizabeth I (1533–1603) and Elizabeth II (b. 1926), two of the greatest monarchs of Great Britain. Elizabeth Bennet was as full of pride as Darcy is prejudiced in Jane Austen's *Pride and Prejudice*.

ELIZABETH TAYLOR aka Princess Dandyridge Brandywine, the Cavalier King Charles Spaniel from the HBO series *Sex and the City*.

ELKANAH God has purchased (Hebrew). Husband of Hannah in the Books of Samuel in the Old Testament.

ELLA True to all (Gaelic). Ella Fitzgerald (1917–1996), the "First Lady of Song," was arguably the greatest American female jazz vocalist of her time. Her career spanned three decades and her tone was pure as the driven snow; indeed, no one could sing "scat" like "Lady Ella." She began her solo career in 1942 after six years with Chick Webb's Orchestra (renamed Ella Fitzgerald and Her Famous Orchestra after his death in 1939) at Harlem's Savoy Ballroom. The rest is history.

Her bebop recording of "Oh, Lady Be Good" (1947) catapulted her to fame, and her recordings of Gershwin, Cole Porter, and Duke Ellington songbooks remain to this day unparalleled classics. Perfect for a dog that can bark an octave above B-flat.

ELLE She, hers (French).

ELLIE Diminutive of **Eleanor**.

ELMA Protection, helmet (Italian).

ELMER Famous (Old English). Elmer Fudd, Looney Tunes cartoon character who has failed to hunt down Bugs Bunny each and every time since 1937.

ELMO Helmet, protection (Italian). Muppets' red, furry monster.

ELNORA Foreign (Italian).

ELODIE Propensity, richness (Gaelic).

ELOF Descendant (Old Norse).

ELOISA Healthy, fit (Italian).

ELPIDIO Hope (Italian).

ELROY *See* Leroy.

ELSA Noble (English). Elsa Lanchester (1902–1986), British character actress who started her career in World War One and played the original Bride of Frankenstein opposite Boris Karloff in the 1935 film. She was married to the great English actor Charles Laughton. Diminutive for **Elizabeth**. **Elsie** is the affectionate version.

ELSIE Elsie Hughes, housekeeper of *Downton Abbey*, played by the amazing Scottish actress Phyllis Logan. Her firm but loving hand administers the smooth running of the staff, but it's her kind compassion that makes "downstairs" a family, albeit a dysfunctional one.

ELSPETH Another affectionate name for **Elizabeth**.

ELVIRA All, true (Spanish).

ELVIS Wise (Old Norse).

ELWOOD A Chinese Crested–Chihuahua mix voted the world's ugliest dog in 2007.

EMBER Soviet space dog. *See* Dog Names by Category: History.

EMERALD Green (Hebrew). Considered one of four "precious" gemstones (the others are diamond, sapphire, and ruby).

EMERSON Son of Emery (English).

EMIKO Blessed, beautiful child (Japanese).

EMIL Rival (Latin). **Emilio** is the Italian version and **Emilie**, the feminine.

EMILY Industrious (English). Emily Brontë (1818–1848), English novelist who only wrote one book, *Wuthering Heights,* and died too young—like her heroine, Catherine Earnshaw.

EMIR Commander, general, prince (Arabic).

EMMA All embracing (Germanic). One of Queen Elizabeth II of England's Corgis. English actress Emma Watson famously played Hermione Granger in the Harry Potter series of films.

EMMELINE Work (Old English).

EMMETT English surname derived from Emma.

EMORY Powerful (Germanic).

EMPEROR Monarch (French). Derived from the Latin word *imperator*. The Japanese Chin is known as "the dog of emperors" and is an ancient breed that first came to Japan when the Emperor of China presented the Emperor of Japan with a gift of a pair of these dogs.

EMRYS Immortal (Welsh).

ENAM Gift from God (African).

ENAUD M. Arthur Enaud, French sportsman who developed the French Brittany Spaniel breed of dog. Today the breed is simply referred to as Brittany.

ENCHILADA Mexican tortilla served with a spicy sauce, a dish that dates back to Mayan times.

ENDAL Yellow Labrador Retriever and the most decorated dog in the world, including Dog of the Millennium and 2005 Crufts Hero Dog of the Year, for his incredible work as a service dog in Great Britain.

ENDEAVOR Effort, enterprise.

ENDINE "Frugality" in the language of flowers.

ENEKI Eager (Hawaiian).

ENGLISH Despite its name, the Brussels Griffon, according to enthusiasts, understands English, not French, as its primary language.

ENNISKILLEN *See* Fermanagh.

ENO Wild (Hawaiian).

ENRICA Home ruler (Italian). **Enrico** is the male version.

ENZO Italian for **Heinz** or **Henry**.

EOS In Greek mythology, Eos is the goddess of the dawn; her brother is **Helios**, god of the sun. Magnificent white hunting hound chosen to be sacrificed to reconcile the Macedonians after the death of Alexander the Great in the 1981 historical novel *Funeral Games*, by Mary Renault.

EOSTRE Anglo-Saxon goddess of spring.

EPAGNEUL Spaniel (French).

EPCOT Disney's international theme park in Orlando, Florida.

EPH Well's Eph, son of Burnett's Gyp and Hooper's Judge, founding dam and sire of the Boston Terrier breed.

EPIC Grand, classic, period drama.

EPSTEIN One of the oldest Slavic Jewish surnames.

ERASMUS Desiderius Erasmus Roterodamus (1466–1536), Dutch Renaissance classical scholar, Catholic priest, theologian, and leader of the Reformation movement in Europe.

ERASTO Man of peace (African).

EREVU Clever (African).

ERIC Eric Heiden, five-time Olympic gold medalist American speed skater. You could hear cheers around the world when he finished first in his fifth and final meet of the 1980 Olympic Games.

ERIN From the Irish *Éireann*, or Ireland. The Irish Terrier is called the "Terrier of Erin."

ERMINA From the earth (Italian).

ERNEST Dave Barry's dog. Barry, a Pulitzer Prize–winning author, humorist, and syndicated columnist, observed, "Dogs feel very strongly that they should always go with you in the car, in case the need should arise for them to bark violently at nothing right in your ear." Dog in *Dave's World*, the 1993 CBS sitcom inspired by Dave Barry's syndicated column.

ERNESTINA Serious (Germanic). **Ernest** is the male form, **Ernie** is the diminutive.

ERNIE Bert's best friend on *Sesame Street*.

EROS God of love (Greek mythology).

ERROL Nobleman, prince, warrior (Old English); Errol Flynn (1909–1959), Australian-born Hollywood actor and writer best-known for his swashbuckler films, including *The Adventures of Robin Hood*, *The Sea Hawk*, and *Captain Blood*. Flynn became a naturalized United States citizen in 1942. Desperate to serve the country he had come to love, he attempted to enlist in the American Armed Forces. But unbeknownst to many, Flynn was not a well man; he suffered from chronic tuberculosis, recurrent malaria, chronic back pain, and an enlarged heart, among other maladies. He was turned away by all four branches. During World War Two he made fifteen movies, most of them war movies such as *Objective Burma!* (1945), *Dive Bomber* (1941), and *Edge of Darkness* (1943), a little known but extraordinarily compelling movie about the Norwegian Resistance movement. He was a guest at a party when, feeling poorly, he excused himself and went into a bedroom to lie down. Before departing from the gathered company, he said, "I will return." Those were his last words. Flynn died shortly after of a massive heart attack at the age of fifty.

ERSILIA Delicate, tender, fragile (Italian). Good name for a Papillon, also known as the Continental Toy Spaniel, Squirrel Spaniel, and Titian Spaniel in days gone by. One of the oldest Toy breeds, its fringed ears gives this spirited, hearty dog a deceivingly delicate appearance. It is fabled that Marie Antoinette carried her Papillon under her arm as she walked to the guillotine. Hopefully, the little dog did not share its mistress's fate.

ESCAPADE Caper, antic, spree.

ESCORT Companion, chaperon.

ESKIMO Northern dwellers of the Inuit and Yupik peoples.

ESMÉ Loved, esteemed (Old French).

ESMERALDA American actress Anne Hathaway's chocolate Labrador Retriever.

ESPERANZA To hope (Spanish).

ESPRESSO Dark, strong, somewhat bitter coffee associated with Italy.

ESSEX *See* Parson.

ESTELLA Spoiled adopted daughter of Miss Havisham, who has a great epiphany at the end of *Great Expectations* by Charles Dickens.

ESTHER Star (Persian). President Grover Cleveland's Cocker Spaniel.

ESTRAMADURA Home of the Spanish Alano breed of dog, related to the Boxer.

ETANA Strong (Hawaiian).

ETTA Etta James (1938–2012), American singer who sang it all—blues, jazz, rock, soul, gospel, and jazz—and was best known for a song many have sung and none equaled, "At Last." Ranked twenty-two in *Rolling Stone's* 100 Greatest Singers of All Time.

ETZEL Etzel von Oeringen (1917–1929), German Shepherd Dog and one of the first canine actors. His screen name was Braveheart.

EUCALYPTUS "To protect" in the language of flowers.

EUFEMIA To speak well (Italian).

EUGENE Eugene Cernan, Thomas P. Stafford, John W. Young, the crew of Apollo 10, which descended to 8.4 nautical miles from the lunar surface in a "dress rehearsal" for the lunar landing of Apollo 11.

EUGENIA Well born (Latin). Feminine of **Eugene.**

EULA Well-spoken (Italian).

EUMAEUS *See* Odysseus.

EUPHORBIA "Persistence" in the language of flowers.

EUPHRATES Longest river in western Asia. It originates in Turkey, joins the Tigris, and empties into the Persian Gulf, encompassing the ancient region known as Mesopotamia.

EUREKA "I have found it!" according to Uncle Henry, when he gives Dorothy the white kitten he has found and tells his niece the meaning of its name in *Dorothy and the Wizard of Oz,* a sequel to L. Frank Baum's *The Wizard of Oz.*

EURIPIDES (480–406 BC) one of the three great writers of ancient Greek tragedies.

EUROPA Wide face (Greek). Phoenician noblewoman and lover of Zeus in Greek mythology who became the Queen of Crete; a moon of the planet Jupiter and also known as Jupiter II.

EVAN *See* Poiret.

EVE To breathe (Hebrew). Adam's wife who listened to a serpent, ate an apple, and ruined mankind's chances for a free pass to Paradise.

EVELYN Life (Hebrew).

EVERETT Sir Everett Millais was the first to introduce the short-legged Basset Hound to England, in 1875.

EVERLASTING "Eternity" in the language of flowers. Best describes the love between a dog and his master.

EWALANI Heavenly woman (Hawaiian).

EWAN Born from the yew tree (Scottish).

EWE Baby sheep. Tender name for a gentle little dog.

EWOK Primeval, curious, friendly furry creatures that live on the Forest Moon of Endor in the *Star Wars* universe.

EX and Ham, one of a pair of Merrie Melodies' animated singing Saint Bernard puppies back in the thirties.

EXCALIBUR Legendary sword of King Arthur, empowered with magic that works only for the rightful sovereign of Great Britain.

EXETER Historic city in Devonshire, England, that was an ancient Roman fortified settlement.

EZE King (African).

EZEKIEL God strengthens (Hebrew).

F

FABLE Legend, story.

FABRIZIA Craftsman (Italian). **Fabrizio** is the masculine name.

FABUMI Gift of God (African).

FAGIN Hook-nosed, long-bearded thief who adds Oliver to his band of juvenile pickpockets in *Oliver Twist*. Sir Alec Guinness portrayed Fagin in David Lean's masterful 1948 film adaptation. You may know Sir Alec better as Obi-Wan Kenobi in *Star Wars*.

FAHIM Learned (African).

FAIRBANKS Douglas Fairbanks (1883–1939), silent screen star married to Mary Pickford. They were Hollywood royalty. Their only child, Douglas Fairbanks Jr., was likewise an accomplished actor. One of his most famous performances was in *Gunga Din*, the remarkable 1939 adventure film starring Cary Grant, Victor McLaglen, and Joan Fontaine. Fairbanks Jr., a highly decorated American naval officer, had been assigned to Lord Louis Mountbatten's commando staff in England in World War Two.

FAIRY *See* Laverack.

FAITH Trust, devotion, allegiance.

FAITHFUL President Ulysses S. Grant's Newfoundland.

FAJITA Mexican dish of cooked meat rolled inside a tortilla.

FAKIH Intellectual (African).

FALA President Franklin Delano Roosevelt's Scottish Terrier.

FALAFEL National dish of Israel, a deep-fried ball of chickpeas garnished with vegetables and sauces.

FALCON *See* Dog Names by Category: Breed; Crufts.

FALCOR Doglike "Luck Dragon" in the 1984 German-American children's fantasy film *The NeverEnding Story*, based on the wonderful book by Michael Ende.

FALKIRK *See* Bruce.

FALLOW English word referring to land that is left unplowed for a season to let it restore its fertility.

FANCY Like, inclination, embellishment (English).

FANDANGO Quick-paced, rhythmic couples dance that originated in Spain or Portugal in the early eighteenth century, usually accompanied by castanets, clapping, and emotional singing.

FANG Canine tooth in mammals, snakes, some spiders and most dragons and vampires. Along with **Grip** and **Wolf**, Fang was one of the three fierce dogs that protected Farmer Maggot's mushroom farm in the Shire in J. R. R. Tolkien's *The Fellowship of the Rings*. *Columbo*'s dog in the television detective series starring the inimitable American actor Peter Falk. American actress and comedienne Phyllis Diller (b. 1917) joked about her husband, "Fang," in her routines—a fictitious spouse that resembled neither of Diller's real-life husbands. Hagrid's enormous pet Mastiff in the Harry Potter series; *Fang: A Maximum Ride Novel*, by American author James Patterson.

FANNY Fanny Brice (1891–1951), American radio, stage, and film actress, comedienne, and singer, daughter of Hungarian Jewish immigrants, who paved the way for women in comedy. Brice started her career in burlesque, went on to headline Broadway's *Ziegfeld Follies*, then went to Hollywood. With the exception of Rose Marie, no female comedic entertainer had a more diverse or inspiring career. *See* Rose Marie.

FANSOME First English Springer Spaniel bitch to be awarded a Challenge Certificate, in 1898.

FANTASIA Cutting-edge 1940 Walt Disney animated film featuring music by the Philadelphia Symphony Orchestra, conducted by maestro Leopold Stokowski.

FANTÔME NOIRE Alias of Poker, a Miniature Black Poodle in James Thurber's short story "How to Name a Dog."

FARGO Largest city in North Dakota.

FARHANI Happy (African).

FARMANN Traveler (Old Norse).

FARO Burt Lancaster directed and starred in the touching 1955 family film *The Kentuckian*. Faro, a black and white mixed breed that plays the Wakefield family's dog, won a PATSY (Picture Animal Top Star of the Year) Award for his performance; seventeenth-century French card game played for stakes.

FARTHINGALE Stiff, hooped skirt that originated in the fifteenth century. The term was also used for a heavily braided Hussars jacket during the Crimean War. Terrific name for a corded-coat dog, such as a Komondor.

FASKALLY *See* Buccleuch.

FATHER WOLF Raises the human child Mowgli as his own cub in *The Jungle Book*, by Rudyard Kipling.

FATIMA Great Dane in the 2000 Farrelly brothers' comedy film *Me, Myself & Irene*, starring Jim Carrey and Renee Zellweger.

FAULTLESS *See* Dog Names by Category: Breed; Westminster.

FAUN Rustic forest god in Roman mythology that's half man, half goat. C. S. Lewis brought the faun to life in *The Chronicles of Narnia* with the character Mr. Tumnus, tenderly portrayed by Scottish actor James McAvoy in the gorgeous 2005 film adaptation.

FAUNA Wildlife, nature's creatures.

FAUNE *See* Dog Names by Category: Breed; Crufts.

FAUST Protagonist of the German legend about a doctor who went into league with the devil. "He laid the Holy Scriptures behind the door and under the bench, refused to be called doctor of Theology, but preferred to be styled doctor of Medicine." *The Tragical History and the Life and Death of Doctor Faustus* was written by English playwright Christopher Marlowe and published posthumously in 1604. German writer and Renaissance man Johann Wolfgang von Goethe wrote his version in 1805 as the tragic morality play *Faust*, and Elizabeth Taylor and Richard Burton made a brilliant but sadly forgotten film version in 1967, inspired by the original Marlowe story.

FAUX PAS False step, misstep (French).

FAVE Provenchères-sur-Fave a region in northeastern France chronicled as early as the thirteenth century by the Romans; slang for *favorite*.

FAVELL Jack Favell, Rebecca's conniving cousin and implied lover in Daphne du Maurier's intriguing psychological drama *Rebecca*. The role was convincingly played by English actor George Sanders.

FAWN Natural name for a dog with a light brown coat such as a Cardigan Welsh Corgi.

FAY Fairy (Middle English, from the word *faie*).

FAY RAY Much-photographed Weimaraner owned by photographer William Wegman, who named the dog after *King Kong* actress Fay Wray. Fay Ray appeared on *Sesame Street* in 1989 and had a litter of puppies, **Battina**, **Crooky**, **Chundo**, and **Chip**, who also appeared on the PBS show.

FEARNOUGHT *See* Dog Names by Category: Breed; Westminster.

FEATHER Best-selling English author Jilly Cooper's beloved Greyhound, a rescue dog.

FEDERICA Peaceful ruler (Italian). **Federico** is the masculine version.

FEDORA Men's felt hat with a crease down the crown made popular by American film actor Humphrey Bogart.

FEISTY Spirited, full of life.

FELICIANO Happy, full of joy (Italian).

FELICITA Good fortune, lucky (Italian).

FELICITY *See* Dog Names by Category: Breed; Westminster.

FELINA Princess Orzana of Storybook Mountain's cat in *The Magical Mimics in Oz*, one of the thirteen sequels to *The Wonderful Wizard of Oz*, by L. Frank Baum.

FELIX Lucky, successful (Latin).

FELLER President Harry S. Truman received the blond Cocker Spaniel as a gift.

FELLOW Companion, partner.

FELLOWES Julian Fellowes (b. 1949), the heart, soul, and genius behind the critically acclaimed Carnival Films television period drama *Downton Abbey*. A real-life Conservative Peer of the Realm known as Baron Fellowes of West Stafford, the gifted screenwriter, novelist, and sometime actor wrote the scripts for *The Young Victoria* (2009), *Vanity Fair* (2004), and Robert Altman's English period mystery set in 1932, *Gosford Park* (2001).

FENNEL Vegetable whose seeds are used in seasoning.

FENRIS Fame-wolf or monster of the River Ván in Norse mythology. A wolf-dog in *Prose Edda* and *Heimskringla*, written in the thirteenth century by Snorri Sturluson.

FENTON *See* Dog Names by Category: Breed; Crufts.

FENWAY Boston's baseball park and home of the Red Sox.

FERDINAND Brave journey (Germanic). **Fernando** in Spanish.

FERDINANDA Wanting peace (Italian).

FERGUS Man of vigor (Gaelic).

FERGUSON Son of Fergus (Gaelic).

FERMANAGH Jason Hazzard of Timaskea, County Fermanagh, first bred Irish Setters in the early eighteenth century, along with Sir St. George Gore and the Earl of Enniskillen, confirmed in records dated 1812.

FERN "Fascination" in the language of flowers.

FERRARI Italian sports car company founded by Enzo Ferrari in 1929, renowned for its Formula One race cars.

FERRO Built of iron (Italian).

FESS Young pageboy in the House of Gules in *Merry Go Round in Oz*, by Eloise Jarvis McGraw and Lauren McGraw Wagner, the last "official" book in the "Famous Forty" series authorized by *Oz* creator L. Frank Baum to be written after his death.

FEZZIWIG The young Scrooge's jovial, generous employer, "an old gentleman in a Welsh wig . . . Scrooge cried in great excitement: 'Why, it's old Fezziwig! Bless his heart; it's Fezziwig alive again!'" in Charles Dickens's *A Christmas Carol.*

FIALA *See* Shackleton.

FIAMMETTA Little bird (Italian).

FIDDLE Colloquial term for "violin." The first fiddle was the bowed lira, a tenth-century instrument from Ancient Persia. Also used as a verb, meaning "to play a string instrument" or "fiddle around," which means "to fool around." **Fiddler** is a person who plays the fiddle.

FIDELE The dog in Russian writer Nikolai Gogol's short story "Diary of a Madman," published in 1835.

FIDGET The restless puppy in the Walt Disney animated film *101 Dalmatians*.

FIDO Fidelity (Latin). Mixed-breed dog whose master, Carlo Soriani, died in an air raid near Florence, Italy, during World War Two. Every day for fourteen years, Fido waited for the bus his master used to take home from work, never losing faith that one day they would be reunited; in faith, they were. Dog in Johnny Gruelle's *Raggedy Ann Stories*. Abraham Lincoln's mixed-breed dog.

FIESTA Party, celebration (Spanish).

FIFI Minnie Mouse's dog and Pluto's girlfriend. Ill-tempered Poodle in the 2006 computer animated film *Open Season 2*.

FIGARO Protagonist in French playwright Pierre-Augustin Caron de Beaumarchais's plays *The Barber of Seville* (1775), *The Marriage of Figaro* (1784), and *The Guilty Mother* (1792). Mozart and Rossini adapted Figaro into their operas.

FIGGY Figgy pudding, a Christmas dessert made with figs that originated in sixteenth-century England, traditionally served to carolers (i.e., "Now give us some figgy pudding..." from "We Wish You a Merry Christmas").

FIGHTER Boxer, someone who engages in fighting.

FILBERT "Reconciliation" in the language of flowers.

FILBERTO Extremely bright (Italian). Clever name for your intelligent Spinone Italiano.

FILIPO Lover of horses (Italian).

FILIPPONI Bolognese merchant and early breeder of Papillons.

FILIUS Professor Filius Flitwick, vertically challenged Charms professor at the Hogwarts School of Witchcraft and Wizardry, and head of Ravenclaw House in the Harry Potter series.

FINA Serpent (Italian).

FINGAL First Schnauzer known to have been imported to the United States.

FINN Fair, white (Irish). Huckleberry Finn. Mark Twain first had him appear in *The Adventures of Tom Sawyer* and then chronicled the troublesome boy's own exploits in *Adventures of Huckleberry Finn* (1885).

FINNEGAN Descendant of Fionnagán (Irish). Character in *Finnegan's Wake*, by James Joyce (1939).

FIOLMENA Easygoing friend (Italian).

FIONA Female version of Finn, from the Irish word *Fion*.

FIONOULA Singer-songwriter Billy Joel's Boston Terrier.

FIORALBA Early blooming flower (Italian).

FIORE Flower (Italian).

FIORELLA Little flower (Italian).

FIORENZA To blossom (Italian).

FIRE CHIEF Famous Bull Terrier in England in 1901. Highest-ranking officer at a firehouse.

FIRECRACKER Paper-wrapped explosive that soars into the air emitting vibrant flashes of fire. Developed by the Chinese to celebrate their New Year, known as the "Spring Festival" or *Pinyin*.

FIREHOUSE The Dalmatian is the traditional firehouse dog.

FIRMINO Steadfast, true (Italian).

FIRTH Fjord, creek, coastal waters (Scottish). Colin Firth (b. 1960), Academy Award–winning British actor (*The King's Speech*) who interprets his characters with depth and insight.

FITZGERALD Ruler of the spear (Norman).

FITZGILBERT Richard Fitz Gilbert (c. 1035–1090), much-favored Norman lord who accompanied William the Conqueror to England and fought at the Battle of Hastings in 1066. For his courage and fidelity, William bestowed upon him huge land grants. This would be an exceptional name for a Bullmastiff, a dog of English origin bred to protect. *See* Hamilton.

FITZWILLIAM Colonel Fitzwilliam, steadfast, devoted, commonsensical cousin of Darcy in Jane Austen's *Pride and Prejudice*.

FIVE Fifth of Edward Henshaw Hobbie's beloved Springer Spaniels. Four and Three preceded my dearest's Five, of course.

FIZZ Effervescent, bubbly.

FLAG Long fringe on the tail of a dog like a Rough Collie—and good name for one.

FLAITH Ancient Gaelic word for prince or king. Fitting name for a King Charles Spaniel.

FLAME First dog honored with a PATSY Award, in 1951, for his role as Pal in the RKO *My Pal* series of films. The PATSY awards were originated by the Hollywood branch of the American Humane Society to honor exceptional animal actors. Flame of the Miramichi, bred by the late Andre Godin at the Miramichi Inn on that fabled Canadian salmon-fishing river, is my Irish Setter.

FLAN Spanish custard and great name for a Basque Shepherd Dog, which originates in Spain and has a custardy yellow-colored coat.

FLANAGAN Red, ruddy (Gaelic). Swell name for an Irish Setter.

FLANDERS *A Dog of Flanders* was written in 1872 by "Ouida," the pen name of English novelist Marie Louise Ramee (1839–1908). It is the heartwarming story of a boy named Nello and his Bouvier des Flandres, Patrasche, and has inspired several movies, most recently the 1999 film starring Jack Warden, Jon Voight, and, as Patrasche, the canine actor Napoleon.

FLANNEL Soft carded wool, usually dyed gray to make tailored flannel pants. Perfect name for a Wirehaired Pointing Griffon.

FLAPPER Liberated breed of women in the Roaring Twenties that bobbed their hair, hiked up their skirts, wore blood-red lipstick, and danced the night away.

FLAVIANUS *See* Quintus.

FLAVIO Yellow hair (Italian).

FLAX "Domesticity" in the language of flowers. Wonderful name for a Norfolk Terrier.

FLEALICK Wheelchair-bound Jack Russell Terrier in the 1998 film *Babe: Pig in the City*, the sequel to 2005's endearing live-action film *Babe*. Other breed dogs in this canine-studded sequel are an English Bulldog, French Poodle, German Shepherd, Italian Greyhound, Neapolitan Mastiff, Pit Bull Terrier, Doberman Pinscher, Boxer, and a Beagle. *See* Fly; Rex.

FLEETFOOT *See* Dog Names by Category: Breeds; Westminster.

FLETCH Protagonist who inherits a fortune and stumbles into trouble in the 1974 mystery novels by Gregory McDonald and adapted into the 1985 comedy film starring comic genius Chevy Chase.

FLEUR Flower (French). Soames Forsyte's only child in *The Forsyte Saga*, a series of three books by English novelist John Galsworthy, published between 1906 and 1921 and the inspiration for several television and film adaptations.

FLICKER Light that glimmers, like the flicker of a match.

FLINDERS Sir William Matthew Flinders Petrie (1853–1942), English archeologist and author who pioneered modern archeological techniques including sequence dating, which he applied at numerous sites in Egypt and at Stonehenge in his native country.

FLIRT To tease with playfully romantic intent.

FLO Rough Collie in the 1989 animated film *All Dogs Go to Heaven*.

FLODDEN *See* Flute.

FLOPSY One of Peter's well-behaved siblings in *The Tale of Peter Rabbit*, by Beatrix Potter.

FLORA Roman goddess of flowers and spring.

FLORABELLE "Unpretentious" in the language of flowers.

FLORENZ *See* Glinda.

FLOSSIE Dog in D. H. Lawrence's scandalous and most famous novel, *Lady Chatterley's Lover*, published in 1928.

FLOWER A bloom, blossom or flowering plant.

FLUFFY Dog in *Gold Diggers of 1933*, Warner Brothers motion picture starring Ruby Keeler, Dick Powell, and Ginger Rogers. Three-headed dog, perhaps from a litter sired by Cerberus, that Rubeus Hagrid purchased from a "Greek chappie" in *Harry Potter and the Sorceror's Stone*.

FLUKE Stringy mongrel cur that wandered the streets of the city in the best-selling thriller of the same name, by English writer James Herbert.

FLURRY Prince, king (Gaelic).

FLUSH Spaniel owned by Elizabeth Barrett Browning and fictionalized in Virginia Wolf's endearing 1933 novel *Flush*.

FLUTE James Joicey, First Baron of Flodden of County Durham, Ireland, established Flodden Kennels, where he raised Labrador Retrievers, notably Flute of Flodden, born in 1922, a dual UK champion (bench and field trial).

FLY Farmer Hoggett's female Border Collie who adopts Babe the Pig as one of her own in *The Sheep-Pig*, by Dick King-Smith, adapted into the 1995 Australian-American film *Babe*. Nine dogs were trained to play Fly at various times in the movie.

FOGEY Old English Sheepdog in Walt Disney's *101 Dalmatians*. Two different dogs played Fogey in the 1995 live-action film version.

FOIE GRAS Fat liver (French). A great French delicacy.

FONDUE French or Swiss dish of cheese melted over a spirit lamp and served with chunks of fresh-baked bread.

FONSIE Noble and ready (Italian).

FONTAINE Miss Joan Fontaine (b. 1917), great and elegant lady of the silver screen, three-time Academy Award Best Actress nominee, and the only actor to win an Academy Award in a movie directed by Alfred Hitchcock (for 1941 Best Actress for *Suspicion*). She also starred in *Gunga Din*, *The Women*, *Rebecca*, *Jane Eyre*, and *Ivanhoe*. Before Grace Kelly, there was Joan Fontaine.

FONZIE Arthur Herbert Fonzarelli, better known as "the Fonz," the cool, hip, leather-swaddled guy with the greased-back hair that Henry Winkler brought to life for a decade in the popular American 1974 sitcom *Happy Days*.

FOO Foo Dogs are Chinese guardians represented in art, pottery, and sculpture by the Chow Chow breed of dog, called *Songshi Quan*, or "puffy-lion dog," in Chinese; also by the Japanese Chin, Pekinese, Pug, Shar Pei, Tibetan Spaniel, and the Shih Tuz, called *Chzi Gou*, or "lion dog" in Chinese.

FOO-FOO Miss Piggy's dog on *The Muppet Show*.

FORBES American publishing house founded in 1917 by Bertie Charles "B. C." Forbes (1880–1954), a Scottish financial journalist. *Forbes* magazine, known as "the Capitalist Tool," grew to become a leading world financial forecaster under the astuteness of B.C.'s son, the late Malcolm Forbes.

FORGET-ME-NOT "Remember me always" in the language of flowers.

FORMOSA Island in the western Pacific off the coast of China.

FORREST Woodsman, of the forest, forest-keeper (Gothic).

FORSETI Norse god of mediation.

FORSYTE Aristocratic family in *The Forsyte Saga*, by John Galsworthy. *See* Fleur.

FORSYTHIA "Expectation" in the language of flowers.

FORTUNE Immense wealth.

FOXHALL Parish in Suffolk, England, recorded in AD 1086 in *The Domesday Book*.

FOXY Affectionate name for a Fox Terrier.

FOZZIE Fozzie Bear, stand-up Muppet comedian that always ruins the punch line.

FRA MAURO Crater and highlands on the moon named for Fra Mauro, the fifteenth-century Italian monk and mapmaker. This was the intended landing site for the aborted Apollo 13 mission and the successful landing site of Apollo 14, crewed by Alan B. Shepard Jr., Stuart A. Roosa, and Edgar D. Mitchell.

FRABJOUS Add "fair," "fabulous," and "joyous" and you have "frabjous," a word invented by Lewis Carroll for *Alice's Adventures in Wonderland*.

FRACAS *See* Resy Patricia.

FRAGONARD John-Honoré Fragonard (1732–1806), prolific French Rococo painter. He died a forgotten man; it was not until he was rediscovered at the end of the nineteenth century by French Impressionists such as Renoir, who greatly admired Fragonard's use of color composition, that he was deemed one of the great masters of French painting.

FRANCESCA Italian feminine form of Frank.

FRANCIS *See* Phineas.

FRANCISCO Free man (Latin). *See* Goya.

FRANCO Spear (French); from France (Latin).

FRANÇOIS François Truffaut (1932–1984), iconic French director, actor, screenwriter, and producer who made his filmmaking debut in 1959 with *The 400 Blows*, considered the defining film of French New

Wave cinema, which he cofounded. A diversely talented man, he appeared in more than twenty-five films, notably as scientist Charles Lacombe in the 1977 Steven Spielberg film *Close Encounters of the Third Kind*.

FRANQUEVILLE *See* Mons Lane.

FRANK SINATRA Actress Reese Witherspoon's English Bulldog.

FRANK THE PUG Smart-alecky alien Pug dog in *Men in Black I* and *Men in Black II* (1997, 2002), starring Tommy Lee Jones and Will Smith.

FRANKLIN Franklin Delano Roosevelt, thirty-second president of the United States and the only president to be elected to four terms of office.

FRECKLES Dog in *Being a Public Character*, by American humorist Don Marquis. Great name for a Dalmatian.

FRED Lucy and Desi's Cairn Terrier on the mother of all sitcoms, *I Love Lucy*, starring Lucille Ball and Desi Arnaz and produced by Desilu, the couple's production company. Cledus "Snowman" Snow's Basset Hound in the 1977 film *Smokey and the Bandit*, starring Burt Reynolds, Sally Field, and the great Jackie Gleason.

FREDERICK Frederick the Great, King of Prussia (1712–1786), owned an Italian Greyhound. The dog never left his side. On one occasion, during the Seven Years' War, Frederick was forced to hide from the enemy under a land bridge. The little dog didn't utter a sound; had he barked just once, the lives of the king and all of Prussia might have ended then and there. So distraught was Frederick upon the death of his canine companion that he dug the little dog's grave with his own bare hands, on the grounds of his palace in Berlin, Sanssouci. Frederick was affectionately called **Old Fritz** by his people.

FREDI Peace (Old Norse).

FREEWAY The name of the Löwchen belonging to Jonathan and Jennifer in the 1979 Aaron Spelling action-adventure television series *Hart to Hart*, starring Robert Wagner and Stefanie Powers. Freeway was a stray found on the freeway. Fact is, the Löwchen is one of the rarest breeds of dog; surely someone would have put up a "lost" poster offering a reward.

FRENCHIE Affectionate name for the French Bulldog.

FREUD Dr. Sigmund Freud (1856–1939), Austrian neurologist who founded psychoanalysis, the evaluation of the unconscious mind, through dialogue between a patient and a psychoanalyst. Stricken with cancer, Freud died from a physician-assisted lethal injection of morphine.

FREYA Goddess of fertility in Norse mythology.

FRIAR Friar Tuck, man of the cloth and one of the greatest (in spirit and girth) of Robin Hood's Merry Men in Sherwood Forest.

FRIDAY Jack Russell Terrier in *Hotel for Dogs*.

FRIGG Wife of Odin, "All-Father" in Norse mythology.

FRISBEE Round disc invented by Walter Frederick Morrison in 1938 that can provide unending joy for your dog for as long as you keep tossing it to him.

FRISKY Playful, energetic.

FRITH Butler at Manderley in Daphne du Maurier's *Rebecca*. British genre painter William Powell Frith, R.A., whose monumental 1862 canvas *The Railway Station* features several dogs.

FRITZ Peaceful ruler (Germanic). Diminutive of **Frederick**.

FRODO BAGGINS Hobbit of the Shire who inherited Sauron's Ring from his uncle Bilbo Baggins and set forth to destroy it in the fires of Mount Doom in J. R. R. Tolkien's *Lord of the Rings* trilogy.

FROLIC *See* Dog Names by Category: Breed; Westminster.

ENGLISH SETTER PUPPIES

FROLICK Romp, gambol (Old English).

FRONTIER Region beyond a settled area.

FROOFIE Fictional dog from *Inside the Mind of Bill Cosby*, the comedian's 1972 comedy album.

FROST Wonderful name for a dog with a white coat such as the Great Pyrenees, known as Pyrenean Mountain Dog. This breed dates from the fifteenth century in the Pyrenees Mountains of southern France and northern Spain and used by Basque shepherds as herding dogs.

FUCHSIA "Good taste" in the language of flowers.

FUDGE Sinfully delicious chocolate confection. Sweet name for a chocolate Labrador Retriever.

FUFU A thick paste made from boiled vegetables that is a staple of West and Central African cooking.

FULLER Scottish word for a millworker who cleanses raw wool of oils and dirt as part of the woolen cloth-making process. The process is known as "fulling" or "waulking." A fuller is also known as a "tucker" or "walker," also good names to consider for your dog.

FULTON Bird-catcher's town (Old English).

FULVIA Yellow (Italian).

FUZZ Ziggy's small white dog in the Tom Wilson comic strip *Ziggy*, which was syndicated in 1971. Fuzzy, President Ronald Reagan's Belgian Sheepdog.

G

GABBY Diminutive of **Gabriel**.

GABRIEL Gabriel hounds from Welsh mythology—Cŵn Annwn, or "hounds of Annwn"—hunt only on the feast days of Saint John, Saint Martin, Saint Michael the Archangel, All Saints, Christmas, New Year, Saint Agnes, Saint David, and Good Friday, and in the autumn and winter, though some say Arawn only hunts from Christmas to Twelfth Night. Cŵn Annwn escorts the souls of the dead on their journey to the Otherworld. **Gabrielle** is the feminine form of the name.

GADGET Small device or tool that may derive from the French word *gâchette*, which means firing mechanism, or *gagée*, a small tool.

GAELFORCE *See* Dog Names by Category: Breed; Westminster.

GAELIC General term for the ancient Irish, Manx, and Scottish languages.

GAIETY Jovial, merry.

GAINSBOROUGH Thomas Gainsborough (1727–1788), masterful English portrait and landscape artist who painted Henry Scott, Third

Duke of Buccleuch, around 1770 with his Old English Sheepdog. Gainsboro gray, a bluish shade of grey, was named after the artist. This would make a great name for a Neopolitan Mastiff or a Bearded Collie.

GALADRIEL Mightiest of all the Elves that remained in Middle-earth after the death of Gil-galad and "the greatest of all elven women" in J. R. R. Tolkien's *The Lord of the Rings*.

GALAHAD Sir Galahad, knight of King Arthur's legendary Round Table, one of the three achievers of the Holy Grail and illegitimate son of Lancelot and Elaine of Corbenic. Prince Galahad of Wyndham, a Bull Terrier played by Wildfire in the movie *It's a Dog's Life* (1955), starring Edmund Gwenn and Dean Jagger.

GALILEO Galileo Galilei (1564–1642), Italian physicist, mathematician, and philosopher who is known as the "father of modern observational astronomy."

GALINA Goddess of calm seas in Greek mythology. Galina Kulakova of the Soviet Union won eight medals for cross-country skiing in the Olympic Games from 1972 to 1980.

GALSWORTHY John Galsworthy (1867–1933), prolific English novelist, playwright, and author of *The Forsyte Saga*. Contemporary of George Bernard Shaw and friend of Joseph Conrad, Galsworthy lived a life that was the stuff of which his books were made. An aristocrat by birth, he had a decade-long affair with his cousin's wife. When it ended in divorce, they married and remained married until his death from a stroke at the age of sixty-six, six weeks after he won the Nobel Prize in Literature.

GALUMP To move with a clumsy and heavy tread (Old English).

GALWAY Comte de Tournon of France sent two Basset Hounds to Lord Galway in 1866. Named **Basset** and **Belle**, they were the first Basset Hounds imported to Great Britain.

GAMBA Warrior (African).

GAMBLER Person who gambles, risk taker, high roller, adventurer.

GAMBOGE Dark mustard-yellow color. Pretty name for a Golden Retriever with that shade of coat.

GAMBOL Cavort, frolic, dance.

GAMEKEEPER Person who manages the land and the wildlife it supports for the purpose of hunting. Good name for a hunting dog.

GAMIN Ch. Nellcote Gamin, foundation dog for the French Bulldog breed in America.

GAMLE Gamle Bamse Gram, prepotent sire of the modern grey Norwegian Elkhound, born in 1865 and owned by Consul Jens Gram of Ask.

GANDALF Great and wise wizard in J. R. R. Tolkien's *The Hobbit* and *The Lord of the Rings*, the last of the "Istari." Quenya for "Wise Ones."

GANDER Newfoundland mascot of the Royal Rifles of Canada whose heroic action saving soldiers' lives at the Battle of Lye Mun on Hong Kong Island in World War Two cost him his own. He was posthumously awarded a Dickin Medal.

GANDHI Mohandas Karamchand Gandhi (1869–1948), political and ideological leader of India during the Indian independence movement. He advocated nonviolence in his pursuit of civil unification and peace in India. His daughter, Indira, succeeded him.

GARBO Greta Garbo (1905–1990), born Greta Lovisa Gustafsson, the most elusive, mysterious actress to come out of Hollywood. Her first film, *Torrent*, was made in 1926 and her last, *Two-Faced Woman*, was in 1941. Nominated four times for a Best Actress Oscar, she was presented with a Lifetime Achievement Award in 1954 by the Academy of Motion Picture Arts and Sciences, for her "unforgettable screen performances"—a gracious nod to a career that, alas, did not survive World War Two.

GARCIA Actor Owen Wilson's Australian Cattle Dog.

GARDENIA "Admiration" in the language of flowers.

GARETH Sir Gareth, chivalrous, ill-fated younger brother of Sir Gawain, likewise a legendary knight of King Arthur's Round Table.

GARFIELD James A. Garfield, twentieth president of the United States. The world's most famous cat, who was created in 1978 by cartoonist Jim Davis. Garfield's owner is Jon Arbuckle and Jon's dog—and Garfield's best buddy—is **Odie**. *Garfield* is recognized as the world's most widely syndicated comic strip by *The Guinness Book of World Records*.

GARGERY Joe Gargery, Pip's brother-in-law and his most devoted friend in Charles Dickens's *Great Expectations*. Joe, a blacksmith, may have been an illiterate man, but he possessed a literal understanding of human nature and applied it to life with a combination of common sense and pure, unadulterated kindness.

GARLIC Pungent species of onion whose bulb is grated or chopped for cooking.

GARM Garm is the dog in J. R. R. Tolkien's medieval fable *Farmer Giles of Ham,* written in 1937 but not published for twelve years. Four-eyed dog that guarded Helheim, the Icy Underworld and Land of the Dead in Norse mythology. "Garm, a Hostage," by Rudyard Kipling, an endearing short story about a dog named Garm.

GARNET Dark red (Middle English). Red gemstone used in jewelry since Roman times.

GARRYOWEN The Citizen's dog in *Ulysses*, by Irish novelist James Joyce.

GARY Spear (Old English).

GASPARE Treasure bearer (Italian).

GASPODE Very clever talking dog in the *Discworld* novels by Terry Pratchett.

GASTON The Cocker Spaniel was first mentioned by Gaston III of Foix-Béarn in his fourteenth-century work *Livre de Chasse*.

GASTONE From Gascony (Italian).

GATOR Greyhound in *A Greyhound's Tale: Running for Glory, Walking for Home*.

GATSBY Tragic central character in F. Scott Fitzgerald's great American novel *The Great Gatsby*, first published in 1922. *Gatsby* recognized the new, liberal, carefree generation of young men and woman whose lives were defined by the excesses and abundances of the Jazz Age. Fitzgerald could not have known what was to come when he wrote *Gatsby*, but in a very real sense, Gatsby's fate was symbolic of America's as the black storm clouds of the Great Depression hovered over the horizon.

GAULLIE President John F. Kennedy's Poodle.

GAVIN Hawk of May (Welsh).

GAWAIN Sir Gawain, nephew of the legendary King Arthur, knight of the Round Table and head of the Orkney clan.

GAZALI Majestic (African).

GAZELLE Fast-running species of antelope indigenous to the grasslands of Africa.

GAZPACHO Cold summertime soup made with fresh tomatoes.

GEEZER Slang for an eccentric old man.

GEHRIG Henry Louis "Lou" Gehrig (1903–1941), "The Iron Horse," American Major League Baseball first baseman who played out his entire seventeen-year baseball career for the New York Yankees (1923–1939), setting several Major League records, including the most career grand slams (twenty-three). The saddest day in American baseball was when Gehrig said good-bye to his fans in 1939, at the age of thirty-six, stricken with amyotrophic lateral sclerosis, today known as Lou Gehrig's disease. That same year he was inducted into the Baseball Hall of Fame—and remains the greatest first baseman to ever play ball.

GEISHA Female performing Japanese entertainers since the seventh century, magnificently robed, who wear white pancake makeup, red lipstick, and black kohl-outlined eyes.

GELERT Tragic Welsh legend of a faithful hound that is just too woeful to relate.

GELVIRA Truthful, true soul (Old English).

GEM A dog of indiscriminate genes belonging to President Teddy Roosevelt. Diamonds, rubies, emeralds, and sapphires. *See* Gemma.

GEMINI Constellation in the night sky represented by the twins, **Castor** and **Pollux**, of Greek mythology.

GEMMA Gem, precious stone (Medieval Italian).

GEN Spring (Japanese).

GENERAL Military officer of high rank.

GENESEE Genesee Valley hunting hounds, famous pack of English Foxhounds.

GENGHIS Genghis Khan, thirteenth-century emperor of the Mongol Empire who succeeded in uniting the nomadic tribes of northeast Asia through wholesale slaughter and massacre.

GENIE Supernatural creature in Arab folklore capable of granting wishes, most notably the one that was trapped in a lamp that Aladdin found, hilariously voiced by Robin Williams in the 1992 Walt Disney animated feature film *Aladdin*.

GENIUS Mastermind, prodigy, person of great intellect.

GENKI Brief era in Japanese history from 1570–1573 ruled by emperor Ōgimachi-tennō.

GEORGE Farmer, earth-worker (Greek). Dog in Howard Hawks's 1938 screwball comedy *Bringing Up Baby*, starring Katharine Hepburn and Cary Grant.

GEORGE TIREBITER Stray dog who became the unofficial mascot of the University of Southern California from 1940 to 1950.

GEORGES Georges Miez of Switzerland won eight Olympic medals for gymnastics in games held between 1924 and 1936.

GEORGETA Georgeta Damian of Romania won five Olympic gold medals for rowing in the 2000 and 2004 games.

GEORGIA Georgia O'Keeffe (1887–1986), twentieth-century American abstract painter known for her stylized, sensual interpretation of flowers.

GEORGIANA Georgiana Darcy, devoted sister whose protective brother, Darcy, saves the young innocent from the foul machinations of Wickham in Jane Austen's *Pride and Prejudice*.

GERALD Ruler of the spear (Germanic).

GERALDINE Feminine form of Gerald.

GERANIUM "Folly" in the language of flowers.

GERBERA "Cheerfulness" in the language of flowers.

GERDA Protector (Old Norse).

GERLAND Saint Gerland of Arigento (d. 1100), Bishop of Sicily canonized in 1159. Good name for an Italian Greyhound or other breed of Italian origin.

GERMANO From Germany (Italian).

GERONIMO (1829–1909) Native American leader of the Chiricahua Apache tribe, which fought against Mexico and the United States during the Apache Wars. Great Dane owned by Italian book cover model Fabio.

GERSHWIN George Gershwin (1898–1937), American composer and pianist who wrote some of the greatest music of his day or any day. His lyricist was his brother, Ira. They wrote fifteen Broadway plays and the American opera *Porgy and Bess*. Gershwin's *Rhapsody in Blue* branded his style, his jazz, and his generation.

GERT Gert Fredricksson of Sweden won eight Olympic medals in canoeing in the games held between 1948 and 1960. Gertie, Elliott's sister, played by a young Drew Barrymore, in Steven Spielberg's classic family sci-fi film, *E.T.: The Extra-Terrestrial*.

GERTRUDE Spear of strength (Germanic). Hamlet's mother in the Shakespearean tragedy; **Gertie** is the diminutive.

GERWN Mr. A. T. Williams of Ynis-y-Gerwn, a sportsman, brought attention to the Welsh Springer Spaniel in field trials in 1900 in England. His conformation show champion, Corrin, was the first of his breed to ever be photographed, in 1903.

GESUNDHEIT Bless you (German). Common response to someone who has sneezed.

GETSOM Getsom and Gotsom appear in *The Yellow Knight of Oz*, by Ruth Plumly Thompson, one of the L. Frank Baum–authorized sequels to *The Wonderful Wizard of Oz*. Cute names for a pair of puppies.

GHALIB Winner (African).

GHOST Striking name for a white-coated dog.

GIANNI God is gracious (Italian). Also **Giovanni**.

GIANT GEORGE Great Dane recognized as the world's tallest dog by *The Guinness Book of World Records*, standing forty-three inches.

GIDDY Silly, flighty.

GIDEON To make or shape an object with an axe (Hebrew).

GIDGET The Taco Bell Chihuahua and Bruiser's mother in the 2001 comedy film *Legally Blonde*, starring Reese Witherspoon.

GIG A horse-drawn, two-wheeled carriage.

GIGGLES Outburst of short, hysterical, happy laughter.

GIGI Diminutive of **Georgina**.

GILBERT Rev. Gilbert White, Rector of Selborne, England, wrote the first description of a Chow Chow in 1780 in his treatise *Natural History and Antiquities of Selbourne*. He imported two from Canton.

GILDA Sacrifice (Italian).

GILES Major Giles Lacy, simple but goodhearted brother-in-law of Maxim de Winter in Daphne du Maurier's psychological thriller, *Rebecca*.

GILLIE Lad, servant (Scottish Gaelic). Man or boy who assists a sportsman in field or stream.

GILLIGAN *Gilligan's Island*, popular TV sitcom about seven disparate castaways stranded on a desert island.

GILLIKINS Northern part of the kingdom of Oz in *The Wonderful Wizard of Oz*, by American author L. Frank Baum. Cute name for a little dog.

GILLIS Gillis Grafstöm of Sweden won the gold medal for men's figure skating in the 1920, 1924, and 1928 Olympics and the silver in the 1932 Lake Placid games. He is the only three-time gold medalist in the sport.

GIMBLE To make holes (English). If your puppy starts to dig holes in your backyard, his name should be Gimble.

GIMLI Dwarf warrior who accompanies Frodo through his perils and adventures in J. R. R. Tolkien's *The Lord of the Rings*.

GIN Silver (Japanese).

GINGER Dog in E. L. Konigsburg's Newbery Award–winning children's novel *The View from Saturday*.

GINGER PYE Newbery Medal for excellence in American children's literature by Eleanor Estes about a Beagle named Ginger Pye. Its sequel is **Pinky Pye**.

GINGERSNAP Thin twice-baked ginger-flavored biscuits.

GINGHAM Medium-weight checkerboard woven cotton cloth.

GINNUNGAGAP "Yawning abyss," the vast, primordial void before the creation of the universe in Norse mythology.

GINO Little farmer (Italian).

GINSENG Chinese herb used as a cure for a variety of ills and conditions.

GIOCONDA Happy (Italian). Also **Giola**.

GIOFFREDA God's peace (Italian).

GIORGIO Farmer (Italian).

GIOVANNA God is gracious (Italian).

GIPPER George "the Gipper" Gipp, American college football player for Notre Dame. He died at the age of twenty-five from a strep infection. "Win just one for the Gipper," became Ronald Reagan's political slogan in 1988. He had a right to use it—Reagan played Gipp in the 1940 movie, *Knute Rockne, All American*. But here's how it really went: Gipp was on his deathbed; Rockne, his coach, went to see him in the hospital. Notre Dame, the underdog, was up against the undefeated US Army team. Here's what Gipp said: "I've got to go, Rock. It's all right. I'm not afraid. Sometime, Rock, when the team is up against it, when things are wrong and the breaks are beating the boys, ask them to go in there with all they've got and win just one for the Gipper. I don't know where I'll be then, Rock. But I'll know about it, and I'll be happy." Notre Dame won.

GIRALDA *See* Dog Names by Category: Breed; Westminster.

GIRL Lass, female child.

GIRMA Majesty (African).

GISELLA To pledge (Italian).

GIULIANA Descended from Jupiter (Italian).

GIUSEPPE He will add (Hebrew). Italian form of **Joseph**.

GIUSTINA Fair, just (Italian).

GIZMO Gadget, invention. Unbelievably, among the top thirty male dog names.

GLADIATOR Swordsman (Latin). In Roman times, an armed soldier or combatant at the Coliseum.

GLADIOLUS "Generosity" in the language of flowers.

GLADSTONE William Gladstone (1809–1898), liberal statesman and prime minister during the reign of Queen Victoria.

GLEE *See* Dog Names by Category: Breed; Westminster.

GLEN President Herbert Hoover's Collie.

GLENCOE Village in the glen (Scottish).

GLENLYON Famous early Scottish Terrier foundation dog registered in America, along with **Whinstone**, both belonging to John Naylor.

GLENMERE *See* Goelet.

GLINDA Glinda, the Good Witch of the North, was played by stage and screen actress Billie Burke, who also played Clara Topper in both *Topper* comedy films and starred in George Cukor's *Dinner at Eight*. She was married to Broadway producer Florenz Ziegfeld.

GLOXINIA "Love at first sight" in the language of flowers.

GLYNN Mr. Glynn set the standards of the Cairn Terrier breed and referred to them as having "Cairnishness."

GNAISH The wild dog in *Thunder Oak*, a 1997 heroic fantasy by British novelist Garry Kilworth.

GNASHER Blend of characters and virtues (Old English). Gnasher, the dog that stars in the 1938 British comic strip *The Beano*, which features Dennis the Menace and his family. Gnasher's son is **Gnipper**.

GNIPPER *See* Gnasher.

GO GO GIRL Dog in *Weetzie Bat*, a young adult novel written by Francesca Lia Block in 1989.

GODDARD Jimmy's robotic dog in the 2002 animated children's series *Jimmy Neutron: Boy Genius*.

GOELET Robert Goelet first imported the West Highland Terriers to America, Kiltie of Glenmere and Rumpus of Glenmere, in 1907.

GOETHE Johann Wolfgang von Goethe (1749–1832) is considered the greatest figure in modern German literature. *See* Faust.

GOLDENROD "Take care" in the language of flowers. A good name for a Golden Retriever.

GOLDIE Cute name for a puppy with a gold-colored coat.

GOLIATH Davey's talking dog in the sixties stop-motion animated children's Christian television series *Davey and Goliath*, produced by the Lutheran Church of America.

GOMER Complete (Hebrew).

GONZO Gonzo the Great, a Muppet performance artist of dubious talent who has no clue but keeps trying anyway.

GOOD NEWS *See* Dog Names by Category: Breed; Westminster.

GOOFY Born Dippy Dawg on May 25, 1932, then renamed George Geef, but the world knows him as Mickey Mouse's best friend, Goofy.

GORDON Green hill (Gaelic). Captain Gordon Murray established the points and breed standards of the Scottish Terrier in 1877.

GORO Fifth (Japanese).

GOS Dog (Catalan).

GOTHAM Homestead or water meadow (Old English).

GOTSOME *See* Getsome.

GOTTHARD St. Gotthard Pass, ancient route forged by Romans over the Alps. Rottweilers accompanied the Roman Army on their expeditions through the Pass, protecting their cattle. Obviously, an historical name for a Rottweiler.

GOVERNOR *See* Dog Names by Category: Breed, Westminster.

GOYA Francisco Goya (1746–1828), Spanish Romantic painter who depicted Toy Poodles in his paintings.

GRACE Grace, Her Serene Highness of Monaco (1929–1982), American film star, one of Alfred Hitchcock's blondes and one of the most beautiful women in the world, she turned her back on Hollywood to marry Prince Rainier. Basset Hound belonging to Kit Kittredge, an American Girl doll.

GRACIE Gracie Allen (1895–1964), whose husband, George Burns, was her "straight man" in the famous couple comedy team, Burns and Allen, first teaming together in 1922. Media mogul Oprah Winfrey's beloved Golden Retriever whom she lost due to an accidental death.

GRACO *See* Dog Names by Category: Breed; Crufts.

GRADY Noble (Gaelic).

GRAHAM Homestead (Old English); American inventor, engineer and scientist Alexander Graham Bell (1847–1922), inventor of the telephone. Both his mother and his wife were deaf, inspiring his work in speech and elocution and fueling his revolutionary advances in the development of optical communications. Interestingly, he refused to permit a telephone in his study. He was a founding member of the National Geographic Society.

GRAIUS Grecian (Greek). Good name for a Greyhound, a breed held in high esteem by the ancient Greeks.

GRAM *See* Gamle.

GRANGER Hermione Jean Granger, Muggle-born Gryffindor student and, with Harry and Ron, one of the three protagonists in the Harry Potter series.

GRANT *See* Dog Names by Category: Breed; Crufts.

GRANTHAM The Right Honourable Robert Crawley, Earl of Grantham, patriarch and lord of the manor in the British period drama series *Downton Abbey*. Actually, there was an Earl of Grantham in real life. The title was created in 1698 but became extinct in 1754 when both the earl's sons and his three brothers predeceased him. However, the peerage has been resurrected on television, at least, by the marvelous British actor Hugh Bonneville.

GRANVILLE Large town (Old French).

GRAY DAWN *See* Terhune.

GRAZIA Pleasing, acceptable (Italian).

GRECH Dog (Old English), from which the name of the Greyhound breed was derived.

GREER Greer Garson (1904–1996), Superb English actress who epitomized courage and perseverance during World War Two in films such as *Mrs. Miniver*, for which she won an Academy Award, and *Random Harvest*.

GREGORY Watchful, alert (Greek). Diminutive is **Greg**.

GRETCHEN Little pearl (Germanic). *See* Dog Names by Category: Breed; Westminster.

GRETEL With her brother, Hansel, must not give in to the old witch in the Brothers Grimm fairy tale *Hansel and Gretel*.

GREY BROTHER One of Mother and Father Wolf's cubs in *The Jungle Book*, by Rudyard Kipling.

GREYFRIARS BOBBY The Skye Terrier whose love for his beloved master never wavered. Every evening for fourteen years, no matter the weather, the wee dog slept on his master's grave in Greyfriars Churchyard, Edinburgh, Scotland, quietly whimpering. A statue memorializing the devoted dog stands near the graveyard today. Walt Disney produced the memorable family film *Greyfriars Bobby*, in 1961.

GRIFLET Sir Griflet, knight of King Arthur's legendary Round Table and one of Arthur's closest advisors. Arthur instructed Griflet to return his sword, Excalibur, to the Lady of the Lake upon his death.

GRIFTER Con artist. Personified by Paul Newman and Robert Redford as grifters Henry Gondorff and Johnny Hooker in the 1973 film *The Sting*.

GRIM President Rutherford B. Hayes's Greyhound.

GRINCHY *See* Stump. The *Grinch*.

GRIP With Fang and Wolf, the fierce dogs that stood watch over Farmer Maggot's mushroom patch in *The Lord of the Rings*.

GRITS Grits Gresham (1922–2008), internationally renowned American sportsman, author, photographer, and television radio personality and a real gentleman. Grits cohosted ABC's *American Sportman* TV series from 1966 to 1979 with Curt Gowdy.

GRIZZLE Elizabeth Dalloway's dog in *Mrs. Dalloway,* a novel by Virginia Woolf.

GROENENDAEL There are six varieties of Belgian Sheepdog. The Groenendael is the one with the long black coat.

BELGIAN SHEEPDOG PUPPY

GROMIT The intelligent foil to his absentminded inventor-master in the British animated films *Wallace and Gromit*.

GROUCHO Groucho Marx, born Julius Henry Marx (1890–1977), American comedian and film star who, as the quick-witted, mustachioed, twitching eyebrowed, cigar-chomping member of the Marx Brothers, made thirteen feature films with his siblings and afterwards embarked upon a successful television career with his quiz show *You Bet Your Life*.

GROVER Blue monster that's "self-confident, furry, and cute" on *Sesame Street*.

GRYFFINDOR One of the four student houses at Hogwarts School of Witchcraft and Wizardry in the Harry Potter series. Gryffindor's values are "courage, bravery, loyalty, nerve, and chivalry."

GUARDIAN Guardian of the Gates stands guard in the gatehouse in the wall of the Emerald City in *The Wonderful Wizard of Oz* by L. Frank Baum. Good name for a German Shepherd Dog or Saint Bernard.

GUERINO Shelter, cover (Italian).

GUERNSEY Bailiwick of Guernsey (Celtic), British crown dependency off the coast of Normandy, France. The island is rich in military history from medieval times. The Nazis occupied Guernsey in World War Two.

GUIDE To lead, escort.

GUIDITTA Praised (Italian).

GUIDO Wide (Italian). How about this for a name for a dog with wide shoulders, like a Bulldog?

GUINEVERE King Arthur's beautiful but unfaithful queen who gave it all up when she fell in love with Lancelot.

GUINNESS Celebrated Irish brewery founded in 1759 by Arthur Guinness, who shrewdly signed a 9,000-year lease for an abandoned brewery, Saint James Gate Brewery, in Dublin. Guinness is served in hospitals due to its high nutritional value.

GUISACHAN Scottish estate of Lord Tweedmouth. *See* Dudley.

GULLIVER *Gulliver's Travels into Several Remote Nations of the World, in Four Parts. By Lemuel Gulliver, First a Surgeon, and then a Captain of Several Ships,* more simply known as *Gulliver's Travels,* written by English clergyman Jonathan Swift in 1726.

GUMBALL Round, candy-coated chewing gum usually sold in vending machines.

GUNDE Gunde Svan of Sweden took home six medals in cross-country in the 1984 and 1988 Olympic Games. He is also an auto racing driver.

GUNGA DIN Rudyard Kipling's 1892 narrative poem, related by a British soldier, about a native water-carrier in India during the British Raj, Great Britain's rule of India. Gunga Din, desperate to become a British soldier himself, forewarns a British regiment of soldiers of an imminent attack; his courage costs him his life. The last bars of the poem are immortal: "Tho' I've belted you and slayed you, By the livin' Gawd that made you, You're a better man than I am, Gunga Din!" The classic 1939 film adaptation starred Cary Grant, Victor McLaglen, Douglas Fairbanks Jr., Joan Fontaine, and in the title role, Sam Jaffe. Hollywood, don't bother trying to remake this movie ever again. Even though it's in black and white, it could never be surpassed. *See* Bhisti.

GUNMETAL Good, solid name for a German Wirehaired Pointer, which is the color of gunmetal and a sporting breed too.

GUNNAR *See* Olaf.

GUNNER Black-and-white Kelpie whose hearing was so acute that he could detect Japanese bombing raids over Darwin Air Force Base during World War Two before the planes even appeared on radar.

GÜNTHER Warrior (Germanic).

GURU One who has great wisdom and knowledge (Sanskrit).

GUS Force, strength, energy (from the Scottish word *Aonghus*). Virgil I. "Gus" Grissom died during a launch rehearsal onboard Apollo 1 when a cabin fire broke out, killing him and his crew members, Edward White and Roger B. Chaffee, on January 27, 1967.

GUSTO With enthusiasm, a zest for life.

GUSTY Affectionate name for Gustavus Adolphus in Jerome K. Jerome's *Idle Thoughts from an Idle Fellow*, a collection of humorous essays published in 1886.

GUY Sir Walter Scott (1771–1832), Scottish novelist and admirer of the Dandie Dinmont Terrier and celebrated the breed in *Guy Manner-*

ing or the Astrologer, published anonymously in 1815. Of the breed, Sir Walter wrote: "I had them a' regularly entered, first wi' rottens, then wi' stots or weasles, and then wi' the tods and brocks, and now they fear naething that ever cam' wi' a hairy skin on't."

GWEN Blessed (Welsh).

GWYNNE White (Welsh).

GYASI Wonderful (African).

GYÖZÖ Gyözö Kulsár of Hungary won six Olympic medals in fencing in games from 1964 to 1976.

GYP Burnett's Gyp, called Kate, owned by Mr. Edward Burnett of Southboro, Massachusetts, was bred to Hooper's Judge to establish the modern breed standard of the Boston Terrier.

GYPSY Dog in *The Tale of Little Pig Robinson*, by Beatrix Potter.

GYRE Circular or spiral movement, to whirl, a circular ocean current. Good name for an Irish Water Spaniel.

HAAMID Grateful (African).

HABEN Pride (African).

HABIB Beloved (African).

HACHI Good fortune (Japanese). *Hachi: A Dog's Tale (Hachiko Monogatari*, a 2009 film starring Richard Gere based upon the true story of an Akita named Hachikō, who waited every day at the train station for his master to return home from work. One day on the way to work, his master died of a heart attack. For nine years, until the dog himself died, Hachikō waited at the station. Hachikō has come to symbolize loyalty in Japan.

HADES God of the Underworld in Greek mythology represented by a three-headed dog.

HADLEY Apollo 15 took off July 26, 1971, the first "J Series" mission to make a three-day stay on the moon to undertake extensive geological exploration. David Scott, Alfred Worden, and James Irwin were the first to use the Lunar Rover, driving over seventeen miles of the pock-marked lunar surface. Apollo 15 landed at Hadley-Apennine, a lava plain bordered by mountains.

HADRIAN Roman Emperor from AD 117 to 138, third of the "Five Good Emperors," who built the famous wall across Great Britain that bears his name. His reign lasted more than two decades.

HAGOS Joy (African).

HAIKU Japanese poem.

HALCYON "Hey, ho—halcyon days," a phrase that refers to the tranquil, untroubled, uncluttered days of the past.

HALE *See* Jonathan.

HALEY *See* Hickory.

HALIA Fond memory (Hawaiian).

HALO An optical phenomena caused by ice crystals known as "diamond dust."

HAM Ham and Ex were Merrie Melodies's singing St. Bernard puppies in the 1935 animated short "I Haven't Got a Hat."

HAMAN Yasha the Magician's dog in Isaac Bashevis Singer's novel *The Magician of Lublin*.

HAMILL Dorothy Hamill of the United States, 1976 women's figure skating Olympic gold medal champion was "America's sweetheart" with her bobbed haircut and sunny disposition. She invented the skating move known as the "Hamill camel," a camel spin that goes into a sit spin.

HAMILTON Clan Hamilton, or the House of Hamilton, were large landholders in southern Scotland descended from Walter Fitzgilbert of Cadzow.

HAMISH Scottish version of **James**.

HAMISI Born on Thursday (African).

HAMLET *The Tragical History of Hamlet, Prince of Denmark,* written by William Shakespeare around 1600, is a Freudian recipe for misery: one part each of moral corruption, incest, problems with mom, treachery, and a dash of revenge.

HAMPTON Home or high settlemen (Old English).

HAN The Chow Chow is a hunting breed that dates back to the Han Dynasty, about 150 BC in China.

HANA Bud, blossom (Japanese).

HANAI Lucky (Hawaiian).

HANCOCK John Hancock (1737–1793), patriot of the American Revolutionary War, Boston merchant, and president of the Second Continental Congress, whose flourishing signature on the United States Declaration of Independence so King George could see it produced the phrase "Put your John Hancock on that," meaning sign your name boldly.

HANDEL George Frideric Handel (1685–1759), German British Baroque composer born the same year as Johann Sebastian Bach. Mozart said, "Handel understands 'affect' better than any of us. When he chooses, he strikes like a thunderbolt." Beethoven said, "He was the master of us all . . . the greatest composer that ever lived. I would uncover my head and kneel before his tomb." Handel's most popular work was the *Messiah*, which he feverishly wrote in twenty-four inspired days. The tradition of standing for the Hallelujah Chorus came about when King George II was so moved when it was first performed in London that he rose to his feet.

HANDSOME Good-looking, attractive. Handsome Dan, Bulldog, mascot of Yale University.

HANK The dog in the *Hank the Cowdog* series, by John R. Erickson.

HANNAH Favor, grace (Hebrew).

HANNES Hannes Kolehamainen of Finland won five Olympic medals for athletics in game held from 1912 to 1920.

HANS Writer Hans Bols refers to the English Setter for the first time in *Partridge Shooting and Partridge Hawking*, published in 1582.

HANSA The kind of name that would suit a German Pinscher puppy.

HANSEL Gretel's brother in the Brothers Grimm's 1812 fairy tale, "Hansel and Gretel," which translates to "Little John and Little Margaret," are lured deep into the forest to the gingerbread house of a hungry, anthropophagus witch.

HAPPY West Highland Terrier that played Happy on the Emmy-award winning television show *7th Heaven*. White German Shepherd Dog owned by the late exercise and fitness guru Jack La Lanne.

HARDY The Otterhound has been described as having the coat of an Irish Water Spaniel and is as hardy as a Bulldog.

HARLEQUIN If you have a dog that has black patches on an otherwise white coat or two distinctly different colors, then that's a Harlequin coat and a good name for your dog.

HARLEY Harley-Davidson, American motorcycle company founded at the beginning of the twentieth century in Wisconsin, considered the Cadillac of motorcycles.

HARLOW *See* Lionel.

HARMONICA Also called a blues harp or mouth organ, a harmonica is a hand-sized reed instrument played with the mouth and, in the hands of Little Walter and George "Harmonica" Smith, breathes music from the very depth of the soul.

HARMONY In agreement, of one mind.

HAROLD Leader of the army (Old English).

HARPER A Scottish surname associated with the Buchanan clan. Harper Lee (b. 1926), 1960 Pulitzer Prize–winning author of *To Kill a Mockingbird*, one of the most beloved American novels of all time. Lee was awarded the Presidential Medal of Freedom in 2007; *Mockingbird* is the only book she ever wrote.

HARPO Arthur Adolph "Harpo" Marx (1888–1964), the speechless Marx Brother who communicated by whistling or honking a horn, was the second of six sons of "Frenchie" and Minnie Marx, European Jewish immigrants. Harpo made thirteen films with his brothers. A self-taught harpist, he touched millions with the musical interludes he played in most of those films. Harpo married for keeps, unlike the rest of his brothers, to actress Susan Fleming in 1936. The couple had four adopted children. In 1948, comedian George Burns asked Harpo how many children he planned to adopt. He replied, "I'd like to adopt as many children as I have windows in my house. So when I leave for work, I want a kid in every window, waving good-bye."

HARRIET Harriet Beecher Stowe (1811–1896), abolitionist and author of twenty books. The most famous was *Uncle Tom's Cabin*, written in 1852. She was born the seventh of thirteen children to a passionate preacher in Litchfield, Connecticut. Her passion for the abolition of slavery was fueled by her husband, Calvin Ellis Stowe, a biblical scholar and educator who became her literary agent. The couple was part of the Underground Railroad, giving shelter and food to slaves as they made their way to freedom.

HARRIS Home ruler (Old English).

HARRISON Son of Harry (Old English).

HARROD American actress Rue McClanahan's Scottish Terrier.

HARRY Prince Harry of England (b. 1984), popular second son of Charles, Prince of Wales and the late Lady Diana Spencer. Diminutive of **Harold**.

HARRY POTTER The world's most famous wizard and "the boy who lived," born from the imagination of British author J. K. Rowling.

HARTENSTEIN Herr Max Hartenstein of the Plavia Kennels was an early breeder of the Standard Schnauzer.

HARU One born in the spring (Japanese).

HARUKI Shining brightly (Japanese).

HARUKO Firstborn (Japanese).

HARVEY Hound that is the mascot of the Calgary Flames National Hockey League team. Elliott's Golden Retriever in Steven Speilberg's 1982 family sci-fi movie *E.T.*

HASANI Handsome (Swahili).

HASTINGS The Sussex Spaniel was first bred in 1795 in Hastings, East Sussex, England, at Rosehill Park.

HATHI Indian elephant in *The Jungle Book*, by Rudyard Kipling.

HAUKALIMA Ice cream (Hawaiian).

HAVANA Capital of Cuba. Cigars are sometimes called Havanas, but correctly, it is the Cuban state tobacco company, Habanos, SA, that controls the export of Cuban cigars.

HAVERFORDWEST The town in Wales where the Sealyham estate, owned by Captain John Edwards in the nineteenth century, originated the Sealyham Terrier breed.

HAWICK Near Hindlee, Scotland, where James Davidson established the Dandie Dinmont Terrier breed.

HAWK The hawk is a large species of bird that includes goshawks, sparrow hawks, buzzards, and eagles.

HAWKER Colonel Hawker, a noted British sportsman, first hunted with the precursor of the Labrador Retriever, which he described as "very large, strong of limb, rough hair, and carries tail high," and "by far the best for any kind of shooting." The Labrador Retriever has remained the most popular dog in America for two decades, according to the American Kennel Club.

HAWKEYE Captain Benjamin Franklin "Hawkeye" Pierce, fictitious army surgeon and principal protagonist of *M*A*S*H: A Novel About Three Army Doctors*, by Richard Hooker, about his experiences as a doctor attached to a US Mobile Army Surgical Hospital in Korea during the Korean War. When director Robert Altman made *M*A*S*H* into a major motion picture in 1970, Donald Sutherland portrayed Hawkeye; then *M*A*S*H* came to television (1972–1983) and Alan Alda flat-out owned "Hawkeye" Pierce.

HAYDEN Hay valley (Old English).

HAYLEY Hay clearing (Old English).

HAZEL Witch hazel is a flowering shrub. It is also a color, brown tinged with green and gold, the color of autumn. Fine name for a brown English Cocker Spaniel.

HAZELNUT *See* Dog Names by Category: Breed; Crufts.

HAZZARD *See* Fermanagh.

HEATHCLIFF Tortured, brooding, Byronic main character in *Wuthering Heights*, by Emily Brontë.

HEATHER Coarse, dense wild ground shrubs that spring white or lavender flowerets that carpet the moors of Scotland. *See* Dog Names by Category: Breed; Crufts.

HEAVEN The place we all hope will be our Final Destination.

HÉBÉ Pomeranians Hébé and Boby, painted in 1915 by the artist F. Sinet, reflect the substantial changes made to the breed during the reign of Queen Victoria of England. Today a Pomeranian weighs between three to seven pounds; however, before the breed was introduced to Victoria, Pomeranians weighed up to thirty pounds. The Queen, a very small woman, preferred small dogs and thereby helped influence the modern standards. The F. Sinet painting is in the American Kennel Club collection.

HEBEL Breath, to breathe (Hebrew).

HECTOR The scowling Bulldog in the Looney Tunes and Merrie Melodies animated cartoons from 1945. President Grover Cleveland's black French Poodle.

HECUBA Wife of King Priam of Troy in Greek mythology who bore him nineteen children. She was caught scowling by the gods and as punishment, turned her into a barking dog. Can you blame her for scowling after having that many kids?

HEIDI Noble and kind (Germanic). Dachshund in the United States that lived to be almost twenty-one years old. President Dwight D. Eisenhower's Weimaraner.

HEIMDALL Guardian of the bridge in Norse mythology.

HEISS Carol Heiss (b. 1940), American skater who earned a silver medal for women's figure skating at the 1956 Winter Olympics. She refused to turn professional until she won a gold medal in memory of her mother, who died of cancer. She fulfilled her dream: between 1956 and 1960 Heiss virtually owned the sport, winning five world championships, four US titles—and won the 1960 Olympic gold medal in her mom's memory. Heiss was the first female skater to perform the double axel in competition.

HELEN Helen of Troy, daughter of Zeus in Greek mythology, whose abduction by Paris brought on the Trojan War.

HELGA Holy, blessed (Old Norse).

HELIOS God of the sun and brother of Eos, goddess of the dawn in Greek mythology.

HELIOTROPE "Devotion" in the language of flowers.

HÉLOÏSE Hale, healthy. *See* Abélard.

HELVETIA Roman name for Switzerland, place of origin of the Saint Bernard Dog.

HEMINGWAY Ernest "Papa" Hemingway (1899–1961), whose adventurous life and understated writing style produced works such as *For Whom the Bell Tolls* and *The Old Man and the Sea*. The son of a physician father and a musician mother, he became a Red Cross ambulance driver in World War One and a war correspondent during the Spanish Civil War and World War Two. A world-class sportsman, he embraced fishing, hunting, women, and Scotch. He lived large. But his demons caught up with him; it was the business end of a W&C Scott Monte Carlo B twelve-gauge pigeon gun that turned out the literary luminary's light.

HENRI Equestrian Henri Saint Cyr of Sweden won four gold medals in the 1952 and 1956 Olympics.

HENRIETTE Queen Marie Henriette, wife of Leopold II of Belgium, was a devoted owner of Schipperkes.

HENRY Home ruler (Germanic). Henry I of England who, in 1077, encouraged Flemish weavers to immigrate to southwest Wales; Sir Henry Pottinger hunted foxes with Norwegian Elkhounds.

HEPBURN Katharine Hepburn (1907–2003), Connecticut-born, four-time Academy Award–winning actress once reviewed by humorist Dorothy Parker as having given "a striking performance that ran the gamut of emotions from A to B." Not quite. Hepburn's body of work ranged from comedies such as *Bringing Up Baby* to drama, and her greatest film, *The African Queen* with Bogart. One day, while wearing very high heels, she was introduced to actor Spencer Tracy by director Joseph Mankiewicz. "I'm afraid I'm too tall for you, Mr. Tracy," Hepburn quipped, whereupon Mankiewicz warned her, "Don't worry, he'll soon cut you down to size." He did. Though Tracy never divorced his Catholic wife, he and Hepburn became one of Hollywood's iconic couples, on-screen and off, making nine movies together.

HEPHAESTUS Greek god of blacksmiths and all metalworkers, the lord of the forge, God of technology whose skills were so fine that he made Achilles his armor—but missed a spot at the heel.

HERA Goddess of childbirth and marriage, and wife of Zeus in Greek mythology.

HERBERT Bright army (Old English).

HERBY Medical doctor in *The Giant Horse of Oz*, another sequel to *The Wonderful Wizard of Oz*.

HERCULE Hercule Poirot, Agatha Christie's Belgian detective who solved mysteries with his "little grey cells" in thirty-three novels and fifty-one short stories published between 1920 and 1975.

HERCULES aka "The Beast," a baseball-eating, 300-pound English Mastiff belonging to Mr. Mertle, voiced by the inimitable James Earl Jones, in the 1993 family movie *The Sandlot*.

HERMA Herma Szabo of Austria won the 1924 Olympic gold medal in women's figure skating and five consecutive World championships from 1922 to 1926, the most medaled Austrian figure skater in history.

HERMAN Army man (Germanic).

HERMES God of mischief, messenger of the Greek Gods, who gets a kick out of playing tricks on mere mortals.

HERMIT Recluse, a loner.

HERO Champion, victor.

HERODOTUS Greek writer who mentions Mastiffs as early as 550 BC and speaks of an episode in which a Mastiff attacked an elephant—incredibly, the elephant was so frightened, it lay down on the ground as an admission of defeat

HERSHEY Delicious name for a chocolate Labrador Retriever.

HESTIA Sister of Zeus, goddess of home and hearth.

HEXEN Witchcraft (Pennsylvania German).

HIBISCUS "Consumed by love" in the language of flowers. A white flower used in traditional Indian medicine. Very pretty name for a dog with a white coat.

HICKORY The Kansas farmhand who became the Tin Man in *The Wizard of Oz*. Played by stage, radio, and film star Jack Haley, he made two memorable movies with Shirley Temple and worked until a week before his death at the age of eighty-one in 1979. He was married for fifty-eight years to Florence McFadden, a beautician who owned a successful Hollywood beauty parlor frequented by many movie stars—and affectionately called "Flo Haley's House of Correction."

HIDALGO Spanish title of people of nobility. Riveting 2004 fact-based film starring Vigo Mortensen as American Frank Hopkins, who rides his mustang, Hidalgo, to victory in the "Ocean of Fire," a 3,000-mile race across the Najd Desert that up until then, had only been run by Arabian horses.

HIDE Excellent (Japanese).

HIGGINS Mixed-breed dog that played Benji and also starred in the CBS television series *Petticoat Junction* from 1963 to 1970.

HIKARI Light (Japanese).

HILARY Happy, cheerful (Greek). Hilary of Poitiers (AD 300–368), Bishop of Poitiers, father of Abra and Universae Ecclesiae doctor of the Catholic Church. The son of pagans, he sought to better himself, got a good education and wrote theological doctrines that remain integral to the Church to this day. Moral: get an education—any way you can, any age you are.

HILDA Battle (German). Hilda and King whelped Turk. *See* Turk.

HILDEBRAND Battle sword (Germanic).

HILL *See* Laverack.

HILLBILLY *See* Rimshot.

HINDLEE Scottish town where a farmer named James Davidson raised "the immortal six" terriers that were foundation line of the Dandie Dinmont Terrier.

HINKS James Hinks, an early breeder of the Bull Terrier.

HIROKO Magnanimous (Japanese).

HIROSHI Generous (Japanese).

HISANO Open plain (Japanese).

HIT AND MISS *See* Breed; Crufts.

HITARI *See* Dog Names by Category: Breed; Crufts.

HOBBES *See* Calvin.

HOBBIT Small, brave, simple folk with rather large, hairy feet that J. R. R. Tolkien gave birth to in the Shire in *The Lord of the Rings*. **Frodo Baggins**, **Samwise Gamgee**, **Peregrin Took**, and **Meriadoc Brandybuck** were the Hobbit friends that set out to dispose of the Ring.

HOBO Black Labrador Retriever with the Second Battalion the Royal Gurkha Rifles, British Army, a bomb-sniffing dog that was hit three times with shrapnel when his unit came under fire in Nahr-e Saraj, Afghanistan, in July 2011. He recovered completely from his wounds and returned to active duty.

HOD The blind god in Norse mythology.

HOGWARTS Hogwarts School of Witchcraft and Wizardry where Harry Potter studies and where much of the action of the J. K. Rowling books takes place.

HOKU Star (Hawaiian).

HOLDEN A Labrador Retriever beloved by actress Gwyneth Paltrow.

HOLLAND Holland & Holland, founded in 1835, field sport supplier holding several British Royal warrants. A good name for a sporting dog; the Keeshonden is the national dog of Holland.

HOLLY "Domestic happiness" in the language of flowers. One of Queen Elizabeth II of England's beloved Corgis.

HOLLYHOCK "Abundance" in the language of flowers.

HOLMES Who is the greatest detective the world has ever known? Elementary, my dear Watson. It is, of course, Sherlock Holmes.

HOMER Ancient Greek epic poet who wrote the *Iliad* and the *Odyssey*. Scholars are unsure when he lived—some say 850 BC, while others say closer to the time of the Trojan War, in the early twelfth century BC. No matter. People are still reading Homer today.

HOND Dog (Dutch).

HONDO *See* Sam.

HONEY TREE EVIL EYE Bull Terrier canine actor famous as Spuds MacKenzie in the Budweiser beer commercials. By the way—I hate to break this to you—Spuds is a bitch (female dog).

HONEY Term of endearment.

HONEYFLOWER "Sweet disposition" in the language of flowers.

HONEYSUCKLE "Bond of love" in the language of flowers.

HONEYWOOD *See* Parson.

HONG KONG PHOOEY Alter ego of mild-mannered Penrod Pooch, canine superhero adept in the Chinese martial arts that saved the world in 1974 Hanna-Barbera animated shorts.

HOOCH Dogue de Bordeaux sidekick of Tom Hanks in the 1989 action comedy *Turner & Hooch*. At least the dog was unforgettable. Hooch is played by Beasley, who died in 1992 at the age of fourteen.

HOOPER Hooper's Judge, owned by Mr. Robert C. O'Brien around 1885, is considered the true modern Boston Terrier and foundation dog of the breed standard. He was actually a cross between an English Bulldog and a white English Terrier.

HOPE Hope is the one thing you can hold on to when the future is bleak.

HORACE Hour, time, season (Latin). Horace E. F. Slughorn, Potions Professor at Hogwarts School of Witchcraft and Wizardry.

HORAND Horand von Grafrath, first registered German Shepherd Dog and the foundation sire of the breed.

HORNET Another of the hounds that "were singing" in Frederick Watson's book *In the Pink* (1932).

HORRIE Horrie the Wog Dog was the unofficial mascot of the 2/1st Machine Gun Battalion. His ability to detect incoming enemy aircraft at long range bought time for the battalion's defense, and spared lives.

HORSFORD *See* Avendale.

HORTON *See* Seuss.

HOSHIKO Star (Japanese).

HOTDOG Jughead's dog in the *Archie* comics, first published in 1939.

HOTEL FOR DOGS Dogs in the 2009 children's film *Hotel for Dogs* include **Friday**, a Jack Russell Terrier; **Georgia**, a Boston Terrier; **Lenny**, an English Mastiff; **Cooper**, an English Bulldog; **Georgia**, a Boston Terrier; **Shep**, a Border Collie; **Romeo**, a Chinese Crested; **Henry**, a Beauceron; **Juliet**, a Poodle; **Viola** and **Sebastian**, Dachshunds; **Rocky**, a Bull Mastiff; **Chelsea**, an American Pit Bull Terrier; **Coco**, a Wirehaired Pointing Griffon; **Harley**, a Beagle and two Pugs, **Fric** and **Frac**.

HOUDINI Harry Houdini (born Erik Weisz, 1874–1926) Budapest-born American magician and escape artist and master of the art.

HOUND The Penderwicks dog in *The Penderwicks: A Summer Tale of Four Sisters, Two Rabbits and a Very Interesting Boy*, by Jeanne Birdsall.

HOWARD From the words *high* (há) and *guardian* (varðr) in Old Norse. Scruffy old dog that narrates the *Bunnicula* series of children's books, by James Howe, about a vampire bunny rabbit that sucks the juice out of vegetables.

HOWE *See* Lorna.

HOWLER One of Tonka's Pound Puppies.

HOWLIN' WOLF (1910–1976), American blues singer, guitarist, and harmonica player who stood six feet, six inches and ranked number fifty-one in *Rolling Stone* magazine's "100 Greatest Artists of All Time." Record producer Sam Phillips once remarked, "When I heard Howlin' Wolf, I said, 'This is for me. This is where the soul of man never dies.'" Listen to "Smokestack Lightnin'" and darn if you don't agree. Proper name for a Wolfhound.

HUAN The great wolfhound of Valinor, companion of Beren and Lúthien, in J. R. R. Tolkien's novel *The Silmarillion*.

HUBBLE aka Canid 3942, a Border Terrier voiced by Matthew Broderick in the 2003 Jim Henson–MGM motion picture *Good Boy!* featuring Vanessa Redgrave as the voice of the all-powerful Greater Dane, Delta Burke as the pampered Poodle **Barbara Ann**, Carl Reiner as **Shep**, a Bernese Mountain Dog, Cheech Marin as a Chinese Crested henchman, a Boxer named **Wilson**, and an Italian Greyhound named **Nelly**.

HUBERT Saint Hubert, patron saint of hunters.

HUCK *See* Finn.

HUCKLEBERRY HOUND Hanna-Barbera's Bluetick Southern hound in *The Huckleberry Hound Show*, which first aired in 1958.

HUDDERSFIELD BEN (1865–1871), foundation sire of the Yorkshire Terrier, owned by Mr. and Mrs. M. A. Foster of Yorkshire, England. Celebrated dog painter George Earl (father of dog artist Maud Earl), a noted authority on the breed, wrote in 1891, "Huddersfield Ben was the best stud dog of his breed during his life-time, and one of the most remarkable dogs of any pet breed that ever lived; and most of the show specimens of the present day have one or more crosses of his blood in their pedigree."

HUDSON Angus Hudson, authoritative Scottish butler played to perfection by the late Gordon Jackson in the incomparable 1971 BBC television series aired on PBS, *Upstairs Downstairs*, created by two amazing actresses, Jean Marsh and Dame Eileen Atkins.

HUEJOTZINGO Monastery of Huejotzingo on the highway from Mexico City has carved stones with images of the Techichi-Chihuahua breed that date to the year 1530.

HUFFLEPUFF One of the four student houses at Hogwarts School of Witchcraft and Wizardry in the Harry Potter series. Hufflepuff's values are "hard work, tolerance, loyalty, and fair play." That would be a good name for just about any dog.

HUGH Heart, mind, spirit (Old English). Hugh Laurie (b. 1959), who for eight riveting seasons *was* Gregory House, M.D., chief of diagnostic medicine and mentally and physically tortured curmudgeon at a fictitious hospital in New Jersey in FOX-TV's amazingly popular television series *House*. Laurie, an Englishman who sings "God Save the Queen" to the tune of "Our Country 'Tis of Thee," is a prolific, diverse actor, whether in comedy (as Bertie Wooster opposite his longtime pal, Stephen Fry, in the ITV adaptation of P.G. Wodehouse's *Jeeves*); in period drama (as in *Sense and Sensibility* as the long-suffering husband, Mr. Palmer, in his friend Emma Thompson's award-winning adaptation of the Jane Austen novel); or in PG-rated films, hilariously as Jasper, in the 1995 live action version of *101 Dalmatians*. However, it's his music that's closest to this complex and gifted man's soul. Listen to his breakout album, *Let Them Talk*, or—appropriate to this book—*Police Dog Blues*. Here's another bloke, like Eric Clapton, who can belt out the Blues from somewhere deep and dark in his soul. Stay with the music, Hugh, and Godspeed. This is your time. By the way, Mr. Laurie owns a chocolate Labrador Retriever.

HUGO Victor-Marie Hugo (1802–1885), French poet, playwright, and novelist whose parallel careers as a statesman and human rights activist are reflected in two of his most famous works, *Les Misérables* and *The Hunchback of Notre-Dame*.

HULA Hawaii's native dance form.

HULME John Hulme of Manchester, England, is said to have originated the Manchester Terrier breed by crossing a Whippet with a Terrier.

HUMMEL German manufacturer of collectible bisque figurines.

HUMPHREY Peaceful warrior (English).

HUND Dog (Danish, German, Norwegian, Swedish).

HUNDA Dog island (Old Norse, feminine). Uninhabited island in the Orkneys of Scotland.

HUNDI Dog (Old Norse, masculine).

HUNDOLF Wolf-dog (Old Norse). Great name for a Wolfhound.

HUNDUR Dog (Icelandic).

HUNG KWONG *See* Dog Names by Category: Breed; Crufts.

HUNK One of Auntie Em's farmhands, who becomes the Scarecrow in Oz, played in the 1939 motion picture by that wonderful song-and-dance man Ray Bolger, who later starred with Judy Garland in *The Harvey Girls*. Bolger was the last surviving main cast member of *The Wizard of Oz*.

HUNTER A man who hunts, from the Middle English word *huntere*. A woman who hunts is a **Huntress**. Excellent names for hunting dogs.

HUNTSMAN *See* Dog Names by Category: Breed; Crufts.

HURRICANE Storm, tempest.

HUSH PUPPY Along with Lamb Chop and Charlie Horse, endearing puppets on the sixties children's television program *The Shari Lewis Show*.

HUTCHINSON General William Hutchinson, author of *Dog Breaking*, published in London in 1885.

HUZZAR Janus was bred to Mouche, the Wirehaired Pointing Griffon that established the breed and produced Huzzar, the only puppy in the litter. *See* Mouche.

HYACINTH "Jealousy" in the language of flowers (the yellow hyacinth). The hyacinth is dedicated to the Greek god Apollo.

HYDRANGEA Large, globelike flowers that come in an assortment of colors. Great name for a white Poodle.

I

IAN Ian Fleming (1908–1964), British writer who embellished his personal experiences as a naval intelligence officer to create the world's greatest spy, James Bond, Agent 007. His own life reads like one of his fourteen Bond novels—indeed, even more exciting and perhaps just as romantic. Fleming also wrote a delightful children's story that was adapted into a 1968 feature film starring Dick Van Dyke and Sally Ann Howes called *Chitty Chitty Bang Bang*. It is said to be among the Queen of England's favorites and screened every Christmas for the Royal Family.

IBSEN Henrik Ibsen (1828–1906), nineteenth-century Norwegian playwright and poet heralded as "the father of modern drama," best known for his plays *A Doll's House* and *Hedda Gabler*.

ICARUS His father, master craftsman Daedalus in Greek mythology, constructed wings of wax so Icarus could escape from Crete. Dad Daedalus warned his son not to fly too close to the sun, but boys will be boys and guess what happened.

ICE TEA A name to consider for a Pomeranian puppy or any dog with a coat the color of a glass of ice tea.

ICEMAN *The Iceman Cometh*, 1939 play by Eugene O'Neill. Good name for a Siberian Husky.

IDI Born during the Id-ul-Fitr festival (African).

IDRISSA Immortal (African).

IDUN Keeper of the apples of youth in Norse mythology.

IGNATIUS Fire (Latin).

IGNAZIO Innocent (Italian).

IGOR Assistant to Dr. Frankenstein, none better than English comedian-writer Marty Feldman (1934–1982), who played Igor (*eye*-gor) so side-splitting hilariously in Mel Brooks's 1974 film parody of the Mary Shelley story, *Young Frankenstein*. The film also starred Gene Wilder, Teri Garr, Cloris Leachman, and Madeline Kahn.

IKE Nickname for Dwight David "Ike" Eisenhower (1890–1969), five-star general and Supreme Commander of the Allied Forces in Europe in World War Two, supreme commander of NATO, and thirty-fourth president of the United States. Other than Colonel Theodore Roosevelt, Eisenhower was the only commanding officer elected president in the twentieth century.

IKKI Asiatic brush-tailed porcupine in *The Jungle Book*, by Rudyard Kipling.

ILARIA Joyful, happy (Italian).

INARI Shrimp (Japanese). Great name for any of the Toy breeds.

INCA Last sovereign empire among the Andean civilizations of South America to fend off the conquistadores before they disappeared into oblivion by the sixteenth century.

INDIANA Henry Walton "Indiana" Jones Jr., PhD, adventurous archaeological professor who frequently gets himself into really difficult, dangerous situations. Harrison Ford first breathed life into the character created by George Lucas and Steven Spielberg in 1981's *Indiana Jones and the Lost Ark*. It was revealed in *Indiana Jones and the Last Crusade* (1989) that Indiana was actually the name of the Jones family's dog.

INDIGO Deep shade of blue.

INDO One of Will and Jada Pinkett Smith's Rottweilers.

INDRA Ruler over all gods in India.

INES Chaste (Italian).

INEZ *See* Madame de Pompadour.

INGE Bringer of happiness (Nigerian). Inge de Bruijn of the Netherlands won eight Olympic medals for swimming in the 2000 and 2004 games.

INGRID Beautiful (Scandinavian).

INK Good name for a black dog.

INNISFREE *See* Dog Names by Category: Breed; Westminster.

INTREPID Fearless, courageous.

INUIT *See* Kotzebue.

IPO Sweetheart (Hawaiian).

IPOMOEA "I am yours forever" in the language of flowers.

IPPTY, Royal Scribe of Rash, character in the kingdom of Oz in *The Hungry Tiger of Oz*, written by the authorized chronicler of Oz after the death of L. Frank Baum, Ruth Plumly Thompson.

IPYANA Grace (African).

IRINA Peace (Russian). Fine name for a Borzoi or Samoyed; both are Russian breeds.

IRIS "Wisdom and courage" in the language of flowers. The yellow iris is a beautiful flower and would be a lovely name for a female Pomeranian.

IRMA World War Two search and rescue dog. She was awarded the Dickin Medal for finding more than one hundred people buried in the rubble during the London Blitz.

IRON WILL Walt Disney family adventure movie based on the 1917 Winnipeg-to-Saint Paul dogsled race.

IRONSIDE Sir Ironside, the "Red Knight of the Red Lands" of King Arthur's legendary Round Table.

IRVING Irving Berlin (1888–1989), American Jewish composer whose music you've listened to all your life, and so did your parents and your grandparents, who wrote "White Christmas," "There's No Business Like Show Business," "Alexander's Ragtime Band," "This Is the Army, Mr. Jones," and "God Bless America." His music bolstered American spirits through two world wars, the Great Depression, Korea, and Vietnam. He wrote nineteen Broadway shows, eighteen Hollywood musicals, and 1,500 songs. George Gershwin called him "the greatest songwriter that has ever lived," but perhaps Jerome Kern said it best: "Irving Berlin has no place in American music—he *is* American music."

ISABEL Medieval Provençal form of Elizabeth. Isabelle Adjani (b. 1955), French film actress, singer, and the only woman in the history of the Cannes Film Festival to win a Palm d'Or for Best Actress for two movies in one year, 1981.

ISABELLINE This is a very interesting name for a white dog. The word is often associated with a white or light Palomino horse; however, there's a story that goes like this: Isabella, Archduchess of Austria (1566–1633), the daughter of Philip II of Spain (1527–1598) was married to Albert VII, Archduke of Austria (1559–1621), who laid siege to Ostend in 1601. Isabella announced to the court that the victory would be so speedy, that she vowed not to change her underwear until Ostend was taken. Well, things didn't move as quickly as she expected—in fact, the siege lasted a little over three years, finally ending in 1604. Her underwear surely became discolored, but perhaps a bit more than the color Isabelline, a pale off-white, suggests.

ISHMAEL God will hear (Hebrew). Appropriately, the name of the protagonist in Herman Melville's great American classic *Moby Dick; or The Whale* (1851). The first line reads, "Call me Ishmael." Gregory Peck played Ahab and Richard Baseheart played Ishmael in the 1956 film masterpiece directed by John Huston. Orson Welles has a brief, deeply moving appearance as Father Mapple.

ISOBEL Mrs. Isobel Crawley, Matthew Crawley's mother in the addictive British television series *Downton Abbey* and superbly portrayed by English actress Penelope Wilton. Mrs. Crawley is generally right, but when it comes to the hospital and shared family matters, she comes up against her match—Violet, the Countess of Grantham, played by the legendary British actress Maggie Smith.

ISSA God saves (African). A Maltese that belonged to Publius, the Roman governor of Malta at the time of the Apostle Paul. On his way to Rome, Paul was shipwrecked on Malta. He preached to Publius and converted him to Christianity. Issa was always with Publius and was therefore known to Paul. Marcus Valerius Martialis (b. AD 38) commemorated Issa, "Issa is more frolicksome than Catulla's Sparrow. Issa is purer than a dove's kiss. Issa is gentler than a maiden. Issa is more precious than Indian Jems."

ISTARI *See* Wizard.

IT Dog (Azerbaijani).

ITALIA The Italian Greyhound is believed to have been the earliest and only pet dog in Italy for several centuries.

ITALO From Italy (Italian).

ITCHY Itchy Itchiford, Charlie B. Barkin's best friend, the nervous Dachshund in the 1989 animated film *All Dogs Go to Heaven*.

ITSY BITSY Means teensy weensy. Cutesy wootsey name for a whittle twoy dwog.

IVAN God is gracious (Slavic). **Ivana** is the feminine form, **Ivanka** is the affectionate form. **John** is the English version of the name.

IVANHOE Hero in Sir Walter Scott's romantic novel the story of Saxon nobles battling the Normans in AD 1194 at the time of the Crusades and Richard I of England.

IVAR Ivar Ballangrud of Norway won seven Olympic medals in speed skating in games held between 1928 and 1936.

IVORY Good name for a dog with an ivory-colored coat. The tusks of an elephant or a walrus, and the teeth of sperm whale are ivory.

IVY "Friendship" in the language of flowers. The Saluki in the family film *Cats & Dogs* was played by two canine actors, **Fancy** and **Mia**.

IZAAK Sir Izaak Walton wrote with fond admiration about dogs in *The Compleat Angler* (1653).

J

JABARI Fearless (African).

JABARL Valiant (African).

JABBERWOCKY Nonsense verse in Lewis Carroll's *Through the Looking-Glass, and What Alice Found There* (1872), recited by the Jaberwock to Alice: "Twas bryllyg, and ye slythy toves, Did gyre and gymble in ye wabe: All mimsy were ye borogoves; And ye mome raths outgrabe." You tell me.

JABIR Comforter (African).

JABULANI Happy (African).

JACK *Jack Russell: Dog Detective* series by Darrel and Sally Odgers. Only son of English writer Rudyard Kipling. *See* Kipling. Bulldog mascot of Georgetown University. Teddy Roosevelt's son Kermit's dog.

JACKET The coat of Jack Russell Terriers and other short-furred Terriers is called a jacket. Great name for such a dog.

JACKIE Dalmatian mix owned by Finnish businessman Tor Borg. In 1941, shortly before the invasion of the Soviet Union by Germany, it came to the attention of the Nazis that Borg's dog would raise a paw to mimic a Nazi salute whenever the name Hitler was mentioned. A frenzy of communication erupted between the German Foreign Office in Finland and the Nazi Party Chancellery in Munich. Borg and his wife, Josefine, known to have anti-Nazi sentiments, were harshly interrogated. When no proof could be found to support the accusation, the Nazis set out to destroy Borg's business. In *A Dog Named Hitler*, historian Klaus Hillenbrand wrote, "There were two or three dozen people discussing the affair of the dog rather than preparing for the invasion of the Soviet Union."

JACKSIE C. S. Lewis's childhood dog that died in an accident when Lewis was only four years old. The young Lewis began calling himself Jacksie—and as a result, he was known as Jack to friends and family for the rest of his life.

JACKSON An English surname that means "son of Jack," Jack is the affectionate name for John, John is derived from the Latin form of the Greek, which means Yahweh is gracious; Andrew Jackson was the seventh president of the United States.

JACOB May God protect (Hebrew).

JACQUES Jacques du Fouilloux, writer who wrote about dogs in 1561 in *La Venerie*, in which the Scottish Terrier is first mentioned in print.

JADE Stone of the flank (Greek). The Ancient Greeks believed jade could cure kidney stones.

JAEGAR Hunter (Germanic).

JAFRAK *See* Dog Names by Category: Breed; Crufts.

JÄGER Hunter (German). Great name for a hunting dog, especially a German Shorthaired Pointer, which is of German origin.

JAGGERS Tough, brusque lawyer who hides his tender heart, in Charles Dickens's *Great Expectations* (1860).

JAJA Respectable (African).

JAKE Everything's all right (English slang).

JAMAICA Land of woods and water (Spanish). Island nation in the Caribbean.

JAMAL Elegance (African).

JAMAR Handsome (African).

JAMES King James I had a half-dozen Scottish Terriers sent to France as a present, though to whom is unclear; it is assumed that they were a gift to the French king.

JANE One of Queen Elizabeth of England's first Corgis. Beautiful eldest daughter of Mr. and Mrs. Bennet who finally does marry Mr. Bingley in Jane Austen's classic novel of love won and lost and won back, *Pride and Prejudice*.

JANET God is gracious (Hebrew). The Slavic version is **Janica**.

JANICA Janica Kostelić of Croatia won six Olympic medals for Alpine skiing in the 2002 and 2006 games.

JANUARY First month of the year in the Julian and Gregorian calendars. *Captain January*, an 1891 children's novel by Laura E. Richards and adapted into the delightful 1936 Shirley Temple movie of the same name, with Guy Kibbee, one of Hollywood's most popular character actors (*Mr. Smith Goes to Washington, 3 Godfathers*).

JANUS Roman god of beginnings and transitions. Woolly-haired Wire-haired Pointing Griffon whelped from Mouche. *See* Mouche.

JAPONICA "Sincerity" in the language of flowers.

JASMINE "I attach myself to you" in the language of flowers. Aromatic white or yellow flower. Sweet name for a Pembroke Welsh Corgi, which has a white chest and yellow saddle.

JASON Leader of the Argonauts who set out on a quest for the Golden Fleece in Greek Mythology.

COCKER SPANIEL PUPPY

JASPER Max de Winter's black Cocker Spaniel at Manderley in Daphne du Maurier's *Rebecca*. Actor John Forsythe's dog in the popular television series *Bachelor Father*, which ran from 1957 to 1962.

JAVA Island in Indonesia.

JAWARA Peace loving (African).

JAZZ Popular rhythmic, big-beat music born in the American South in the early 1900s and identified with Billie Holiday, Louis Armstrong, Ella Fitzgerald, Tommy Dorsey, Bing Crosby, Frank Sinatra, and other legends who defined the genre.

JE T'AIME I love you (French).

JEAN "Jean the Vitagraph Dog," Hollywood's first leading canine star, who appeared in movies produced by the American Vitagraph studio from 1908 to 1913.

JEAN-CLAUDE Jean-Claude Killy of France, perhaps the most charismatic and famous men's skier of all time, winning all three Alpine gold medals at the 1968 Olympics and two World championships.

JEAN-JACQUES Jean-Jacques Rousseau (1712–1778), influential writer and philosopher during the French Revolution.

JEANNIE Scottish Terrier in American humorist James Thurber's story "The Dog That Bit People."

JEBEL Jebel Musa ("Mountain of Moses"), between the Gulf of Suez and the Gulf of Akaba on the Sinai peninsula, where Jehovah delivered the tablets to Moses, is believed to be the place of origin of the Afghan Hound.

JED Jed (1977–1995), canine actor that appeared in the films *The Journey of Natty Gann* and *White Fang*.

JEDI Futuristic knights in the *Star Wars* epics who employ light sabers and use the Force in their crusade against the Dark Side.

JEEP-JEEP Popeye's dog.

JEEVES Reginald Jeeves, a valet or rather, "gentleman's personal gentleman" to Bertie Wooster in a long series of humorous novels by P. G. Wodehouse that began in 1915, parodying the British class system.

JEFFERSON Thomas Jefferson (1743–1826), principal author of the United States Declaration of Independence, third president of the United States (1801–1809), inventor, architect who built Monticello, his Virginia plantation whose vast land holdings were farmed by hundreds of slaves, despite the fact that he was a proponent of abolitionism. Jefferson included an abolition clause in his draft of the Declaration, which was struck when it caused a threat to its required unanimous approval by Congress. Jefferson had six children by one of his slaves, Sally Hemmings, the mixed-race, half-sister of his wife, Martha, who died at the age of thirty-four in childbirth after bearing him six children. Only three lived to see their twenty-fifth birthdays.

JEKYLL *Strange Case of Dr. Jekyll and Mr. Hyde*, a novella written in 1886 by Scottish author Robert Louis Stevenson, about a scientist who chemically self-induces a split violent personality. Over 125 stage, screen, comic book, and radio adaptations have been made of Stevenson's story, including the 1941 film version starring Spencer Tracy, Ingrid Bergman, and Lana Turner.

JELANI Powerful (African). Name to consider for a Great Dane.

JELLIA JAMB Head housemaid in the Palace of the Emerald City in *The Road to Oz*, *Oz* sequel by L. Frank Baum's authorized Oz historian, Ruth Plumly Thompson.

JELLY ROLL Jelly Roll Morton (1890–1941), American ragtime and early jazz pianist, composer, and bandleader best known for his foxtrot "Jelly Roll Blues." Catchy name for a Fox Terrier.

JEMIMA Dove (Hebrew). Lovely name for a female Weimaraner which has a dove-colored coat.

JENNIE *Higglety-Pigglety Pop! Or, There Must Be More to Life* by the late author -illustrator Maurice Sendak. Sendak's inspiration was his Sealyham Terrier, Jenny. Published in 1967, the book was adapted in 2010 by Warner Home Video in an animated feature voiced by Meryl Streep, Forest Whitaker, and Spike Jonze.

JENNY JUMP Teenage girl who discovers a leprechaun stealing her cheese and sets out from there upon a great adventure in four *Oz* sequels.

JENÖ Jenö Fuchs of Hungary won four gold medals for fencing in the 1908 and 1912 Olympic Games.

JERICHO Village mentioned in the Old Testament of The Holy Bible.

JERRY LEE Dog detective sidekick of actor Jim Belushi in the 1989 movie, *K-9*. Jerry Lee Lewis (b. 1935), rock and roll and country music singer and songwriter best known for his explosive song "Great Balls of Fire."

JERRY Hero dog of Jack London's *Jerry, Dog of the Islands*.

JESS Jenny Miles's dog in the *Jess the Border Collie* series of books by Lucy Daniels.

JESSE Gift (Old English). Jesse Owens, African American track and field athlete. Owens was a prominent figure in the 1936 Berlin Olympics even before the games begun. His presence alone defied the host country's Aryan ideals. Owens won four gold medals—a veritable slap in the face to Adolf Hitler. **Jessie** was President Theodore Roosevelt's Scottish Terrier.

JET Jet-black mineral (Gothic). Alsatian attached to the British Civil Defence Service, awarded the Dickin Medal in 1945 for assisting in the rescue of persons trapped under bombed buildings during the London Blitz in World War Two. Wonderful name for a black Labrador Retriever or any jet-black dog. President Rutherford B. Hayes's dog, breed unknown.

JETHRO Abundance (Hebrew).

JEWEL Precious stone.

JEZEBEL The name has come to mean a woman with loose morals. *Jezebel* was a 1938 Bette Davis movie about such a woman. In the Holy Bible, Jezebel was the evil wife of Ahab, King of Israel. She got on the wrong side of her husband, was thrown out the window, and eaten by a pack of dogs. On second thought, this might not be such a good name for a dog after all.

JIGGS English Bulldog, mascot of the US Marine Corps from 1922. Subsequent USMC mascots have included Jiggs II, Smedley, and his successors (1930–1955), and Chesty and his descendants to the present day.

JIGGY *Real Housewives of Beverly Hills* star Lisa Vanderpump's little dog that suffers some sort of skin allergy, poor thing. Lisa is the voice of reason on the otherwise out-of-touch-with-reality show.

JIMI Jimi Hendrix (1942–1970), universally considered the greatest guitarist in music history. Influenced by the early blues guitarists, he gave a voice to the guitar that has never been emulated. He died from complications resulting from a drug overdose and left us way too young.

JIMINY Jiminy Cricket, Disney's top-hatted, umbrella-totting, talking cricket who first appeared in the animated feature film *Pinocchio*, in which he (voiced by Cliff Edwards) sings the most famous of all Disney songs—indeed, the song that ranks seventh in the American Film Institute's 100 Greatest Songs of Film History, "When You Wish upon a Star," sung by Edwards and written by Leigh Harline and Ned Washington. It became Disney's signature song and anthem of hope.

JIMMY Jimmy Carter, thirty-ninth president of the United States. Diminutive of **James**.

JIN Tenderness (Japanese).

JING Jing Guo Jingjing of China won four gold and two silver Olympic medals in diving in games held between 2000 and 2008. Great name for a Shar Pei.

JINGLE Alfred Jingle, engaging charlatan and braggart who hardly ever completes a sentence in Charles Dickens's first novel published in 1836, *Pickwick Papers*.

JINJUR Female warrior who leads the "Army of Revolt" in *The Marvelous Land of Oz*, an *Oz* sequel by L. Frank Baum.

JINNICKY Jinnicky the Red Jinn, little fellow who lives inside a ginger jar in Ruth Plumly Thompson's sequels to *The Wonderful Wizard of Oz*. Great name for a small ginger-colored dog, such as a Pomeranian.

JINX Curse placed upon a person or event.

JINX A curse.

JINXY Eva Longoria's Maltese.

JIP Pampered lapdog belonging to David's first wife, the pretty, childish Dora Spenlow in Dickens's *David Copperfield*. One of Doctor Doolittle's animal companions in the charming books by Hugh Lofting.

JIRO Second male (Japanese).

JOCK Jock of the Bushveld, Staffordshire Bull Terrier from South Africa whose owner, Sir James Percy Fitzpatrick, chronicled his travels in 1880 in the Transvaal accompanied by Jock. Scottish Terrier in Walt Disney's 1955 animated motion picture *Lady and the Tramp*.

JOCKO Ch. Jocko von Stolzhafen, twice National Field Champion, appeared in the 1978 film *Days of Heaven*. Tragically, Jocko disappeared the following year, feared stolen.

JOE A Corded Poodle painted in 1889 by Lucy Waller, it was one of the most important dogs of its breed. The painting hangs in the Collection of the American Kennel Club; Joey is the affectionate form of **Joe** and the diminutive of **Joseph.**

JOE WILLIE Joseph William Namath (b. 1943), aka "Broadway Joe." American football quarterback for the University of Alabama under coach Paul "Bear" Bryant, he joined the New York Jets in 1965 then, in 1977, on the downslope of his career, signed on with the Los Angeles Rams, retiring after a single season. Namath played 140 games, threw 173 touchdowns, had 220 interceptions, and completed 1,886 passes for 27,663 yards in a career that included three division championships, one league championship—and, in one of the greatest upsets in sports history, Super Bowl III.

JO-FI Chow Chow belonging to Dr. Sigmund Freud. Jo-Fi often sat in on therapy sessions. His presence had a way of calming anxious patients. Most dogs do that; beats medication.

JOHANN God is merciful (German).

JOHN JOINER The terrier that rescued Tom Kitten from being made into a pudding by rats in Beatrix Potter's *The Roly-Poly Pudding*.

JOHN BULLDOG and "Mike's inseparable companion" in P. G. Wodehouse's humorous novel *Psmith in the City* (1910).

JOHNNY Austro-Hungarian-born American Johnny Weissmuller won five gold medals and one bronze for the United States in swimming and water polo in the 1924 and 1928 Olympic Games. The man best known as Tarzan in the twelve motion pictures he made swinging through the jungle with Jane, was one of competitive swimming's greatest athletes, winning fifty-three US National Championships and setting sixty-seven world records.

JOHNNY Johnny Depp (b. 1963), extremely popular American actor, producer, and musician, universally known as Captain Jack Sparrow in the films spawned by Disney's billion-dollar "Pirates of the Caribbean" franchise. He's purported to be one of the highest-paid actors in history. Depp hand-picks the projects he immerses himself in, which range from his long, deep-rooted collaboration with director Tim Burton, to his quirky film adaptations of the work of Hunter S. Thompson. It's said he cherishes his children, family, and friends above work and for that reason, a dog named Johnny or, for that matter, Depp, would be just the ticket for your devoted dog.

JOHNSON Gift of God (English). Also means "Son of John." Andrew Johnson, seventeenth president of the United States.

JOICEY *See* Flute.

JOKER Jester, someone who makes jokes.

JOLANDA Violet flower (Italian).

JOLLY Robert Southey's dog in "Letters from England" (1807).

JON Jon Olsen of the United States won five medals for swimming—four of which were gold—in the 1992 and 1996 Olympic Games.

JONATHAN Siberian Husky and the University of Connecticut's mascot, named after the State of Connecticut's first governor, Jonathan Trumbull, who served from 1769 to 1784—before *and* after the American Revolutionary War. A close friend and advisor of General George Washington, Trumbull gave Nathan Hale his first commission as a lieutenant in a Connecticut militia. A year later, on September 22, 1776, Hale was hanged by the British in New York, the first American spy to be executed in history.

JONES Common Welsh surname, first recorded in 1279.

JONQUIL "Love me and I shall love you" in the language of flowers.

JOSÉ Joseph (Spanish). *See* Napa.

JOSEPH Joseph Paul "Joltin' Joe" DiMaggio (1914–1999), aka "The Yankee Clipper." American Major League Baseball center fielder who played his entire thirteen-year Major League Baseball career for the New York Yankees, winning with his team ten pennants and nine world championships. His 56-game hitting streak (May 15 to July 16, 1941) record has never been broken. DiMaggio was inducted into the Baseball Hall of Fame in 1955. His personal life was no home run. His second marriage, to Marilyn Monroe, ended 274 days after their wedding in 1954. Joe never remarried.

JOSEPHINE The Lord increases (Latin).

JOSHUA Sir Joshua Reynolds (1723–1792), noted British painter who depicted a Schnauzer in one of his most famous works.

JOWLS The English Bulldog is famous for its hanging jowls. Another good name would be **Chops.**

JOY Joy Freer saved the Sussex Spaniel when the breed was almost made extinct in the Second World War. All Sussex Spaniels today are descended from her kennels' bloodline.

JUB Trotting gait of a horse (Old English).

JUBILEE Celebration.

JUDE Praised (Hebrew).

JUDY Judy (1937–1950), a purebred liver-and-white English Pointer war dog aboard the HMS *Grasshopper*, a Locust class British gunboat in World War Two. Judy was responsible for saving crewmembers when the boat was attacked by the Japanese and sank south of Singapore. She was captured by the Japanese, the only dog to be registered as a prisoner of war during WWII, and was sentenced to death but escaped, finally reuniting with her crew. Important Dachshund painted by the eminent English artist George Earl; the Royal Family of England's Tibetan Lion Dog.

JULIA Youthful

JULIAN Down-bearded youth. Good name for a Scottish Terrier, Miniature Schnauzer or other puppy with a beard.

JULIET Shakespeare's lovesick heroine who *so* loved Romeo that she sacrificed her life. If you have a boy dog and a girl dog, cleverly name them Romeo and Juliet and be sure that they, unlike Shakespeare's tragic characters, live happily ever after.

JULYAN Colonel Julyan, fair-minded county magistrate and friend of Maxim's in *Rebecca*, by Daphne du Maurier.

JUNIOR Son who shares his father's name.

JUNIPER "Eternal love" in the language of flowers. A tree from the cypress family that produces berries used in cooking.

JUNKYARD Staffordshire Bull Terrier–Lab mix in the 2009 Walt Disney family thriller *Race to Witch Mountain*.

JUNO Wife of Jupiter and queen of the gods in Roman mythology. John and Abigail Adams's dog and President Rutherford B. Hayes's hunting dog. *See* Dog Names by Category: History.

JUNON Wirehaired Pointing Griffon whelped from Mouche. *See* Mouche.

JUPITER Ruler over all gods in Roman mythology. His queen is Juno. Fifth planet from the sun and the largest in our solar system. Grand name for a Great Dane or other really large dog.

JUST NUISANCE Great Dane and only dog officially enlisted in the Royal Navy. He served in World War Two onboard the HMS *Afrikander*, a Royal Navy shore establishment in Simon's Town, South Africa.

JUST RIGHT *See* Dog Names by Category: Breed; Westminster.

JUSTIN "The father of the modern Irish Water Spaniel" was breeder Justin McCarthy of Dublin in the 1830s.

JUSTUS Just, fair (Latin). Fourth Bishop of Canterbury in the seventh century.

K

K-9 Green Martian dog in the Looney Tunes animated cartoons. Robotic dog in the perpetually running British television science fiction series *Doctor Who*.

KAA Indian Python in *The Jungle Book*. *See* Kipling.

KABUMPO Wise elephant in *Kabumpo in Oz*, a Ruth Plumly Thompson sequel to *The Wonderful Wizard of Oz*—her second Oz book but the first in which she is credited as author.

KAEOMON Joyful (Japanese).

KAFKA Franz Kafka (1883–1924), Prague-born novelist believed to have suffered from schizophrenia and whose name inspired the term "Kafkaesque," an adjective that means senseless, menacing, and disturbingly impersonal.

KAGAMI Mirror (Japanese).

KAHILI Feather (Hawaiian).

KAHLÚA Sweet, coffee-flavored Mexican liqueur.

KAI Sea (Hawaiian).

KAIDA Little Dragon (Japanese).

KAIKO Recollection (Japanese).

KAISER Emperor, leader (Germanic).

KAIYA Forgiveness (Japanese). **Kaiyo** is the male version.

KALANI Royal (Hawaiian).

KALE Strong (Hawaiian).

KALEA Bright (Hawaiian).

KALEI Garland (Hawaiian).

KALIDAH Fictitious animal with the head of a tiger and the body of a bear in *The Wonderful Wizard of Oz*, by American author L. Frank Baum.

KALOKE Carrot (Hawaiian).

KAMIN Joyful (Japanese).

KANA Powerful (Japanese).

KANIN Kaninchen Teckel is a German strain of miniature Dachshund.

KAORI Strong (Japanese).

KAORU Fragrant (Japanese).

KAPONO Goodness (Japanese).

KARAIT Common. Karait is a character in *The Jungle Book,* by Rudyard Kipling.

KAREN Pure (Danish). Danish female given name for **Katherine**.

KARI Curly-haired (Old Norse).

KARL Free man (Old German).

KARMA "For every event that occurs, there will follow another event whose existence was caused by the first" in Indian religions. The notion that one will surely reap what one sows.

KASHMIR The valley between the Himalayas and the Pir Panjal mountain range in northwest India.

KASHTANKA Dog in Anton Chekhov's short story of the same name.

KATA Worthy (Japanese).

KATARINA Katarina Witt of Germany won the 1984 and 1988 Olympic gold medals in Women's Figure Skating and four World championships.

KATE Diminutive of **Katherine**, also **Katie**. One of the thirty most popular female dog names.

KATHERINE Each of two (English name derived from the Greek *Hekaterine*). Katherine Minola, Shakespeare's shrew and Petruchio's romantic challenge in *The Taming of the Shrew.*

KATHRIN Kathrin Boron of Germany won five Olympic medals in rowing in games held between 1992 and 2008.

KATMANDU Ancient capital of Nepal associated with Buddha.

KATO Sawao Kato of Japan won twelve Olympic medals for gymnastics in games held between 1968 and 1976.

KATRIN Katrin Wagner-Augustin of Germany won five Olympic medals in canoeing in the 2000, 2004, and 2008 games.

KAWASZ Armed guard of the nobility (Turkish). The Kuvasz breed of dog gets its name from this word.

KAY Sir Kay, knight of King Arthur's legendary Round Table and one of its greatest warriors, known for his sharp tongue and churlish ways.

KAZAK Hound in *The Sirens of Titan*, by Kurt Vonnegut.

KAZAKH Selena MacIntosh's Seeing Eye dog in *Galápagos*, by Kurt Vonnegut.

KAZAN Wolf dog in James Oliver Curwood's 1914 novel *Kazan the Wolfdog*.

KEANU Cool mountain breeze (Hawaiian).

KEEPER The Old English Bullmastiff is known as "the keeper's nightdog." Tawny Bull Dog that belonged to English author Emily Brontë.

KEIGHLEY *See* Skipton.

KEIJI Lead cautiously (Japanese).

KEIKO Blessed one (Japanese).

KEILAH City in the lowlands of Judah where David sought Jonathan "and strengthened his hand in God."

KEITARO Blessed (Japanese).

KEITH Wood (Scottish).

KELB Dog (Maltese).

KELLAN Powerful (Swahili).

KELLER Keller and Kraemer, eminent zoologists who maintained the Mastiff breed originated in Asia.

KELLY Gene Kelly (1912–1996), charismatic actor, singer, director who codirected and starred in the 1952 *Singing in the Rain* with America's eternal sweetheart, American actress-singer Debbie Reynolds.

KELPIE Legendary Celtic water horse that haunts the rivers and lakes of Ireland, Wales, and Scotland. In Wales it is known as **Ceffyl Dŵr**, in Scotland and Ireland it is **Colpach** and in Orkney, **Nuggle**.

KENDI Loved one (Swahili).

KENDŌ *See* Samurai.

KENNEDY Armored head (Gaelic name *Cinnéidigh*).

KENNY Born of fire (from the Gaelic, *Cináed*).

KENSINGTON Kensington Palace, London, a royal residence of the British monarchy since the seventeenth century. Home of the Duke and Duchess of Cambridge, affectionately known as **Will** and **Kate**.

KENT Clark Kent, alias Superman.

KENTUCKIAN *See* Dog Names by Category: Breed; Crufts.

KEP Rough Collie in Beatrix Potter's *The Tale of Jemima Puddle-Duck* and also the name of the English children's author's real-life Border Collie.

KERMIT Son of Diarmaid (Irish). Kermit the Frog, chief Muppet, created by visionary puppet master, Jim Henson (1936–1990).

KERNOCHAN James Kernochan imported Beagles from northern England in 1896 to refine the breeding of his pack and breed standards in America.

KERRY County Kerry, Ireland, is the place of origin of the Kerry Blue Terrier.

KERSURCK The Lakeland Terrier was introduced at the Kersurck Dog Show in 1912.

KEUL Dr. Keul of the Veterinary School of Brussels first called attention to the many distinguished qualities of the Bouvier des Flandres.

KEVIN Beautiful at birth (Gaelic).

KHAFRA *See* Sphinx.

KHAKI Dust, ash-colored (Persian). Fabric from which military uniforms were made in the British Indian Army.

KI Tea (Hawaiian).

KIBBEE *See* January.

KIBBLE Ground meal pressed into small, easily digested pieces for dog food. Cute name for a little dog.

KIBWE Blessed (Swahili).

KICHE The mother of White Fang in Jack London's 1906 classic tale of the Yukon, *White Fang*.

KID Child (American English slang). A baby goat.

KIKI Griffon Bruxellois dog in the 2001 Robert Altman film *Gosford Park*.

KILIMANJARO Little white hill (Swahili). Mount Kilimanjaro in Africa was the setting for Ernest Hemingway's story of big game hunting and tragedy in Africa, *The Snows of Kilimanjaro*.

KILO Prefix in the metric system denoting "one thousand."

KILOGRAM Basic unit of mass in the metric system (2.2056 lbs. equals 1,000 grams).

KILTIE *See* Goelet.

KIM Rudyard Kipling's novel *Kim*, published in 1901, is about the vagabond life of the orphaned son of an Irish soldier in India, whom Kipling describes as "a poor white, the poorest of the poor."

KIMBERLY Cyneburga's field (Old English).

KIMI She who is without equal (Japanese).

KIN Relative, family member.

KING BUCK Labrador Retriever who competed in an unprecedented sixty-three consecutive series in the National Championship Stake and was the first to win two consecutive National Retriever Field Trial Club championships (1952 and 1953), a feat that was not duplicated for nearly forty years. King Buck was also the first dog to be honored on a United States postage stamp.

KING Cole, Nat "King" Cole (1919–1965), baritone and jazz pianist, one of America's national treasures. He smoked three packs a day, which he believed created that rich layer to his incomparable voice; it also caused his early death at the age of forty-five. One of the most poignant duet performances ever was his daughter Natalie singing "Unforgettable" with her father against his recorded image superimposed on film. Cole was the first black American to host a television show. "The Christmas Song" ("Chestnuts Roasting on an Open Fire") is second only to Bing Crosby's "White Christmas" come the holiday season. "Mona Lisa" is one of pop's greatest love songs. He sang it all—gospel, blues, jazz, even classical and he played with them all— Ella, Bing, Frank Sinatra, Tony Bennett, Eartha Kitt, Peggy Lee, Harry Belafonte, usually with his longtime collaborator Nelson Riddle and his orchestra. A dog should be named King Cole if he's got a smooth and easy disposition.

KING COLE President Calvin Coolidge's German Shepherd.

KING JOHN *See* Twici.

KING TUT President Herbert Hoover's Belgian Shepherd.

KING Important Mastiff sired by T. H. V. Lukey's Rufus out of Nell III, King and Hilda produced one of the renowned litters of the day. One of the puppies was Turk.

KINGSLEY King's wood (Old English). Cannon Kingsley may have been inspired by the champion English Foxhound, Gambler, when he wrote: "The result of nature not limited, but developed by a high civilization. Next to an old Greek statue there are few such combinations of grace and strength as in a fine foxhound."

KINGSTON Kingston Trio, popular American folk group whose first album was released in 1958.

KIOKO Meets world with happiness (Japanese).

KIPLING Rudyard Kipling (1865–1936), English author and journalist. *The Jungle Book*, his classic collection of children's stories, was inspired by everything Kipling "knew or heard or dreamed about the Indian jungle." Great Britain's Nobel laureate, he spent his early years in India, the only bright spot of his childhood. He adored children; tragically, two of his own three would die young: Josephine, at the age of six, of pneumonia, and his only son Jack, eighteen, went missing in action during the Battle of Loos in World War One. Kipling's poem "My Boy Jack" (1915) will tear your heart out; his grief tore out his—Kipling never recovered from the loss of his children. English actor David Haig brilliantly adapted this tragic portion of Kipling's life into a play that was subsequently made into a television drama, with himself as Kipling and American actress Kim Cattrall just incredible as his wife, Carrie.

KIPPAX *See* Dog Names by Category: Breed; Westminster.

KIPPER Airedale in the Walt Disney animated and live-action films *101 Dalmatians*.

KIRABO Gift (Swahili).

KIRBY Church settlement (Old Norse).

KIRSCH Cherry brandy.

KISSES What you give someone you love.

KIT Christopher Houston "Kit" Carson (1809–1868), American frontiersman, trapper, and guide in the Missouri Territory who left home at the age of sixteen to carve out a life in the American West.

KIVA White Poodle in the 2000 Ben Stiller movie *Zoolander*.

KIWI Five species, all endangered, of a flightless New Zealand bird that lays the largest egg relative to its size of any bird. Luscious golden-skinned fruit with bright green flesh, also known as the Chinese **Gooseberry**.

KJETIL Kjetil André Aamodt of Norway won eight medals in Alpine skiing in the Winter Olympic Games held between 1992 and 2006.

KLEOBIS One of two earthly brothers in Greek mythology.

KLONDIKE The Alaskan Malamute was a sled dog during the Klondike Gold Rush of 1896.

KNAVE A male servant. The Jack in a deck of playing cards.

KNIGHT *See* Peers.

KNOOKS The Knooks of Burzee, friends of Santa Claus in *The Road to Oz: In Which Is Related How Dorothy Gale of Kansas, The Shaggy Man, Button Bright and Polychrome the Rainbow's Daughter Met on an Enchanted Road and Followed It All the Way to the Marvelous Land of Oz*, fifth sequel to The *Wonderful Wizard of Oz*, by American author L. Frank Baum.

KNOX Round hill (Old English).

KNUR *See* Dog Names by Category: Breed; Crufts.

KOBE Japan's sixth largest city, founded in the Meiji Era.

KOBUK Northern Light Kobuk, first Siberian Husky AKC champion.

KOER Dog (Estonian).

KOFI Born on Friday (Swahili).

KOHANA Little Flower (Japanese).

KOIRA Dog (Finnish).

KOJO Born on Monday (Akan, African).

KOKO Stork (Japanese).

KOKOLEKA Chocolate (Hawaiian).

KOKOMO *See* Dake.

KOMETKA Soviet space dog.

KONI Russian Prime Minister Vladimir Putin's Labrador Retriever.

KÖNIG King (Scandinavian).

KOPA'A Sugar (Hawaiian).

KOPE Coffee (Hawaiian).

KOPEK Dog (Greek).

KORBEL Korbel Champagne Cellars, a winery based in Guerneville, California, founded in 1882 by two Czechoslovakian brothers.

KORNELIA Kornelia Ender of East Germany won four gold and four silver medals in swimming in the 1972 and 1976 Olympic Games.

KORTHALS Original breeder of the Wirehaired Pointing Griffon.

KOSUKE Kosuke Kitajima of Japan won six medals for swimming in the 2004 and 2008 Olympic Games.

KOTICK White seal in *The Jungle Book*, by Rudyard Kipling.

KOTO Harp (Japanese).

KOTZEBUE Kotzebue Sound in the upper western corner of Alaska is the native home of the Alaskan Malamute, dog of the Inuits.

KRASAVKA Soviet space dog.

KRISTALL Very precious, crystal (English).

KRISTI Kristi Yamaguchi of the United States won the gold medal in women's figure skating at the 1992 Albertville Olympics—an amazing achievement when you consider Kristi was born with club feet. She began skating at a very early age as therapy to correct her birth defect. Obviously, it worked.

KRISTIN Kristin Otto of East Germany won six gold medals in swimming at the 1988 Olympics in Seoul.

KRYPTO Krypto the Superdog, Superman's white German Shepherd, first appeared in March 1955, in *Adventure Comics* #210.

KUDRYAVKA Soviet space dog.

KUJŌ One of the five regent houses of Japan.

KU-KLIP *See* Munchkin.

KUMA Grandmother, grandfather, or grandparents (Serbian).

KUMIKO Braid (Japanese). Perfect name for a Komondor.

KUMU Tree (Japanese).

KUNIKO Child from the country (Japanese).

KÜNZLI Dr. Künzli, Dr. Sigmund, and Max Siber, noted authorities on the Saint Bernard, determined the standards for the breed at the International Congress in Zurich in 1887.

KURA Treasure house (Japanese).

KURI Chestnut (Japanese).

KURZHAAR Smooth-coated Dachshund.

KUTYA Dog (Hungarian).

KYLE Gru's rather strange dog in the fabulous animated movie *Despicable Me*. Gru is voiced by the inimitable Steve Carrell.

KYOKO Mirror (Japanese).

KYRA Black (Irish, from *ciar*). Kyra and Chalcy are a pair of Weimaraners that posed with actress Angelina Jolie in a fashion advertisement. Great name for a black female dog.

KYTE The Belgian Tervuren that played **Wellard** in *EastEnders*, one of Britain's most popular television soap operas.

L

LA Sun (Hawaiian).

LA BEALE Dog belonging to Sir Tristram in *Le Morte d'Arthur* (1478) by Sir Thomas Malory.

LACE Lace is generally white or ecru and very delicately made, so this might be a very fine name for a small, white, little dog.

LACEY Surname derived from Lassy, a town in Normandy, France.

LAD Author Albert Payson Terhune's Rough Collie, portrayed in his *Lad of Sunnybank* novels.

LADDIE Queen Victoria's beloved Scottish Terrier. Laddie Boy, President Warren G. Harding's Airedale Terrier.

LADY *Lady and the Tramp*, Disney's 1955 animated film, is a canine romance about a purebred American Cocker Spaniel named Lady who falls for a stray mutt named Tramp. Other canine characters are **Jock**, **Joe**, **Bulldog**, **Dachsie**, **Policeman**, **Trusty**, **Tony**, **Darling**, **Peg**, **Toughy**, **Pedro**, and **Professor**.

LADY Lady Willoughby de Eresby, who lived in Greenthorpe, Lincolnshire, was an early breeder of the Pug in England. Skeeter's dog, a Basenji, in the 1956 film *Good-bye, My Lady*, starring Walter Brennan and Sidney Poitier.

LADY EDITH Lady Edith Crawley, middle daughter on the British period television drama *Downton Abbey*, who was despicable in Season One but evolved into a very useful person in Season Two. She is portrayed by the attractive and talented British actress Laura Carmichael.

LADY GAGA (b. 1986), New York–born singer and songwriter whose camp, eyebrow-raising costumes unnecessarily distract the audience from appreciating her incredibly superb voice, music, and lyrics and hide her natural beauty. But, hey, the world loves her that way. Great name for a bitch that regularly has to go to the grooming salon, like a female Toy Poodle.

LADY HOWE Owner of early dual champions (Field Trial and Bench Show) Labrador Retrievers Banchory Bolo, Bramshaw Bob, and Banchory Painter.

LADY JANE Queen Elizabeth's dog when she was a princess.

LADY MARY Lady Mary Josephine Crawley, eldest daughter of Lord and Lady Grantham in the hit British television series *Downton Abbey*, played with texture and grace by English actress Michele Dockery.

LADY SYBIL Lady Sybil Crawley Branson, youngest and pretty daughter of Lord and Lady Grantham, who is political—as is the chauffeur, who she ups and marries, causing social class mayhem in the acclaimed British period television series *Downton Abbey*.

LADYBIRD The Hill family's Bloodhound, in the animated family, *King of the Hill*. Lady Bird Johnson (1912–2007), much-admired wife of President Lyndon B. Johnson. Recognized for her love of flowers, she spearheading national beautification projects while First Lady and after, in her home state of Texas. "Where flowers bloom, so does hope," she said.

LADYBUG Little red beetle with black spots.

LAEKEN Short-coated, fawn-colored strain of Belgian Sheepdog.

LAELAPS A hunting dog in Greek mythology that was a gift from Zeus to Europa. Laelaps never failed to catch his prey.

LAFAYETTE Marie-Joseph Paul Yves Roch Gilbert du Motier, Marquis de La Fayette, (1757–1834), known as Lafayette, was a French aristocrat and a general in the Continental Army during the American

Revolutionary War. George Washington, who never had any natural children of his own, looked upon Lafayette as a son. Lafayette gave two Great Pyrenees to his friend, J. S. Skinner, as a gift in 1824. Basset Hound that is Napoleon's companion in the 1970 Walt Disney animated feature *The Aristocats*.

LAIKA Soviet space dog.

LAIRD King James I wrote to the Laird of Caldwell to have Scottish Terriers selected from the kennel of the Earl of Montieth and sent to him in the early seventeenth century.

LAKA Gentle (Hawaiian).

LALIA Well-spoken (Italian).

LAMB CHOP Adorable, smarty-puss puppet on the children's television series *The Shari Lewis Show*, which originally aired on NBC from 1960 to 1963.

LAMBERT Daniel Lambert, an English sportsman, who developed a line of black English Pointer hunting dogs.

LANCE Knight's attendant (English). Dog in the 1958 Western *The Proud Rebel*, starring Olivia de Havilland and Alan Ladd.

LANCELOT The bravest of King Arthur's Knights of the Round Table who broke the king's trust—and heart—when he and Queen Guinevere fell in love.

LANGHAAR Langhaar is the long-haired strain of Dachshund.

LANI Sky, heavens (Hawaiian). Diminutive of the Hawaiian female name, **Nolani**.

LANTANA "Rigorous" in the language of flowers.

LARA An important Mastiff painted in 1882 by H. Hardy Simpson. The portrait is in the collection of the American Kennel Club. Canine member of the Spy Dog organization in *The Secret Files of the Spy Dogs*, whose members set out to save the world. The leader is **Dog Zero**.

Elizabeth Taylor with Lassie in *Courage of Lassie* (1946)

Other members include **Ralph, Mitzy, Scribble, Angus, Von Rabie, Frank, Stahl, Catastrophe, Baron Bone, Ernest Anyway, Mistress Pavlov,** and **Pookie.** The 1999 American animated series was created by Jim Benton.

LARISA Larisa Latynina, Soviet gymnast, won eighteen Olympic medals that included nine gold in the 1956 and 1964 Olympic Games; Larisa Lazutina of Russia won seven Olympic medals for cross-country skiing in games held between 1992 and 1998.

LARKSPUR "Pure and open heart" in the language of flowers.

LASKA Levin's old grey dog in Leo Tolstoy's *Anna Karenina*.

LASSIE The legendary Rough Collie in Eric Knight's novel *Lassie Come Home* that became the classic 1943 film starring Roddy McDowall, the canine actor Pal, a stellar cast, and, as the Duke of Rudling's granddaughter, an eleven-year-old child actress in her first major motion picture—Elizabeth Taylor.

LATIF Gentle (African).

LAU Leaf (Hawaiian).

LAUD *See* Dog Names by Category: Breed; Westminster.

LAURA Popular English female given name since the thirteenth century.

LAUREL AND HARDY Stan Laurel (1890–1965) and Oliver Hardy (1892–1957), the greatest comedy team that ever made us break our ribs with laughter. Their collaboration began in silent films and lasted more than thirty years. Great names for a pair of dogs, one thin, one fat.

LAUREL "Glory" in the language of flowers. The leaves of the laurel tree were used by the Romans to make crowns and garlands.

LAURIE Opera star Beverly Sills's Welsh Corgi, of whom she said, "As soon as I arrive at the house, Laurie starts running, hits my chest, knocks me down, and licks my face. It's become a family ritual."

LAVA Mixed-breed dog adopted by the 1st Battalion 3rd Marines Unit, nicknamed the Lava Dogs, during the war in Iraq.

LAVENDER "Loving devotion" in the language of flowers. Aromatic flower that is said to soothe and calm the soul.

LAVERACK Edward Laverack, developed the modern Setter from **Ponto** and **Old Moll**, obtained from Rev. A. Harrison in 1825. Ponto and Old Moll produced **Prince**, **Countess**, **Nellie**, and **Fairy**. Laverack's foundation dogs were **Dash** and **Hill**.

LAWLESS One of the Hounds that "were singing" in Frederick Watson's *In the Pink* (1932).

LAWRENCE *See* Prescott.

LAYLA Rock's eternal love song, first released in 1970 by Derek and the Dominos, with a scorching guitar coda by the legendary rock, blues, and soul guitarist Eric Clapton. Clapton composed the song as an ode to Pattie Boyd, the wife of his best friend, George Harrison. From there it gets complicated.

LAZARUS "God has helped" (Ancient Greek). Man raised from the dead four days after his death by Jesus Christ, according to the Gospel of John.

LE BEAU President John Tyler's Italian Greyhound.

LE DIABLE Clever—indeed notorious—dog that smuggled lace and other valuable items across the French border during the French Revolutionary War (1792–1802).

LEAD BELLY Huddie William "Lead Belly" Ledbetter (1888–1949), American blues singer, guitarist, and songwriter. Lead Belly did jail time as the result of a quick temper that stayed with him all of his life. In the realm of blues, he was called "the Father of Delta Blues" and "the King of the Twelve-string Guitar." He also played mouth organ, violin, accordion, and mandolin. Listen to "House of the Rising Sun" or the racially controversial "Titanic." An obvious name for a Bulldog because of the breed's stout build. But if your dog has music in his soul, name him Lead Belly.

LEAD *See* Maupin.

LEADER *See* Dog Names by Category: Breed; Crufts.

LEAH Weary (Hebrew).

LEAO Mixed-breed dog that refused to leave the grave of his mistress, Cristina Cesário Maria Santana, who died in the January 2011 deadly landslides caused by heavy rain in Brazil.

LED "Learned English Dog" in Thomas Pynchon's 1997 novel *Mason & Dixon*.

LEDA Beautiful English Setter painted by eminent dog artist Percival Leonard Rosseau in 1906. The painting is in the collection of the American Kennel Club.

LEGH *See* Peers.

LEGOLAS Legolas Greenleaf, son of Thranduil, King of the Woodland Realm of Northern Mirkwood, elf and one of the nine members of the Fellowship of the Ring in the J. R. R. Tolkien legendarium, *The Lord of the Rings*.

LEIF Leif Eriksson (AD 980–1020), Norse explorer who is believed to have discovered America five hundred years before Columbus. Good name for a Norwegian Elkhound.

LEIKO Arrogant (Japanese).

LEMI Lemon (Hawaiian).

LEMON BLOSSOM "Fidelity" in the language of flowers.

LEMON Yellow citrus fruit and a cute name for a Chow Chow. "Blind" Lemon Henry Jefferson (1893–1929), American blues guitarist and singer. Born blind and one of eight children of sharecroppers, he became a street musician while barely in his teens, playing his guitar in front of barbershops and depending upon the kindness of whores and bootleggers who'd toss a nickel or dime into his cup. He met up with blues great Lead Belly in Dallas and taught T-Bone Walker the nuances of blues guitar. Around Christmas of 1925, he went to Chicago to record songs that became blues classics, such as "Got the Blues" and "Long Lonesome Blues" and most famously, "See That My Grave Is Clean," later recorded by Bob Dylan, the Grateful Dead, B. B. King, and Peter, Paul and Mary. There are conflicting stories of his tragic death at the age of thirty-six. What a name for a yellow dog that sees poorly.

LENCHO Lion (African).

LENNY German Shepherd mix that appeared with actor David Duchovny in *Best Friend Forgotten*, a 2004 documentary about homeless pets. Yellow Labrador Retriever in the 2005 film *Lenny the Wonder Dog*.

LEO Lion (Latin)

LEONARDO *See* Da Vinci.

LEONORA Foreign (Italian).

LEONTIEN Leontien van Moorsel of the Netherlands won six Olympic medals for cycling in the 2000 and 2004 games.

LEPRECHAUN An Irish fairy, usually portrayed as a little old man in red or green garb, who safeguards a pot of gold at the end of the rainbow.

LEROY The King (French); also **Elroy**.

LES AMIS Friends (French). Les Amis du Briard ("Friends of the Briard"), a French breed club that sets the standards for the Briard breed of dog.

LESEDI Light (African).

LESLIE Garden of holly (Scottish).

LETIZIA Happiness (Italian).

LEVI Attached (Hebrew).

LEWIS Carl Lewis, sprinter and long jumper, won ten Olympic medals (nine gold and one silver) in the games between 1984 to 1998 and ten World Championship medals during that period.

LEX Active duty military working dog granted early retirement to be adopted by the family of his handler, United States Marine Corps handler Corporal Dustin J. Lee, after Lee was mortally wounded in the Iraq War.

LHASA The sacred Tibetan city where the Lhasa Apso originated.

LI Li Xiaopeng of China won five Olympic medals in gymnastics in games between 2000 and 2008.

LIAM Irish form of William.

LIBBY Diminutive of **Isabel**.

LIBERTY Freedom, the most precious commodity of man. President Richard M. Nixon's Golden Retriever.

LIDIA Lidia Skobilkova of the Soviet Union won six gold medals in speed skating in the 1960 and 1964 Olympic Games.

LIEBCHEN Sweetheart, dear (German).

LIFESAVER Steve Martin's dog in the 1979 Carl Reiner comedy *The Jerk*.

LIGHTNIN' Lightnin' Hopkins (1912–1982), Texas-born singer, songwriter and guitarist who "felt the blues in him" with "Rock Me Baby" and "Trouble in Mind." He may have had trouble in his mind, but he had poetry in his soul. Great name for a dog that runs like lightning, such as a Saluki or a Greyhound.

LIGHTNING Flash of light discharged in an electrical storm. Good name for a fast dog.

LIKO Bud (Hawaiian).

LILAC Harold's Old English Sheepdog in *Harold and the Purple Crayon*, the series of children's books first published in 1955 by Crockett Johnson, produced by HBO in 2002 as an animated TV series narrated by Sharon Stone. Tree that blossoms in spring, producing large clusters of flowerets that range in color from deep purple to white.

LILI "Lili Marleen," famous World War Two song sung by Marlene Dietrich. *See* Dietrich.

LILLIAN Dam of Toledo Blade, an important English Setter. *See* Toledo.

LILLIBET Affectionate name for **Elizabeth**.

LILY "Purity of heart" in the language of flowers. The white lily was born from Eve's tears as she was leaving the Garden of Eden. Legendary American actress and singer Liza Minnelli's Scottish Terrier.

LIMBO The otherworldly place where the souls of the righteous that died before the birth of Jesus Christ wait for the Judgment Day. A Caribbean dance that requires a bar or rope and a lot of dexterity.

LINA Early Wirehaired Pointing Griffons related to Mouche, the breed's foundation bitch.

LINCOLN Abraham Lincoln (1809–1865), sixteenth president of the United States, whose conviction that all men should be free cost him his own life.

LINDA Soft, tender (Germanic).

LINDBERGH Charles Lindbergh (1902–1974), aka "Slim," "Lucky Lindy," "The Lone Eagle." Lindbergh was a twenty-five-year-old US Mail pilot in the Midwest before he successfully made the first nonstop flight across the Atlantic Ocean in his single-engine plane, *Spirit of Saint Louis*, from Roosevelt Field, Long Island, to Le Bourget Airport in Paris where he landed on May 21, 1927.

LINDSAY A Scottish clan that acquired "the lands of Crawford" in Lanarkshire in AD 1120.

LINEN Linen, a woven cotton fabric, is a warm shade of white and the name could be just perfect for a dog with a coat that color.

LINK Connection, tie, bond.

LINNAEUS In 1792, Carolus Linnaeus, the father of taxonomy, observed the Maltese as "being about the size of Squirrels."

LINNET One of Queen Elizabeth of England's Corgis.

LINUS Flax (Greek). Son of Apollo and a Muse in Greek mythology, Linus is the symbolic inventor of melody and rhythm. Charlie Brown's wise, thumb-sucking best friend in the timeless Charles M. Schulz comic.

LION Henry Gowan's noble dog in Charles Dickens's novel *Little Dorrit*, published in 1855. The Pekingese is called the "Lion Dog" because it resembles a lion with a heavy mane and is just as brave.

LIONEL Lionel Barrymore (1878–1954). Best Actor Academy Award Winner of 1931 and famously known as Henry Potter, James Stewart's nemesis in Frank Capra's classic 1946 film *It's a Wonderful Life*. One of Hollywood's most prolific and beloved actors, he starred in *Key Largo* with Humphrey Bogart and Lauren Bacall, *Captains Courageous* with

Spencer Tracy, *Treasure Island* with Wallace Beery and Jackie Cooper, and as Dr. Leonard Gillespie in the *Dr. Kildare* movies with Lew Ayres. Few today realize that Barrymore, brother of actors John and Ethel, was also a prolific classical composer of piano and orchestral works. Married twice, he had two daughters, neither of whom survived infancy. His marriages didn't survive either. His loss was compounded when Jean Harlow, who looked upon Barrymore as a father, died of kidney disease in 1937 at the age of twenty-six. Barrymore owned a Scottish Terrier named Johnny.

LISA Soviet space dog.

LISICHKA Soviet space dog.

LITTLE ANN Little Ann and **Old Dan**, Billy's Red Bone Coonhounds in Wilson Rawls's children's novel *Where the Red Fern Grows*.

LITTLE BEAR Star of the series of children's books by Else Holmelund Minarik, illustrated by Maurice Sendak.

LITTLE BROTHER Mulan's dog in the 1998 Walt Disney animated film *Mulan*.

LITTLE MAN Along with **Ace**, one of the two hunting hounds in the 2002 family adventure film *Gentle Ben*, produced by Animal Planet.

LITTLE MUSTARD *See* Auld.

LITTLE PEPPER *See* Auld.

LITTLE SISTER *See* Dog Names by Category: Breed; Westminster.

LIVINGSTONE Dr. David Livingstone (1813–1873), Scottish missionary, medical pioneer, and explorer who failed to find the source of the Nile River but made many important geographical discoveries in southern Africa nonetheless. When his whereabouts became unknown, Henry Morton Stanley, a newspaperman for the *New*

York Herald, set out to find him and did, famously addressing him, "Dr. Livingstone, I presume?" Livingstone refused to return to Great Britain with Stanley, maintaining that his work was incomplete. He became fatally ill and died in the land he cherished. Chief Chitambo's tribe, which revered Dr. Livingstone, refused to return his body to England for burial. Pressed, the Chief finally relented. When the body arrived, a note was found in the chest cavity. It said, "You can have his body, but his heart belongs in Africa!" His remains are interred in Westminster Abbey; his heart is buried in Africa.

LIZZIE Diminutive of **Elizabeth**.

LLOYD Captain Lloyd, a nineteenth-century English sportsman wrote about hunting with Norwegian Elkhounds, which heightened interest in the breed. W. Lloyd-Thomas of Mabws Hall, Llanrhystyd, Cardiganshire, South Wales, spent twenty years documenting the history of the Corgi.

LOBENGULA Lobengula, king of the Matabele people of South Africa was so smitten by an Italian Greyhound owned by a Mr. Luscombe Searelle that he begged to buy the dog—which Searelle reluctantly sold for two hundred head of cattle.

LOCHINVAR Loch on the hilltop (Scots Gaelic). *See* Terhune.

LOFTUS Mrs. Loftus Allen first exhibited the Pekinese breed of dog in England in 1893.

LOGAN Little hollow (Gaelic).

LOHENGRIN Knight of the Holy Grail in German Arthurian literature. An opera by Richard Wagner, first performed in 1850.

LOKI Norse god of fire and ally of the frost giants.

LOLA A Bulldog, one of Ozzy and Sharon Osbourne's canine family.

LOLLIPOP Candy on a stick. "The Lollipop Kid," American actor Jerry Maren (b. 1920), a featured Munchkin who represented the Lollipop Guild in the 1939 film *The Wizard of Oz*. Maren enjoyed an amazing career that spanned more than sixty years.

LOLLY Adrien Brody's Chihuahua.

LOMAX Squire Lomax of Clitheroe was known to have the best-trained pack of Otterhounds that ever hunted in England in the 1860s.

LONDON German Shepherd Dog who played Hobo in *The Littlest Hobo*, the 1963 Canadian television series.

LONESOME DOVE *See* Dog Names by Category: Breed; Westminster.

LONSDALE Lord Lonsdale had a Lakeland Terrier that, in 1871, crawled twenty-three feet underground in pursuit of an otter.

LOONY Stubby's black Spaniel who's always getting into trouble in Enid Blyton's *Famous Five* series of twenty-one children's novels, written between 1942 and 1963.

LORD Bread-keeper or loaf-ward (Germanic). Originally from the word *hláfweard*, the word refers to the Germanic tribal custom that the chief provides bread to his tribe. A Lady was called a "loaf-kneader." "Lord" and "Lady" later became the titular terms for British nobility or peers of the realm.

LORD Master, ruler, member of the British peerage, landowner. **Laird** in Scotland.

LORELEI A rock on the River Rhine where a beautiful siren sits combing her long, luxurious hair, according to German folklore. This distracts sailors, whose vessels crash into the rock. That's one way to get a man's attention.

LORENZO Lorenzo de' Medici (1449–1492), "Lorenzo the Magnificent," early Italian Renaissance ruler of the Florentine Republic and patron of the arts who supported the work of many painters and sculptors, including Michelangelo and Leonardo da Vinci.

LORNA Lorna, Countess Howe, a supporter of the Club for Curly Retrievers before World War Two.

LOTEKI *See* Dog Names by Category: Breed; Westminster.

LOTHARIO Seducer of women. Character in *Don Quixote*, by Miguel de Cervantes.

LOTUS "Forget the past" in the language of flowers. British sports car.

LOU Beagle voiced by Tobey Maguire in *Cats & Dogs*, a 2001 family comedy starring Jeff Goldblum and Elizabeth Perkins. Lou is played by canine actor Prada, who also appeared as **Porthos** in *Star Trek: Enterprise*. Four canine actors rotated with Prada to play Lou: Buddy, Confusion, Coco, and C.J.

LOUIS Famous warrior (French). Louis Doberman, the first breeder of the Doberman Pinscher in the German state of Thuringia after the Franco-Prussian War, around 1890. A tax collector who also ran the Apolda dog pound, he mated dogs that exhibited "strength, loyalty, intelligence, and ferocity" to breed a canine companion that could accompany him on his often-dangerous rounds.

LOURDES Chateau of Lourdes used Great Pyrenees as guard dogs in the fifteenth century.

LOUVOIS The Marquis de Louvois issued a decree that "the Dog of the Shepherd of the Pyrenees (Pyrenean Shepherd) was the companion pet of the nobility."

LOVELL Jim Lovell, Frank Borman, and William A. Anders took off December 21, 1968, on Apollo 8, the first manned lunar flight, completing ten lunar orbits in twenty hours. They were the first humans to see the far side of the moon and "earthrise." The world saw it, too—in live television pictures broadcast to Earth.

LOVELY Enchanting, comely.

LUA Goddess in Roman mythology to whom soldiers sacrificed enemy weapons seized in battle.

LUATH Yellow Labrador Retriever who joins Bodger, an old, partly blind English Bull Terrier, to make *The Incredible Journey*. The novel, by Shelley Burnford, was published in 1961 and inspired two Walt Disney film adaptations.

LUCA Very sensitive dog who guards the house next door to Garfield's in *Garfield: The Movie*.

LUCAN Sir Lucan, a knight at King Arthur's legendary Round Table.

LUCAS Lucas Cranach the Elder tapestry maker who portrayed Schnauzers as early as 1501.

LUCIANA Light (Italian).

LUCIEN Lucien Gaudin of France won four gold and two silver Olympic medals in fencing in games held between 1920 and 1928.

LUCIFER Tempter of mankind, the Devil (Latin).

LUCINDA Light (Latin).

LUCIUS Lucius Malfoy, husband of Narcissa, father of Draco: a Death Eater who ultimately turns his back on Voldemort when he decides to protect his family in the finale of the Harry Potter series.

LUCKY and **Flo** Two black Labrador Retrievers trained to detect optical discs by scent as part of a Motion Picture Association of America initiative to combat copyright infringement of the illegal production and sale of motion pictures onto DVD.

LUCKY Only member of a four-dog team serving in the British Royal Air Force to survive tracking terrorists in Malaya from 1949 to 1952. John Travolta's Shepherd mix, played by canine actor Sebastian, in the 2009 Disney movie *Old Dogs*. Fifteenth and last biological puppy born to Pongo and Perdita in Disney's *101 Dalmatians*. Dr. Doolittle's dog in the 1998 film starring Eddie Murphy. President Ronald Reagan's dog.

LUCKYSTAR *See* Dog Names by Category: Breed; Crufts.

LUCREZIA Wealthy (Italian).

LUDGER Equestrian Ludger Beerbaum of Germany won four gold medals in Olympic Games from 1988 to 2000.

LUDMILLA Ludmilla Tourischeva of the Soviet Union won nine Olympic medals in gymnastics between 1968 and 1976.

LUDOVICA Feminine of **Ludovico**, famous warrior (Italian).

LUDOVIK Famous warrior (Albanian).

LUDVIG Famous in battle (Swedish, Norwegian).

LUFFRA Yet another one of the dogs in Sir Ector's kennels in T. H. White's 1958 Arthurian novel *The Once and Future King*.

LUIGI Famous warrior (Italian).

LUIS Drooling Bulldog in the 2011 children's animated movie *Rio*.

LUKE and Duke Julie's two little dogs in the 1995 action comedy *Bad Boys*, starring Will Smith and Martin Lawrence.

LULU Affectionate form of **Louisa**.

LUNA Moon, beautiful woman (Latin). The Roman name of the Greek goddess of the moon, Selene. Luna Lovegood, good friend of Harry Potter and daughter of Xenophilius Lovegood, a widower and magazine editor of *The Quibbler*. Luna sees some things that Harry can see but others cannot.

LUPIN Wolf (Latin).

LUPO Wolf (Hawaiian).

LUTALO Warrior (African).

LUTHER The dog that could smell Heaven in the 1988 comic fantasy novel *Fool on the Hill*, by Matt Ruff.

LUXOVIUS In Gallo-Roman religion, the god of the spring-waters of Luxeuil.

LYDA *See* Nic.

LYDIA Ancient Greek name meaning "From Lydia," an Iron Age kingdom in western Asia Minor where coins were thought to have first been used around 600 BC. Foolish, shallow sister of Elizabeth Bennet who, much to his regret, marries Wickham in Jane Austen's novel *Pride and Prejudice,* first published in 1813.

LYME *See* Peers.

LYNDON Lyndon Baines Johnson, thirty-sixth president of the United States.

LYNK Left-handed (Old English).

LYUBOV Lyubov Yegorova of Russia won nine Olympic medals for cross-country skiing in the 1992 and 1994 games.

M

MA BARKER Leader of a gang of Doberman Pinchers that attempts a bank heist in the 1972 film *the Doberman Gang.*

MA GERTRUDE "Ma" Rainey (1886–1939), the "Mother of Blues" and the earliest known blues performer and recording artist. Powerful, dynamic, and thrilling, she was known for her "moaning"—notably on "Deep Moaning Blues." She recorded with Louis Armstrong, among others.

MAALIK Experienced (African).

MABEL Loveable (Latin).

MABWS *See* Lloyd.

MAC Son of (Gaelic). One of the Siberian Huskies in the 2002 Disney feature film *Snow Dogs.*

MACBETH *The Tragedy of Macbeth*, commonly called *Macbeth*, is Shakespeare's shortest tragedy and was first performed at the Globe Theatre in 1611. Although some of the greatest actors in history have played Macbeth and Lady Macbeth, two of Shakespeare's most complex characters, many believe the play is cursed and therefore will only ever refer to it as "the Scottish play."

MACHIAVELLI Niccolò di Bernardo dei Machiavelli (1469–1527), Italian Renaissance historian, philosopher, and humanist whose *The Prince* (*Il Principe*, 1513) is universally considered the first work of modern political philosophy. His name became the basis of the word *Machiavellian*, which, according to the Oxford English Dictionary, means "the employment of cunning and duplicity in statecraft or in general conduct." In short, anything goes.

MACHIKO Fortunate one (Japanese).

MACKINTOSH Aunt Agatha's West Highland Terrier in P. G. Wodehouse's series of humorous Jeeves & Wooster novels

MCINTOSH Michael McIntosh (1945–2010), well-known American outdoor writer, author of twenty-nine books, avid wing shooter and fly fisherman, staunch friend who loved dogs, Scotch, women, and the woods in autumn.

MACMILLAN Commander Donald B. MacMillan, famous explorer who drove a team of Eskimo dogs one hundred miles in eighteen hours at a speed sometimes in excess of twenty miles per hour.

MACNAMARA Captain Macnamara had a Newfoundland that protected him in an 1803 "Incident in Hyde Park," a poem by Edmund Blunden.

MACTAVISH A fitting name for a feisty, affectionate, and smart Scottish Terrier such as mine.

MADAME French polite title for a married woman.

MADAME AUGOT Hector and Mouche, the Wirehaired Pointing Griffons that established the breed. Their daughter was Madame Augot.

MADAME CURIE Maria Skłodowska-Curie (1867–1934), Polish physicist and chemist, was the only woman, and one of only four individuals, awarded two Nobel Prizes: for Physics in 1903 and for Chemistry in 1911.

MADAME DE POMPADOUR (1721–1764), "official" chief mistress of King Louis XV of France. She owned two Papillons, **Inez** and **Mimi**.

MADDY Rough Collie belonging to the Duke of Gordon, foundation dam of his line of Gordon Setters.

MADEMOISELLE French polite title for an unmarried woman.

MADGIE A dog in Gogol's *Diary of a Madman*.

MADISON Labrador Retriever that played Vincent on the ABC television series *Lost*.

MADRA Dog (Irish).

MAEKO Truthful child (Japanese).

MAEMI Honest child (Japanese).

MAESTRO Reverent appellation for a master teacher, professor, or conductor of western classical music and opera.

MAETERLINCK Maurice Polydore Marie Bernard Maeterlinck (1862–1949), Belgian playwright, poet, and 1911 winner of the Nobel Prize in Literature. He wrote affectionately about the Belgian Sheepdog in his short story "Our Friend the Dog."

MAFALDA Mighty in battle (Italian).

MAGENTA Purplish-red color and a popular Crayola crayon.

MAGGIE A Japanese Chin in Ozzy and Sharon Osbourne's canine family. Canine actor in the 2001 movie *Cats & Dogs*.

MAGIC Magic Slim (b. 1937), American blues guitarist and vocalist. He lost his little finger in a cotton gin accident but that hasn't stopped Mississippi-born Morris Holt from playing a soulful blues guitar and making magic with songs like "Going to Mississippi" and "I'm a Bluesman."

MAGNOLIA "Nobility, lover of nature" in the language of flowers. Beautiful name for any white dog.

MAGNUM *Magnum in parvo*, Latin for "much in little" is often used to describe the big personality of the little Brussels Griffon, a Toy breed.

MAGWITCH Abel Magwitch, convict turned successful sheepherder and Pip's benefactor who turns out to be Estella's father in Charles Dickens's classic novel *Great Expectations. See* Pip.

MAHARI Forgiver (African).

MAHINA Moon (Hawaiian).

MAI TAI A rum-based alcoholic cocktail served in glasses adorned with little umbrellas and orchids and exotic stuff like that.

MAI Brightness (Japanese).

MAI'A Banana (Hawaiian).

MAIDA Beloved deerhound of Sir Walter Scott, who called her "the most perfect creature of Heaven."

MAINTENON *See* Dauphin.

MAISIE First in a series of ten films from 1939 to 1947 that starred American actress Ann Sothern as a young, adventurous woman who always finds trouble.

MAISON The Schipperke has often been referred to as "*le meilleur chien de maison*"—that's French for "the best house dog."

MAJESTY Greatness (Latin, from *maiestas*). Royal term for Her Majesty Elizabeth, Queen of England, abbreviated "H.M."

MAJOR Rank of a commissioned military officer.

MAJORA President Franklin Delano Roosevelt's German Shepherd.

MAKENNA Gift of God (Hawaiian).

MAKO Genus of mackerel sharks in the *Lamnidae* family, which also includes the Great White shark.

MAKOTO Sincere, honest (Japanese).

MALCHIK A mongrel stray that made its home in a Moscow railroad station and endeared himself to the commuters. He was brutally killed, inciting enormous public outrage and grief.

MALCOLM There were four kings of Scotland with this name, who reigned between 943 and 1165. Regal name for a Scottish Deerhound.

MALCOME The West Highland Terrier originated at the estate of Captain E. D. Malcome in Poltallock, Scotland, from dogs descended from the kennels of King James I of England.

MALIBU Twenty-one-mile-long oceanfront community in Los Angeles that includes some of the priciest real estate in the world.

MALINES The town in Belgium where the Malinois variety of Belgian Sheepdog originated. The Malinois has a short, brindle coat.

MALLARD Wild species of waterfowl called a dabbling duck. Swell name for water dogs such as the Labrador Retriever, Chesapeake Bay Retriever, and Nova Scotia Duck Tolling Retriever.

MALLOW "Sweetness" in the language of flowers.

MALMESBURY *See* Earl.

MALO Winner (Hawaiian).

MALTA The Maltese is known as "Ye Ancient Dogge of Malta," and for more than twenty-nine centuries has been considered one of the aristocrats of the canine world.

MALYSKA Soviet space dog.

MAMELO Patience (African).

MAMIE Mamie Eisenhower (1896–1979), wife of President Dwight D. Eisenhower and First Lady of the United States from 1953 to 1961. Affectionate name for **Mary**.

MAMMY Scarlett O'Hara's indispensible, devoted, fussy nanny in *Gone with the Wind*.

MAN RAY Weimaraner owned by photographer William Wegman, who used his dogs as the subject of many of his works.

MANA Power, authority (Spanish, Hawaiian).

MANCHU Black Pekingese given as a gift to Alice Roosevelt, daughter of President Theodore Roosevelt, by the last Empress of China.

MANCS Male German Shepherd rescue dog working with the Spider Special Rescue Team of Miskolc, Hungary. Mancs had the remarkable ability to locate buried earthquake victims; he was sent around the world on rescue missions.

MANDRAKE Used in pagan rituals at least a century before the birth of Christ. Legend says when a mandrake root is uprooted, it will kill any who hears its awful cry. Titus Flavius Josephus (AD 37–100), a first-century Romano-Jewish historian, wrote detailed instructions on how to properly do it: "A furrow must be dug around the root until its lower part is exposed, then a dog is tied to it, after which the person tying the dog must get away. The dog then endeavours to follow him, and so easily pulls up the root, but dies suddenly instead of his master. After this the root can be handled without fear." Pomona Sprout, professor of Herbology at Hogwarts School of Witchcraft and Wizardry, knew just how to handle a mandrake root in J. K. Rowling's Harry Potter series.

MANDY Another one of Tonka's Pound Puppies.

MANFRED Mighty Manfred the Wonder Dog, Tom Terrific's companion on *Captain Kangaroo*, the longest-running children's television show of its day, which ran from 1955 to 1984.

MANFREDO Strong peace (Italian).

MANG A bat in *The Jungle Book*, by Rudyard Kipling.

MANGO Sweet, fleshy tropical fruit.

MANLIO Morning (Italian).

MANNERS Polite conduct.

MANSELL *See* Noailles.

MANTON Joseph Manton, innovative nineteenth-century British gunmaker credited with inventing the modern sporting shotgun.

MANU Bird (Hawaiian); second born (African).

MANXOME Fearsome, manly (Manx).

MAPLE Deciduous shade tree that can grow up to 145 feet tall. King of the New England woods, its five-point leaves turn bright red in autumn. Sugar maple trees are tapped in the early spring. The sap is collected and, when boiled, thickens into maple syrup. It takes forty liters of sap to make one liter of syrup. This is the right name for a dog with a maple-colored coat, such as a Rhodesian Ridgeback.

MARASCHINO Bright red, sweet cherries used in cocktails and in baking. Bittersweet, clear liqueur made from Marasca cherries.

MARCELLA Of the sea (Italian).

MARCO POLO (AD 1254–1324), Venetian merchant who recorded his travels in *Il Milione*, in which he describes his adventures in the unchartered Far East. Marco Polo was the first European to open trade between Europe and the Far East.

MARCUS *See* Issa.

MAREA Erigone's dog who helped her find her father in Greek mythology.

The magazine cover that launched a career. The magazine wanted to photograph this cute puppy and needed a little girl—but it was the little girl that got the attention and launched the career of child actor Margaret O'Brien in 1941. Photo courtesy of Miss Margaret O'Brien.

MARGARET Margaret O'Brien (b. 1937), Oscar-winning actress best known for the films she made during her childhood. *The Canterville Ghost, A Journey for Margaret, Jane Eyre, The Secret Garden, Our Vines Have Tender Grapes,* and *Little Women* are among the forty films in which Miss O'Brien starred—twelve made during World War Two. She received an Academy Juvenile Award as Outstanding Child Actress of 1944 for her role as Judy Garland's sister, Tootie, in the classic MGM musical, *Meet Me in St. Louis* (1944). Miss O'Brien was five years old when she began her extraordinary career. Her films continue to enthrall audiences of all ages and around the world.

MARGHERITA Pearl (Italian).

MARIA My beloved (Egyptian). Also a female given name in Mexican, African, Arab, Armenian, Bulgarian, Catalan, Croatian, English, German, Greek, Italian, Maltese, Norwegian, Polish, Portuguese, Russian, Romanian, Pakistani, Afghan, Serbian, Swedish, and Spanish.

MARIUS Roman name for the mother of Jesus Christ. In Hebrew it is **Miriam**.

MARIBEL Bitter, sour (Hebrew).

MARIBELLA Character in the kingdom of *The Wonderful Wizard of Oz*, by L. Frank Baum.

MARIE ANTOINETTE (1755–1793), Queen of France who was beheaded with her husband, Louis XV, in the French Revolution, but not before she purportedly proclaimed, "Let them eat cake."

MARIE LOUISE *See* Flanders.

MARIELLA Obstinate, rebellious (Italian).

MARIETTA Little rebel (Italian).

MARIGOLD "Sorrow" in the language of flowers. Pretty name nonetheless for a dog with a yellow coat.

MARIKO Circle (Japanese).

MARIT METTE Harrison's Black Lab in *The Princess and the Hound*.

MARJETTA *See* Dog Names by Category: Breed; Westminster.

MARJORAM "Joy" in the language of flowers.

MARJORIBANKS *See* Dudley.

MARK Consecrated to the god of Mars (Latin).

MARLENE Beloved (Germanic). Female given name derived from **Magdelene**.

MARLEY Loveable, practically untrainable yellow Labrador Retriever in the 2005 *New York Times* best-seller *Marley & Me: Life and Love with the World's Worst Dog.*

MARLIN Large game fish with a spearlike bill that can reach up to sixteen feet in length and weigh 1,500 pounds.

MARLOWE Author Stephen King's Pembroke Welsh Corgi, believed to be his inspiration for Oy in his fantasy series *The Dark Tower.*

MARMADUKE Great Dane in Brad Anderson's comic strip of the same name that spun off a movie with talented American actor Owen Wilson as the voice of Marmaduke.

MARMALADE Fruit preserve made from oranges. Good name for a dog with orange markings or an orangey-gold coat.

MARMIE The brave, devoted mother who holds the family together in Louisa May Alcott's beloved novel set in the time of the American Civil War, *Little Women.*

MARPLE Agatha Christie's detective Miss Marple, the elderly spinster whose extensive knowledge of human nature comes from closely observing life in her small English village.

MARQUIS *See* Lafayette.

MARSHALL Horse, servant (Old French).

MARSHMALLOW White, puffy confection impaled on a stick and roasted over a campfire.

MARTA Lady, mistress (Italian).

MARTHA Dog in the 2008 PBS children's animated series *Martha Speaks*, based on the nineties books by Susan Meddaugh. Paul McCartney's dog, said to have inspired the Beatles' "Martha My Dear."

MARTIN Martin Van Buren, eighth president of the United States.

Martini A popular vodka cocktail that James Bond orders shaken, not stirred.

Mary Mary Cassatt (1845–1926), celebrated American painter known for her paintings of children and mothers. Cassatt had no children. She chose to remain unmarried, commenting that marriage would not conform to her chosen lifestyle.

Maryscot *See* Dog Names by Category: Breed; Westminster.

Marzipan A confection made with sugar and almond meal. Adorable name for a French Bulldog.

Masako Justice (Japanese).

Maso Twin (Italian).

Mason Along with Dakota, two nearly identical Rough Collies that played *Lassie* in the 2006 remake of the movie classic; dog in the 2003 Jerry Bruckheimer action comedy *Bad Boys II*.

Massimo Greatest (Italian).

Master McGrath Champion Irish Greyhound that was granted an audience with the British Royal Family.

Master The Masters of Foxhounds Association of England dates to before the year 1800.

Matabele *See* Lobengula.

Matador Spanish bullfighter.

Mate Chum, buddy.

Matilda Children's book by Welsh writer Roald Dahl, published in 1988.

Matin Matin de Terceira is a breed of dog from the Azores that is related to the Boxer.

MATISSE Henri-Émile-Benoît Matisse (1869–1954), French painter and student of English painter J. M. W. Turner. Border Collie in the 1986 Disney comedy *Down and Out in Beverly Hills,* starring Bette Midler, Richard Dreyfuss, and Nick Nolte.

MATSU Pine (Japanese).

MATT Matt Biondi of the United States won eleven Olympic medals for swimming from 1984 to 1992.

MATTEO Gift of God (Italian).

MATTHIAS Matthias I, who ruled Hungary from 1458 until 1490, always traveled in the company of at least one Kuvasz dog. His kennels at Siebenbürgen were the most impressive in Europe.

MATTI Earth in Telugu, a primary language of India.

MATZOBALL Comic actor Adam Sandler's late dog. Babu followed.

MAUD Maud Earl (1864–1943), noted British-American painter whose dog paintings are among the most valued by fine art collectors.

MAUI A Border Collie mix played by a canine actor named Murray in the Paul Reiser and Helen Hunt NBC sitcom *Mad About You* (1992–1999). Second largest island in the Hawaiian chain.

MAUNA KEA White mountain (Hawaiian). Volcano on the island of Hawaii.

MAUPIN General Maupin got a Beagle from East Tennessee called Tennessee Lead, which he bred with an English Hound imported from England to produce the Walker Hound.

MAURA Dark-skinned, Moorish (Italian). **Maurice** is the male version; also **Mauro**.

MAVERICK A rebel, nonconformist.

MAX The Grinch's devoted dog in Dr. Seuss's *How the Grinch Stole Christmas!* Jim Carrey's faithful Jack Russell Terrier in *The Mask* (1994), played in real life by a dog named **Milo**.

MAX GOOF Son of Disney's goofy dog Goofy.

MAXIM Maxim de Winter, Rebecca's tormented husband in Daphne du Maurier's psychological thriller *Rebecca*.

MAY Fifth month of the year according to the Gregorian calendar and female given name. Also spelled **Mae**.

MAYA Mother, precious one, great woman (Old English).

MAZATLAN Place of origin of the Mexican Hairless breed of dog.

MAZURKA Fast-paced, lively folk dance.

MBWA Dog (Swahili).

McBARKER Angesis McBarker, Mr. Magoo's dog in the 1970 animated television series *What's New, Mr. Magoo*.

McCARTHY *See* Justin.

McGONAGALL Professor Minerva McGonagall, headmistress of Hogwarts School of Witchcraft and Wizardry in the Harry Potter series, played in the movie adaptations by one of England's great actresses, Dame Maggie Smith.

McGRUFF McGruff the Crime Dog was a cartoon Bloodhound in the 1980 ad campaign for the National Crime Prevention Council. His slogan was "Take a bite out of crime."

McKINLEY William McKinley, twenty-fifth president of the United States. Assassinated in his second term, he was succeeded by Theodore Roosevelt.

MEA'ONO Cookie (Hawaiian).

MEADOW Field of grass, land upon which cows and horses graze.

MECHLINBURG The marketplace in Mechlinburg, Germany, has a statue of a hunter with a Schnauzer crouched at his feet. Schnauzers were used to guard farm carts in German marketplaces.

MEDDLE *"Wha Daur Meddle Wi' Me,"* the motto of the Skye Terrier Club of Scotland.

MEEKA Beautiful fragrance (Japanese).

MONS MEG Huge medieval cannon made in 1449 and still standing at Edinburgh Castle, Scotland.

MEGARGEE *See* Bixby.

MEGGIE The Scottish Terrier that Franklin and Eleanor Roosevelt owned when they first moved into the White House. It is said that Meggie bit a senator, and Roosevelt granted his dog a presidential pardon.

MEHITIBEL Alley cat in humorist Don Marquis's long-running newspaper column, *Archy and Mehitibel.* She believed she was Cleopatra reincarnated.

MEKA Eyes (Hawaiian).

MEL "Peerless Mel" Sheppard of the United States won five Olympic medals in the 1908 and 1912 games, four gold, in the men's 800- and 1,500-meter relays.

MELANIA Black, dark (Italian).

MELANIE Melanie Hamilton Wilkes, Ashley Wilkes's compassionate, emotionally strong but physically fragile wife in *Gone with the Wind,* by Margaret Mitchell, who received the Pulitzer Prize for Literature in 1937 for her epic book of the American South at the time of the Civil War. In the movie, Melanie was played by Academy Award–winning actress Olivia de Havilland.

MELI Honey (Hawaiian).

MELLOW Warm, rich, smooth.

MELODY Musical theme of a song or composition.

MELON Sweet fruit with a hard rind.

MELTON *See* Otho.

MEMPHIS It is believed that Afghan Hounds were sent to Memphis as gifts to the pharaohs.

MENTHON Saint Bernard of Menthon, first established breeder of the Saint Bernard, after whom the breed is named.

MERCEDES German luxury car manufacturer and maker of trucks, founded in 1926, a leader in the automotive industry.

MERCHANT A trader or seller of goods.

MEREDITH Sea lord (Welsh, from *meredydd*).

MERIADOC Meriadoc Brandybuck. *See* Hobbit.

MERLE Mottled-colored coat of a dog.

MERLIN Legendary wizard in Arthurian legend.

MERLYN Another of the dogs in Sir Ector's kennels in T. H. White's *The Once and Future King* (1958).

MERMAN *See* Dog Names by Category: Breed; Crufts.

MERRIWETHER A character in *Gone with the Wind.*

MERRY A term of affection for the Cocker Spaniel breed is the "the merry cocker."

MERYL Meryl Streep (b. 1949), American stage and screen actress, and three-time Academy Award winner for Best Actress. A classy lady in a class all her own.

MESRODIA *See* Aibe.

MESSENGER Irish Terriers were important war dogs in World War One. Lieutenant Colonel E. H. Richardson, commander of the War-Dog

School wrote, "I can say with decided emphasis that the Irish Terriers of the service more than did their part. Many a soldier is alive today through the effort of one of these very Terriers."

METRO Abbreviation for metropolitan—not a bad name for a city dog.

METTE Common female name in Norway.

MEX First canine mascot of the University of Oklahoma.

MHINA Joyful (African).

MIA Mine (Italian, Spanish).

MICAWBER One of Charles Dickens's most colorful characters, Wilkins Micawber, who is facing debtors' prison, advises the young David Copperfield: "Annual income twenty pounds, annual expenditure nineteen pounds nineteen and six, result happiness. Annual income twenty pounds, annual expenditure twenty pounds ought and six, result misery." It is advice Mr. Micawber never takes himself—and advice we all would be better served if we did.

MICHAEL "Who is like God?" (Hebrew)

MICHELANGELO Saint Bernard Dog Beethoven's twin in *Beethoven's 4th*, a canine spoof of Mark Twain's humorous *The Prince and the Pauper*.

MICHELLE Michelle Kwan of the United States, the woman figure skater with the most medals: five world titles (1996–2003), a record nine US championships, a silver medal at the 1998 Nagano Olympics, and a bronze at the 2002 Salt Lake City Olympic Games. Her signature move is her change-of-edge spiral.

MICHI Righteous way (Japanese).

MICHIKO Beauty, wisdom (Japanese).

MICK THE MILLER The first Greyhound to run a 525-yard course in under thirty seconds.

MICKEY Mickey Mouse was created by Walt Disney and first appeared in the early cartoon short "Steamboat Willie"—one of the first with synchronized sound—in 1928. Walt founded an empire upon the shoulders of that little mouse.

MIDA Bouldogue du Mida, relation of the Boxer from the south of France.

MIDAS King in Greek mythology with the golden touch that proved to be a double-edged sword. Great name for a dog with a gold-colored coat.

MIDGET Of short stature; a cute name for a Dachshund.

MIDNA Character in the Nintendo game *The Legend of Zelda: Twilight Princess*.

MIDNIGHT Middle of the night, twelve o'clock p.m. Marvelous name for a black dog.

MIDORI Green (Japanese).

MIEKO Already prosperous (Japanese).

MIGHTY The Lhasa Apso was "kept in the homes of the mighty."

MIGNON Lisa Douglas's Yorkshire Terrier on the 1965 CBS sitcom *Green Acres*, starring Eddie Albert and Eva Gabor.

MIKADO Gilbert and Sullivan operetta. Great name for a Japanese Chin.

MIKE President Harry S. Truman's dog.

MIKI Flower stalk (Japanese).

MIKIE Active (Hawaiian).

MIKLÓS Nicholas (Greek).

MILDRED Shasta Fay Hepworth's dog in Thomas Pynchon's novel *Inherent Vice*.

MILES Soldier (Latin).

MILIANI Gentle caress (Hawaiian).

MILKY Milky Way, constellation of stars in the night sky. Good name for a dog with a coat the color of milk.

MILLARD Millard Fillmore, thirteenth president of the United States.

MILLICENT Strength (Germanic).

MILLIE George and Barbara Bush's Springer Spaniel. *See* Dog Names by Category: History.

MILNE A. A. Milne (1882–1956), prolific English writer best known for his ageless bear, Winnie-the-Pooh.

MIMI *See* Madame de Pompadour.

MIMOSA "Secret love" in the language of flowers; see Ah Cum.

MIMSY King George VI's yellow Labrador Retriever.

MINA South (Japanese). British composer Sir Edward Elgar's Cairn Terrier, for whom he named his final orchestral work.

MINERVA Virgin Roman goddess of poetry, medicine, wisdom, commerce, weaving, crafts, and magic and the inventor of music. Some busy lady.

MING Ruling dynasty in China from 1368 to 1644. Regal name for a Chinese breed of dog.

MINI Miniature, tiny. What better name for a toy breed?

MINIUS A crossbreed dog from Poland that lived to be over twenty-six years old.

MINIVER *Mrs. Miniver*, the 1942 wartime movie nominated for twelve Academy Awards (winning six, including Best Picture, Greer Garson for Best Actress, and William Wyler for Best Director) was based on a series of semiautobiographical newspaper columns by Jan Struther (the pen name of Joyce Anstruther) about "an ordinary sort of woman who leads an ordinary sort of life."

MINKAH Justice (African).

MINKE Treasured possession, very own (Old English).

MINNIE Minnie Mouse, Mickey's paramour in the universe of Disney.

MINOR Canis Minor, the "Little Dog" in the constellation Orion.

MINSTREL Troubadour, singer.

MINUS Poko's pet dog in the Canadian animated TV series *Poko*.

MIRABELLE Boston Terrier in the children's book *The Adventures of Mirabelle*.

MIRACLE Something, someone, or a happening that is full of wonder. If you've a dog that's come to you in a wonderful way, call her Miracle.

MIRANDA Yorkie-Poodle mix that was abandoned by her snobby owner because "she didn't match the drapes" on the PBS children's cartoon series, *Martha Speaks*.

MIRELLA To admire (Italian).

MIRÓ Joan Miró (1893–1983), Spanish Surrealist painter and sculptor and contemporary of Picasso who declared an "assassination of painting" by upsetting the visual elements of art with a complex arrangement of stylized objects.

MISCHA Diminutive of **Mikhael**, which is **Michael**, in Russian.

MISO Japanese seasoning produced from fermented beans and rice. Good name for a Japanese Chin.

MISS BEASLEY President George W. Bush's family dog.

MISS HUD Actor Matthew McConaughey's Labrador Retriever–Chow mixed-breed canine companion for twelve years.

MISS LEMON Poirot's meticulous secretary in Agatha Christie's Hercule Poirot mysteries.

MISS PIGGY Kermit's paramour and Muppet diva who swings a hard right hook and sings flat.

MISSE A Whippet presented to King Louis XV of France.

MISSIS One of the Dalmatians in *The Hundred and One Dalmatians*, by Dodie Smith, which inspired the Walt Disney feature films.

MISSISSIPPI The longest river in the continental United States.

MISSY Beethoven's girlfriend in *Beethoven's 2nd*.

MISTER Mister Peabody of "Mister Peabody's Improbable History," a segment in the animated *Rocky and Bullwinkle* cartoon show televised in the fifties and sixties.

MISTY A puppy from Liberty's litter that President Richard M. Nixon's family kept for themselves.

MISTY ISLE Romantic name for the Isle of Skye, home of the Cairn Terrier.

MITCH Short for Mitchell.

MITCHELL *Gone with the Wind*, Margaret Mitchell's unparalleled novel about the impact of the Civil War on life in the South was published in 1936. Tragically, Mitchell, who won the Pulitzer Prize for her breathtaking book, was struck and killed by a speeding car in 1939. Katie Scarlett O'Hara Hamilton Kennedy Butler, called Scarlett, is the story's protagonist. She married Charles Hamilton, Frank Kennedy, and the dashing Captain Rhett K. Butler but secretly pined for the Ashley Wilkes, who is married to Melanie Wilkes, sister of Scarlett's vapid first husband. Unlike the movie, Scarlett has three children in the book, one by each husband. Among the colorful minor characters are Aunt Pittypat Hamilton, Melanie and Charles Hamilton's fluttery spinster aunt; Mammy, Scarlett's beloved and domineering nanny since birth; Mrs. Merriwether, Aunt Pittypat's friend and fellow gossip; and Big Sam, the strong, hardworking field slave from Tara who saves Scarlett's life.

MITE *See* Dog Names by Category: Breed; Crufts.

MITHE Greyhound in *Chroniques*, by Jean Froissart.

MITSUO Mitsuo Tsukahara of Japan won nine Olympic medals in gymnastics in games held from 1968 to 1976.

MITZY Grandma had a Miniature Poodle named Mitsy.

MIYA Sacred house (Japanese).

MIYOKO Beautiful child (Japanese).

MOBRAY *See* Otho.

MOCHA Coffee beverage that's a bit milkier than caffe latte, made up of one third espresso, two thirds steamed milk, and a wallop of chocolate. It's all in the milk. Got chocolate Lab?

MODENA *See* Beatrice.

MODESTO Sober (Italian).

MOE Dark-skinned (Roman). Short for **Morris**, derived from the Ancient Roman name **Maurus**. Short, sweet name for a dog with a brown or black coat.

MOHAWK Haircut named after the people of the Mohawk nation in which the head is short or shaven, leaving a longer center strip from the brow to the nape of the neck. American GIs, notably the 101st Airborne Division during World War Two, adopted the hairstyle of the fierce, fighting Mohicans. Mohawk or Mohican would be an appropriate name for a Rhodesian Ridgeback, which has a strip of fur running along its back.

MOHEGAN "People of the wolf." Algonquin tribe that lived in the Connecticut Valley.

MOIRA Star of the sea (Gaelic).

MOJAVE High desert that encompasses much of southeastern California, as well as parts of Arizona, Utah, and Nevada. Its border is partly outlined by the unstable San Andreas Fault. Sandy, parched, the Mojave incredibly supports 2,000 species of plants. A sandy-colored dog could be called Mohave.

MOLLY Affectionate form of **Moira.**

MOLOSSER Predecessor of the Saint Bernard breed.

MOLOSSUS Original bloodline of the Boxer breed.

MOMBI Wicked Witch of the North who first appears in *The Marvelous Land of Oz*, a sequel of *The Wonderful Wizard of Oz*, by American author L. Frank Baum.

MON AMI My friend, my dear (French).

MON PETITE My little one (French).

MONA LISA Mona Lisa, familiar name for *La Gioconda*, Portrait of Lisa Gherardini, wife of Francesco del Giocondo, the most famous portrait in existence, painted by the Italian artist Leonardo da Vinci sometime between 1503 and1519. It hangs in the Louvre in Paris. If you can't make out what your dog is thinking, perhaps you should name her Mona Lisa.

MONARCH Mastiff out of Wynn's Norah, owned by English breeder M. B. Wynn, who wrote the early standards of the breed in the mid-1800s.

MONARQUE Clonmel Monarque, son of Ch. Warland Whatnot, an Airedale Terrier.

MONDRIAN (1872–1944) Pieter Cornelius Mondrian, a Dutch painter who spearheaded the De Stijl ("the Style") movement of nonrepresentational abstract art known as "Neo-Plasticism." If you have a Drentsche Patrijshond (Dutch Partridge Dog), Mondrian is just the name.

MONEKE *See* Monkey.

MONGOL The Russian Wolfhound was known to Genghis Khan in the thirteenth century.

MONICA Advisor (Latin, from *moneo*).

MONKEY FACE "Monkey Face" was the affectionate name Cary Grant gave Joan Fontaine in the 1941 Alfred Hitchcock suspense thriller *Suspicion*, for which Miss Fontaine won a Best Actress Academy Award.

MONKEY A primate whose name may have originated from Moneke. Son of Martin the Ape in the sixteenth-century European fable called "Reynard the Fox."

MONROE James Monroe, fifth president of the United States.

MONS LANE Mons Lane of Franqueville near Boos, one of the largest breeders of Basset Hounds in France.

MONSIEUR Mister (French).

MONSON *See* Calgary.

MONT BLANC Switzerland's "white mountain."

MONTAGNES Le Grand Chien des Montagnes, or Le Chien des Pyrenees—French names for the Great Pyrenees, known in England as the Pyrenean Mountain Dog.

MONTE Long-haired Chihuahua voiced by Opera tenor Placido Domingo in the 2008 Disney film *Beverly Hills Chihuahua*.

MONTEZUMA King of the Aztecs who figures in the history of the Chihuahua dogs. Big name for such a little dog.

MONTGOMERY Gumarich's mountain (Norman).

MONTIETH *See* Laird.

MONTMORENCY Dog in Jerome K. Jerome's *Three Men in a Boat*.

MONTRAVIA *See* Dog Names by Category: Breed; Crufts.

MONTY Diminutive of **Montgomery**.

MOONBEAN Light from the moon.

MOONHILL *See* Dog Names by Category: Breed; Crufts.

MOONIE Chihuahua canine actor that played Reese Witherspoon's dog Bruiser in both *Legally Blonde* and *Legally Blonde 2*.

MOONLIGHT Perfect name for a hound that brays to the moon at night.

MOONSHADOW Nice name for a dog with a black and some white in his coat, such as a Border Collie.

MOONSTONE *The Moonstone*, by English writer Wilkie Collins, written in 1868, is considered the first mystery novel written in the English language.

MOORE Dr. Bond Moore of Wolverhampton is considered the man most responsible for developing the standard for the Flat-Coated Retriever.

MOOSE Jack Russell Terrier that starred interchangeably with his son, Enzo, in the 2000 film *My Dog Skip*, based on the 1995 Willie Morris memoir, in which Skip was actually a Fox Terrier.

MOP The pure strain of English Springer Spaniel was bred in 1812 by the Boughley family of Aqualate, Shropshire, England, from the breed's foundation dog, Mop.

MOPSY Flopsy, Mopsy, and Cottontail, children of Mrs. Josephine Rabbit and siblings of Peter in Beatrix Potter's timeless 1902 children's story *The Tale of Peter Rabbit*.

MOR An Indian peafowl in *The Jungle Book*, by Rudyard Kipling.

MORDRED Sir Mordred the Traitor, knight of King Arthur's legendary Round Table.

MORGAN Traditional Welsh name derived from the words *mor* for "sea" and *cant* for "circle."

MORGOTH Dark Lord in J. R. R. Tolkien's Middle Earth legendarium.

MORIARTY Professor Moriarty, nemesis of Sherlock Holmes and criminal mastermind, who challenges, the celebrated nineteenth-century detective created by Sir Arthur Conan Doyle.

MOROCCO Constitutional monarchy in North Africa whose national symbol is the Barbary Lion. Morocco's largest city is Casablanca, setting of the 1942 *film noir* starring Humphrey Bogart and Ingrid Bergman.

MORRIS Morris Motor Company, a British automotive manufacturer founded in 1910 by bicycle manufacturer William Morris. Such marvelous little cars!

MORRISON J. B. Morrison drew up the standards for the Scottish Terrier Kennel Club in 1880, which largely remain unchanged to this day. Mr. Morrison of Walham Green and Lady Willoughby de Eresby were early breeders of the Pug in England.

MORSEL A little bit, tidbit.

MORTIMER Mortimer Smith contributed tirelessly to developing the Field Spaniel breed in the early twentieth century.

MOSELEY Jonny Moseley took Olympic gold in the moguls at the 1998 Nagano Games. He was the first Puerto Rican to become a member of the US Ski Team.

MOSES Chihuahua-Yorkie mix who "has the sublime ability and urge to mate with anything that moves" in the 2004 star-studded comedy *Meet the Fockers*.

MOTHER TERESA Newfoundland in the 2005 romantic comedy *Must Like Dogs*, played interchangeably by canine actors Molly and Mabel. Their namesake, Mother Teresa, the Roman Catholic nun and founder of the Missionaries of Calcutta, was beatified by Pope John Paul II in 2003 after her death (in 1997 at the age of eighty-seven) and given the name Blessed Teresa of Calcutta. She was presented with the Nobel Peace Prize in 1979.

MOUCHE A seven-year-old gray and brown Griffon bitch that E. K. Korthals of Holland acquired to establish the Wirehaired Pointing Griffon breed of dog in 1874 from M. G. Armand of Amsterdam, for sixty florins, about twenty-five dollars. Mouche's ancestry was vague. Over the next three years, Korthals purchased **Janus**, **Hector**, **Satan**, **Junon**, and **Banco** to further establish the foundation line of the breed.

MOUNTAIN BOY President Woodrow Wilson's Greyhound.

MOUSE Harry's dog in *The Dresden Files*.

MOUSTACHE Moustache or **Mous** (1799–1812), French Poodle war dog whose courage in the French Revolution and Napoleonic Wars became legend.

MOUTON Dog artist Nelson Arthur Loraine painted a particolored Poodle named Mouton in 1892. The painting is in the collection of the American Kennel Club.

MOWGLI Young jungle boy hero of *The Jungle Book*, by Rudyard Kipling.

MOXIE Spunky, a go-getter. Early popular soda since 1876.

MOZART Wolfgang Amadeus Mozart (1756–1791), a child prodigy, was one of the greatest classical composers of all time, producing more than six hundred works over his very short lifetime. Joseph Haydn, a contemporary of Mozart, wrote that "posterity will not see such a talent again in one hundred years." We're still waiting.

MR. ATLAS Wirehaired Fox Terrier played by Skippy in the 1938 sequel to the classic screwball comedy *Topper*, which, like its sequel, starred Constance Bennett, Roland Young, Billie Burke, but alas, not Cary Grant, who played George Kirby in the original.

MR. BEEFY The talking bulldog in *Little Nicky*, the 2000 comedy starring Adam Sandler.

MR. BONES Stray dog that narrates *Timbuktu*, by Paul Auster.

MR. BUCK *See* Nash.

MR. JAGGERS Pip's trustee who withholds a dark secret until he comes of age in *Great Expectations*, by Charles Dickens.

MR. MAGOO Quincy Magoo, legally blind, wealthy retiree voiced by one of Hollywood's most versatile actors, Jim Backus, best known for his "Locust Valley lockjaw" accent as the millionaire castaway Thurston Howell III on the 1964 television series *Gilligan's Island*.

MR. PEABODY Talking canine genius and history expert in *The Rocky and Bullwinkle Show*.

MR. SMITH Frank Capra's classic 1939 drama *Mr. Smith Goes to Washington*, in which James Stewart, with the help of Jean Arthur, exposes corruption on the floor of the Senate. What a notion . . . and the name, by the way, for Cary Grant and Irene Dunne's Wirehaired Fox Terrier (once again played by Skippy) caught in the midst of divorce between the two of them in the hilarious 1937 comedy *The Awful Truth*, directed by Leo McCarey.

MR. WEENIE Dachshund in the 2006 computer animated film *Open Season 2*.

MR. WHISKERS Canine star of the Disney Channel's 2004 children's animated television series *Brandy and Mr. Whiskers*.

MR. WINKLE "A very small dog of uncertain breed" that has achieved national fame through images captured by her owner, photographer Lara Jo Regan.

MRS. DANVERS Her obsessive devotion to her mistress consumes her in Daphne du Maurier's novel *Rebecca*.

MRS. DINGLEY "Pray steal me not, I'm Mrs. Dingley's, whose heart in this four-footed thing lies." So states the inscription on the dog collar of writer Jonathan Swift's beloved dog.

MRS. JOE Pip's mean and miserable much older sister in *Great Expectations*, by Charles Dickens.

MUDDY Muddy Waters (1915–1983), "the father of Chicago blues," inspired the British music explosion of the sixties and influenced pretty much every blues singer and rocker with songs like "Hoochie Coochie Man" and "I Just Want to Make Love to You." Great name for a water dog with a brown coat, such as a Chesapeake Bay Retriever.

MUFFIN Individual-size breakfast cupcake.

TWO LABRADOR RETRIEVERS ENJOYING THE OUTDOORS

Muffy This is, like, a really cute name for, like, a little dog from Southern California, like, by the beach or Rodeo Drive, ya know?

Mugsy Gangster (American slang).

Mugwort "Happiness" in the language of flowers.

Mulberry "Prudence" in the language of flowers.

Mumbles Ancient Roman part of Swansea, Wales.

Munchener Early name of the Schnauzer.

Munchkin The fictional natives of Munchkinland in the *Wizard of Oz*. Some of the fictitious names that would be adorable for little dogs are **Algernon Woodcock, Nimmie Amee, Boq, Jinjur, Ku-Klip, Ojo the Lucky, Queen Orin of the Ozure Isles, Dr. Pipt**, and **Unc Nunkie**.

Mura Village (Japanese).

Murphy Sea Warrior (Gaelic Irish, from *Ó Murchadha*). No name could suit an Irish Water Spaniel better.

Murray Lord and master (Gaelic). Great name for a Scottish Terrier dog. *See* Gordon.

Musa Drawn out of the water (Hebrew).

Muse Goddess that inspires the creation of art and poetry.

Mushka Soviet space dog.

Mushroom The Peltzer family's dog in the 1984 Steven Spielberg horror-comedy *Gremlins*.

Music The elements of sound and rhythm combined to create harmonious compositions.

Mustard Good name for a Vizsla or a dog with a mustard-yellow coat. or a Dachshund, which is affectionately called the "frankfurter dog."

MUTTLEY Dick Dastardly's dog in the Hanna-Barbera animated cartoon *Dastardly and Muttley in Their Flying Machines*, a takeoff on the film *Those Magnificent Men in Their Flying Machines*.

MUTTNICK Soviet space dog.

MYCROFT Mycroft Holmes, Sherlock Holmes's older brother (by seven years) in Sir Arthur Conan Doyle's stories of the greatest detective in fiction (along with Agatha Christie's Hercule Poirot). Of Mycroft, Sherlock said: ". . . he has no ambition and no energy. He will not even go out of his way to verify his own solutions, and would rather be considered wrong than take the trouble to prove himself right."

MYLES Soldier (Latin). Also **Miles**.

MYRNA Myrna Loy (1905–1993), recipient of the 1991 Motion Picture Academy Lifetime Achievement Award and 1988 Kennedy Center Lifetime Achievement Award, the Montana-born American actress is best known as Nora Charles in the *Thin Man* movies with William Powell and based on the Dashiell Hammett books. Loy had a tough act to follow playing opposite Skippy the dog, which was Nick and Nora Charles's dog Asta in the movies.

MYRTLE Myrtle and Lassie, dog artist Sir Edwin Henry Landseer's own dogs. Lassie was his constant companion.

MYSTIC A person who practices the occult.

N

NAASIR Defender (African).

NABER John Naber of the United States won five Olympic medals for swimming in the 1976 games.

NAC Dog (Serbian).

NADIA Hope (African).

NAG Male king cobra in *The Jungle Book*, by Rudyard Kipling.

NAGAINA Female king cobra, Nag's mate, in *The Jungle Book*, by Rudyard Kipling.

NAIROBI Capital and largest city in Kenya.

NAJIB *See* Terhune.

NAMATH *See* Joe Willie.

NAMI Wave (Japanese).

NAN Beautiful (Hawaiian).

NANA Motherly Newfoundland that dotes over the Darling children in *Peter Pan*, by J. M. Barrie.

NANOOK Sam's dog in 1987 teen cult film *The Lost Boys*. Sam was played by the acclaimed Canadian actor and Hollywood teen heartthrob, Corey Haim.

NANSEN A Samoyed sledge dog.

NAPA Lush wine country of Northern California Napa Valley discovered in 1823 by Padre José Altimira, founder of Mission San Francisco Solano in Sonoma.

NAPOLEON Napoleon Bonaparte (1769–1821), French military leader who crowned himself emperor only to be exiled by his people. Ideal name for a small dog with a big personality.

NARCISSUS "Selfishness" in the language of flowers.

NARIKO Thunder (Japanese).

NASA National Aeronautics and Space Administration, established in 1958 to commence American space exploration.

NASH Nash Buckingham (1880–1971), Tennessee-born conservationist, sportsman, and hunting dog enthusiast whose collection of bird-hunting stories, *De Shootinest Gent'man*, remains a hallmark of outdoor literature. He was affectionately known as "Mr. Buck."

NASSOR Victorious (African).

NASTURTIUM "Victorious in battle" in the language of flowers.

NATALE Birthday (Italian).

NATALIE Christmas Day (French).

NATIVIDAD Christmas Day (Spanish).

NAVAJO Good name for a Redbone Coonhound or other American breed.

NAYLOR John Naylor is credited with first introducing the Scottish Terrier to the United States, in 1883.

NEAL The intoxicated Saint Bernard in the television series *Topper*, based on the popular motion picture.

NEBUCHADNEZZAR (634–562 BC), King of the Neo-Babylonian Empire, conqueror of Judah and Jerusalem who sent the Jews into exile, and builder of the Hanging Gardens of Babylon, he was called the "destroyer of nations." Might be just the name for a puppy that destroys your furniture.

NECESSITY *See* Dog Names by Category: Breed; Crufts.

NECKAR Although the Rottweiler is a Roman cattle dog, the breed got its name from Rottweil, in Wurttemberg, a township that sits on the left bank of the Neckar River South of Germany.

NEDO Nedo Nadi of Italy won six Olympic medals in fencing in games held from 1912 to 1920.

NEEDLES Spanish Needle is a yellow flower. Great name for a dog with a rough coat, such as a Wirehaired Pointing Griffon or a Wire Fox Terrier.

NEGASI Royalty (African).

NEGUS Emperor (African); Scottish Terrier belonging to Hitler's mistress and wife of one day, Eva Braun.

NELL Nell III, grandmother of King, an important English Mastiff.

NELLA Hereditary name for a Bouvier des Flandres. *See* Zola.

NELLCOTE Superb name for a French Bulldog. *See* Gamin.

NELLIE Very good name for a Labrador Retriever. *See* Laverack.

NELLO *See* Patrasche.

NEMO Nemo A534, German Shepherd Dog who served in the United States Air Force during the Vietnam War at Tan Son Nhut Air Base, which fell under attack on December 4, 1966. Nemo attacked Viet Cong soldiers, losing one eye and suffering a gunshot wound to the nose before saving the life of his handler, Airman Robert Throneburg.

NOELANI Mist of heaven (Hawaiian).

NEON An inert noble gas. If your pup is the tenth puppy born in a litter, then Neon's a good name for him.

NEOS Neapolitan Mastiff in the Harry Potter series.

NEREZA Darkness (Italian).

NERINA Water (Italian).

NERIO Wet one (Italian). Good name for a water dog.

NERO Scottish satirical writer Thomas Carlyle's dog. Nero died in 1849. Saint Bernard who comes to live with the Wilder family in Laura Ingalls Wilder's *The First Four Years*.

NESSIE Affectionate name for the Loch Ness Monster, a shy aquatic creature said to live in Loch Ness, a long, haunting, mist-shrouded lake in northern Scotland. Too many people have seen Nessie to doubt that she exists.

NETTLE The flower of the nettle is white, which makes this a name to consider for a dog with a white coat. Miss Nettles was Dr. Snuggles's friend on the *Dr. Snuggles* animated television series that aired in 1980, with Sir Peter Ustinov as the voice of Dr. Snuggles.

NEVILLE Neville Longbottom, pureblood Gryffindor student and good friend of Harry Potter who always tries to improve himself, even at the cost of a sense of humor.

NEVINS The dog in the 2003 live-action film adaptation of the Dr. Seuss classic *The Cat in the Hat*, starring Mike Myers as the unstoppable, wise-guy Cat.

NEVIO Spotted (Italian). Great name for a Dalmatian or a dog with spots.

NEW BABY Japanese Chin in Ozzy and Sharon Osbourne's canine family.

NEWCASTLE "Carry coals to Newcastle" means to do something unnecessarily.

NEWS Latest new bulletin, newsflash.

NEWTON Sir Issac Newton (1642–1727), English physicist, mathematician, astronomer, natural philosopher, alchemist, and theologian, one of the most influential scientists in history.

NIBBLES Wee name for a wee dog that takes wee bites from his wee meals.

NIC Ch. Nic de Sottegem, first shown in 1920 at the Olympic Show in Antwerp, did much to revive the Bouvier des Flandres breed after the Great War. Distinguished descendants of Nic, the foundation breed sire, are **Prince D'or**, **Droya**, **Corshe**, **Goliath**, **Lyda**, **Norah**, **Siske**, and **Dragon de la Lys**.

NICHOLAS Saint Nicholas, a true Greek saint, embodies the celebratory spirit of Santa Claus.

NICK Nick Carter, famous man-trailing Bloodhound in the forties.

NICKLEBY *Nicholas Nickleby*, Charles Dickens's third novel written in 1838, about a fine young Englishman who protectively undertakes the care of his mother and sister Kate after the untimely death of his father. This forces the threesome to be uprooted from their comfortable life in Devonshire. They have no choice but to seek the charity of Nicholas and Kate's father's brother, Ralph Nickleby, one of Dickens's most despicable characters, and unless you read the book, you can't imagine all else that happens. So, read the book.

NICO Victor of the people (Italian).

NICOLA Heroine of the people (Italian).

NICOLE Equestrian Nicole Uphoff of Germany won four gold medals in the 19988 and 1992 Olympic Games.

NIETZSCHE Friedrich Nietzsche (1844–1900), German Existentialist who searched for the true meaning of life and the idea of life affirmation in his philosophical writings.

NIGEL Nigel Bruce (1895–1953), British character actor best known as Dr. Watson to Basil Rathbone's Sherlock Holmes, such as *The Voice of Terror* and *The Hound of the Baskervilles* on radio and in movies in the forties and as the Duke of Radling in *Lassie Come Home* (1943) and *Son of Lassie* (1945).

NIGHTHAWK Small nocturnal bird that flies from the late evening to the dawn.

NIGHTINGALE Wild bird also known as the "night songstress" because of its trills, whistles, and warbles.

NIGHTSHADE "Truth" in the language of flowers. Lovely name for a black Labrador Retriever.

NIKKI *Nikki, Wild Dog of the North*, the 1961 Walt Disney family adventure film about a dog's survival in the wilds of the Yukon.

NIKKO Head Flying Monkey of the Wicked Witch of the West's band of flying monkees in *The Wonderful Wizard of Oz*, by L. Frank Baum.

NIKOLAI Victory of the people (Russian). Nickolai Andrianov of the Soviet Union won fifteen Olympic medals in gymnastics from 1972 to 1980.

NILE North-flowing river in Africa, considered the longest river in the world. Running through ten countries, it is 4,130 miles long. Its two major tributaries are the White Nile and the Blue Nile. Historical name for an Afghan Hound. *See* Blackstone.

NIMMIE AMEE Love interest of the Tin Woodman in *The Wonderful Wizard of Oz*, by L. Frank Baum.

NINA God is gracious (Italian). Spanish for *girl*, and **Nino** is the male version, for *boy*.

NIP Nip and **Tuck**, pair of dogs in Damon Runyon's 1937 short story "The Bloodhounds of Broadway."

NIPPER HMV, "His Master's Voice," famous trademark dog of the Gramophone Company, established in 1899.

NISHI West (Japanese).

NITRO Nitroglycerin, active ingredient in the manufacture of explosives such as dynamite.

NIU Coconut (Hawaiian).

NIXE Mermaid or sprite in Germanic legend.

NIXON Richard Milhous Nixon, thirty-seventh president of the United States.

NJAL A great and mighty hound in Celtic legend.

NJORD Norse god of the sea.

NOA Freedom (Hawaiian).

NOAH It is told in Genesis that Noah was instructed by God to build an ark, and to take aboard one male and one female of each species from his kingdom before the rains that would last forty days and forty nights and destroy the heathen of the earth. It is believed the ruins of the ark are atop Mount Ararat in Turkey; indeed, satellite photos confirm the ruins of a structure that resembles such a vessel. One of the canine actors in *Cats & Dogs*.

NOAILLES The Duc de Noailles was believed to have given his kennel of Clumber Spaniels to the Duke of Newcastle at Clumber Park in Nottinghamshire at the outbreak of the French Revolution. The Duke of Newcastle's gamekeeper, William Mansell, is credited with the development and improvement of the breed.

NOBEL Alfred Nobel (1833–1896), inventor of dynamite, who dedicated his enormous fortune to the establishment of the Nobel Prize, the most prestigious of all international honors, awarded in the fields of peace, physics, chemistry, literature, physiology, and medicine.

NOBLE Aristocratic (Latin); distinguished by rank or title.

NOËL Christmas (French).

NOEMI My delight (Italian).

NOIRE Blooming, pleasant, verdant (Old English).

NOME Home of the Borden Cup Race, a sled dog marathon a distance of 26 miles and 385 yards held in Nome, Alaska.

NONA Grandmother (Italian). Roman goddess of pregnancy.

NOODLE Wide strand of spaghetti. If it's wide, it's German; if it's thin, it's Chinese. Noodle is also an affectionate name for someone who has done something silly.

NOP Border Collie, from the novel *Nop's Trials*, by Donald McCaig.

NORAH Ch. Wynn's Norah, dam of Monarch, a champion Mastiff. *See* Monarch.

NORD North (French). M. Fontaine, vice president of the Club Saint Hubert du Nord, invited many noted experts to set the standard of the Bourvier des Flandres at a meeting in August 1912. Among those who attended were M. de Hautvert of Levita, Baron van Zeiglen of Weymons, and M. Van Herreweghe.

NORDIC The blood of the Norwegian Elkhound has remained untainted for over six millennia.

NORMAN Northman (Viking). **Norma** is the feminine version, as in Norma Jean Baker, whom the world knew as Marilyn Monroe. The Harrier is of Norman origin.

NORSK The Norwegian language and the best name for an Norwegian Elkhound.

NORWICH In the fifteenth century, Edward of Norwich, Second Duke of York of England, wrote about the Cocker Spaniel: "Another kind of hound there is that be called hounds for the hawk and spaniels, for their kind cometh from Spain, notwithstanding that there are many in other countries." Obvious name for a Norwich Terrier.

NOSEGAY "Gallantry" in the language of flowers.

NOTTS *See* Dog Names by Category: Breed; Crufts.

NOVA A nuclear explosion in a white dwarf star.

NUGENT Playful Rottweiler in *Over the Hedge*, the 2006 Dreamworks animated family film voiced by Bruce Willis, Garry Shandling, Steve Carell, William Shatner, Wanda Sykes, Nick Nolte, and Avril Lavigne—great voice cast.

NUGGET Tidbit, a little piece. Sweet name for a small dog.

NUGGLE is the Orkney name for the legendary British water horse. A water dog with a smooth coat such as a Labrador Retriever or Chesapeake Bay Retriever could have this name, or a smooth-coated dog, since a Nuggle likewise has a smooth coat like a seal.

NUNZIO Corgi on the television series *Dharma and Greg*.

NURU Born at night (African).

NUTMEG Spice from the Spice Islands of Indonesia that's most often found in custards and apple desserts. The warm brown color would of course make a swell name for a dark brown dog.

O'HARA Mr. O'Hara, Scarlett's father from whom she gets her hot Irish temper in *Gone with the Wind*.

O'NEIL Descendant of a champion (Gaelic). The original O'Neil is believed to be O'Neil, High King of Ireland, in the fifth century.

O'TOOLE Old Irish family that traces its roots to the Celtic Uí Dúnlainge dynasty, which lived in the region known today as County Wicklow.

OAK "Hospitality" in the language of flowers.

OBAMA Barack Obama, forty-fourth president of the United States.

OBI Heart (African).

OBO Ch. Obo, foundation sire of the English Cocker Spaniel. His son, Ch. Obo II, was the foundation sire of the American Cocker Spaniel line.

OCHI Laughter (African).

OCHRE Warm yellow color. Good name for a Golden Retriever.

O'CONNOR Dog in Samuel Beckett's novel *Watt*.

OCTAVIA (69–11 BC) Sister of the first Roman emperor, Augustus, fourth wife of Mark Antony, grandmother of Claudius, and great-great grandmother of Nero, she possessed, it is said, all the true feminine qualities of womanhood—and certainly patience, to have had to put up with that bloody lot.

OCTOBER Tenth month of the year in the Julian calendar. Shortened to Tober, it is an ideal name for a New England bird dog. The late writer Corey Ford had a dog named Tober, his last dog. Tober was given a good home but nonetheless mourned his master terribly—and died on the first anniversary of Ford's death. Ford immortalized Tober in many humor stories, including "My Dog Likes It Here" and "Every Dog Should Have a Man."

ODIE Fictional yellow, brown-eared Beagle in Jim Davis's comic strip *Garfield*. In the two live-action Garfield movies, Odie is portrayed by a Dachshund.

ODIN Bloodhound painted by William Mangford in 1872, one of the most important dogs in the development of the modern breed. Father of the Norse gods who ruled over mortal men. Solid name for a Norwegian Elkhound.

> **ODYSSEUS** Odysseus left behind his devoted dog Argos when he left home for the Trojan War. Homer immortalized Argos in *The Odyssey*: "'This dog,' answered Eumaeus, 'belonged to him who has died in a far country. If he were what he was when Odysseus left for Troy, he would soon show you what he could do. There was not a wild beast in the forest that could get away from him when he was once on its tracks.'" Argos is a superb name for a hunting dog.

OFFICER Good name for a guard dog such as a German Shepherd Dog.

OGIER *See* D'Artagnan.

OH BOY Mrs. Warren G. Harding's English Bulldog.

OHIN Chief (African).

OJO Ojo the Lucky, a Munchkin in *The Wonderful Wizard of Oz*, by L. Frank Baum.

OKI Ocean (Japanese).

OLAF In the tenth century in early Celtic literature, Olaf, a Norwegian prince, said to his friend, Gunnar, in the *Saga of the Burnt Njal*, "I will give thee a hound that was given to me in Ireland; he is big, and no worse than a stout man. Besides, it is part of his nature that he has a man's wit, and he will bay at every man whom he knows to be thy foe, but never at thy friends . . . This hound's name is Sam."

OLD CRAB Foundation sire of the Yorkshire Terrier breed that was mated to a bitch named Kitty.

OLD DAN Red Tick Hound, with Little Ann, in *Where the Red Fern Grows*.

OLD DRUM American Foxhound immortalized by Senator George Graham Vest's "Eulogy to a Dog" (see page xvii).

OLD FRITZ *See* Frederick.

OLD HEMP Early Border Collie that established the breed standard.

OLD JACK Siberian Husky in *Eight Below*.

OLD JOCK Old Jock and **Old Trap**, Smooth-haired English Terriers that lived in the 1860s and are considered the ancestors of the modern Fox Terrier breed.

OLD JOLYON Patriarch of the Forsyte Family in the *Forsyte Saga*, by John Galsworthy.

OLD MOLL *See* Lavarack.

OLD SHEP The Border Collie that observed the coffin of his master loaded onto a train in Fort Benton, Montana, in 1936 and for the next six years until his death, remained at the station awaiting his master's return (a similar story to Hiachi).

OLD TRAP Ancestor of the modern Fox Terrier. *See* Old Jock.

OLD YELLER The yellow mongrel played by a canine actor named Spike, in the 1957 Walt Disney movie of the same name, which starred Fess Parker and Dorothy McGuire.

OLE Ole Einar Bjørndalen of Norway won eleven Olympic medals for the biathlon in the games held from 1998 to 2010.

OLEANDER "Be cautious" in the language of flowers.

OLGA Blessed (Slavic).

OLINA Joyous (Hawaiian).

OLIVE "Peace" in the language of flowers.

OLIVIA Olive tree (Germanic, from *Olaf*). **Oliver** is the masculine version.

OLIVIER Sir Laurence Olivier (1907–1989), one of the greatest English actors of stage and screen, his repertoire was vast, and his Shakespearean performances set the bar for excellence.

OLSEN Ole Liloe-Olsen of Norway won six Olympic medals for shooting in the 1920 and 1924 games.

OLYMPIA Site of the first Olympic Games in 776 BC.

OMARR Long living (African).

OMEGA The twenty-fourth and last letter in the Greek alphabet. An appellation of Jesus Christ, in which it is recorded in Book of Revelation that He states, "I am the Alpha and Omega, the first and the last."

OMELETTE An egg dish that's a meal unto itself. If you love to cook and you have a yellow dog, then Omelette (or **Omelet**) is the perfect name.

OMOREDE Prince (African).

ONSLOW The Fourth Earl of Onslow bought a litter of Basset Hound puppies from Lord Galway in 1867.

ONYX Claw, nail (Greek). A mineral that is usually black in color. Good name for a Flat-Coated Retriever or other black dog.

OPAL Colorful, vibrant semiprecious stone, national gemstone of Australia, and a grand name for an Australian Sheepdog.

OPHELIA Promised in marriage to Prince Hamlet, she is yet another of Shakespeare's tragic women. She drowns. If you name your water dog Ophelia, be sure she's a good swimmer.

ORABELLA Golden, beautiful (Italian).

ORAZIO Keen of vision (Italian).

ORCHID "I care about you" in the language of flowers. The white orchid is one of the most elegant flowers. A beautiful white female Pointer should be called Orchid.

OREO What better name for a black-and-white dog like a Japanese Chin than the name of the black, cream-filled cookie? Nabisco, maker of Oreo Cookies, celebrated the brand's hundredth anniversary in 2012.

ORFORD Ford of cattle (Old English).

ORIENT Rising in the east (Latin). The Three Kings of the Orient followed the Star of the East to Bethlehem.

ORION The great huntsman of Greek mythology. A swell name for a keen hunting dog.

ORLANDO Famous land (Italian).

ORRY Orry and **Dockleaf** were two top Bulldogs that, in 1891, competed against one another in a famous walking race in England. Dockleaf won.

ORSINA Like a bear (Italian). Great name for a Saint Bernard, which is almost as big and certainly as fuzzy as a bear. Orso is the male version of the name and **Orsola** means "little she-bear."

ORSON Black Labrador Retriever in *Seize the Night* and *Fear Nothing*, by Dean Koontz.

ORTHROS Another one of the dogs in Sir Ector's kennels in T. H. White's *The Once and Future King*.

ORTHRUS Orthrus and **Cerberus** were the "Demons of the Pit," also known as the "Hounds of Hades" in Greek mythology.

OSCAR Oscar the Grouch, resident pessimist who lives in a garbage can on PBS Children's Television Workshop's *Sesame Street*.

OSHKOSH President Calvin Coolidge's Rough Collie.

OSMUNDA "To old dear, cherish" in the language of flowers.

OTHELLO Tragic Moor, a general in the Venetian military, in Shakespeare's tragedy of the same name. He and his wife, Desdemona, had a bit of a misunderstanding. Othello and Desdemona would be interesting names if you have a male dog and a female dog, providing you don't care about what happens at the end of *Othello*.

OTHO Captain Otho Paget of Melton Mobray, a nineteenth-century breeder of Beagles, is considered the "dean of all beaglers."

OTIENO Born at night (African).

OTIS Pug in *The Adventures of Milo and Otis*.

OTLEY Good name for an Airedale. *See* Skipton.

OTTER Otter is the obvious name for an Otterhound, a large, rough-coated hound bred to hunt otters, one of the oldest breeds to originate in Great Britain.

OTTO Sargent Snorkel's army dog in *Beetle Bailey*. Terrier cross in the UK that lived to be over twenty-one years old.

OTVAZHNAYA Soviet space dog.

OUIDA Pseudonym of English author Marie Louise de la Ramée. *See* Patrasche.

OUTBACK The Australian frontier, generally referring to vast, unpopulated or hardly populated stretches of land.

OUTLAW Desperado, bandit.

OVID Ovid wrote about the Greyhound in 63 BC.

OWAIN One of King Arthur's Knights of the Round Table.

OWD BOB *See* Tailless Tyke.

OWEN Youth (Welsh).

OWNEY Official United States Postal Service dog.

OXFORD Ancient and famous university in Oxford, England.

OZ Magical land where Dorothy finds true friends, great adventure—yet in the end, realizes "There's no place like home."

OZZY Ozzy Osbourne (b. 1948) British "godfather of heavy metal," lead guitarist of Black Sabbath. Osbourne and his family, who had their own reality television show in America from 2002 to 2005, are devoted dog lovers.

P

PAAVO Paavo Nurmi of Finland won nine gold medals for a total of twelve for track in the Olympic Games held between 1920 to 1928.

PABLO *See* Picasso.

PACO Spanish diminutive masculine name for Francisco.

PADDINGTON The Golden Retriever in Bush's Baked Beans commercials. Paddington Bear, the marmalade sandwich–loving teddy bear was abandoned in Paddington Station, London, and found on Christmas Eve 1956 by the Brown family, who adopted him. Since then, Paddington has delighted children the world over in Michael Bond's books, charmingly illustrated by Peggy Fortnum.

PADDY Irish diminutive of **Patrick**.

PADFOOT Name given to Sirius Black when he transforms into a dog in the Harry Potter series by J. K. Rowling.

PADUA The oldest city in northern Italy, established by a Trojan prince around 1100 BC.

PAGET Young servant (English).

PAIGE Servant (English).

PAINTER Artist who paints with oil paints, watercolor, acrylics, or gouache, any colored medium requiring a brush. *See* Lady Howe.

PAISLEY Largest town in historic Renfrewshire, the center of weaving in Scotland.

PAL The Collie that played Lassie in the 1943 MGM film *Lassie Come Home*, starring Roddy McDowall, based on the novel by Eric Knight. Dog on the PBS animated children's educational series *Arthur*, which first aired in 1996. The Welsh Terrier has been called the "pal for either Town or Country."

PALE Short name for a dog with a pale yellow coat, such as a Great Dane. *The Pale Horse*, a mystery by Agatha Christie.

PALL MALL Ch. Pall Mall His Majesty, established the American breed standard for the Pomeranian.

PALO ALTO President Calvin Coolidge's bird dog.

PALOMA Dove (Spanish). Lovely name for a dog with a gray coat, such as a Weimaraner.

PANAMA Southernmost country of Central America. The Panama Canal, which took ten years to build beginning in 1904, was an American engineering project. It is the "throughway" that connects the Atlantic and Pacific oceans.

PANDA Black-and-white bear that inhabits the mountains of central China. An endangered species, very few have been born in captivity. If you have a black dog with white markings, Panda's the name for her.

PANDORA The first woman, created from a gift given by each of the Greek Gods. She opened a jar (*pithos*, not a box) and all the evils and illnesses of mankind escaped. But Pandora closed the jar before Hope could escape.

PANFILO Friend of all (Italian).

PANINI Italian luncheon sandwich.

PANSY The Mastiff in the *Burke* crime fiction novels by Andrew Vachss. Vachss owns a Pit Bull named Honey.

PANTHER Leopard in Africa and Asia, cougar or Mountain Lion in North America, and jaguar in South America, this is a sleek, fast, and stealthy animal. Good name for a Greyhound.

PANZER Armor (German). *Panzernashorn* means rhinoceros in German. The rhino's armorlike skin inspired the name of the German tank. Armored military forces are called panzer divisions.

PAOLA Small (Italian).

PAPAYA Terrific name to consider of an American Staffordshire Terrier or any sweet dog with an orange coat the color of a papaya.

PAPI Chihuahua voiced by George Lopez in the 2008 Disney film *Beverly Hills Chihuahua*.

PARADISE Place of beauty, heaven.

PARCHEESI American board game adapted from the Indian cross and circle game *Pachisi*.

PARD The crippled mutt in the 1919 silent film *In Wrong*.

PARIS City of romance, capital of France, first settled in 4200 BC, which means people have been drinking fine wine, eating gourmet food, singing, dancing, and making love in Paris for over six millennium.

PARKER Dorothy Parker (1893–1967), American humorist and a founding member of the Algonquin Round Table. Her great wit and enormous success was offset by a tumultuous and tragic life.

PARSIFAL *See* Dog Names by Category: Breed; Westminster.

PARSLEY Green leaf herb used as a garnish, often with potatoes, rice dishes, and essential in homemade Italian meatballs—but it has to be fresh and chopped fine.

PARSON Parson Philip Honeywood of Essex originated the modern breed of Beagle in the mid-nineteenth century.

PARTNER Companion, pal.

PARTRIDGE Partridge Pea is a yellow flower. Good name for a dog with a yellow coat, especially a hunting dog like a yellow Labrador Retriever or a Lemon Belton Setter.

PAS Dog (Croatian).

PASHA President Richard M. Nixon's daughter, Trisha, had a Yorkshire Terrier named Pasha.

PASTEUR Louis Pasteur (1822–1895), French chemist and microbiologist who created the first vaccine for rabies and anthrax, and the pasteurization process for milk.

PASTORIA Rightful King of Oz in *The Wonderful Wizard of Oz*, by L. Frank Baum.

YORKSHIRE TERRIER MOTHER AND PUPPY

PAT First of several Irish Terriers called Pat owned by Canadian Prime Minister William Lyon Mackenzie King. King held séances to communicate with Pat after her death. President Herbert Hoover's German Shepherd Dog. *See* Dog Names by Category: History.

PATCH Plot of land. Spot, piece of fabric, rubber, or other material used to repair a hole or tear. Great name for a dog with patches of color on a solid colored coat, like a Dalmatian. Also **Patches**.

PATCHWORK Patchwork Girl first appears in *The Patchwork Girl* of Oz, a sequel to *The Wonderful Wizard of Oz*, by L. Frank Baum, and later is reunited with the Scarecrow.

PATIENCE Persistent, enduring under difficult circumstances, unflappable. Common woman's name in Victorian times.

PATINA Dog with a silvery coat, such as a Siberian Husky.

PATOU Generic name for the Great Pyrenees. Patou means shepherd in French.

PATRASCHE A novel published in 1872 by English author Marie Louise "Ouida" de la Ramée about a Flemish boy named Nello and his dog Patrasche.

PATRICK President Herbert Hoover's Irish Wolfhound.

PATRIOT Loyal to one's country. Good name for a devoted dog.

PATSY Patsy's, famous Italian restaurant in New York City where Frank Sinatra ate whenever he was in town. One of Frank's favorite dishes was named after him, "Frank's Clams Posillipo."

PATTER From Henry Wadsworth Longfellow's poem, "The Children's Hour"—"I hear in the chamber above me, The patter of little feet, The sound of a door that is opened, And voices soft and sweet."

PATTON General George Patton (1885–1945), Commander of the Western Task Force of the US Army in World War Two. He survived the war but died as a result of a car accident shortly after.

PAUL Paul Cushing Child (1902–1994), an OSS agent who met his wife, Julia McWilliams, during World War Two when they were both stationed in Ceylon. After the war, Child worked for the United States Information Agency, during which time the Childs lived in France, Germany and Norway, returning to the United States in 1955. Extraordinarily supportive of his wife and her consummate love of cooking, Paul was a frequent guest on his wife's television show, *The French Chef*, which first aired in the seventies. Paul and Julia Child were married almost fifty years. Paul Pry, President Calvin Coolidge's Airedale Terrier.

PAULINE Humble (Latin). Feminine version of **Paul**.

PAULO Place of rest (African).

PAVAROTTI Luciano Pavarotti (1935–2007), great Italian operatic tenor who crossed over into popular music and became perhaps the most financially successful opera singer of all time.

PAVLOVA Anna Pavlova (1881–1931), considered the greatest classical ballet dancer in history. If your dog prances, name her Pavlova.

PAWS Such an obvious name for a dog—but nonetheless a catchy one.

PAYNE Payne's Grey is an oil paint color, a dark grey, often used in painting the sky—and therefore a wonderful name for a Skye Terrier.

PCHELKA Soviet space dog. *See* Dog Names by Category: History.

PCHYOLKA Soviet space dog. *See* Dog Names by Category: History.

PEACHES Fuzzy-skinned fruit with a huge pit in the middle. Adorable name for a peach-colored coat.

PEANUT Cute name for a Chihuahua.

PEANUTS Charles M. Schulz's syndicated comic strip, which ran for a half century, from 1950 to 2000, when Schulz died at the age of seventy-seven. But Charlie Brown, his dog Snoopy, and the gang continue to live on in comics, books, and television. Charles Schulz was an important benefactor of Canine Companions for Independence, a nonprofit organization that breeds, trains, and pairs assistance dogs with physically challenged adults and children. His wife, Jean, continues to be an active supporter of the charity (www.cci.org). Margaret O'Brien, one of film's greatest child actors, is an enthusiastic advocate of CCI. She has lent her name to a children's fund, the Margaret O'Brien CCI Children's Initiative, which earmarks funds toward the cost of dogs that will be given to physically challenged children.

PEARL Natural iridescent gem produced from oysters and exceedingly rare. Cultured pearls also come from oysters, but a graft is inserted into the live oyster, around which nacre forms. Good name for a dog with a white coat like a Great Pyrenees.

PEBBLES Redhaired daughter of Fred and Wilma Flintstone in the sixties' Hanna-Barbera animated cartoon series *The Flintstones*. The family dog—a dinosaur with doglike characteristics—was named **Dino**.

PECKSNIFF Charity Pecksniff who is ill-fated in love in Charles Dickens's 1943 novel *Martin Chuzzlewit*.

PEDRO Stone (Spanish).

PEEK To catch a glimpse of, look through a crack. Peekaboo, a children's game when you hide your face behind your hands and then peek out, exclaiming "Peekaboo!" Cute name perhaps for a Pekingese.

PEERS Sir Peers Legh, Knight of Lyme Hall, was wounded on October 25, 1415, in the Battle of Agincourt. His Mastiff ferociously protected him for many hours from his enemies, but in the end her master died from his wounds. The knight's faithful dog was returned to Lyme Hall, where the most famous strain of Mastiff continues to be bred to this day.

PEETIE Peetie Wheatstraw (1902–1941), American blues singer who recorded 161 songs during the Great Depression. Listen to his "You Can't Stop Me from Drinking." Name a dog Peetie who's confident, humorous, and life-loving. Sadly, Peetie's was cut short when the car in which he was a passenger was struck by a train.

PEEWEE Pint-sized, tiny, of course a fitting name for a toy breed; small woodland songbird.

PEG Lhasa Apso in Walt Disney's 1955 animated motion picture *Lady and the Tramp*.

PEGGO Character in the kingdom of *The Wonderful Wizard of Oz*, of which there were thirteen sequels written by American author L. Frank Baum.

PEGGOTTY Clara Peggotty, Master Davey's lovingly devoted nurse who eventually marries Barkis, who was willing, in Charles Dickens's classic novel *David Copperfield*.

PEGGY Peggy Fleming of the United States (b. 1948), one of the most beloved names in women's figure skating, the Audrey Hepburn of the ice, won five US titles (1964–1968), three World titles, and the 1968 Olympic gold medal in women's figure skating. She went on to become a popular television commentator for the sport. A breast cancer survivor, she publicly shared her story and became a prominent activist and proponent of early detection by self-examination and prompt treatment.

PELLEAS A little short-lived Bull Dog in "Our Friend the Dog," by Maurice Maeterlinck.

PELLEGRINO Wanderer (Italian). Italian bottled water.

PEMBROKE Pembroke Welsh Corgi, a herding dog and the favorite breed of Queen Elizabeth of Great Britain.

PENCIL Peggy's dog in the 2007 black comedy *Year of the Dog*, starring Molly Shannon.

PENELOPE Wife of Odysseus who fended off suitors while her husband was away at war in Homer's *Odyssey*. Her name signifies marital fidelity.

PENISTONE The first pack of Harriers in England.

PENNY Canine friend of Minnie Mouse. *See* Dog Names by Category: Breed; Westminster.

PEP Any dog with pep and vigor.

PEPE He shall add (Hebrew). Italian for Joseph. Diminutive of **Giuseppe**. Female version is **Giuseppina**.

PEPPER Faithful Bull Mastiff in *The House on the Borderland*, by William Hope Hodgson.

PEPPERMINT "Amiability" in the language of flowers. Hybrid mint plant with a high menthol content that has many uses, including candy, medicine, tea, and toothpaste.

PEQUOD Captain Ahab's doomed whaling schooner in the American novel *Moby-Dick*, by Herman Melville, written in 1851.

PERCHINA Good name for a Russian Wolfhound. *See* Romanoff.

PERCIVALE Sir Percivale, second most pious of King Arthur's knights after Sir Galahad.

PERCY Pet Pug of Governor Ratcliffe in the Walt Disney animated film *Pocahontas*.

PERDITA Mother Dalmatian in *101 Dalmatians*.

PEREGRINE Bird, traveler, wanderer (Old English).

PERFECTION *See* Dog Names by Category: Breed; Westminster.

PERITAS Alexander the Great's "dog of huge size" given to him by the King of Asia.

PERIWINKLE "Sweet remembrance" in the language of flowers.

PERRO Dog (Spanish).

PERRY *See* Commodore.

PERSEPHONE Queen of the Underworld in Greek mythology.

PERSEUS Legendary founder of Mycenae.

PERSIA The Saluki is known as the Royal Dog of Eygpt, but it is also called the Persian Greyhound—therefore, a wonderful name for a Saluki or Greyhound.

PERTRONELLA Little rock (Italian).

PES Dog (Czech).

PETALS American actress Sigourney Weaver's Italian Greyhound.

PETE President Theodore Roosevelt's Bull Terrier. He bit so many people that he was exiled from the White House and sent to live at the Roosevelt family's Oyster Bay, New York, home, Sagamore Hill.

PETE THE PUP Also known as **Petey**, the ring-eyed Pit Bull in the *Our Gang* ("Little Rascals") movies of the twenties and thirties.

PETER Rough Collie with England's Civil Defence Service. Peter rescued people trapped in bombed buildings during the London Blitz in World War Two. He was awarded the Dickin Medal in 1945.

PETER PAN . . . *or, The Boy Who Wouldn't Grow Up.* Title of the 1904 London stage play by J. M. Barrie. He expanded the story in his novel published in 1911. Peter first appeared in 1902 in Barrie's novel *The Little White Bird.* Had he grown up, Peter would be well over a century old today. President Calvin Coolidge named his Terrier Peter Pan.

PETER PIPER Peter Piper, **Black Prince**, and **Sultan**, important Mastiffs that helped establish the breed in America around 1900.

PETRA A mixed-breed that was the first dog to appear on *Blue Peter*, the world's longest-running children's television show, which has aired on the BBC since 1958. Other *Blue Peter* dogs have included an Irish Setter–Dachshund mix called **Barney**, a Border Collie named **Shep**, and **Lucy**, a Golden Retriever.

PETULA Pug from the *Molly Moon* series.

PETUNIA "You are my comfort" in the language of flowers.

PHARAOH An ancient ruler of Eygpt.

PHELPS Michael Phelps, United States Olympic champion won a total of sixteen medals—fourteen of which were gold—in swimming in the games held in 2004 and 2008.

PHILIDOR François André Danican Philidor (1726–1795), French composer who was considered the best chess player of his day. A checkmate method was named after him. *See* Chess.

PHILIP Lover of horses (Greek). Prince Philip, Duke of Edinburgh (b. 1921), husband of Queen Elizabeth II of England and one of the most influential, independent, and admired members of the Royal

Family along with the Queen. He is an accomplished equestrian and participant in horse driving trials.

PHINEAS The low-slung variety of Field Spaniel was developed by Phineas Bullock from dogs purchased from Sir Francis Burdett, a breeder of black English Cocker Spaniels.

PHIZ Boston Terrier given to Helen Keller by her classmates at Radcliffe College.

PHLOX "A happy partnership" in the language of flowers.

PHOEBE A bitch named Phoebe, acquired in 1920 by Joseph Ainsley from a friend in Alnwick, is believed to be the foundation dam of the Bedlington Terrier breed of dog.

PHOENIX Sacred, mythological firebird dating to the fifth century BC. Dumbledore's Phoenix, Fawkes, also rose from the ashes periodically in J. K. Rowling's, Harry Potter series.

PHOMELLO Succeed (African).

PICABO Picabo Street, American women's alpine racer, dominated the World Cup circuit and won a silver and gold medal respectively at the 1994 and 1998 Olympic Games.

PICASSO Pablo Diego José Francisco de Paula Juan Nepomuceno María de los Remedios Cipriano de la Santísima Trinidad Ruiz y Picasso (1881–1973), known as Picasso. Unless your exposure to art is limited to cave paintings, you know Picasso to be the greatest twentieth-century artist and one of the most influential of all time.

PICCADILLY London's most famous boulevard and square. Piccadilly was called Portugal Street up until the seventeenth century.

PICCOLO An Italian mongrel that lived to be over twenty-three years old.

PICKFORD Mary Pickford (1892–1979), "America's sweetheart," Canadian-born American actress who dominated silent films. One of the thirty-six founders of the Academy of Motion Picture Arts and Sciences, which bestows the coveted Oscar for excellence in the film industry. Pickford married Douglas Fairbanks, one of Hollywood's most celebrated actors. The marriage lasted eighteen years and produced one son, Douglas Fairbanks Jr., an important Hollywood actor in his own right and World War Two hero. *See* Fairbanks.

PICKLES Terrier that kept shop with **Ginger** the cat in Beatrix Potter's *Ginger and Pickles*.

PICKWICK Samuel Pickwick, portly, congenial, easily befuddled founder of the Pickwick Club in Charles Dickens's classic farce of the English middle class, *Pickwick Papers*.

PICKZWAURT Fine name for a Bouvier des Flandres. *See* Zola.

PICTS The Scottish Deerhound is a descendant of Hounds of Picts. The Picts were an ancient people believed to have roamed Great Britain in AD 150.

PIDGEON Walter Pidgeon (1897–1984), Canadian-born American actor and one of Hollywood's true gentlemen, who starred in many important films including *How Green Was My Valley* (1941), *Advice and Consent* (1962), and *The Bad and the Beautiful* (1952). He was famously paired with actress Greer Garson in films that included *Mrs. Miniver* (1942) and its sequel, *The Miniver Story* (1950), *Madame Curie* (1943), *That Forsythe Woman* (1949), *Julia Misbehaves* (1948), and *Blossoms in the Dust* (1941).

PIEBALD The piebald coat of a dog or horse has patches of black on white fur. A nice name if your dog's coat is like that.

PIERCE Franklin Pierce, fourteenth president of the United States.

PIERRE Peter (French).

PIERS Peter (Medieval).

PIES Dog (Polish).

PIGGY Scottish Terrier in *Gone to the Dogs*, by Susan Conant.

PILOT Mr. Rochester's dog in Charlotte Brontë's classic romantic novel of desire and despair, *Jane Eyre*.

PIM Ch. Mr. Pim of Johnstounsburn, important Yorkshire Terrier with a steel-blue coat and winner of many championships.

PING Peaceful (Chinese).

PINNY Pinny Penny, prime minister of Oz in *The Wishing Horse of Oz*, a sequel to *The Wonderful Wizard of Oz*.

PINO GRIGIO Crisp, dry, aromatic white wine and great name for a white Poodle.

PINO The coniferous tree, the mighty pine (Spanish).

PINSENT Matthew Pinsent of Great Britain claimed four rowing gold medals in Olympics held between 1992 and 2004.

PINYIN Dog (Chinese).

PIO Pious, holy (Italian).

PIP The central character in Charles Dickens's 1860 classic *Great Expectations*, raised by his much older sister, Mrs. Joe, who "brought him up by hand," until the young Pip is told one day that he has a secret benefactor and that he should anticipate great expectations as he is meant to be groomed to be a gentleman. However, his future is marred by difficulties. Other memorable characters in what is universally cherished as one of Dickens's most endearing books are: Joe Gargery, Uncle Pumplechook, the Convict, Estella, Miss Havisham, Herbert Pocket, Mr. Jaggers, Biddy, and Abel Magwitch.

PIPER Daughter of Phoebe, matriarch of the Bedlington Terrier breed.

PIPPA Sister of the Duchess of Cambridge and darling of the London society and worldwide tabloids.

PIPPI Pippi Longstocking, eight-year-old girl in Swedish author Astrid Lindgren's series of books first published in 1945. The final *Pippi* story was published in 2000.

PIPPIN Dog in the *Pippin and Mabel* series of picture books by K. V. Johansen.

PIPSQUEAK Code name for an IFF (Identification Friend or Foe) system used by the Royal Air Force during the Battle of Britain in World War One. Small child or thing—good name for a very small dog.

PIRATE Dog in *The Tale of Little Pig Robinson* by Beatrix Potter.

PISCES Twelfth sign of the zodiac.

PITCH Colonel Thornton Pitch in 1790 first recorded the Fox Terrier, an ancient breed of English origin; black as pitch—great name for a black Labrador Retriever.

PITTER PATTER *See* Dog Names by Category: Breed; Westminster.

PITTYPAT Rhythmic beating of the heart, sometimes resulting from feelings of romance. Aunt Pittypat, Melanie's aunt in *Gone with the Wind*.

PIUS Dutiful (Latin). Twelve Catholic popes were named Pius.

PIXEL Tiny dot of light that is the unit of measurement for image definition and clarity on televisions and computer screens.

PIXIE Mystical sprite in Cornwall legend.

PIZZAZZ Sparkle! Zest! Flair!

PLATINUM White precious metal, and a name to think about for a dog with a short, shimmering coat such as a Siberian Husky.

PLATO (424–347 BC) Ancient Greek philosopher and student of Socrates who laid the foundation of Western philosophy and learning through his timeless writings.

PLAVIA *See* Hartenstein.

PLAYER Competitor, participant. Good name for a playful puppy.

PLINY (AD 23–79) Roman author, naturalist, and philosopher who studied and wrote about geographic phenomena in *Pliny's Natural History*.

PLUM PUDDING traditional Old English steamed dessert served at Christmastime.

PLUMBER Skilled workman who repairs and installs water pipes. Splendid name for a Portuguese Water Dog.

PLUTARCH (AD 46–120) Greek-born Roman historian, magistrate, and ambassador whose biographies of the Roman emperors proved an invaluable chronicle of ancient times.

PLUTO and **Juno** Pair of Pointers belonging to Colonel Thornton in the early nineteenth century. The dogs could hold a point on a bird for a very long time; one was timed at one hour and fifteen minutes. One day, Colonel Thornton was hunting on the moors when one of the dogs got lost. Unable to find him, Thornton reluctantly gave up. The dog was never found but a year later, as the story goes, Thornton was hunting near the same spot when he came upon his dog's skeleton—pointing at the skeleton of a bird! This story has been "adopted" by various outdoor writers to the present day, but this is believed to be the original tale. Whether it's true or not is another story!

PLUTO Mickey Mouse's pet dog that first appeared in 1930 and has remained one of Disney's most popular and endearing cartoon characters.

POACHER Lyme Hall Kennels, English breeder, one of the oldest breeders of Mastiff. Poacher, painted by Richard Ansdell in 1868, was one of the kennel's most important dogs. Bull-Mastiffs were bred in the mid-1800s and trained to attack poachers of wild game on English estates.

POCKET Herbert Pocket, Pip's devoted friend in Charles Dickens's *Great Expectations. See* Pip.

POCO American country rock band that Richie Furay and Jim Messina formed after the end of Buffalo Springfield in 1968.

POET Someone who writes poetry and is privy to the secret workings of the heart.

POGO Immensely popular daily syndicated newspaper comic strip created by Walt Kelly (1913–1973), which ended two years after his death. By then it had spawned forty-five books of collected cartoon strips.

POIRET M. Poiret of Ghent was the first breeder to show the Bouvier des Flandres at the International Dog Show in Brussels in 1910. He showed two dogs, Nelly and Evan.

POKY *The Poky Little Puppy*, a classic children's book by Janette Sebring Lowry, illustrated by Gustaf Tenggren.

POLICE Appropriate name for the German Shepherd Dog, a preferred breed used in law enforcement for crowd control, rescue, drug and explosives detection, and other tasks.

POLICEMAN Law enforcement officer. Good name for a German Shepherd dog. *See* Lady.

POLINA Polina Astakhova of the Soviet Union won ten Olympic medals for gymnastics in games held from 1956 to 1964.

POLK James Polk, eleventh president of the United States.

POLLUX Twin brother of **Castor** in Greek and Roman mythology and constellations in the night sky.

POLO "The king of sports" (perhaps because you have to be about as rich as one to afford to play), described as "hockey on a horse."

POLONAISE Stately formal couples' dance. The word also applies to the music that accompanies the dance.

POLTALLOCK West Highland Terrier originated in Poltallock, Scotland.

POM Affectionate name for the Pomeranians.

POMONA Pomona Sprout, professor of Herbology at Hogwarts School of Witchcraft and Wizardry in J. K. Rowling's Harry Potter series.

POMPEII The Italian Greyhound is known to have been a pet as far back as the time Pompeii, the southern Italian city that was buried by Mount Vesuvius in AD 79.

POMPEY Heroic Pug that thwarted an assassination attempt on William I, Prince of Orange (1533–1584).

POM-POM Great name for a Poodle. *See* Tam O'Shanter.

PONGO Dalmatian dad in Dodie Smith's novel *The Hundred and One Dalmatians* and the Walt Disney film adaptations of the book. *See* Disney.

PONTO Historic name for an English Setter. *See* Lavarack.

PONTOU Town in the Douron Valley of France and birthplace of the French Brittany Spaniel.

PONZIO Of the sea (Italian).

POOCH Affectionate name for any dog.

POOH Winnie-the-Pooh came to life in 1926 through the pen of writer A. A. Milne. The real Pooh was a much-loved stuffed animal that belonged to the writer's son, Christopher Robin Milne.

POOLE James Edwin Harris, Second Earl of Malmesbury, acquired his dogs from a man named Poole in Newfoundland, Canada. Harris, an avid waterfowl hunter, bred the dogs at Heron Court on the south coast of England around 1800, commenting that the dog has a "close coat which turns water off like oil" and a tail "like an otter" that acts like a rudder when his dogs swam to retrieve a fallen duck. That dog came to be known as the Labrador Retriever.

POOTZY Runyon Jones's lost dog in *The Odyssey of Runyon Jones*, a radio play that aired in 1941.

POPEYE He's Popeye the sailor man, created by Elzie Crisler Segar and first appeared in 1929 in a daily King Features comic strip called *Thimble Theater*. Popeye is one of America's longest-lived cartoon heroes, brought to life by Robert Altman in the 1980 major motion picture starring Robin Williams. His nemesis is Brutus, his paramour is Olive Oyl, daughter of Castor Oyl, and his best friend is hamburger-loving J. Wellington Wimpy (Vickers Wellington bombers were nicknamed "Wimpy" in World War Two). His foster daughter is **Swee' Pea**, his father is **Poopdeck Pappy**, and he has four lookalike nephews named **Peepeye**, **Pupeye**, **Pipeye**, and **Poopeye** and, last but not least, a dog with a bulbous red nose named **Jeep-Jeep**.

POPOV Alexander Popov of Russia won nine Olympic medals for swimming in games held between 1992 to 2000.

POPPET Affectionate term for "sweetheart."

POPPY Poppy Pomfrey, magical Healer and Matron and nurse of the Infirmary at the Hogwarts School of Witchcraft and Wizardry in J. K. Rowling's Harry Potter series. In the film versions, the role is played by the superb English actress Gemma Jones.

POPS What our grandchildren call my husband. *See* Satchmo.

PORK Head houseman at Tara and afterward, in Atlanta with Scarlett and Rhett in *Gone with the Wind*.

PORTHOS J. M. Barrie's dog in the bittersweet, semibiographical account of his love for Sylvia Llewelyn Davies, a young, terminally ill widow, in the 2004 motion picture *Finding Neverland*, with tender performances by Johnny Depp and Kate Winslett.

PORTIA Beautiful, rich, intelligent Shakespearean romantic heroine in *The Merchant of Venice* who has a rather nasty temperament.

POSEIDON God of the sea in Greek mythology.

POSSUM Mr. Culbertson of Minnesota was a well-known breeder of Schipperkes and used them to hunt possums and raccoons.

POSTBOY A dog in *The Tale of Little Pig Robinson*, by Beatrix Potter.

POSTSCRIPT Westminster Kennel Club champion. *See* Dog Names by Category: Breed; Westminster.

POTTER *See* Dog Names by Category: Breed; Crufts.

POUCH *See* Dog Names by Category: Breed; Westminster.

POUND PUPPIES Tonka Toy collection of puppies that whelped a 1986 animated television series—and $300 million in sales. The dogs included **Cooler**, Golden Retriever; **Nose Marie**, a Boxer; **Howler**, a Chihuahua mix; **Whopper**, a Schnauzer; **Beamer**, a Scottish Terrier–Siberian Husky mix; **Barkerville**, a Shetland Sheepdog; **Reflex**, a Yorkshire Terrier; **Uncle J.R.**, another Schnauzer and Whopper's uncle; **Biff Barker**, a Basset Hound; **Zazu**, the Fairy Dogmother; **Teensy**, a tiny puppy; **Sparky**, a Golden Retriever; **Lucy**, an expectant bitch who had three puppies, **Candy**, **Mandy**, and **Andy**; and **Rusty**, the father of Lucy's pups, **Princefeld** and **Toots**.

POWDER Field Trial Ch. Velox Powder, important dog from the Bougley line of English Springer Spaniels.

PRADA One of three Beagles canine actors that, along with **Breezy** and **Windy**, interchangeably played **Porthos**, Captain Archer's dog on *Star Trek: Enterprise*. Prada also starred as **Lou** in the film *Cats and Dogs*.

PREACHER Offspring of Jack and Jill Russell in the *Jack Russell, Dog Detective* books, by Darrel and Sally Odgers.

PRECIOUS The ring in the J. R. R. Tolkien *Lord of the Rings* legendarium that Gollum (originally called Smeagol), a Stoor Hobbit of the River-folk who lived near the Gladden Fields, was so obsessed with that it cost him his humanity—and finally, his life.

PRECIOUS BABY One of Hollywood actor Randal Malone's precious dogs. *See* Randal.

PRESCOTT Prescott Lawrence first imported Welsh Terriers to America in 1888. One was named **T'Other**. The other was named **Which**.

PRESIDENT Important Newfoundland that helped establish the breed, depicted in an 1868 painting by Horatio Henry Couldery in the collection of the American Kennel Club. President Franklin Delano Roosevelt's Great Dane. *See* Dog Names by Category: History.

PRESLEY Elvis Presley (1935–1977), Mississippi-born "king of rock and roll" whose songs revolutionized American popular music. His first single, "That's Alright Mama" was recorded in 1954 and his first number-one pop record and million-dollar seller, "Heartbreak Hotel," released by RCA, was the best-selling single of 1956. From that point on, his life was a rollercoaster ride, and the burden of fame contributed to his early death at the age at forty-two. He left behind "Love Me Tender," "Don't Be Cruel," "Hound Dog," and his haunting gospel redition of "Peace in the Valley." Long live the King.

PRESTON Evil canine robot in the stop-action animated movie *Wallace and Gromit*.

PRETTY BOY Pretty Boy Floyd and five other Doberman Pinschers that attempt a bank heist in the 1972 film *The Doberman Gang*.

PRETTY Beautiful, attractive

PRETZEL A knotted, crusty, salted rope of baked or fried dough.

PRIDE *See* Dog Names by Category: Breed; Crufts.

PRIMA DONNA *See* Dog Names by Category: Breed; Westminster.

PRIMO First (Italian).

PRIMROSE "Inconstancy" in the language of flowers.

PRINCE ALBERT Prince Albert of Saxe-Coburg and Gotha (1819–1861), the Prince Consort and husband of Queen Victoria of Great Britain and Ireland. First cousins, their marriage was arranged, but it proved to be a deeply loving and commited one and was further bound by a large family of nine children. Clearly, Albert was the power behind the throne. His premature death at the age of forty-two devastated Victoria, and she dressed in mouring for the rest of her long life. She remains the longest-sitting monarch on the British throne—although Queen Elizabeth II is fast catching up. *See* Dog Names by Category: Breed; Westminster.

PRINCE D'OR Historical name for a Bouvier des Flandres. *See* Nic.

PRINCE TERRIEN Dog in the novel and 2007 film *Bridge to Terabithia*.

PRINCE The Prince of Orange, or Prinsgeziden, was pitted against the Patriots, or Patriotten, in the class war preceding the French Revolution. The Keeshonden was identified with the Patriotten as "the dog of the people." Because the Prinsgenziden triumphed, the Keeshonden lost popularity until 1920, when the Baroness van Hardencroek took an interest the breed, which was thought to be almost extinct. She was surprised to discover riverboat captains and farmers had maintained the integrity of the breed. Through her efforts, the Keeshonden was revived; Jasper King's dog in Margaret Sidney's novel *Five Little Peppers and How They Grew*.

PRINCESS Wife of a prince, such as Princess Grace of Monaco or daughter of a queen, such as Princess Anne, Princess Royal of England. Princess is among the thirty most popular female dog names.

PRINCESS OZMA Raven-haired rightful ruler of Oz in *The Marvelous Land of Oz*, a sequel to *The Wonderful Wizard of Oz*, by L. Frank Baum.

PRINZ Prinz Hartmuth, important dog in the Seppel line of Schnauzers.

PRISSY Scarlett's useless housemaid in *Gone with the Wind*.

PROCYON "Before the dog" (Latin) Yellow-white star and eighth brightest in the night sky.

PROFESSOR Scholar, teacher, person who professes to be an expert on a subject. Professor Marvel, who is a carnival performer in Kansas, is none other than the Great Oz himself, the Wizard of Oz, in the Land of Oz. Dr. Roy Hinkley, called "The Professor" and portrayed by American actor Russell Johnson, was one of the seven castaways in the television series *Gilligan's Island*.

PROMISE *See* Dog Names by Category: Breed; Westminster.

PROSPERO *See* Tempest.

PROTECTOR Stories abound of how the Newfoundland saved numerous men, women, and children on sinking boats from a watery grave, and how the St. Bernard saved avalanche victims in the Alps. Protector is a strong name for a guard or rescue dog.

PRUDENCE Prudence Primm, President Calvin Coolidge's Rough Collie.

PRUNELLA A purple-headed flower with the healing abilities of an antiseptic.

PRUSSIA *See* Frederick.

PRYSE Prince (Old English).

PUA Flower (Hawaiian).

PUB The oldest single-breed specialty club was the Bulldog Club, formed in 1878 in England. Meetings were held at the Blue Post Pub on Oxford Street, London.

PUBLIUS Historical name for a Maltese. *See* Issa.

PUCKSHILL *See* Dog Names by Category: Breed; Crufts.

PUDDING A British savory dish, steamed or boiled, that includes Yorkshire pudding, black pudding, suet pudding, steak and kidney pudding, and on the sweet side, Christmas pudding and figgy pudding.

PUDDLES An accumulation of rainwater.

PUDEL German word for the Poodle.

PUDGE Character in the kingdom of *The Wonderful Wizard of Oz*, of which there were thirteen sequels written by American author L. Frank Baum. Good name for a pudgy little puppy.

PUDGY Cartoon character Betty Boop's dog.

PUGNAX A mutt that can read in *Against the Day*, by Thomas Pynchon.

PULSAR A pulsating star that emits brief surges of visible radiation.

PULU Ball (Tibetan). The word for the game of polo comes from *pulu*.

PUMPLECHOOK Uncle Pumplechook, pompous relative who first brings Pip to see the eccentric Miss Havisham in *Great Expectations*, by Charles Dickens. *See* Pip.

PUNCH Jack London's childhood dog that he reminisces about in *The Road* (1907).

PUNCH and **Judy** A pair of Boxers responsible for saving two British officers in Israel from a terrorist attack. They were awarded the Dickin Medal in 1946.

PUP Affectionate name for puppy.

PUP DOG CHILE Puppy from Walt Kelly's comic, *Pogo*.

PURCELL Mr. R. L. Purcell Llewellin founded the Llewellin strain, around 1870 when he acquired a number of Mr. Laverack's best show dogs from the Dash-Moll and Dash-Hill bloodlines.

PURDEY James Purdey & Son, founded in 1814, British fine sporting goods and firearms maker. A good name for a traditional English gun dog, such as an English Pointer or English Springer Spaniel.

PUSHINKA President John F. Kennedy's dog.

PUSSY GALORE Yorkshire Terrier that played Truffles, Mildred's terrier, in the British sitcom *George & Mildred* (1976–1979).

PWYLL Pwyll, Prince of Wales, a contemporary of King Arthur, is believed to have bred Beagles.

PYCOMBE Historical name for a Curly-Coated Retriever. *See* Sable.

PYM Magnus Pym, fictitious British spy in the 1986 novel *A Perfect Spy*, by literary spymaster John le Carré.

Q

QEN Dog (Albanian).

QIQIRN Dog in Inuit mythology.

QUAASHIE Born on Sunday (African).

QUAIL Wild game bird; quail eggs were considered a delicacy in Victorian and Edwardian England. Good name for a sporting dog.

QUAKER One of the most celebrated Mastiffs in England, his portrait was painted in 1882 by renowned dog artist John Sutcliffe (Collection of the AKC). Mastiffs were war dogs in the fifteenth century. It is recorded that King Henry VII of England presented four hundred Mastiffs to King Charles V of France as a gift.

QUEEN LURLIE Character in the kingdom of *The Wonderful Wizard of Oz*, of which there were thirteen sequels written by American author L. Frank Baum.

QUEEN Queen Elizabeth II of England has had a royal household full of dogs all her life. She was a ten-year-old princess when her Uncle Edward abdicated the throne of England in 1936 for "the woman I love." (Never crowned king, his reign lasted a mere 326 days.) At that point, the young princess's life changed dramatically. Her father, King George VI, an example of unwavering fortitude to his people in World War Two, died at the age of fifty-six, and Elizabeth, a young mother, succeeded him. One of the constants in her tumultuous and demanding life was, and continues to be, her dogs. Princess Elizabeth, her sister, Margaret Rose, and her parents, when Duke and Duchess of York, had a canine household comprising: **Lady Jane,** a reddish-brown Pembroke Welsh Corgi (from whom all the queen's Corgis were bred or descended), and another Corgi, **Dookie;** a Tibetan Lion Dog named **Choo-Choo,** a Golden Retriever named **Judy** and a black Cocker Spaniel named **Ben;** her father's particular dogs were **Mimsy,** a yellow Labrador Retriever, and her son and daughter, **Stiffy** and **Scrummy.**

QUEENIE The subject of J. R. Ackerley's memoir about fifteen years with his beloved German Shepherd Dog, Queenie.

QUEEQUEG Headhunter from the fictional island of Kokovoko in the South Seas and Ishmael's stalwart mate aboard the *Pequod* in *Moby-Dick,* by Herman Melville, written in 1851. Although he is associated with coastal New England and the seafaring life, Melville was born and raised in New York City. But his family roots were deep in Boston—in fact, his paternal grandfather was a leader of the Boston Tea Party.

QUERIDA Early Wirehaired Pointing Griffons related to Mouche, the breed's foundation bitch. *See* Mouche.

QUIBBLE Nit-pick, fuss. If your puppy is a finicky eater, then Quibble might be just the name.

QUICKSILVER Operation Quicksilver, deception plan created by General George Patton in World War Two to divert Nazi attention away from Normandy and the Allied landings in June 1944. Thick, silver-colored element that is the only metal to remain liquid at normal temperatures. Wonderful name for a Siberian Husky.

QUIDDITCH You need two teams of seven, mounted on fast broomsticks, four balls, and six goals suspended in midair, to play this popular wizards' game in J. K. Rowling's Harry Potter series.

QUIGLEY *Quigley Down Under*, perennially popular 1990 cowboy movie set in the Australian Outback starring Tom Selleck and Alan Rickman, two incredibly fine actors. Rickman is best known, perhaps, for his role as Professor Snape in the Harry Potter films.

QUINCY Saer de Quincy, First Earl of Winchester (1155–1219), who helped lead the insurrection to topple King John of England from the throne. A major figure in Scotland and England at the end of the twelfth century, he joined the Fifth Crusade to the Holy Land, where he died from an illness.

QUINN Chief (Irish Gaelic).

QUINT Shark hunter played by the British actor Robert Shaw in Steven Spielberg's thriller, *Jaws*.

QUINTUS Roman Consul Quintus Aurelius Symmachus was given a gift of seven Irish Wolfhounds by his brother, Flavianus, commenting, "All Rome viewed them with wonder."

R

RAB *Rab and His Friends*, a short story written by Dr. John Brown in 1859 about a huge Mastiff in the Lowlands of Scotland—"old, grey, brindled as big as a Highland bull."

RACHEL Ewe (English).

RADAR Detection system developed in World War Two that utilizes electromagnetic waves to detect direction, speed, altitude, and range of moving or fixed objects.

RADCLIFFE Daniel Radcliffe (b. 1989), actor who brought Harry Potter to life onscreen from the pages of J. K. Rowling's marvelous and magical books.

RAFA Bull Terrier in the 2008 Disney film *Beverly Hills Chihuahua.*

RAGS Mascot of the US 1st Infantry Division in World War One. He ran messages between rear headquarters and the front lines, most notably during the Meuse-Argonne Campaign. While delivering a vital message he sustained injuries and became partially blinded by gas, but got through nevertheless.

RAIDER Robber, thief, and great name for a dog that tries to nuzzle open the refrigerator, like my hundred-pound Labrador Retriever, Teal, used to do.

RAIMI Kind (African).

RAIN Water that tumbles down from the heavens.

RAINBOW Arched spectrum of light. Dorothy sang about somewhere over the rainbow, Leprechauns bury their pots of gold at the end of it, and when you see one, make a wish!

RAISA Raisa Gorbachova (1932–1999), much-admired wife of Mikhail Gorbachov, General Secretary of the Communist Party of the Soviet Union from 1985 until 1991. To the Western World, she was the first elegant, approachable wife of a Russian premier and esteemed for her work on behalf of research into children's leukemia. Good name for a Russian breed, such as a Borzoi.

RAISIN A dried-up, wrinkled grape and great name for a dog with baggy skin, like a Chinese Shar-Pei.

Captain Edward John Smith, captain of the *Titanic*, with his Borzoi. Both master and dog perished after the ship collided with an iceberg on April 14, 1912.

RAJAH New Zealand's first police dog, a German Shepherd also known as Methven's Wonder Dog, lived and worked with his master, Constable John Robertson, in the town of Methven during the thirties.

RAK Large, talking flying winged creature who can run like a deer and swim like a fish in *Tik-Tok of Oz*, a sequel to *The Wonderful Wizard of Oz*, by L. Frank Baum.

RAKE Irish Water Spaniel that helped establish the modern standard of the breed, painted in 1879 by renowned English artist George Earl.

RAKSHA The Mother wolf who raises Mowgli as her own cub in *The Jungle Book*, by Rudyard Kipling

RALPH Unnamed terrier that belongs to Ralph Touchett in Henry James's *Portrait of a Lady*. Scottish Terrier in Booth Tarkington's short story "Blue Milk."

Hollywood actor, president of the Southern California Motion Picture Arts Council, and dog lover Randal Malone with his canine family outside Malone Manor, Hollywood. Randal has owned many dogs in his lifetime, all rescue dogs. Erica Jong wrote, "Dogs come into our lives to teach us about love. They depart to teach us about loss. A new dog never replaces an old dog; it merely expands the heart. If you have loved many dogs, your heart is very big." Randal's heart is very big.

RAMAYANA One of the two great ancient Sanskrit epics of India.

RAMÓN Ramón Fonst of Cuba won five Olympic medals for fencing in the 1900 and 1904 games.

RAMSES Born of the sun (African).

RANDAL Randal Malone, celebrated Hollywood cult star (the "king of B-rated horror films"), president of the Southern California Motion Pictures Council, costar of MTV's hit nineties show *Singled Out* with Carmen Electra, philanthropist, and cherished friend of many in the entertainment industry, has been owned by dogs all his life. Each one has come from a very famous kennel: the animal shelter. "All my dogs are rescue dogs," Randy explains. The dogs that currently reside at "Malone Manor" are **Duke,** the Duke of Malone Manor, a German Shepherd Dog and his consort, **Duchess,** a Golden Retriever; **Page,** a black Chihuahua whose godmother was the late silent film star Anita Page, "the girl with the most beautiful face in Hollywood," in the twenties; and **Sparky** Malone, a Terrier, born on the fourth of July. "My darling **Henry** died at nine," Malone mourns almost a decade after his white Miniature Poodle's death. **Precious Baby,** a Toy Poodle, also has passed. "I rescued her when she was six months old. She had a very bad heart. The vet said if we were lucky, she'd live another year. I kept her on a special diet and carried her everywhere. She never once set foot on the grass or pavement." Precious Baby died at the age of twelve. Recently added to Malone's canine family is a very small Toy Poodle named **Herman,** a gift from his dear friend, legendary Hollywood actress Margaret O'Brien.

RANDOLPH Labrador Retriever in *A Dog About Town*, *A Dog Among Diplomats*, and *A Dog at Sea*, by J. F. Englert.

RANGER Member of a the elite force of highly trained US Army soldiers whose history goes back to King Philip's War in 1676.

RANIA Queen Rania (b. 1970), Queen Consort of King Abdullah II of Jordan, who does much to develop education and health among the children of her country.

RANN A kite in *The Jungle Book*, by Rudyard Kipling.

RAREBIT Welsh rarebit, a traditional British dish made with melted cheese and a little beer, poured over warm, thickly sliced bread.

RASCAL Little scoundrel, scallywag.

RASHIDI Thinker, counselor (African).

RATTLE A rhythm instrument, a baby's rattle, and a good name for a dog whose jowls rattle against his teeth when he shakes his head.

RATTLER Canine actor that played Chance in *Homeward Bound: The Incredible Journey*, voiced by actor Michael Fox.

RAUHHAAR Wire-haired variety of Dachshund.

RAUL Wise (Italian).

> **RAVEN** Large black birds. Six ravens protect the Tower of London and the Crown. When Henry VIII ordered the execution of his wife, Anne Boleyn, it is said the ravens fled before the bloody axe was wielded. Superstition says if the ravens leave the Tower, doom shall soon descend upon the royal house. It would probably be a good idea if someone clipped the ravens' wings. Great name for a black dog.

RAVENCLAW One of the four student houses at Hogwarts School of Witchcraft and Wizardry in *Harry Potter*. Ravenclaw's values are intelligence, creativity, learning, and wit.

RAVENWOOD Marion Ravenwood, Indiana Jones's tough ex-girlfriend played by Karen Allen in Steven Spielberg's *Raiders of the Lost Ark*. Good name for a black Labrador Retriever.

RAVISHER To seize by force and carry away. One of the hounds that "were singing" in Frederick Watson's 1932 hunting book *In the Pink*.

RAWDON Rawdon B. Lee, great authority on the Scottish Terrier breed, who wrote "The Scottie is the oldest variety of the canine race indigenous to Britain . . . For generations he had been a popular dog in the Highlands."

RAWHIDE American Western series that aired on CBS beginning in 1959 and starred a young actor with shrewd eyes and a quick draw named Clint Eastwood.

RAY Ray Charles Robinson, known as Ray Charles (1930–2004), perhaps the greatest African-American singer, pianist, and composer of all time. He did it all—soul, rhythm and blues, gospel, rock and roll, country and pop. Frank Sinatra called Charles "the only true genius in show business." The son of a sharecropper and railroad worker, Charles was blind from glaucoma by the age of seven. His Baptist roots influenced his musical career, which began for all intent and purposes at the age of fifteen, when he left home in Florida upon the death of his mother. At his death at the age of seventy-three, he achieved an unparalleled musical legacy—and left a void in music that never can be filled.

RAYCROFTS *See* Dog Names by Category: Breed; Crufts.

RAYMOND Advice, protector (Germanic).

REAGAN Ronald Reagan (1911–2004), fortieth president of the United States, thirty-third governor of California, whose nonpartisan politics and "Reaganomics" economic initiatives were part of an enormous legacy defined by ending the Cold War with Russia.

REBA Reba McEntire (b. 1955), flame-haired popular country & western singer and actress.

REBECCA *Rebecca*, Alfred Hitchcock's 1940 film noir based on the psychological thriller by the great English author, Daphne du Maurier. In a nutshell: a young, naïve, homely, underpaid female companion (whose name is never mentioned) is thrown together with a handsome, rich, middle-aged English aristocrat named Maxim de Winter in Monaco. On the spur of the moment they marry. He whisks her off to Manderley, his imposing family estate on the coast of Cornwall. But Max has a dark secret. And I'm not telling. Has to do with his deceased first wife, Rebecca. Rent the movie starring Joan Fontaine and Laurence Olivier or read the book or both, because the endings are different.

REBEL Renegade, nonconformist.

RECKLESS The Waltons' family dog on the 1972 CBS television series.

RECRUIT Apprentice, conscript, someone drafted into service. *See* Dog Names by Category: Breed; Crufts.

RED Primary color and obvious name for a red-coated dog, like Big Red.

RED BARON Manfred Albrecht Freiherr von Ricthofen (1892–1981), famously known as the Red Baron. Imperial German Army Air Service fighter pilot and flying ace in World War One, his eighty record air combat victories set a record. *See* Dog Names by Category: Breed; Westminster.

RED PALM First Welsh Terrier to be exhibited in America.

RED SOX Founded in 1901, the Red Sox is Boston's professional baseball team and member of the American League Eastern Division. A Red Sox fan is invincible in spirit. *See* Babe.

RED WINE Consider this name for a dog with a dark, reddish brown coat, especially a Dogue de Bordeaux.

REDDY Dog in Hanna-Barbera's *Ruff and Reddy*.

REFLEX One of Tonka's Pound Puppies.

REGINALD Advice, decision (Germanic).

REGULUS To rule (Latin).

REILLY Irish surname from the Gaelic *Ó Raghallaigh*. The meaning of the word is unknown.

REINAGLE German strain of English Bulldog, established in 1803. Noted nineteenth-century artist who painted the old Rough-haired Water Dog of England, which resembles a modern unclipped Poodle and was, in fact, a hunting dog used to retrieve waterfowl.

REINER Equestrian Reiner Klimke of Germany won eight Olympic medals at the games held between 1964 and 1988.

REIVER Historical name for a Bloodhound. *See* Sleuth.

REMBRANDT Rembrandt Harmenszoon van Rijn (1606–1669), Dutch painter. Rembrandt depicted Schnauzers in several of his paintings. Considered one of the great masters, he developed chiaroscuro, a painting technique depicting high contrast between darkness and light, which made a dramatic impact on art.

REMEDY To cure. The love of a dog cures about anything. *See* Dog Names by Category: Breed; Westminster.

REMINGTON Frederic Remington (1861–1909), American artist who captured the spirit of the Old West on canvas and in bronze. He lived the life he depicted in his art, wild and adventurous, but tragically died at the age of forty-eight during an emergency appendectomy.

REMO Swift (Italian).

REMUS LUPIN Defense against the Dark Arts professor at Hogwarts School of Witchcraft and Wizardry, he suffers from lycanthropy (turns into a werewolf), but he doesn't allow it to put a crimp in his style. Remus was a good friend of Harry Potter's parents and godfather, Sirius Black. He marries Nymphadora Tonks but their marriage is tragically short-lived.

RENATA Reborn (Italian).

RENÉ Born again (French, from the Latin, *renatus*). Dr. René Belloq, Indiana Jones's nemesis played by Paul Freeman in Steven Spielberg's *Raiders of the Lost Ark*. René is a great name for any dog of French origin.

RENOIR Pierre-Auguste Renoir (1841–1919), French painter and leader of the Impressionist movement. His vibrant use of color and his images of bucolic life in France have made his work popular down through the ages.

RESY PATRICIA Swiss dam from which Fracas Franconia, the first American Schnauzer champion, was whelped.

RETH King (African).

REUBEN Sir Peter Paul Rubens (1577–1640), Flemish Baroque painter known for his mythological and religious allegories. His court paintings are a veritable window into seventeenth-century life.

REVEILLE Collie, mascot of Texas A&M University.

REX Fictitious dog in DC Comics's *The Adventures of Rex the Wonder Dog*, published from 1952 to 1959. Hollywood canine actor that appeared in numerous silent films in the twenties. Farmer Hoggett's sheepdog and father of Fly's puppies in the 1995 Australian-American family film *Babe*. Irish novelist D. H. Lawrence's beloved Fox Terrier, whom he celebrated in his short story "Rex." Rexx, canine star of the 2007 family film *Firehouse Dog*. Rex Harrison (1908–1990), much-awarded and, indeed, knighted, English stage and screen actor best known for his portrayal of Professor Henry Higgins in *My Fair Lady* on both stage and screen.

REYNOLDS English surname as early as the fourteenth century. *See* Joshua.

RHAPSODY Rapture, ecstasy. *See* Gershwin.

RHEANNA Great queen (Celtic). Goddess of fertility in Welsh mythology.

RHETT Protagonist in *Gone with the Wind* who meets his match in Scarlett O'Hara. Nominated for a Best Actor Academy Award for his role, Clark Gable *was* Rhett Butler in the movie and to millions of adoring fans.

RHINESTONE Originally rhinestones were rock crystals harvested from the River Rhine in Europe that were then cut and polished to look like diamonds or colored gemstones—hence the name. Cute name for a dog that wears a rhinestone collar.

RHODES Island off the coast of Greece in the Aegean Sea with a colorful ancient history. Obvious name for a Rhodesian Ridgeback.

RHODODENDRON "Caution" in the language of flowers and rather a long name for a dog, but you can always call her Rhoddie.

RHOEBE English Setters from the Duke-Rhoebe-Laverack lines are generally known as Llewellin Setters in America.

RHONDA Woman from Rhodes (Greek). *See* Yankee.

RHOSDDU Ch. Rhosddu Royalist, foundation dam of the Airedale Terrier breed.

RHYTHM Beat, tempo. *See* Dog Names by Category: Breed; Westminster.

RIBSY Henry Huggins's canine companion in Beverly Cleary's books for young readers.

RICCARDO Powerful ruler (Italian).

RICKY A Welsh Collie injured by shrapnel that continued to work locating unexploded mines along the bank of the Nederweert Canal in the Netherlands during World War Two. He was awarded the Dickin Medal in 1947.

RICO Border Collie studied at the Max Planck Institute for Evolutionary Anthropology in Leipzig by animal psychologist Juliane Kaminski. She confirmed that the dog understood a remarkably large vocabulary of words and commands. Rico died at the age of fourteen in 2008.

RIFF Australian Shepherd Dog in British TV series *Tractor Tom*.

RIFF RAFF Rottweiller gangster (originally portrayed as a wolf) in the animated children's television series, *Underdog*.

RIFLEMAN Rifleman Khan, an Alsatian belonging to the British 6th Battalion Cameroonians that rescued a drowning soldier under heavy shellfire during the assault of Walcheren in World War Two. He was awarded the Dickin Medal in 1945.

RIGO Most influential dog in the early breeding of Schnauzers, a son of Sierger Rex von Den Gunthersburg.

RIKKI-TIKKI-TAVI Indian Mongoose in *The Jungle Book*, by Rudyard Kipling.

RILEY Courageous (Irish).

RIMSHOT Ernest P. Worrell's dog in the films *Ernest Goes to Jail* (1990) and *Ernest Scared Stupid* (1991), starring the wonderful comic actor, Kentucky-born "hillbilly" Jim Varney (1949–2000). He made America laugh out loud in television commercials, which launched his film career, most notably a dozen *Ernest* movies and as the voice of Slinky Dog in *Toy Story 1* (1995) and *Toy Story 2* (1999). He left us too soon, dying of lung cancer. His last words before he died were "Please leave the window open."

RIN TIN TIN Shell-shocked puppy found in a bombed-out dog kennel in France by American serviceman Lee Duncan, who adopted him, brought him home to LA—and the rest, as they say, is the stuff Hollywood movies are made of. This German Shepherd Dog and his heirs appeared on radio and television, helping establish law and order in the American West to an audience of riveted viewers across the generations.

RINALDO Wise ruler (Italian).

RINGO Apple (Japanese).

RIO River (Spanish).

RIP A stray found during the London Blitz in 1940 that, though never trained in search and rescue, succeeded in saving the lives of more than one hundred people trapped beneath the rubble of bombed buildings. He became the unofficial mascot of the Southill Street Air Raid Patrol.

RIQ Traditional instrument in Arabic music that resembles a tambourine.

RISE AND SHINE *See* Dog Names by Category: Breed; Westminster.

RITA SKEETER Obnoxious reporter for the *Daily Prophet* whose Quick-Quotes Quill feverishly jots down notes during her overly inquisitive interviews in the Harry Potter series.

RITZ César Ritz (1850–1918), "king of hoteliers, and hotelier to kings," Swiss hotelier and founder of the exclusive Hôtel Ritz in Paris and in London.

RIVER Waterway, brook, stream. *See* Dog Names by Category: Breed; Westminster.

ROALD Roald Dahl (1916–1990), author of children's books that equally enchant adults, such as *Charlie and the Chocolate Factory*, *James and the Giant Peach*, *The Fantastic Mr. Fox*, and the screenplay of *Chitty Chitty Bang Bang*. His body of work goes far beyond that; indeed, it was enormous. And that was only part of his life. Born in Wales to Norwegian parents, Dahl was an RAF pilot and intelligence agent during World War Two. He was married to the late actress Patricia Neal, with whom he had five children.

ROAN Good name for a Pointer with roan-colored markings.

ROB Rough Collie, war dog No 471/322, that served as a messenger and guard dog in the Special Air Service, a Special Forces unit of the British Army during World War Two. Rob, the first canine parachutist, made over twenty parachute jumps during the North African Campaign. He was awarded the Dickin Medal in 1945.

ROB ROY President Calvin Coolidge's Rough Collie.

ROBBIE Diminutive of **Robert** or **Robin**.

ROBERTA Bright, fame (Italian).

ROBERTO Basset Hound in *Open Season 2*.

ROBIN HOOD Legendary outlaw from Sherwood Forest who, with his Merry Men, robbed from the rich to give to the poor. Beloved canine companion, a Spaniel, of Jim Corbett, big game hunter, conservationist, and colonel in the British India Army who saved countless lives from man-eating tigers and leopards.

ROBINSON Jack Roosevelt "Jackie" Robinson (1919–1972), first black player in Major League Baseball. Robinson broke baseball's color line when he signed on with the Brooklyn Dodgers in 1947, ending segregation in professional baseball. But that's not why he was inducted into the Baseball Hall of Fame in 1962. Robinson played in six World Series and helped clinch the 1955 pennant for the Dodgers—the only time the team won a World Series in Brooklyn. It was the last one the Dodgers would play in before moving to the West Coast.

ROBOT Dog owned by a boy named Simon who discovered prehistoric cave paintings in Lascaux, France in 1940.

ROCCO Rest (Italian).

ROCHESTER Eddie "Rochester" Anderson (1905–1977), black American actor and comedian best known as Jack Benny's sidekick on the radio and on television. He described himself as a descendant of slaves who escaped the Civil War South through the Underground Railroad. If any man broke the racial barrier, it was Rochester. His filmography spans thirty years, his last film being the star-studded 1963 comedy *It's a Mad, Mad, Mad, Mad World*. But his greatest role wasn't in Frank Capra's *You Can't Take It with You* with James Stewart and Jean Arthur, or *Cabin in the Sky* with Ethel Waters and Lena Horne (two incomparable ladies of screen and song), but as a charitable man. He left the bulk of his estate to fund a foundation to help troubled men transition into society at the Rochester House in Los Angeles. In literature, he is the tormented romantic hero of Charlotte Brontë's haunting 1847 novel *Jane Eyre*.

ROCK Historical name for a Beagle. *See* Royal.

ROCKET Fly, hurtle, missile. *See* Dog Names by Category: Breed; Westminster.

ROCKY *Rocky* (1976), first in a series of films starring Sylvester Stallone, about an uneducated, small-time Philadelphia boxer who aspires to win the heavyweight championship title. This emotionally charged film brought audiences to their feet.

RODEO Competition in which cowboys demonstrate their skills in roping and tying down cows, riding broncos and bulls, and barrel racing.

RODERIGO Sire of Toledo Blade, an important English Setter. *See* Toledo.

RODNEY Ch. Rodney Stone, first English Bulldog to command a $5,000 price tag, around 1900—the equivalent of about $60,000 today. Must have been some dog.

ROGER American actor and writer Steve Martin's canine companion, a yellow Labrador Retriever.

ROGUE Scoundrel, rascal.

ROHO Soul (African).

ROI Louis XIV (1638–1715), the Sun King (Le Roi Soleil), King of France and Navarre, the French monarch whose reign began at the age of four and lasted over seventy-two years. He proclaimed the Great Pyrenees the royal Court Dog.

ROLAND Famous land (Germanic).

ROLLO President Theodore Roosevelt's Saint Bernard.

ROLLY Young boy in *The Rundelstone of Oz*, an *Oz* sequel by Eloise Jarvis McGraw, authorized successor of American author L. Frank Baum. Lively name for a roly-poly puppy.

ROMAN War dog of the ancient Romans.

ROMANI Latin word for the ancient Romans. *See* Traveller.

ROMANOFF Perchina Kennels, breeder of the Russian Wolfhound, was owned by the Grand Duke Nicholas of Romanoff.

ROMEO *See* Juliet.

ROMULUS Founders of Rome. Twins conceived by the goddess Rhea and abandoned, the babies were discovered by a she-wolf who raised them to manhood.

RON Ronald Bilius Weasley and Hermione Granger are Harry Potter's best friends and fellow protagonists in J. K. Rowling's Harry Potter series. Ron was played in the eight film adaptations by British actor Rupert Grint, whom the world met when he was twelve years old and said good-bye to when Ron was twenty-two. But it's okay: Ron marries Hermione and they live a happy life. We want Rupert to have one, too. He gave countless millions a great deal of pleasure.

RONNIE Ronnie Neary, Roy's wife played by Teri Garr, in Steven Spielberg's *Close Encounters of the Third Kind*.

RONTU Dog in *Island of the Blue Dolphins* by Scott O'Dell.

ROOBARB Title character of a British cartoon series.

ROONEY Andy Hardy, the fictitious youth that Mickey Rooney brought to life in sixteen MGM movies over twenty years, beginning in 1937. Mickey Rooney was the most popular actor of the forties and the reason was clear: he was there when America needed him most—a stalwart, compassionate, upstanding young man braving a troubled time—and for that, he can never be thanked enough.

ROSA Rosa Henderson (1896–1968), American jazz and blues singer and musical comedian who was the first female singer to be recorded singing with a big band—on Fletcher Henderson's Jazz Five recording of "Do That Thing" (Vocalion, 1924). Fletcher and Rosa were not related.

ROSABELLA Beautiful rose (Italian).

ROSCOE Doe wood (Old Norse).

ROSE MARIE (b. 1923), best known as Sally Rogers on the popular television sitcom *The Dick Van Dyke Show*, which ran from 1961 to 1966. "The First Lady of Vegas," Rosie started her career as Baby Rose Marie with her own radio show at the age of three. "I had the same voice then as I have now," the actress said about her unmistakable, deep, gravelly voice. She worked on Broadway, in Hollywood, and all across America with every major comic actor and singer, was hired by Bugsy Siegel to open the Flamingo, the first casino hotel on the Vegas strip, and continues to enjoy one of the longest careers in entertainment history. If there was such a thing as entertainment royalty, Rose Marie would be the queen. Pookie, "a fuzzy little white dog," and Spatz, a Golden Retriever mix, are Rosie's canine family. Both are rescue dogs.

ROSEBUD "Purity" in the language of flowers; Golden Retriever in *Snow Buddies*.

ROSELLE Species of hibiscus with medicinal properties.

ROSEMARY "Remembrance" in the language of flowers. Rosemary Clooney (1928–2002), American jazz–pop singer and actress whose signature song was "Come On-a My House," cowritten by playwright William Saroyan, and who visits us every holiday season in *White Christmas* (1954) as Betty Haynes, Bing Crosby's love interest. Her voice was like poured cream. For twenty years after the war, Clooney's songs topped the charts. Despite personal tragedies and illness with bipolar disease, she remained a lady throughout. Her nephew is Academy Award–winning actor and director George Clooney.

ROSENEATH Roseneath Terrier, original name of the West Highland Terrier.

ROSIE Among the thirty most popular female dog names.

ROSS *The Cairn Terrier*, by Florence M. Ross, the earliest book on the breed, published in 1876.

ROSSEAU Dogs imported from France and Ireland in 1830 by a breeder named Rosseau became the foundation line for the Henry-Birdsong and Trigg strains of Beagle.

ROTHBURY Rothbury Terrier, early name for the Bedlington Terrier.

ROTHSCHILD The great eighteenth-century German-Jewish banking family.

ROTWEIL Oldest town in the federal state of Baden-Württemberg near the Black Forest in southwest Germany and place of origin of the Rottweiller, a working breed known as "Rotweil butcher dogs" (*Rottweiler Metzgerhund*) because they were used to herd cattle and pull butchers' carts as early AD 73, when Rotweil was founded by the Romans.

ROVER Standard-issue dog name. *The Rover Boys*, extremely popular series of thirty books by Edward Stratemeyer published between 1899 and 1926 about the escapades of brothers Tom, Sam, and Dick Rover, students at a military boarding school. Their children Fred, Jack, and Tom's twins Andy and Randy, began the second series with Volume 21. *The Hardy Boys*, *Tom Swift*, and *Nancy Drew* took over in popularity. Humorist Corey Ford pariodied the books in *Vanity Fair* magazine, calling them "The Rollo Boys." Stratemeyer attempted to sue.

ROWETT General Rowett imported the Hare Hound from England to refine the bloodlines of the American Beagle in the mid-1800s.

ROWLF Rowlf the Dog, wise-cracking, piano-playing Muppet who also plays Doctor Bob in *Veterinarians Hospital*, the Muppet soap opera.

ROXANNE Bright dawn (Greek).

ROXIE Early Scottish Terrier bitch that helped establish the breed in the United States.

ROY Professor Presbury's Wolfhound that attacks his master, providing the great English detective Sherlock Holmes with an important clue in *The Adventure of the Creeping Man*, by Sir Arthur Conan Doyle.

ROYAL Mr. Arnold of Rhode Island imported Royal Rock Beagles from northern England in the 1880s to refine the bloodline of his American kennel.

RUBENS Peter Paul Rubens, sixteenth-century Flemish painter who depicted Papillons and other dogs on his canvases. Other painters that painted Papillons were seventeenth-century French painters Jean-Antoine Watteau, Jean-Honoré Fragonard, and François Boucher.

RUBEUS Rubeus Hagrid, Gamekeeper and Keeper of Keys and Grounds of Hogwarts School of Witchcraft and Wizardry, a giant of a man who is devoted to Harry Potter and endearingly played by Scottish actor Robbie Coltrane, one of Great Britain's most respected actors. Indeed, Coltrane ranked sixth in a poll as "the most famous Scot" after the Loch Ness Monster, Robert Burns, Sean Connery, Robert the Bruce, and William Wallace. Since three of that number are dead and it's unsure whether or not one really exists, that puts Coltrane in the No. 2 spot after Sean Connery.

RUBY Chestnut red coat of some English Toy Spaniels. Good name for a female Irish Setter; Ruby Rough, President Calvin Coolidge's Rough Collie.

RUDDY A Nova Scotia Duck Tolling Retriever has a ruddy coat and this name would suit him, or any dog with a thick coat that color.

RUDO Love (African).

RUDOLF Wolf (Germanic). Santa's reindeer with the shiny nose. **Rudy** is the diminutive.

RUDYARD *See* Kipling.

RUFARO Joy (African).

RUFF Dennis the Menace's loveable Sheepdog. The comic strip debuted in 1951 and since then, spun-off a television series and 1993 motion picture starring Walter Matthau. At first, Ruff was called Gnasher.

RUFFIAN (1972–1975), "Queen of Fillies," one of the greatest thoroughbred racehorses of all time, certainly the greatest female, who put her heart into racing with such force that it cost her her life.

RUFFINO Redhaired (Italian). Good name for an Italian Spinone.

RUFFLE Early Pomeranian first shown in England by Mrs. Barrett and then, in America, by Mrs. Smythe.

RUFUS Rudolph Chambers Lehmann's beloved spaniel in "To Rufus: A Spaniel." Rufus was also the sire of King, an important English Mastiff. *See* King.

RUGGLES Best-selling novel serialized in 1914 in *Saturday Evening Post* by Harry Leon Wilson about an English butler named Marmeduke Ruggles who journeys to the American West. The book was adapted into a 1935 hit comedy film starring the great English actor Charles Laughton. Go to YouTube and watch Laughton recite Lincoln's Gettysburg Address, excerpted from this movie. If this doesn't bring a tear to your eye or fill you with pride, then, my friend, you are no American.

RUMBA A combination of the musical traditions of Cuba and Africa that produce highly rhythmic music.

RUMPUS Historic name for a West Highland Terrier. *See* Goelet.

RUNAKO Handsome (African).

RUNNER Good name for a fast-running dog like a Greyhound or Saluki.

RUNT The smallest dog in a litter.

RUPERT Bright fame (Gaelic).

RUSSELL Little red one (French).

RUSSET Fine name for a dog with a russet coat, such as an Irish Setter.

RUSTLER A cattle thief and not a bad name for a sheepdog.

RUSTY James McDivitt, David Scott, and Russell "Rusty" Schweickart were the astronauts of Apollo 9, which spent ten days orbiting the Earth. Liftoff was March 3, 1969.

RYA Dragon (Japanese).

RYL "The Yellow Ryl" is a short story by L. Frank Baum, written in 1905.

RYZHIK Soviet space dog.

S

SAAD Good luck (African).

SABATO Born on Saturday (Italian).

SABER Long, thin, extremely sharp sword with a large hand guard believed to have originated in Eastern Europe in the seventeenth century.

SABI Female black Labrador Retriever trained to detect improvised explosive devices (IEDs) for Australian forces stationed in Orūzgā Province during the war in Afghanistan. She was missing in action for fourteen months before being recovered by American troops in 2009.

SABINA Poppaea Sabina (AD 30–65), Roman empress and second wife of Nero.

SABINE *See* Dog Names by Category: Breed; Westminster.

SABLE If your dog has black tipped-silver, grey, or gold fur like some Siberian Huskys do, then sable describes her coat—and it's a nice name to call a dog, besides; Pycombe Sable, a champion Curly Coated Retriever owned by British Brigadier General F. F. Lance.

SABRE Sword (Old English).

SABRINA Singer-songwriter Billy Joel's Pug.

SABU Sabu Dastagir (1924–1963), India-born American actor who gained fame in boyhood for his roles in Alexander Korda's film adaptations of Rudyard Kipling's *Kim* and *The Jungle Book*. Born the son of an elephant herder, Sabu became a naturalized American citizen, served in the US Army Air Corps in World War Two as a tail gunner on a B-24 with the 307th Bomb Group in the Pacific, and was awarded the Distinguished Flying Cross for Valor and Bravery. He died at the age of thirty-nine of a massive heart attack, leaving his wife and two young children.

SABURAU *See* Samurai.

SACHEM *See* Sagamore.

SACHI Female child of bliss (Japanese).

SADA Female child of purity (Japanese).

SADDLE Great name for a Foxhound—not just because the dog is bred for the hunt, but because of its markings.

SADIE A Labrador Retriever trained to detect explosive devices, attached to the Royal Gloucestershire, Berkshire, and Wiltshire Regiment in Kabul, Afghanistan 2005. Sadie was awarded the Dickin Medal in 2007.

SAFFRON A spice derived from the crocus, an early-blooming spring flower.

SAGA An epic story usually associated with Norwegian legend. Famous sagas include J. R. R. Tolkien's *Lord of the Rings*, John Galsworthy's *The*

Forsyte Saga, the *Star Wars* saga, the Indiana Jones movies, and all of J. K. Rowling's Harry Potter books and movies. Saga would be a good name for a Great Dane or other large dog.

SAGAMORE Chief of the Algonquins, also **Sachem**. Theodore Roosevelt's family home in Oyster Bay, Long Island, New York, today part of the National Park Service and open to the public.

SAGE "Wisdom" in the language of flowers.

SAGRAMORE Sir Sagramore, knight of King Arthur's legendary Round Table. Bing Crosby's sidekick in *A Connecticut Yankee in King Arthur's Court*, played by William Bendix.

SAHARA "The Great Desert" and second largest in the world (believe it or not, Antarctica's desert is the first), covering 3,630,000 square miles of North Africa, which exceeds the size of Europe and the continental United States combined. The Saluki breed of dog originated in the part of this region that extended from the Caspian Sea to Persia and Anatolia, where the Anatolian Shepherd Dog originated.

SAID Happy (African).

SAILOR The Chesapeake Bay Retriever is believed to be descended from two dogs, Sailor and **Canton**, rescued as puppies by the American ship *Canton* from an English brig wrecked off the Maryland coast in 1807. Canton was named after the ship. Sailor Boy, President Theodore Roosevelt's Chesapeake Bay Retriever.

SAKURA Cherry blossom (Japanese).

SALEEM Peaceful (African).

SALEM Peace, holy city (Old English).

SALILYN *See* Dog Names by Category: Breed; Westminster.

SALLAH "The best digger in Cairo" hired by Indiana Jones and played by John Rhys-Davies in Steven Spielberg's *Raiders of the Lost Ark* (1981). Good name for an Pharaoh Hound.

SALLY Labrador Retriever guide dog that led her blind owner down more than seventy flights of stairs to safety when the World Trade Center was destroyed on 9/11. She was awarded the Dickin Medal in 2002. **Roselle**, another Lab, performed a similarly heroic feat.

SALMON Swell name for a fly-fisherman's dog.

SALNIKOV Vladimir Salnikov of the Soviet Union won four gold medals in Olympic Games held between 1980 and 1988.

SALVO White Bulldog descended from Crib and Rose, painted by Frank Paton in 1892. The portrait of Salvo is in the collection of the American Kennel Club.

SAM Alsatian with the Royal Canadian Regiment. Sam held back rioters in Bosnia and Herzegovina in 1998 and was subsequently awarded the Dickin Medal. Old English Sheepdog in *Cats & Dogs*. Sam the Eagle, one of Jim Henson's crankier Muppets. John Wayne's dog in the 1953 movie *Hondo*. Riggs's dog in the 1987 action film *Lethal Weapon*, starring Mel Gibson and Danny Glover.

SAM Sheepdog; Looney Tunes's complacent, slow-moving cartoon Sheepdog who foils Ralph E. Wolf every time with a single punch in the snoot. Another creation of the great animator Chuck Jones, voiced by the immortal Mel Blanc.

SAM SPADE *See* Dashiell.

SAMANTA Heard by God (Italian).

SAMANTHA German Shepherd Dog in the 2007 post-Apocalyptic science fiction film *I Am Legend*, starring Will Smith. Sam is played by canine actor Abbey.

SAMI A good nickname for a Samoyed. As a puppy, the Samoyed looks like "a little white teddy bear" and has been called "the big white dog which carries in its face and heart the spirit of Christmas the whole year through."

SAMMY The dog that belongs to one of the house masters in P. G. Wodehouse's *Mike and Psmith*.

SAMSON Man of the son (Hebrew). A man endowed with phenomenal strength by God to engage combat and to undertake great physical deeds. Among the top thirty male dog names and a strong one for a Great Dane.

SAMUR Bjartur's father-in-law's dog in Halldór Laxness's book *Independent People*.

SAMURAI Military nobility in both China and Japan dating to at least AD 900. Samurai are subject to stringent imperatives known as the Bushidō and the martial art Kendō, which means "the way of the Sword." The word comes from the Japanese term *saburau*; in Japan, *saburai*. A good name for brave male dogs of Japanese or Chinese breeds.

SAMWISE Samwise Gamgee, pivotal character in J. R. R. Tolkien's *Lord of the Ring* saga.

SAND DUNE Nice name for a canine beachcomber with a sand-colored coat.

SAND STORM Another good beach-inspired name for a dog with a sandy coat.

SANDERS Helper of mankind (Germanic). **Alisandre** is the French version, **Zander** is the German. Also spelled **Saunders**. Sign over the dooryard of Winnie-the-Pooh's house.

SANDRINGHAM Breeding of the Clumber Spaniel came to a halt with the Great War but was revitalized at the royal kennels at Sandringham by order of King George V in 1925.

SANDSTORM *See* Dog Names by Category: Breed; Crufts.

SANDY Little Orphan Annie's dog since the Harold Gray comic strip came into being in 1924. President Teddy Roosevelt's daughter, Alice

Roosevelt Longworth, owned a Scottish Terrier named Sandy, as did English children's author Beatrix Potter.

SANS SOUCI Carefree, without a worry in the world (French). Good karma comes from a dog with a name like this.

SANSSOUCI Historical name for an Italian Greyhound. *See* Frederick.

SANTA PAWS Santa Claus's dog in the 2009 Disney film *Santa Buddies*.

SANTA Holy (Italian).

SANTINO Little saint (Italian).

SAPHIRA Eyes like the sapphire (Italian).

SAPPHIRE Radiant dark or cornflower blue gemstone from the Greek word *sappheiros*, which means "blue stone."

SARASOTA Southwestern Florida city discovered in 1513 by Spanish Conquistadores. They called it Zara Zote. Sarasota has a particularly rich and colorful history.

SARIS Captain Saris, a British naval officer, received a dog from the Emperor of Japan to give to King James I of England. Every Japanese ruler since has continued the tradition of presenting a dog descended from that line to the reigning monarch of Great Britain. The breed became known as the English Toy Spaniel.

SASHA Shining upon man (Russian). Diminutive for **Alexandra**.

SASSAFRAS Aromatic deciduous tree native to North America. The leaves are used to make perfume and soap, but the root, which has medicinal qualities when prepared, was a seventeenth-century treatment for syphilis and at one time was the second largest export from the Colonies to Europe.

SASSY Fresh, spunky, vivacious.

SATAN Wirehaired Pointing Griffon whelped from Mouche. *See* Mouche. John and Abigail Adams's dog.

SATCHMO Louis Armstrong (1901–1971), called "Satchmo" or "Pops," the most famous American jazz trumpeter ever, if not the greatest. Born into a poor New Orleans family, the son of a prostitute and a deadbeat father, and the grandson of slaves, he dropped out of school at the age of eleven and went to work for a Lithuanian-Jewish immigrant family in New Orleans by the name of Karnofsky. It was the first time the boy had known kindness—and it is for them that Louis wore a pendant with the Star of David the rest of his life. His gravelly voice and magnetic personality made an indelible mark on American jazz. A consummate entertainer, Armstrong performed on radio, television, and in films such as *The Glenn Miller Story* with James Stewart and *Hello, Dolly!* with Barbra Streisand. He accompanied numerous vocal artists, such as Bing Crosby, Ella Fitzgerald, Danny Kaye, and Bessie Smith; his discography is enormous and his awards too many to list. His signature song, "What a Wonderful World," fit this wonderful man.

SATIN Glossy, silky fabric that shimmers. If your dog's coat is like that, then this may be just the name for her. Great name for a Shih Tzu.

SATIPO South American guide played by Alfred Molina who attempts to betray Indiana in Steven Spielberg's first Indiana Jones movie, *Raiders of the Lost Ark* (1981).

SAUERBRATEN German pot roast. Fun name for a German Shepherd Dog, Great Dane, Spitz, Giant Schnauzer, Poodle, Pomeranian, Weimaraner—any of the many dogs of German origin.

SAUERKRAUT Fermented, shredded cabbage, another German dish and another fun name for a German breed.

SAUL Prayed for (Hebrew). Saul (1079–1007 BC) first king of the United Kingdom of Israel according to the Old Testament, anointed by the prophet Samuel and survived by his son, David.

SAUNDERS Defend and help (Scottish). Good name for a search and rescue dog. Jennifer Saunders (b. 1958), brilliant, multitalented English actress and cocreator-writer of the smash British television comedy series *Absolutely Fabulous*, in which she plays lead character Edina Monsoon. Children of all ages know Saunders as the voice of the Fairy Godmother in *Shrek*.

SAURON Principal antagonist in J. R. R. Tolkien's *The Lord of the Rings* saga.

SAVAGE Sam Bluetick Coonhound and Old Yeller's son in the 1963 Disney film sequel to *Old Yeller* called *Savage Sam*.

SAVANNAH Grassland with low, scattered trees.

SAVIO Clever (Italian).

SAVOY Region of France between Lake Geneva and Monaco.

SAWYER Tom Sawyer, protagonist in *The Adventures of Tom Sawyer*, a semiautobiographical account of Samuel Clemens's life growing up in Hannibal, Missouri, first published in 1876. The author is better known as Mark Twain.

SAXON Germanic settlement of tribes that established themselves in Great Britain in the fifth century. *See* Dog Names by Category: Breed; Crufts.

SAYANTSI Nomadic race of people related to the Mongol and the Finn that reached the Yanesei River after traveling vast tracts of tundra, believed to have first bred the Samoyed as reindeer herders and sledge dogs.

SCALLYWAG A little mischief maker.

SCAMP Puppy born to *Lady and the Tramp* in the classic Walt Disney animated feature film.

SCAMPER Golden Spaniel belonging to Peter and Janet in the *Secret Seven* series of young children's mystery novels by Enid Blyton.

SCARECROW Semblance of a man made of old clothes stuffed with straw, meant to scare away crows. The most famous, certainly, came to life in *The Wizard of Oz*. *See* Hunk.

SCARF Cotton or silk square, oftentimes printed with a design, worn around the head or the neck or tied under the chin. *See* Dog Names by Category: Breed; Crufts.

SCARLETT Unforgettable heroine of *Gone with the Wind*, by Margaret Mitchell, played by Vivien Leigh in the epic film produced by David O. Selznick. *"Tomorrow is another day."*

SCENTWELL George Washington's American Staghound.

SCEPTRE Ornamental baton usually made of gold and studded with gemstones that is held by a ruling monarch during royal engagements and most especially, at a coronation. *See* Dog Names by Category: Breed; Crufts.

SCHIAPARELLI, Elsa (1890–1973), Italian-born Paris couture designer and visionary who saw fashion as art and collaborated with artists such as Salvador Dalí and Giacometti. She came to the United States an impoverished bride, returned to Europe to build her couture empire, then spent most of World War Two in the United States working for the American war effort before returning to Paris. Her granddaughters were actress-model Marisa Berenson and the late Berry Berenson Perkins, American photographer and wife of American actor Anthony Perkins, star of Alfred Hitchcock's suspense film *Psycho*. Tragically, Berry was one of the passengers to die on American Airlines flight 11 on 9/11.

SCHMITT Apollo 17, with astronauts Eugene Cernan, Ronald Evans, and Harrison H. "Jack" Schmitt onboard, landed at Taurus-Littrow, a valley on the near side of the moon. It would be NASA's last Apollo lunar landing and the most recent human flight beyond low Earth orbit. That was December 7, 1972—four decades ago.

SCHNAPPS Swallow (German). German liquor dating to the eighteenth century.

SCHNITZEL Traditional Austrian dish and an adorable name for an Austrian breed, such as an Austrian Shorthaired Pinscher.

SCOOBY-DOO Slobbering, mumble-mouthed animated Hanna-Barbera Great Dane that first burst upon the scene in 1969 and has been mumbling ever since.

SCOOTER Like a bicycle without a seat that you propel with one foot while the other rests on a board that's got two wheels. A motorized scooter cuts out the legwork. Cute name for a dog that gets around; Muppet gopher whose uncle owns the Muppet Theater.

SCORPIO Eighth astrological sign of the zodiac.

SCOTCH Scotch and **Soda** were President Ronald Reagan's Scottish Terriers.

SCOTSMAN The Rough Collie, Scottish Terrier, and Scottish Deerhound originate from Scotland. Fitting name for these breeds.

SCOTTY Montgomery "Scotty" Scott (b. 2222), Scottish-born chief engineer aboard the *Enterprise* who went "where no man has gone before" on the television series and in the series-inspired movies. He was portrayed winningly by Canadian actor James Doohan (1920–2005). Affectionate name for the Scottish Terrier.

SCOUNDREL Rascal, rogue, scallywag. Most puppies are.

SCOUT Dalmatian in the children's book *Finley the Fire Engine*. Singer Sheryl Crow's "part Lab, part deer" rescue dog. Young girl and narrator of the classic American novel *To Kill a Mockingbird*, by Harper Lee

SCROOGE Ebenezer Scrooge. Classic story of a curmudgeon who is visited by three ghosts that attempt to change his penny-pinching, dour, friendless life by subliminally revealing the true meaning of Christmas to him—and to countless millions across the years—in Charles Dickens's immortal *A Christmas Carol.*

SCRUFFY Mrs. Muir's Wirehaired Fox Terrier on *The Ghost and Mrs. Muir,* a 1968 television series based on the hauntingly romantic 1947 film, which was based on the 1945 novel by R. A. Dick, pseudonym of writer Josephine Leslie.

SCRUMMY King George VI of England's beloved yellow Labrador Retriever.

SCUD Sid's "toy-chewing" Bull Terrier in the 1995 animated feature film *Toy Story.*

SCUPPER The dog in *The Sailor Dog,* by Margaret Wise Brown.

SCYLAX Watchdog in *The Satyricon,* by Petronius.

SEA CATCH Northern fur seal and Kotick's father in *The Jungle Book,* by Rudyard Kipling.

SEA COW Steller's Sea Cow, a sea mammal similar to a walrus, in *The Jungle Book,* by Rudyard Kipling.

SEA VITCH A type of walrus in *The Jungle Book,* by Rudyard Kipling.

SEAMAN Meriwether Lewis's Newfoundland that accompanied his master on the Lewis and Clark expedition to the American Northwest.

SEAMUS James (Irish).

SEARCHLIGHT Courageous sled dog in *Stone Fox,* by John Reynolds Gardiner.

SEARELLE Historical name for an Italian Greyhound. *See* Lobengula.

SEASHELL Great name for a shell-white puppy, especially if you live near the ocean.

SEBASTIAN Pug in the 2008 Disney film *Beverly Hills Chihuahua.*

SEKANI Merriment (African).

SEKAYI Laughter (African).

SELENE Moon (Greek).

SELVAGGIA Wild (Italian).

SENG Historical name for a Lhasa Apso. *See* Abso.

SENSATION English Pointer depicted on the logo of the Westminster Kennel Club Dog Show.

SEPIA A reddish-brown and good name for a Rhodesian Ridgeback.

SEPPEL Founding dog of the Schnauzer breed.

SEPTIMUS Septimus Small, Aunt Julia's long-deceased husband in *The Forsyte Saga*, by John Galsworthy. *See* Galsworthy.

SERENA Clear, tranquil, serene, peaceful (Latin).

SERENDIPITY A chance or providential event that happily happens.

SERGEANT Noncommissioned officer in the US Army or US Marine Corps. *See* Stubby.

SESTO Sixth (Italian). Appropriate and rather clever name for the sixth puppy in a litter.

SETTCHEN Along with **Jette von Enz**, the two most famous founding bitches of the Schnauzer breed.

SEUSS Theodor Seuss Geisel (1904–1991), universally loved as Dr. Seuss, gave us *The Cat in the Hat*, *How the Grinch Stole Christmas* (*see* Karloff), *Green Eggs and Ham*, *Horton Hears a Who*, and forty-two other children's books that you still delight in. You may not know that Geisel was a political cartoonist and a commander in the US Army Air Corps in World War Two who was awarded the Legion of Merit. He did not begin writing children's books until after the war with the exception of one, written in 1937, *And to Think That I Saw It on Mulberry Street!* And you know, when you really think about it, Dr. Seuss's message always was, if you try your best and stick with it, you will prevail. He knew this first hand: *Mulberry Street* was rejected twenty-seven times before it was accepted by a publisher. Another author who suffered multiple rejections before her first book was accepted by a publisher was a British author named J. K. Rowling, whose first book was written in 1995 on an old manual typewriter. It was called *Harry Potter and the Philosopher's Stone.*

SEYMOUR Jane Seymour (1508–1537), third wife of Henry VIII, who died two weeks after the birth of her first child, a son, who became King Edward VI, Henry's sole male heir. Jane is the only one of Henry's wives to receive a queen's burial and the only one of his eight to be buried beside him at Windsor Castle.

SGT. TIBBS A tabby cat that helps the Colonel find the *101 Dalmatians* in the Walt Disney animated feature film

SHACKLETON Antarctic explorer Sir Ernest Henry Shackleton (1874–1922) used Samoyeds in his expeditions. Strong, good-humored, fast, and devoted, the Samoyed is said to possess nearly human intelligence. Other polar explorers that also used Samoyeds were Borchgrevinck, Scott, Jackson-Harmsworth, the Duc d'Abruzzi, and Anthony Fiala.

SHADOW Dog in the film *Homeward Bound: The Incredible Journey*, voiced by Don Ameche. Among the top thirty male dog names. Fine name for a dog with a black coat.

SHAGGY *The Shaggy Dog*, a 1959 Disney film that starred beloved American actor Fred MacMurray and bred two sequels. Good name for an Old English Sheepdog or a Bearded Collie.

SHAKESPEARE William Shakespeare (1564–1616), English poet and playwright, known as the "Bard of Avon" after Stratford-upon-Avon, the Cotswold town in which he was born, married, and retired after a successful career in London. He also acted in his own plays, performed by his own acting company called the Lord Chamberlain's Men (subsequently called the King's Men), on his own stage—the Globe Theatre, which he and shareholding actors in the Lord Chamberlain's Men built in 1599 to stage Shakespeare's plays. He wrote thirty-eight—*Hamlet*, *Macbeth*, *Othello*, *Romeo and Juliet*, among them—plus 154 sonnets and other poems.

SHAMBALA *See* Tippie.

SHAMROCK Three-leaf (Irish). Three-and the lucky four-leaf green clover, symbol of Ireland, and a clever name for an Irish Setter or Irish Wolfhound.

SHANE Classic 1953 film starring Alan Ladd and Jean Arthur, in her last movie, based on the story by Jack Schaefer, about a gunslinger romantically drawn to a simple homesteader's wife. Great name for an Australian Cattle Dog.

SHANGRI-LA Utopia hidden high in the Himalayas, where no one grows old or gets ill—unless they leave—in James Hilton's 1933 novel *Lost Horizon*, adapted into Frank Capra's 1937 Academy Award–winning film starring the great English actor Ronald Colman.

SHANNON President John F. Kennedy's Irish Cocker Spaniel.

SHASTA Golden Retriever in the 2001 film *K-Pax*, starring Kevin Spacey and Jeff Bridges. Siberian Husky in the 2008 Disney direct-to-DVD film *Snow Buddies*, part of the *Air Buddies* franchise. The puppies in the film are Golden Retrievers named **Budderball**, **B-Dawg**, **Buddha**, **Mudbud**, **Rosebud**, and **Shasta**. They appear in the fourth film in the series, *Santa Buddies*, along with Santa Claus's dog, **Santa Paws** and his son, **Puppy Paws**.

SHATRAJ *See* Chess.

SHAW George Bernard Shaw (1856–1950), prolific, witty Irish playwright, author, and the only individual to be awarded the Nobel Prize in Literature (1925) and an Academy Award (1938) for *Pygmalion*, which inspired the award-winning musical *My Fair Lady*.

SHAYNA Beautiful (Hebrew).

GOLDEN RETRIEVER PUPPY

SHEBA Shrouded in mystery, but in Matthew 12:42 and Luke 11:31 of the Bible, she appears to be the "Queen of the South" and lived around the 10th century BC.

SHEILA Rough Collie sent into the Cheviot Hills during a blizzard to rescue four American airmen after their plane had crashed. She was awarded the Dickin Medal in 1945.

SHELBY Australian Shepherd that Adrian Monk adopts in the popular television series *Monk*.

SHELLEY The meadow along the riverbank (Old English).

SHELTON *See* Dog Names by Category: Breed; Crufts.

SHEP Dog in the 1954 Rory Calhoun movie *A Bullet Is Waiting*. Almanzo's shepherd dog in Laura Ingalls Wilder's *These Happy Golden Years*. President Rutherford B. Hayes's hunting dog.

SHERE KHAN Royal Bengal Tiger in *The Jungle Book*, by Rudyard Kipling.

SHERIFF Enforcer of law and order in the Old West, senior judiciary representative of the monarch in Great Britain, and chief of police in American counties and towns. Good name for a German Shepherd Dog.

SHERLOCK Bright hair (Old English). Sir Arthur Conan Doyle's violin-playing, cocaine-using detective Sherlock Holmes. Holmes is currently and brilliantly portrayed by British actor Benedict Cumberbatch on PBS.

SHERWOOD Luminous wood (Old English). Ye olde forest from whence Robin Hood cometh.

SHIITAKE Edible mushroom originally from Japan.

SHILOH The 1991 Newbery Medal-winning children's novel by Phyllis Reynolds Naylor about a boy and his love for an abused dog.

SHIMMER Glisten, shine, like the coat of a Siberian Husky.

SHINO Stem of the bamboo (Japanese).

SHIRE The Bedlington Terrier takes its name from Bedlingtonshire in Northumberland, England.

SHIRLEY Bright clearing (Old English). Shirley Knight (b. 1936), Academy Award–nominated American stage and screen actress whose career began its meteoric rise with her second motion picture, the 1959 film adaptation of the Tennesse Williams play *Sweet Bird of Youth*, in which she played Heavenly Finley opposite a young up-and-coming actor named Paul Newman. Most proud of her role in the 1967 film *Dutchman*, her film credits also include *Divine Secrets of the Ya-Ya Sisterhood* (2002) with Sandra Bullock, Ashley Judd, and Maggie Smith; *As Good as it Gets* (1997) with Jack Nicholson and Helen Hunt; and *Our Idiot Brother* (2011) with Paul Rudd. On television she played Phyllis Van de Kamp in *Desperate Housewives* and hilariously, Georgia

Adams, a happy old lady under treatment for an STD by British actor Hugh Laurie as *House.*

SHOESHINE Shoeshine Boy from Disney's version of *Underdog* in 2007 (called Shoshine in the 1960 cartoon series).

SHOGUN Hereditary military dictators in Japan from 1192 to 1867. Great name for an Akita.

SHORT ROUND Resourceful Asian kid played by Jonathan Ke Quan in Steven Spielberg's *Indiana Jones and the Temple of Doom.*

SHORTY Affectionate for a short-legged dog like a Dachshund.

SHOTGUN "Riding shotgun" refers to the passenger sitting in the front seat next to the driver in a car or truck—and likely where your dog wants to sit when he goes for a ride; sporting arm used to hunt wild birds and small game, an age-old sport for which bird dogs were bred.

SHUBERT Franz Peter Schubert (1797–1828), prolific Austrian Romantic composer who died too young but still managed to write nine of the world's most beloved symphonies, and over six hundred Lieder (German songs). Best known for his *Unfinished Symphony.*

SHUG Actress Ashley Judd's Cockapoo (Cocker Spaniel–Poodle mix).

SHUTKA Soviet space dog. *See* History.

SIBERIA Place of origin of the Siberian Husky, which was brought to Alaska in 1909. Good name for a Husky.

SIDNEY Sidney Carton, lawyer and hero who sacrifices himself in Charles Dickens's 1859 heartwrenching novel set during the French Revolution, *A Tale of Two Cities*, adapted into a 1935 film starring Ronald Colman.

SIEGER Sieger Rex von Den Gunthersburg, important foundation dog of the Schnauzer line.

SIEGFRIED Victory, peace (German).

SIENNA Yellow-brown color with a reddish tinge. About the color of the coat of a Chesapeake Bay Retriever.

SIERRA Saw-toothed (Spanish). The first word in the names of mountain ranges in California and in Central and South America, such as the Sierra Madre and Sierra Nevada.

SIF Wife of Thor, Norse god of thunder.

SIGMUND Hero in Norse mythology.

SIGNAL To motion, wave, nod. *See* Dog Names by Category: Breed; Westminster.

SILAS Wood, forest (Latin).

SILKY Soft like silk.

SILVANA From the forest (Italian).

SILVER Precious metal used in jewelry, cutlery, coins and as an electrical conductor. Good name for a dog with a light grey coat.

SILVER BLAZE Not actually the name of a dog but the name of a Sherlock Holmes story in which an unnamed dog exhibits strange behavior that provides the world's greatest detective with a vital clue in Sir Arthur Conan Doyle's *The Adventure of Silver Blaze*.

SILVIA Woods, forest (Latin).

SIMON He who hears the word (Latin). The feminine form is **Simone**.

SIMPLON Simplon-Orient Express, one of the world's most luxurious and legendary trains—and where Hercule Poirot must solve a great mystery in Agatha Christie's *Murder on the Orient Express*.

SINATRA Frank Sinatra (1915–1998), also known as Ol' Blue Eyes and the Chairman of the Board, one of the greatest American popular vocalists of the twentieth century. His smooth, deeply emotional interpretation of the songs he sang have been copied by many and equaled by none.

SINBAD Mixed-breed canine sailor on the US Coast Guard Cutter *George W. Campbell* in World War Two and the Coast Guard's most famous mascot until his death in 1954.

SINCLAIR Sinclair Lewis (1885–1951), American novelist, short story writer, and Nobel Prize winner whose novels (*Dodsworth*, *Elmer Gantry*) are among the greatest American books ever written. Admired by contemporaries such as Hemingway, he lost a lifelong battle with alcohol at the age of sixty-five.

SINFONIA Symphony (Italian).

SINGER Vocalist. If you have a very vocal dog, then this is the name for him.

SIOUXSIE Beautiful flower (Old English).

SIR A good name for an imposing dog with a gentlemanly deportment, such as a Great Dane.

SIRIUS BLACK The heir of the noble House of Black, he rejected his Wizarding family's roots in the Black Arts to lead the opposing forces of the Dark Lord. Bellatrix Lestrange, a Death Eater, was his cousin. He was James "Prongs" Potter's best friend and godfather to his son, Harry Potter.

SIRRAH *See* Dog Names by Category: Breed; Westminster.

SISKE Historical name for a Bouvier des Flandres. *See* Nic.

SISSY Affectionate version of **Sister**. Also **Sis**.

SIXTEN Sixten Hernberg of Sweden won nine Olympic medals in cross-country skiing in games held between 1956 to 1964.

SKEAN A Scottish Terrier that, along with **Bogey**, another Scottish Terrier, and **Peter** and **Pim**, two Westmoreland Terriers, were owned by George, Fourth Earl of Dumbarton. So intrepid and courageous were these little dogs that they were nicknamed "the diehards." When the Earl of Dumbarton's regiment was formed in 1633, it took the name the Royal Scots. Today The Royal Scots is the oldest Infantry Regiment of the Line in the British Army, and its moniker is "Dumbarton's Diehards," after the Earl and his four dogs.

SKEAN American aviator Charles Lindbergh's Scottish Terrier.

SKEET Popular shooting sport in which a clay target is broken by pointing a shotgun and discharging a shotshell at the small flying disk.

SKEEZERS Unlike the "Flatheads," the Skeezers are anatomically normal people that live in an obscure corner of the kingdom of *The Wonderful Wizard of Oz*, by L. Frank Baum.

SKIP Jack Russell Terrier featured in *My Dog Skip*, by Willie Morris, later adapted into a movie. President Theodore Roosevelt's Terrier.

SKIPPER Colloquial name for the captain of a boat. Schipperke (pronounced *Skeeper-ker*) was a famous Belgian barge dog. Skipper is also a type of butterfly, which would make this a great name for a Papillon, whose name means "butterfly" in French.

SKIPPY Wirehaired Fox Terrier canine actor who famously played Asta in the *Thin Man* series and many other movies. *See* Asta.

SKIPTON Skipton, Bradford, Keighley, and Otley are English towns rich in Airedale history.

SKYE The Isle of Skye is the place of origin of the Skye Terrier breed.

SKYLAR Jack Russell Terrier in *Skylar and George Washington*, by Matt Burgess.

SKYWALKER The Force is with the Skywalker family in *Star Wars*—Anakin, his son Luke, and Luke's twin sister, Princess Leia.

SLAMMER Dr. Slammer, surgeon with the 97th Regiment who threatens to fight a duel with Jingle in Charles Dickens's first novel, *Pickwick Papers*.

SLATE Grey metamorphic rock, shade of the color grey, and a wonderful name for a Greyhound.

SLEEVE Pekingese were called "sleeve dogs" because they were carried about in the long, hanging sleeves of kimonos worn in Imperial China.

SLEUTH Bloodhounds were called "sleuth hounds" at the time of Robert the Bruce and William Wallace. These "man trackers" were sent to pursue "border reivers"—thieves and raiders that crossed clan boundaries to pilfer and steal in sixteenth-century Scotland. During the American Civil War, Bloodhounds were used to track runaway slaves.

SLIM Slim Pickens (1919–1983), American actor and former rodeo performer known for his cowboy roles in movies such as the John Wayne version of *Stagecoach*, hilariously in Mel Brooks's classic comedy *Blazing Saddles*, and in Stanley Kubrick's 1964 black comedy film *Dr. Strangelove*. Great name for a slender dog.

SLINKY Slinky Dog, aka Slink, toy Dachshund in the 1995 Disney animated film *Toy Story*.

SLIPPER Lady's Slipper, an orchid also known as the moccasin flower. In the language of flowers, Lady's Slipper means to tease or flirt. In the language of feet, it's what you put on after a long and tiring day.

SLOANE Raid, invade (English).

SLUGGY One of Humphrey Bogart's Scottish Terriers. Sluggy starred with his master in the 1941 film *High Sierra*.

SLUMBER "To sleep, per chance to dream," as Hamlet said. *See* Dog Names by Category: Breed; Westminster.

SLYTHERIN One of the four student houses at Hogwarts School of Witchcraft and Wizardry in the Harry Potter series. Slytherin's values are ambition, cunning, leadership, and resourcefulness.

SMELAYA Soviet space dog.

SMITH Smite, strike (English). Smith and Tinker, characters in the kingdom of Oz.

SMITHER The three aged Forsyte sisters's maid in Galsworthy's *The Forsyte Saga*.

SMITTY Affectionate for Smith.

SMOKEY Blue Tick Hound mascot of the University of Tennessee. Smokey the Bear, spokesbear of the US Forest Service, says "Only you can prevent forest fires."

SMOKY (1943–1957), attached to the 5th Air Force, 26th Photo Reconnaissance Squadron assigned to the South Pacific, the little Yorkshire Terrier flew a dozen air/sea rescue and photo reconnaissance missions. She was credited with twelve combat missions, awarded eight battle stars, survived 150 air raids on New Guinea and a typhoon at Okinawa.

SMYTHE Blacksmith (Old English).

SNAG US Drug Enforcement Administration's drug-sniffing dog who was responsible for 118 drug seizures, the total value of which exceeded $810 million.

SNAPDRAGON "Gracious lady" in the language of flowers.

SNAPE Professor Snape, one of the darkest and definitely the least understood character in the Harry Potter series.

SNAPSHOT Photograph taken "in the moment" that captures something spontaneous or unexpected.

SNEAKERS Rubber-soled athletic and leisurewear shoe. A London policeman invented the first sneaker in the 1800s.

SNEZHINKA Soviet space dog.

SNIF Character in the kingdom of *The Wonderful Wizard of Oz*, a dog-like Iffin who lost his "gr" having originally been a ferocious griffin in *The Marvelous Land of Oz*, one of the numerous sequels to *The Wizard of Oz* by L. Frank Baum. Super name for a Bloodhound or any dog who uses his nose to capture scent—which most dogs do.

SNIFF Siberian Husky in *Snow Dogs*.

SNIP NUA Racing greyhound in the BBC television series *Three Men Go to Ireland*.

SNIPPY Gene and Shannon Simmons's beloved family dog. Shannon had a childhood dog when she grew up in Canada named Lassie.

SNITTER Fox Terrier hero in *The Plague Dogs,* by Richard Adams.

SNODGRASS Augustus Snodgrass, another young friend of Mr. Pickwick's who perceives himself to be a great poet. Just as Mr. Winkle is no sportsman, Augustus Snodgrass is no poet.

SNOOPY The world's most famous Beagle, created by Charles M. Schulz.

SNOW WHITE European fairy tale that inspired Walt Disney's 1937 animated movie, *Snow White and the Seven Dwarfs*. Simple and lovely name for a dog whose coat is as white as snow, such as a West Highland White Terrier.

SNOWBALL Ball made of snow used to toss in play and make snowmen. A lively, fluffy white dog such as a Poodle or Samoyed should be named Snowball.

SNOWDRIFT Excellent name for an alpine mountain dog such as the Great Pyrenees or a Saint Bernard.

SNOWDROP "Hope" in the language of flowers.

SNOWFLAKE Flake of snow and a good name for a Bichon Frise, American Eskimo Dog, or any white dog.

SNOWY Tintin's Wirehaired Fox Terrier in *The Adventures of Tintin,* by Hergé.

SNUGGLES *Doctor Snuggles*, 1980 animated television series and joint Dutch, English, and German production. The late, great Peter Ustinov provided the voice of Doctor Snuggles, an eccentric, adventuresome, and kindhearted doctor who lived in an extra-extraordinary world. Alas, the series consists of only thirteen episodes. It's some of the best children's television ever produced.

SOAMES Possessive "man of property" estranged from his tormented wife Irene in John Galsworthy's *The Forsyte Saga.*

СОБАКА (sobaka) Russian, Ukranian for dog.

SOCCER Jack Russell Terrier that starred in the 1995 PBS children's television show *Wishbone.*

SOCKS Great name for a puppy with contrasting markings on his legs that resemble socks.

SOCRATES Classical Greek philosopher (469–399 BC) and one of the founders of Western philosophy.

SOFIA Wisdom (Italian).

SOLDIER Fighting member of the armed forces of a nation. A solid name for a guard dog or any dog with a strong and courageous nature.

SOLEIL Sun (French).

SOLOMON Peace (Hebrew). King of Israel born in 1011 BC, a man of God possessing great wisdom and wealth who accomplished great things before turning from Yahweh when lust overcame him in the latter part of his life.

SOMERSET County in southwestern England.

SONATA A classical form of music.

SONGSHI *See* Foo.

SONJA Sonja Henie of Norway, "Queen of Ice," won more Olympic (1928, 1932, and 1936) and World Championship (1927–1936) medals than any figure skater in history. She was the first skater in competitive sport to wear the short skirt costume and choreograph her own routines. Her superb technique influenced professional figure skating and raised it to a higher level of difficulty. In 1936 she began an extremely successful film career.

SONNIE President Herbert Hoover's Fox Terrier.

SONOMA County in Northern California famous for its wine region.

SOOT Dust, ash. Terrific name for a black Labrador Retriever or any dog whose coat is as black as soot.

SOPHIA Wisdom (Greek). **Sophie** is the diminutive. Among the thirty most popular female dog names.

SORBET Frozen dessert made with fruit juice.

SORCERER Male wizard with supernatural power. A female wizard is a Sorceress.

SOREL The word usually refers to a horse with a reddish-brown coat, but Sorel makes a good name for a dog with a similarly colored coat or markings, such as a Welsh Terrier.

SOTER In Greek, Soter was the spirit of safety, preservation, and deliverance from harm. One of the fifty watchdogs of ancient Greece, Soter was the only one to survive attack by invaders.

SOUTHPAW Left-handed human. But dogs have two left feet.

SPADE Spades, card game related to Whist.

SPANKY Head of the "Little Rascals" in Hal Roach's series of film shorts.

SPARK Flash, flicker, ember. *See* Darwin.

SPARKLE Shine, glitter, full of enthusiasm.

SPARKY One of Tonka's Pound Puppies.

SPARROW Small bird that is the harbinger of good or bad luck, depending on how things go for you. Captain Jack Sparrow, protagonist in Walt Disney's *Pirates of the Carribean* film series with Johnny Depp as Jack. Depp was influenced by Rolling Stones guitarist Keith Richards when he developed the role, much to the initial shock-horror of Disney producers who, like countless millions, were eventually drawn into Depp's quirky, flamboyant character. And that's the thing about him; Johnny Depp is one of the few actors who *becomes* the character rather than making the character *become* him.

SPATS Traditional footwear accessory still used by the Royal Regiment of Scotland. Great name for a dog with distinctive markings around his paws.

SPATTERDOCK A lovely, bright yellow waterlily and a neat name for a Golden Retriever.

SPAYNEL Original name of the Cocker Spaniel, one of the earliest known breeds of dog, dating to 1386.

SPECK Pee-Wee Herman's dog. Pee-Wee is the alter ego of comedian Paul Reubens.

SPECS Guide dog in *A Labrador's Tale: An Eye for Heroism.*

SPECTACLES If your puppy has contrasting markings around his eyes that give the appearance of eyeglasses, these are called "spectacles"— and that's a charming name for him.

SPENSER Author Robert B. Parker's popular mystery series about a Boston detective called Spenser who has three German Shorthaired Pointers. One is named **Pearl**.

SPHINX Great Sphinx of Giza, the largest monolith statue in the world, has a lion's body and a man's head and was built around 2560 BC by the pharaoh Khafra.

SPICE Condiments, savories, and spices to spice up food.

SPIKE Bull Mastiff in the animated movie *Sinbad: Legend of the Seven Seas*, produced by DreamWorks SKG. Yorkshire Terrier owned by comedienne Joan Rivers. British Bulldog, sometimes also called **Butch** or **Killer**, in the animated cartoon series *The Tom & Jerry Show*. Dwayne "The Rock" Johnson's Bulldog in the 2007 Walt Disney family comedy film *The Game Plan*.

SPIRIT Soul, essence of life, *chi*.

SPLASH Good name for a dog like a Whippet whose markings look like a splash of color on a mostly white coat.

SPORT A good name for a sporting breed, such as a Vizsla, Weimaraner, Wirehaired Pointing Griffon, and Boykin Spaniel.

SPOT *Spot the Dog*, a series of popular children's books by Eric Hill. President George W. Bush's English Springer Spaniel, named after Texas Rangers baseball player Scott Fletcher.

SPOTTED DICK Traditional English steamed suet pudding with currants.

SPOTTY *See* Disney.

SPRINGER One of the most popular and oldest breeds of English sporting dog, first described in Dr. John Caius's 1576 work, *Treatise of Englishe Dogs*.

SPRITE Warland Sprite, sister of the Airedale Terrier, Ch. Rhosddu Royalist, a foundation bitch of the breed.

SPROUT Early growth of a plant. Cute name for a Toy Fox Terrier.

SPUD Potato (American slang). Dog in the *Spy Pups* series, by Andrew Cope.

SPUNKY Cartoon Bull Terrier in *Rocko's Modern Life*, a 1993 children's television series on Nickelodean.

SPY Secret agent, covert operative. What your puppy does when he spies you in the kitchen and follows you, begging for a doggy treat.

SQUASH From the marrow family, steamed with a little butter and brown sugar, maybe some toasted marshmallows on top, traditionally served in the fall and at Thanksgiving. *Scrumptious.*

SQUEAK Jack Russell Terrier that would not leave the body of his murdered master, Zimbabwean farmer Terry Ford, in a political riot in 2002. A photo of the little dog protecting his dead master mustered international awareness over the terrible violence in Zimbabwe.

SQUIRE Errand runner (Gaelic). Historial name for a Bedlington Terrier. *See* Trevelyan.

SQUIRREL Border Collie in *A Dog's Life,* by Ann M. Martin. Soviet space dog.

STANDISH Myles Standish (1584–1656), English military officer hired by the Pilgrims to organize the defense of Plymouth Colony in the New World. He was one of the founders of Duxbury, Massachusetts. "The Courtship of Miles Standish," a 1858 narrative poem by American poet Henry Wadsworth Longfellow, depicts the unsubstantiated love triangle between Miles Standish, Priscilla Mullen, and John Alden.

STANISLAV Stanislav Pozdiniakov of Russia won five Olympic medals for fencing in the games held between 1992 and 2004.

STAR Dog in the *Spy Pups* and *Spy Dog* series of children's books by Andrew Cope. Win and Leah's family dog, son of Flame.

STARLET Young, budding, female movie star. Soviet space dog. *See* History.

STATLER and **Waldorf**, the pair of old men who sit in the front box of every Muppet show and mercilessly heckle the performances.

STEENIE Steenie and **Kates**, dogs belonging to King James I of England.

STEFANO Crown (Italian).

STEFFI Garland, crown.

STERLING Seedley Sterling, considered the finest Rough Collie of all time, was bred in England by R. H. Lord, whose dogs became the foundation stock of some of the best-known Rough Collies in America. Seedley Sterling was painted in 1916 by F. Sinet. The portrait is in the AKC Collection.

STERNCHEN Little star (German). Wonderful name for a dog with a white star marking on its forehead.

STETSON Hat manufactured by the John B. Stetson Company of Missouri in the mid-1800s as a prospector's hat, but in today's culture the Stetson is associated with Westerners. If you're from the West, Stetson is a good name for your puppy dog.

STEVE Crown (Greek). Diminutive of **Steven**, from the Greek given name **Stephanos**.

STEVENS Dr. Stevens, whose 1572 treatise, *The Maison Rustique*, is one of the earliest to mention the Scottish Terrier breed.

STIFFY King George VI's yellow Labrador Retriever.

STIGANDR Wanderer (Old Norse).

STILTON Strong-smelling, heavily veined blue cheese made in Derbyshire, Leicestershire, and Nottinghamshire. If it's not, it can't be the real thing because Stilton is a protected "designation of origin" by the European Commission.

STONY Pebbly, rocky terrain.

STORM Inclement weather, such as a blizzard, typhoon, or hurricane. **Stormy** is another name to consider. Stormy would make a good name for a Weimaraner, which has a coat the color of lowering stormclouds.

STORYTELLER The dog that sits at the feet of the narrator in *Jim Henson's The Storyteller: Greek Myths*.

STRATHBOGIE Pen name of Captain Gordon Murray, responsible for setting the standard of the Scottish Terrier in 1879. *See* Gordon.

STRAW Nice name for a dog with a coat the color of straw, especially if his coat is coarse.

STREAKER One of President John F. Kennedy's many dogs.

STREAM Small river, narrow waterway.

STREGA Witch (Italian).

STRELITZIA Bird of paradise, a brown flower associated with freedom and a clear perspective. Pretty name for a dog with a brown coat.

STRELKA Soviet space dog. *See* History.

STRIDER Also known as **Aragon**, the protagonist in J. R. R. Tokien's legendarium, *The Lord of the Rings*.

STRIKER Mascot of the USA Soccer World Cup.

STRONGHEART Stage name of canine actor Etzel von Oeringen, the German Shepherd Dog that starred in the 1925 film version of the 1906 Jack London novel *White Fang* and then in 1927, starred in *The Return of Boston Blackie*.

STRUDEL German coffee cake and delicious name for a dog.

STUART Royal family of Scotland.

STUBBY Sergeant Stubby (1916–1926), the most famous and highly decorated war dog in World War One.

STUDS Louis "Studs" Terkel (1912–2008), American author, historian, actor, broadcaster, and 1985 Pulitzer Prize winner for *The Good War*. **Stud** is a registered unneutered animal used for breeding.

STUKA Scottish Terrier mascot of the World War Two flight crew of the *Memphis Belle*.

STUMP Ch. Clussexx Three D Grinchy Glee, a ten-year-old Sussex Spaniel affectionately called Stump that won Best in Show at the 133rd Westminster Kennel Club Dog Show. He was the oldest dog in Westminster history to become Top Dog. *See* Dog Names by Category: Breed; Westminster.

STUMPY Dog in *The Tale of Little Pig Robinson,* by Beatrix Potter.

STUTTGART City specific to the origin of the Schnauzer.

SUEDE Leather with a "napped" or smooth surface. Good name to call a Smooth Coat Dachshund, Chihuahua, or Smooth Coated Collie.

SUENING Dog of King Eystein of Norway, who ruled from AD 1104 to 1123. To spite his people, the king put his dog on the throne for three years and had him "sign" royal decrees with with his paw prints.

SUGAR Elizabeth Taylor's Maltese. Taylor almost refused to accept the DBE, Dame Commander Order of the British Empire, from Queen Elizabeth in 1999 when she learned she couldn't bring Sugar with her to accept the honor. "Some of my best leading men have been dogs and horses," Taylor once said, referring to the Rough Collie Lassie,

SHIH TZU PUPPY

with whom she starred in *The Courage of Lassie,* and her horse, The Pie, in *National Velvet.*

SUGAR-PIE Anna Nicole Smith's Shih Tzu.

SUI Staffordshire Bull Terrier owned by the late Steve "Crocodile Hunter" Irwin.

SUKI Beloved (Japanese).

SULTAN Strength, authority rulership (Arabic). *See* Peter Piper.

SUMERIAN Excavations of the Sumarian Empire produced carvings of the Saluki that date to 7000 BC.

SUMMER Warmest of the four seasons of the year.

SUN Pekingese are also called "Sun Dogs" because of their golden coats.

SUNBEAM A ray or beam of sunlight.

SUNDAE Sinfully delicious concoction of ice cream, fruit, syrup, and a dollop of whipped cream with a cherry on top.

SUNDANCE KID Harry Alonzo Longabaugh (1867–1908), bank-robbing outlaw and member of Butch Cassidy's Wild Bunch Gang made famous by Robert Redford's portrayal opposite Paul Newman in the 1969 George Roy Hill film *Butch Cassidy and the Sundance Kid.* A Westminster Kennel Club champion.

SUNDOWN End of the day, when the sun goes down.

SUNFLOWER "Pride" in the language of flowers.

SUNGLOW If you have a female Pharaoh Hound, this is a name to consider for, as you know, the Egyptians were sun worshippers.

SUNNY Nice name for a dog with a yellow coat and a sunny disposition. *See* Terhune; Sunnybank Kennels.

SUNRISE Beginning of the day, when the sun rises.

SUNS Dog (Latvian).

SUNSET The sun goes down in flames of red. Wonderful name for an Irish Setter.

SUNSHINE Name for a dog that brings sunshine into your life.

ŠUO Dog (Lithuanian).

SUPERMAN He came from the planet Krypton in 1932 and has saved, rescued, and protected the good people of Metropolis ever since—in comics, books, radio, television, and film.

SURE GRIP'S RATTLER Registered name of the American Bulldog that played **Chance** in 1993's *Homeward Bound: The Incredible Journey*, voiced by actor Michael J. Fox.

SURRY *See* Dog Names by Category: Breed; Westminster.

SUSAN One of President Theodore Roosevelt's dogs.

SUSANNAH Lily (Hebrew).

SUSHI Japanese food composed of fish, sushi rice, and condiments that can be traced to China two thousand years ago. Good name for a Japanese Chin.

SUSIE Queen Elizabeth II of England's most beloved Corgi, from which all her Corgis have since been bred or descended.

SUSSEX An obvious name for a Sussex Spaniel, a breed that originated in East Sussex England in 1795.

SUZUKI Bell tree (Japanese).

SVEN Boy, Lad (Scandinavian). Sven Fischer of Germany won eight Olympic medals in the biathlon in games held between 1994 to 2006.

SWAFFHAM Swaffham Coursing Society, an elite sporting club organized by the Earl of Orford in 1776, limited to only twenty-five members that own Greyhounds.

SWAN Mating swans remain steadfastly with the same partner for life and grieve profoundly when their partner dies.

SWANSEA JACK Celebrated Flat-Coated Retriever responsible for saving the lives of twenty-seven people from his hometown of Swansea, Wales. He remains the only dog to receive two bronze medals from the Dogs Trust, an animal welfare charity in the UK.

SWASHBUCKLER Errol Flynn was Hollywood's greatest swashbuckler, as Captain Blood and other swordsmen. The term hearkens back to the sixteenth century.

SWAT *See* Babe.

SWEE' PEA *See* Popeye.

SWEET LIPS George Washington's American Staghound.

SWEET PEA "Gratitude" in the language of flowers. Developed by a Scottish nurseryman in Victorian times, the Sweet Pea is a delightful flowering climbing plant. Good name for a dog that participates in American Kennel Club Agility or Rally events.

SWEET POLLY Purebred Underdog's heartthrob in the 1964 animated television series.

SWEETHEART One of King Lear's dogs in Shakespeare's tragic play. The dog in *Diary of a Wimpy Kid: Dog Days*.

SWEETIE Short for sweetheart, a term of affection.

SWEETS Harry "Sweets" Edison (1915–1999), popular American jazz trumpeter for the Count Basie Orchestra, who also played with Buddy Rich, Billie Holiday, and most notably, Ella Fitzgerald, among many other jazz greats.

SWEET-WILLIAM "Gallantry" in the language of flowers.

SWITHIN James's twin brother, a bachelor, and one of the ten original Forsytes in John Galsworthy's *The Forsyte Saga*.

SYBIL Prophetess (Greek).

SYDNEY Wide island (Old English). Also spelled **Sidney**.

SYKES A stray mutt found by stunt dog specialist Gill Raddings in Oxfordshire, England, in 2004. Since then, Sykes appeared in the films *Sweeney Todd: The Demon Barber of Fleet Street*, *The Other Boleyn Girl*, *Young Victoria*, *The Dutchess*, *Alexander*, *Prince of Persia: The Sands of Time*, *Pirates of the Caribbean: The Curse of the Black Pearl*, *The Wolfman*, and *Clash of the Titans*, and in the BBC murder mystery series, *Midsomer Murders*.

SYMMACHUS Greek translator of the Old Testament in the second century. *See* Quintus.

T

T'ANG T'ang emperors maintained the most lavish Chow Chow kennels in the history of the breed, around the seventh century, which housed 2,500 Chow Chows and 10,000 huntsmen.

TABAQUI Indian Jackal in *The Jungle Book*, by Rudyard Kipling.

TACA President Ronald Reagan's Siberian Husky.

TACITO Silent (Italian).

TAD Thomas "Tad" Lincoln (1853–1871), fourth and youngest son of Abraham and Mary Lincoln. The boy was called Tad by his father "because he was as wriggly as a tadpole when he was a baby." A sickly boy, he outlived his father by six years before dying from heart failure at the age of eighteen. Mary's purgatory continued for eleven years after Tad's death until her merciful own. Tad's brothers Edward, age four, and Willie, age twelve, predeceased him. Mary and Abraham Lincoln adored their children, and their loss proved unendurable. Mary was temporarily committed to an asylum by her only surviving child, Robert, after the assassination of her husband. Lincoln had suffered from a condition then called "melancholy" but today known as clinical depression.

TADDEO Courageous, big-hearted (Italian).

TADPOLE Baby frog.

TAFFY Fruit or molasses-flavorings added to boiled sugar and butter, then stretched and rolled into a delicious bite-size candy. Johanna Benthal's devoted, taffy-colored Canine Companions for Independence Labrador Retriever that goes with her everywhere—even into the ICU. Johanna, who suffers from the congenital brain disorder referred to as cavernous angioma (www.angiomaalliance.org), has had over eighty brain surgeries. But she has Taffy, thanks to Canine Companions for Independence (www.cci.org), a nonprofit organization that breeds and raises Labrador Retrievers, Golden Retrievers, and Lab/Golden crosses and trains the puppies that meet CCI's high standards as assistance dogs for physically challenged adults and children. The Margaret O'Brien/CCI Children's Initiative accepts donations for dogs for children. Among CCI's benefactors is author Dean Koontz and the late Charles "Peanuts" Schulz, whose widow, Jean, continues to support this amazing organization.

TAG Child's game where if you're tagged, you're it.

TAHIR Pure (African).

TAHOE Lake Tahoe, largest freshwater lake in the Sierra Nevada, is located between California and Nevada.

TAIKOO Foundation dog of the Lhasa Apso breed.

TAILLESS TYKE Dog in "Owd Bob, the Grey Dog of Kenmuir," written by Alfred Ollivant in 1898.

TAJ Exalted (African).

TAJI Crown (African).

TAKASHI Takashi Ono of Japan won thirteen Olympic medals in gymnastics in games held between 1952 to 1964.

TAKYA First Chow Chow exhibited in America, by a Miss A. C. Derby in 1890. Takya took third place at the Westminster Kennel Club show that year. *See* Dog Names by Category: Breed; Westminster.

TALAVERA *See* Dog Names by Category: Breed; Westminster.

TALBOT A dog that has a keen nose and is an enthusiastic pursuer of game. Fitting name for a terrier, hound, or sporting breed.

TALHUND Descendant of the Roman Molosser, an early Alpine breed of dog associated with the Saint Bernard.

TALIB Seeker (African).

TALLULAH Tallulah Bankhead (1902–1968), American stage and screen actress who claimed that the first performance the Wright Brothers ever saw was one of hers. Her most notable role was in Alfred Hitchcock's 1944 thriller, *Lifeboat*.

TALLYHO! Shout out during a foxhunt.

TALON Strong character (Old English). Sharp claw of a bird.

TAM GLEN First Scottish Terrier dog imported to the United States.

TAMA Whole, Perfect (Japanese).

TAMARA Palm tree (Hebrew).

TAMÁS Tamás Darnyi of Hungary won four gold medals for swimming in the 1988 and 1992 Olympic Games.

TAMASINE Twin (Japanese).

TAMMASO Twin (Italian).

TAM-O'-SHANTER Scottish cap named after a character in a 1790 Robert Burns poem. The tam was worn in both world wars by British infantry troops as a general service cap. The pom-pom in the center is called a toorie. **Toorie** would be a great name for a Poodle. The cap is made of woolen tweed, plaid, or solid woven.

TANCREDO Wise and thoughtful counsel (Italian).

TANDY Pale, frail child isolated in the White Tower of the Wise Men in *The Wonderful Wizard of Oz*, one of the sequels written by American author L. Frank Baum.

TANG Earliest record of the Pekingese, in the Tang Dynasty in China (AD 618–907).

TANGO Golden Retriever that played Bailey in the 2005 Canadian film *Bailey's Billion$*.

TANISHIA Born on Monday (African).

TANK English Bulldog in the 2004 remake of *The Ladykillers*, starring one of Hollywood's most respect and accomplished actors, Tom Hanks.

TANNER One who tans hides (English).

TAO Way, path, route (Chinese).

TAPISSER To cover with heavy fabric (Old French). Woven fabrics depicting scenes and people, dating back to Hellenistic times, French and Flemish tapestries of the sixteenth century often depicted Boxers, as in *The Hunt of the Unicorn*, woven between 1495 and 1505.

TAPSTER Among the hounds that "were singing" in Frederick Watson's 1932 fox hunting book, *In the Pink*.

TARA Plantation home of the O'Hara family in *Gone with the Wind*.

TARRAGON Also known as "dragon's wort," a culinary herb.

TARZAN Fictional British child, son of a marooned British lord and lady, lost in the jungle and raised by the Mangani (great apes) in Edgar Rice Burroughs's novel *Tarzan* (1912). Johnny Weissmuller wasn't the first Tarzan, but he surely was the greatest Tarzan of them all.

TASTER George Washington's Black and Tan Coonhound.

TATTERS Foxhound in *Maria and Some Other Dogs*, by Somerville and Ross, written in 1949. Character in the kingdom of *The Wonderful Wizard of Oz*, by American author L. Frank Baum.

TATTOO Indelible ink design applied to the skin. Joseph Banks, the naturalist aboard Captain Cook's ship the HMS *Endeavour*, wrote in his diary in 1769: "I shall now mention the way they mark themselves indelibly, each of them is so marked by their humor or disposition," referring to natives of the South Pacific islands that Cook explored.

TATTY Tatty Oldbitt, the Sailors' Friend, amorous female Basset Hound who liked to chase sailors in *The Perishers*, the popular British comic strip published in *The Daily Mirror* from 1959 to 1983.

TAU Lion (African).

TAUPE Brownish-grey color. Good name for a Keeshond or any dog with variegated greys and browns in his coat.

TAURUS Second astrological sign of the Zodiac, represented by a bull.

TAWNY Golden yellow. Good name for dog with a tawny colored coat, such as a Skye Terrier. A yellow Labrador Retriever that gave birth to a record eighteen puppies in 1999, her first litter.

TAZ Tasmanian Devil, wild animal the size of a small dog that lives on the Australian island of Tasmania and inspired the Warner Bros. Looney Toon character of the same name, affectionately called Taz.

T-BONE Aaron Thibeaux "T-Bone" Walker (1910–1975), Texas-born blues guitarist, singer, and songwriter of African American and Cherokee descent. Ranked among the 100 Greatest Guitarists of All Time by *Rolling Stone* magazine, he "shocked everyone" with his first single "Mean Old World" (1941). No one played a guitar like T-Bone. Listen to "Hey Baby" and you'll understand why. Great name for any dog that can play a guitar with his teeth . . . like T-Bone did.

TEA Aromatic beverage, served hot or cold, prepared from leaves or spices.

TEAL Blue-winged Teal, a North American migratory bird, is a small, wild dabbling duck after which my dog of a lifetime, Teal, a black Labrador Retriever, was named. Bluish-green color.

TECHICHI Predecessor of the Chihuahua.

TECKEL Teckel Club, German Dachshund Club founded 1888 in Germany to establish the standards for the breed.

TEDDY Golden Retriever in an underrated, beautiful movie, *The Majestic*, starring Jim Carrey, comic genius underestimated for his dramatic abilities, and eminent actor Martin Landau, whose body of work is incredible.

TEENSY Very, very small, tiniest. One of Tonka's Pound Puppies.

TEJAS "Friend" in the language of the Caddo Nation of Oklahoma, from which the name of Texas, the twenty-eighth state, is derived.

TELEK One of President Dwight D. Eisenhower's Scottish Terriers.

TEMPEST Play written by William Shakespeare in 1610 and thought to be his last, in which Prospero, the exiled Duke of Milan, attempts to restore his daughter Miranda to her rightful place. Things get wild when a tempest storms into Act One with its famous shipwreck scene.

TEMPLE Pekingese were literally set upon pedestals in Chinese temples.

TENLEY Dr. Tenley Emma Albright, MD (b. 1935), two-time world champion in women's singles ice skating, two-time North American champion, and US champion from 1952 to 1956. She won the 1952 Olympic silver medal and in the 1956 Cortina d'Ampezzo Winter Olympics, became the first American female skater to win the Olympic gold. She retired after the Olympics, graduated from Harvard Medical School, and became a surgeon.

TENNESSEE Historic name for a strain of hound. *See* Maupin.

TENNYSON Son of Dennis (Old English). *See* Alfred.

TENOCHITITLAN *See* Aztec.

TEOFILO Friend of God (Italian).

TEQUILA Spirit made from the blue agave plant in the region around Tequila, Mexico.

TERESA Harvester (Greek). Teresa Edwards of the United States won five medals in Olympic Games held between 1984 and 2000 in basketball.

TERHUNE Albert Payson Terhune (1872–1942), prolific American dog writer and owner of Sunnybank Kennels, premier breeder of Rough Collies. His dog books include *Lad: A Dog* (1919); *Bruce* (1920); *Buff: A Collie* (1921); *Further Adventures of Lad* (1922); *Lochinvar Luck* (1923); *Treve* (1924); *The Heart of a Dog* (1924); *Wolf* (1925); *Najib* (1925); *Treasure* (1926); *My Friend the Dog* (1926); *Gray Dawn* (1927); *The Luck of the Laird* (1927), republished as: *A Highland Collie* (1950); *Bumps* (1927); *Lad of Sunnybank* (1929); *A Dog Named Chips* (1931); *The Dog Book* (1932); *The Way of a Dog* (1932); *The Book of Sunnybank* (1934), republished as: *Sunnybank: Home of Lad* (1953); *Real Tales of Real Dogs* (1935); *True Dog Stories* (1936); *The Critter and Other Dogs* (1936); and *Wallace: Glasgow's Immortal Fire Dog* (1961).

TERRA Highland of the moon.

TERRENCE Instigator (Irish, from *toirdhealbhach*).

TERRY One of the most beloved of all film dogs, Terry was the Hollywood canine actor better known as Toto, Dorothy's little dog in the immortal 1939 film *The Wizard of Oz*, starring the legendary Judy Garland, who sang "Somewhere Over the Rainbow" to the little Cairn Terrier.

TERVUEREN Long-coated, fawn-colored variety of Belgian Sheepdog.

TERZO Third (Italian).

TESSA Summer harvest (Old English). Diminutive of **Teresa**.

TESSIE My old yellow Labrador Retriever, sleeping at my feet as I write. Postscript: Tessie crossed the river on Good Friday 2012 at the age of sixteen, the gentlest, sweetest dog I've ever known.

TEVIOTDALE The hills where Sir Walter Scott first came upon the Dandie Dinmont Terrier.

THALIA Abundance, good cheer (Greek). One of the Three Graces.

THAMES River that runs through London.

THATCHER British Conservative Prime Minister Margaret Thatcher (b. 1925), called "The Iron Lady" for her no-nonsense political and diplomatic positions. A great true leader, she was prime minister from 1979 to 1990. Like President Ronald Reagan, with whom she maintained a close alliance, she survived an assassination attempt. She received a life peerage after her retirement. Baroness Thatcher made this observation, "I was brought up by a Victorian grandmother. We were taught to work jolly hard. We were taught to prove yourself; we were taught self-reliance; we were taught to live within our income. You were taught that cleanliness is next to Godliness. You were taught self-respect. You were taught always to give a hand to your neighbour. You were taught tremendous pride in your country. All of these things are Victorian values. They are also perennial values. You don't hear so much about these things these days, but they were good values and they led to tremendous improvements in the standard of living." Words to live by.

THELONIOUS Thelonious Monk (1917–1982), American jazz pianist and "one of the giants of American music." One of only five jazz musicians to be featured on the cover of *Time* magazine, he was raised in New York City and started playing the piano at the age of six. He used dissonant cords and poignant silences to express himself in classics such as "Round Midnight" and "Epistrophy." Swell name for a big, imposing dog like a Saint Bernard.

THEODORE Theodore Roosevelt (1858–1919), twenty-sixth president of the United States, founder of the short-lived Bull Moose Party, Harvard graduate, rancher, explorer, historian, author and hunter, after whom the Teddy Bear was named. A man of enormous accomplishment, Roosevelt led the 1st United States Volunteer Cavalry, known as the Rough Riders, in the Spanish-American War. He coined many phrases, chief among them "Speak softly and carry a big stick." His achievements as president included the completion of the Panama Canal and negotiating the end of the Russo-Japanese War, for which he won the Nobel Peace Prize. His greatest legacy was the founding of the National Parks Service, which acquired thousands of acres for conservation and the establishment of parks. A masterful hunter, the trophies he took in Africa and South America became the foundation exhibits of the American Museum of Natural History. A bronze effigy of Roosevelt astride a horse stands at the front entrance. He fathered six children, one during his first marriage, and five with his childhood sweetheart and second wife, Edith Carow. In anticipation of a large family, he built Sagamore Hill in Oyster Bay, Long Island, which the family donated to the National Park Service in 1962. Roosevelt survived an assassination attempt while giving a public address, which didn't stop the great orator from talking for another hour and a half: "I am all right—I am a little sore," he was quoted as saying. "Anybody has a right to be sore with a bullet in him," he quipped. Roosevelt was made a Chief Scout Citizen by the Boy Scouts of America, the only person to hold that honor. When he died at the age of sixty, his son Archie telegraphed his siblings, "The old lion is dead." Roosevelt's last words were "Please put out the light."

THIMBLE Small metal cup with a pockmarked surface worn on the middle finger to facilitate pushing a needle through fabric or leather when sewing. The earliest thimble was found in Pompeii, dating to the first century AD.

THISTLE Flowering plant with sharp prickles around its purple flower. It is the symbol of Scotland and a great name for a dog of Scottish origin.

THOMAS Twin (Aramaic).

THOR Hammer-wielding Norse god of thunder. Great Dane owned by Italian model Fabio.

THORN Alsatian with England's Civil Defence Service in World War Two that located air-raid casualties. He was awarded the Dickin Medal in 1945.

THORNAPPLE "You are in my dreams" in the language of flowers.

THORPE Ian Thorpe of Australia won nine Olympic medals in swimming in the 2000 and 2004 games.

THRILLER Book or movie with a thrilling, suspenseful plot line, like any of Alfred Hitchcock's movies.

THUMPER Bambi's rabbit friend in the 1941 Disney animated film based on the book *Bambi: A Life in the Woods*, by Austrian author Felix Salten.

THUNDER Rumble, roar, boom, and rolling, booming clap of an angry lightning storm. *See* Disney.

THUNDERBOLT German Shepherd in Disney's *101 Dalmatians*.

THYME Herb used by the ancient Egyptians in embalming, the Greeks in incense for courage, and by Medieval Europeans, who placed the herb beneath their pillows to ward off nightmares. Give it a try. It can't hurt.

TIA Goddess of a peaceful death in Haidan mythology. The Haida were an indigenous people of the Pacific Northwest.

TIBBY American actress Bette Davis's Scottish Terrier.

TIBET The Boxer is a descendant of the old fighting dogs of Tibet, which is the birthplace of the Kuvasz breed of dog and the Lhasa Apso, too.

TICH Mongrel that served with the 1st Battalion King's Royal Rifle Corps from 1941 to 1945 and was honored "for courage and devotion."

TIDBIT Delicacy, a goody or treat.

TIFFANY Tiffany & Company, premier American jewelry and silverware company, founded in 1837 in New York by Charles Lewis Tiffany and Teddy Young. Originally a stationery store, its direction changed radically in 1853 when Charles Tiffany took complete control and began selling jewelry. Audrey Hepburn had *Breakfast at Tiffany's*.

TIGE Buster Brown of Buster Brown Shoes's Boston Terrier.

TIGER Dog in *An Antarctic Mystery*, by Jules Verne. Dog in *The Narrative of Arthur Gordon Pym of Nantucket*, by Edgar Allan Poe. The Brady family's dog in the 1969 television series *The Brady Bunch*.

TIGG Montague Tigg is a swindler in *Martin Chuzzlewit*, by Charles Dickens. Good name for a dog that steals your heart.

TIGGER One of Christopher Robin Milne's stuffed animals, an orange tiger with black stripes that his dad, Alan (otherwise known as A. A. Milne) immortalized in *The House at Pooh Corner*. Just so you know, "bouncing is what tiggers do best." If your puppy bounces, name him Tigger.

TIK-TOK Machine-man controlled by a clock that has to be wound up regularly in *The Road to Oz* and other sequels to *The Wonderful Wizard of Oz*, by L. Frank Baum.

TILLY Eustace Tilley, human cartoon mascot of *The New Yorker*. American writer and humorist Corey Ford, the first "On the Town" columnist for Harold Ross's fledgling magazine, gave the erudite, monocled highbrow his name "because he reminded me of my Aunt Tilly."

TIM JOHNSON Rabid dog shot by Atticus Finch in the Pulitzer Prize–winning novel *To Kill a Mockingbird*, by Harper Lee. Tim was singer Shania Twain's German Shepherd Dog.

TIMASKEA Historical name for an Irish Setter. *See* Fermanagh.

TIMBER Wood, lumber. Fine name for a dog that loves walking through the woods with you.

TIMOLEON Dog in *Timoleon Vieta Come Home*, by Dan Rhodes.

TIMOTHY Mongrel in Enid Blyton's *Famous Five* series of children's adventure novels.

TIMOTHY GYP Sheepdog in *The Tale of Little Pig Robinson*, by Beatrix Potter.

TIN MAN Dorothy's companion in *The Wizard of Oz* who pined, "If I only had a heart" and, in the end, proved he had the most tender heart of all. Played in the movie version by the late, great Jack Haley. "Remember, a heart is not judged by how much you love, but by how much you are loved by others." *See* Hickory.

TINKER Smith and Tinker, an inventor and an artist, respectively, in *Ozma of Oz*, a sequel to *The Wonderful Wizard of Oz*, by L. Frank Baum.

TINKERBELL J. M. Barrie's fictitious sprite in his 1904 play *Peter and Wendy*—which has since enchanted children and adults as *Peter Pan*.

TINY Obvious name for a really small dog or, conversely, a very big dog, such as President Franklin D. Roosevelt's Old English Sheepdog.

TINY TIM Crippled youngest child of Bob Cratchit, Scrooge's long-suffering clerk. Though fated to die, Destiny in the form of three ghosts steps in and Tiny Tim gets well in Charles Dickens's *A Christmas Carol,* proclaiming, "God bless us, everyone!" President Calvin Coolidge's Chow.

TIP TOPSY To turn upside down and rightside up. Character in the kingdom of *The Wonderful Wizard of Oz,* of which there were thirteen sequels written by American author L. Frank Baum.

TIPKINS A dog in *The Tale of Little Pig Robinson,* by Beatrix Potter.

TIPLER George Washington's Black and Tan Coonhound.

TIPPERARY Town in Ireland on the River Arra. The name means "the well of Arra." "It's a Long Way to Tipperary" was a British music hall song written in 1912. The Connaught Rangers, the 88th and 94th Regiments of Foot, Irish regiments of the British Army, sang it as they marched through Boulogne in World War One, and it gained popularity soon after that as a wartime anthem.

TIPPI Tippi Hedren (b. 1930), stunning American actress, former fashion model, wild animal activist. Her first role was in the Hitchcock thriller *The Birds,* followed by *Marnie.* Hedren is the founding director of Shambala, an exotic animal preserve northeast of Los Angeles that cares for African and Indian animals that otherwise would suffer or be killed. Michael Jackson's tigers Thriller and Sabu were sent to Shambala from his Neverland Ranch after his death. "I went up and sat with them for a while and let them know that Michael was gone," Tippi explained. "You don't know what mental telepathy exists from the human to the animal. But I hope they understood."

TIPSY A little bit drunk.

TISSINGTON Historical name for an English Springer Spaniel.

TITIAN Tiziano Vecellio (1488–1576), known as Titian, was the pre-eminent Italian painter of the Venetian School noted for his rich use of color. Titian red is named after the artist. It would be a great name for an Irish Setter.

TITO Fire (Italian).

TOASTY Comfortably warm.

TOBACCO Good name for a dark brown dog the color of tobacco. Just don't let him smoke.

TOBER Short for "October." Big, slobbering orange Belton English Setter that inspired many humor books and articles by his devoted master, American writer Corey Ford (1902–1969) in which he pondered what it is to be owned by a dog in humor stories such as "My Dog Likes It Here" and "Every Dog Should Have a Man."

TOBY E. B. White's Scottish Terrier. One of America's greatest humorists, White is best known today as the author of *Charlotte's Web*. On his wedding day, he could not find anyone to watch his dog, so he brought him to church, where Toby proudly stood with the wedding party. The dog that Sherlock Holmes borrows in *The Sign of the Four*, by Sir Arthur Conan Doyle.

TOCK The watchdog in *The Phantom Tollbooth*, by Norton Juster.

TOD Dog in the Walt Disney animated film *The Fox and the Hound*.

TOFU Food made from coagulated soy milk. Healthy name for a white dog.

TOGO Siberian Husky who led the longest track of the famous 1925 serum run to Nome. *See* Balto.

TOKI Time of opportunity (Japanese).

TOLEDO Toledo Blade, sired by Roderigo out of Lillian, an important English Setter in England that won twenty-seven show awards and one field trial award in the late 1800s.

TOLLYDIGGLE Female jailor in the only prison in the kingdom of *The Wonderful Wizard of Oz*, by L. Frank Baum.

TOLTEC Civilization in Mexico in the ninth century that first bred the Chihuahua.

TOMASA Spanish feminine of **Thomas**.

TOMATO Round, red fruit that's a staple of Italian cooking. Cute name for a round, red Pomeranian.

TOMICH Historical name for a Golden Retriever. *See* Trench.

TOMMY-GUN Thompson submachine gun invented in 1919. *See* Dog Names by Category: Breed; Crufts.

TOMY Belgian Sheepdog that received high praise in 1898 from a judge named M. Reul, and is credited as the founder of the short-haired Belgian Sheepdog strain.

TONIO Invaluable, precious (Italian).

TONY Diminuitive of **Anthony** or **Antony**. *See* Lady.

TOODLE Polly Toodle, the "plump, rosy-cheeked, wholesome, apple-faced young woman" in the Charles Dickens novel *Dombey and Son*. **Toodles** is slang for good-bye.

TOORIE *See* Tam O'Shanter.

TOOTS Absentminded classmate of Dombey Jr. in *Dombey and Son*, by Charles Dickens.

TOP Cyrus Smith's dog in Jules Verne's science fiction novel *The Mysterious Island*.

TOPAZ Yellow semiprecious stone that the ancient Roman historian Pliny said was first mined on the legendary island of Topazos in the Red Sea. The word *topaz* may also have been derived from the Sanskrit word *tapas*, which means "heat" or "fire." Nice name for a Beauceron or other dog with a deep reddish brown coat.

TOPAZOS Heat, fire (Sanskrit).

TOPKNOT The tuft of hair at the top of the head of a Poodle is a topknot—in fact, it's just the name for a Poodle.

TOPPER The 1937 movie starring Cary Grant, Constance Bennett, and as Topper, Roland Young. A rich, handsome, carefree couple crashes their car, only to come to life as ghosts that only their stuffy banker, Topper, can see. Light comedy at its best.

TOPSELL E. Topsell, early ornithologist who, in 1607 wrote that the Maltese was no "bigger than common ferrets."

TORNADO Cyclone, twister, destructive, gyrating cone of air.

TORO Iberian bull used in bullfighting.

TOSHI Mirror image (Japanese).

T'OTHER Historical name for the Welsh Terrier. *See* Prescott.

TOTO One of the most famous of all dog names, Toto was Dorothy's little dog in *The Wizard of Oz* without whom her adventures would never have begun. "And Toto, too?" *See* Terry.

TOUBERVILLE Author of the 1570 treatise *The Noble Art of Venerie*, in which the Scottish Terrier is first mentioned.

TOUGHY *See* Lady.

TOULOUSE Henri Marie Raymond de Toulouse-Lautrec-Monfa (1864–1901), French Post-Impressionist painter whose paintings captured Paris life in the late nineteenth century. Only child of an old aristocratic family to survive childhood, he broke both legs around the age of twelve, which stunted his growth (his adult height was four and a half feet). In fact, he had a congenital disease called pycnodysostosis, which subsequently was named after him (Toulouse-Lautrec syndrome). He numbed his anguish over his deformity with liquor and sex, dying from syphilis and alcoholism at the age of thirty-six. Lautrec painted more than seven hundred canvases and five thousand drawings.

TOWZER Christopher Smart's dog mentioned in *Poems on Several Occasions*, published in 1732.

TRACEY *See* Dog Names by Category: Breed; Crufts.

TRACKER The ancestor of the Golden Retriever was a dog known as a Russian Tracker.

TRACY Spencer Tracy (1900–1967), iconic Hollywood actor nominated for nine Academy Awards (winning two) and was one of Hollywood's top box office draws throughout his thirty-seven-year film career. He is ranked ninth as the AFI's greatest male movie star of all time. His films with his life partner, Katharine Hepburn, are as sizzling today as they were when they were made, starting in 1942 with the romantic comedy *Woman of the Year* and ending with *Guess Who's Coming to Dinner*, which was completed seventeen days before his death at the age of sixty-seven.

TRAKR Heroic German Shepherd that found the last survivor in the World Trade Center on September 11, 2001.

TRAMP Schnauzer mixed-breed mutt that falls in love with Lady in Walt Disney's 1955 animated motion picture *Lady and the Tramp*. Dog that starred with Cary Grant and Betsy Drake in the 1952 comedy, *Room for One More*. The Douglas family's sheepdog in *My Three Sons*, the 1960 family sitcom starring Fred MacMurray and William Demarest and second longest-running family television series after *The Adventures of Ozzie and Harriet*.

TRAVELER Another name for *Romanichals*, a Romani people in the United Kingdom, a class and culture of gypsies that have traveled the countryside in caravans since the end of the fifteenth century. They are closely related to the Welsh Kale, which employ a tribal structure led by a chieftain.

TRAVIS Collector of tolls on a bridge or road (English).

TRAY Poor dog Thomas Campbell mourned in *The Irish Harper* (1835).

TREE You may not see the forest for the trees, but surely you know a tree when you see one. Good name for a hound, a breed that "trees" raccoons.

TREETOPS Hotel in Aberdare National Park, Kenya, where Princess Elizabeth learned of the death of her father, King George VI, and became queen of England. *See* Dog Names by Category: Breed; Crufts.

TRENCH Colonel W. le Poer Trench, a famous Golden Retriever breeder in 1908, whose dogs were bred at the Guisachan estate in Tomich, Scotland. The Golden Retriever was first bred at Guisachan by Dudley Marjoribanks, First Baron Tweedmouth.

TRENT Ancient surname of an Englishman who lives by the Trent River.

TREO Labrador trained to locate improvised explosive devices (IEDs) with the Royal Army Veterinary Corps in Helmand Province, Afghanistan in August and September 2008. He received the Dickin Medal in 2010.

TREVE One of the most beloved dog names in literature. *See* Terhune.

TREVELYAN Old Flint, the progenitor of the Bedlington Terrier, whelped in 1782 and owned by Squire Trevelyan. The breed was originally known as the Rothbury Terrier.

TREVOR Large village (Welsh).

TREY One of King Lear's dogs in the Shakespearean tragedy.

TREZÓRKA The dog in Butler's company in Leo Tolstoy's *Hadji Murat*.

TRICK Hoax, deception, pretend. *See* Dog Names by Category: Westminster.

TRICKI WOO Mrs. Pumphrey's pampered Pekingese in *All Creatures Great and Small*, by James Herriot. The poor little dog suffered from "flopbottom," his mistress's term for his digestion problems because she overfed him all the time with rich foods, such as paté.

TRIGG Historical name for a Beagle. *See* Rosseau.

TRILLIUM Lovely white flower and a good name for a dog with a white coat, like a Maltese.

TRINKET Little bauble, a charm on a necklace.

TRIP Travel, vacation; to stumble or prance. A nice name for a dog that has a sprightly step.

TRIPOD Rusty's three-legged dog in the 2000 Disney film *The Kid*, starring Bruce Willis.

TRIXIE Golden Retriever (d. 2007) and purported author of *Life Is Good*, owned by science fiction writer Dean Koontz and his wife. Trixie was a retired Canine Companions for Independence Service Dog. The CCI Southwest Regional Center was rededicated as the Dean, Gerda, and Trixie Koontz Campus in 1996.

TROIKA Russian folk dance where a man dances with two women. The word itself means three-horse team. Very nice name for a Borzoi, also known as a Russian Wolfhound.

TROJAN Inhabitant of the Ancient Greek city of Troy.

TROOPER Private in a British Army cavalry regiment.

TROT Character in the kingdom of *The Wonderful Wizard of Oz*, of which there were thirteen sequels written by American author L. Frank Baum.

TROTTER Alfred Jingle's servant in Charles Dickens's humorous novel *Pickwick Papers*.

TROUT Outdoor writer Corey Ford's "little English Setter that I hunted everywhere with," which met a tragic end, immortalized in Ford's famous open letter, published in 1949 in *Field & Stream* magazine called

"Just a Dog," which prompted an international hue-and-cry in favor of state-enforced hunters's safety practices.

TROUVEE Early Wirehaired Pointing Griffons related to Mouche, the breed's foundation bitch. *See* Mouche.

TROWNEER Another of the dogs in Sir Ector's kennels in T. H. White's *The Once and Future King*.

TRUCKER Someone who drives a truck, professionally or otherwise: in short, a truck driver.

TRUFFLES Underground mushroom called "the diamond of the kitchen," a supreme epicurean delicacy found by truffle-sniffing dogs or pigs. On the open market, truffles command upwards of $2,000 a pound. Superb name for a Fox Terrier or a Jack Russell Terrier that "goes to ground" (underground) to hunt ferrets and rats.

TRUMAN Harry S. Truman, thirty-third president of the United States and vice president under Franklin D. Roosevelt, who succeeded him as president on April 12, 1945, upon FDR's death, three months into his historic fourth term and just weeks before VE Day, the end of World War Two in Europe. With a lowly 36 percent approval rating going into the 1948 election, Truman nonetheless beat Thomas E. Dewey in a surprise upset victory.

TRUSTY Trustworthy. Good name for any dog. *See* Lady.

TRYG Trustworthy (Old Norse).

TSYGANKA Soviet space dog.

TUCK *See* Nip.

TUCKER South African actress Charlize Theron's beloved dog.

TUDOR House of Tudor, English royal dynasty that began with King Henry VII. *See* Dog Names by Category: Breed; Westminster.

TUFFY Good name for a tough dog like an English Mastiff.

TULGEY "Thick, dense, dark," according to Lewis Carroll in *Alice in Wonderland*. Great name for a dog with a thick, dense coat like an Irish Water Dog or Labrador Retriever.

TULIP "I am not worthy of your love" for the white tulip in the language of flowers. J. R. Ackerley's dog in his 1956 memoir *My Dog Tulip*. Good name for a dog with a white coat, such as a Clumber Spaniel.

TUMBLEWEED Rough, dry grass that collects into a ball and is blown by the wind across deserts and arid, open places. Good name for a Norwich Terrier.

TUNDRA Good name for a Siberian Husky. *See* Sayantsi.

TUPMAN Tracy Tupman, member of the Pickwick Club who has a weakness for the fair sex in *The Pickwick Papers*, by Charles Dickens.

TURBO Turbine-powered compressor and good name for a powerful dog like an English Bulldog.

TURK Whelped of Hilda and King, Turk, an English Mastiff, was sold for a record £450 in England in 1868—the equivalent of approximately $60,000 today. One of the dogs in *Swiss Family Robinson*.

TURNER One who works with a lathe (Old English).

TURNIP Bulbous root vegetable and a cute name for a white dog.

TUT King Tutankhamun (1341–1323 BC), the most famous Egyptian pharaoh of the Eighteenth Dynasty. Steve Martin even wrote a song about him. *See* Carnarvon.

TUTU Costume worn by ballerinas.

TUXEDO Elegant men's dinner suit.

TWAIN Mark Twain, pen name of Samuel Langhorne Clemens, who came into the world on Haley's Comet on November 30, 1835, and left on Haley's return on April 21, 1910. You could write an awful lot about Mark Twain—but nothing need more be said than this: he was and remains America's greatest author and humorist.

TWEED Type of woven cloth. *See* Dog Names by Category: Breed; Crufts.

TWEEDLEDEE and **Tweedledum** Fictional twins in Lewis Carroll's *Alice Through the Looking-Glass, and What Alice Found There*. Good name for a pair of dogs.

TWEET It used to mean a bird's song but now it means a post on Twitter.

TWICI A huntsman named William Twici left an account of a pack of Otterhounds in 1307 as, "rough sort of dog, between a hound and a terrier." It is believed King John, who reigned in England from 1199 to 1216, hunted with Otterhounds.

TWIFFLE Character in the kingdom of *The Wonderful Wizard of Oz*, of which there were thirteen sequels written by American author L. Frank Baum.

TWIGGY Paper-thin sixties English high-fashion model.

TWILIGHT That sliver of the day between dusk and sunset when all the colors of the world take on a blue cast. The French call it *l'heure bleue*.

TWINKLE "Twinkle, twinkle little star . . ." English nursery rhyme first published in 1806 that every child knows.

TWO-TONE *See* Disney.

TWYNSTAR *See* Dog Names by Category: Breed; Crufts.

TXAKURRA Dog (Basque).

TY Tyrus Raymond "Ty" Cobb (1886–1961), "The Georgia Peach," Georgia-born American Major League Baseball outfielder who played twenty-two seasons with the Detroit Tigers, the last six as the team's player-manager, finishing his career with the Philadelphia Athletics.

Cobb is widely regarded as one of the best pro baseball players of all time.

TYCOON Capitalist czar, businessman of great wealth, many chronicled in financial periodicals such as *Forbes* magazine.

TYLER John Tyler, tenth president of the United States.

TYPHOON Tropical cyclone that develops in the northwest Pacific. Good name for a really active Japanese Chin or Chow Chow puppy.

TYR Norse god of war.

U

UA Rain (Hawaiian).

UBA Lord (Nigerian).

UBERTO Bright heart, shining spirit (Italian).

UBORA Excellence (African).

UGA Bulldog, mascot of the University of Georgia.

UGGIE Eight-year-old Jack Russell Terrier canine actor that was featured in the 2011 Academy Award Best Picture *The Artist*, and before that, *Water for Elephants*. Uggie was awarded a Palm Dog Award at the 2111 Cannes Film Festival for his role as Jack in the *The Artist*. His "memoir" will be published by Simon & Schuster.

UGOLYOK Soviet space dog.

ULRICH Ulrich Salchow of Sweden created the Salchow jump. He was the first Olympic men's figure skating champion, winning his gold medal in the 1908 London games.

ULSTER Historical name for an Irish Wolfhound. *See* Aibe.

ULYSSES Latin name for Odysseus. *See* Odysseus.

UMAR Longevity (African).

UMBER Reddish-brown pigment. Good name for a Rhodessian Ridgeback.

UMEKO Plum blossom (Japanese).

UNC NUNKIE Elderly Munchkin and uncle of Ojo the Lucky who speaks in one-word sentences. On rare occasions, he will make a long speech using only two words in *The Patchwork Girl of Oz*, a sequel to *The Wonderful Wizard of Oz*, by L. Frank Baum.

UNCLE HENRY Dorothy's uncle, a hardscrabble Kansas farmer, in *The Wizard of Oz*.

UNCLE SAM Patriotic symbol of the United States. He first came onto the American scene during the War of 1812 and has not missed a war since.

UNDERDOG "There's no need to fear—Underdog is here!" Superhero cartoon dog.

UNO One (Spanish) UNO, the United Nations Organization.

UPENDO Love (African).

URBANO From the city (Italian).

URIAH Uriah Heep, antagonist in *David Copperfield*, whose cover as "a humble man" masks a cold, calculating cad who, in the end—as with all of Dickens's bounders—is exposed for his wrongdoings.

URSULA Little Bear (Latin). The Constellation Ursa Minor is known as "little bear."

UTA Poem (Japanese).

V

VAGABOND Gypsy, nomad.

VAL Val Dartie, son of Montague and Winifred Dartie in John Galsworthy's *The Forsyte Saga*.

VALDAMAR Renowned leader (Germanic) Royal name in early Denmark. Also **Waldemar**. *See* Vladimir.

VALENTINA Valentina Vezzali of Italy won seven Olympic medals in fencing for games held from 1996 to 2008.

VALENTINE Greeting card or gift you send to someone you love.

VALENTINO Rudolf Valentino (1895–1926), "the Latin Lover," Italian-born Hollywood silent film star and pop icon. His sudden death at thirty-one (caused by peritonitis complicated by pleurisy) caused a seismic wave of hysteria across the nation. One hundred thousand people lined the streets of New York to pay tribute.

VALERIA Healthy and strong (Italian).

VALETKA Dog in Turgenev's story "Yermolay and the Miller's Wife."

VAN GOGH Vincent Willem Van Gogh (1853–1890), Dutch Post-Impressionist painter, perhaps the most famous of all. His use of color and application of oil paint, often with a palette knife, gave a physical quality to his extraordinary work. But he was impoverished and sick in body and soul, haunted even by his name, which had originally been given to his stillborn brother exactly a year before Vincent's birth. He found living "almost unbearable." His only friends were his devoted brother Theo, artist Paul Gauguin, and the prostitutes of a brothel he frequented. He entrusted one of them with a small package that contained his ear, which he cut off with a razor, telling her to "keep this object carefully." He was thirty-seven when he died from a self-inflicted gunshot wound. His paintings *Still Life: Vase with Twelve Sunflowers* (1888) and *Irises* (1889) make us smile; *The Starry Night* (1889) takes our breath away.

VANDA Wanderer (Italian).

VANILLA Spice used to flavor desserts such as ice cream. Sweet name for a white dog like a Chinese Shar-Pei.

VANITY Prideful, narcissistic. Yet another one of those hounds that "were singing" in Frederick Watson's *In the Pink* (1932).

VANNI God is gracious (Italian).

VAQUERO Cowboy (Spanish).

VE A brother of Odin, the All-Father in Norse mythology.

VEGAS Fertile valley (Spanish).

VELOX Historical name for an English Springer Spaniel. *See* Powder.

VELVET Black Labrador Retriever mix breed who helped save three climbers stranded on Mount Hood in Oregon in 2007.

VENATICI *Canes venatici*, Latin for "hunting dogs" and the name of a constellation.

VENDEE The Otterhound is said to most resemble the old Vendee Hound of France.

VENI VENICONES, a Celtic tribe believed to have settled in the vicinity of Dundee, Scotland, was recorded by Ptolemy. *Venicones* is believed to mean "hunting hounds."

VENUS Pro golfer Amy Alcott's Scottish Terrier.

VĚRA Věra Čáslavská of Czechoslovakia won eleven medals in the Olympic Games held between 1960 and 1968.

VERBENA "Sensibility" in the language of flowers.

VERDELL Brussels Griffon played by canine actor Jill the Dog who infuriates, and then warms the heart of curmudgeon Jack Nicholson in the 1997 romantic comedy *As Good As It Gets*, costarring Helen Hunt.

VERDI Giuseppe Fortunino Francesco Verdi (1813–1901), Italy's greatest composer and one of the most influential composers of the nineteenth century. He wrote twenty-eight operas, almost all of which are performed today. In 1861 he became a figure in Italy's Risorgimento where the revolutionaries' slogan was "Viva, Verdi!" an acronym for Viva Vittorio Emmanuele Re D'Italia (Victor Emmanuel King of Italy), referring to Victor Emmanuel II, then king of Sardinia.

VERDUN BELLE A stray Setter whose devotion to an American soldier that cared for her and her puppies became one of the most moving war dog stories of World War One.

VERNON Alder (Norman, from *vern*). Deciduous tree native to northern temperate regions.

VERONA City in Italy and site of Shakespeare's 1632 play *The Two Gentlemen of Verona*. Great name for a Spinone Italiano.

VERONICA "Fidelity" in the language of flowers.

VERONIQUE She who brings victory (Latin, French).

VESTA Early Wirehaired Pointing Griffon related to Mouche, the breed's foundation bitch.

VESUVIUS The volcano that buried Pompeii and place where the Italian Greyhound may have originated.

VETEROK Soviet space dog.

VETO President James Garfield's dog, breed unknown.

VIC Diminutive of **Victor**. *See* Dog Names by Category: Breed; Westminster.

VICAR Vice deputy (Old English). A vicar is a minister or parish priest in the Anglican religion in England.

VICEROY Colonial official by royal appointment to a country. Louis Mountbatten, First Earl Mountbatten of Burma, was a Viceroy and Governor-General of India when India was under British administration. The favorite uncle of Prince Philip of England.

VICKY President Richard M. Nixon's daughter Julie's French Poodle.

VICO Conqueror (Italian).

VICTOR Winner, conqueror (Old English).

VICTORIA Queen Victoria first saw the Rough-coated Collie in 1860 at her Scotland estate, Balmoral, and immediately fell in love with the breed.

VICTORY President Ronald Reagan's dog.

VIDA Life (Portuguese, Spanish). Doberman Pinscher who lives with Heather, Jaime, and John.

VIDAR Son of Odin, All-Father in Norse mythology.

VIENNA Capital of the Austrian Empire from 1804 until the end of the Great War in 1918 and today, the capital of Austria. A lovely name for a female Austrian Pinscher or an Austrian Black and Tan Hound.

VIKING The Norwegian Elkhound originated at the time of the Vikings.

VIKTOR Viktor Chukarin of the Soviet Union won eleven Olympic medals for gymnastics in the games held in 1952 and 1956.

VILI A brother of Odin, All-Father in Norse mythology.

VILLE Farm (Latin, *villa-rustica*). Ville Ritola of Finland won eight Olympic medals in athletics in the 1924 and 1928 games.

VINCENT To conquer (Italian).

VINEGAR and **Mustard**, two characters in the kingdom of *The Wonderful Wizard of Oz*.

VIOLET "Modesty" in the language of flowers.

VIOLET The Right Honorable Violet, Countess of Grantham, dowager countess, and mother of Lord Grantham in *Downton Abbey*. The part is played by arguably the greatest British actress of our time, the indomitable Maggie Smith.

VIRGINIA Historical name for a Foxhound. *See* Walker.

VISA Government document that allows a foreigner to enter and leave the country.

VISCOUNT Member of British royalty, above a baron but below an earl.

VISTE A skeleton of a Norwegian Elkhound was uncovered in Viste Cave in Jaeren, Norway that dated from 4,000 to 5,000 BC.

VITALY Vitaly Scherbo of Belarus won ten Olympic medals in gymnastics in the games held in 1992 and 1996.

VITTORIO Italian masculine for **Victor**.

VIVA Live! (Spanish).

VIVIEN Vivien Leigh (1913–1967), two-time Academy Award Best Actress winner, the English beauty immortalized the role of Scarlett O'Hara in the film version of Margaret Mitchell's *Gone with the Wind*. As Lady Laurence Olivier, she and her husband were considered royalty in Hollywood, on Broadway, and on the London stage. Vestiges of mental illness and depression had surfaced early in their marriage and became noticeable after World War Two. David Niven commented that Leigh was "quite, quite mad" and playwright Noël Coward wrote in his diary that "things had been bad and getting worse since 1948 or thereabouts." The couple divorced in 1960; Leigh persevered, despite her illness and, in 1967, died from a recurrence of tuberculosis. She was fifty-four years old.

VIXEN Little dog in *Adam Bede* (1859), by George Elliot. Soviet space dog.

VLADIMIR Vladimir Sviatoslavich the Great, known in Old Norse as Valdamarr Sveinaldsson (c. 958–1015), Viking grand prince of Kiev who was forced to flee to Scandinavia after his brother Yaropolk murdered their brother Oleg in order to gain rule of Russia.

VODKA Distilled fermented grains or potatoes with a minimum alcoholic content of 37.5 percent as established by the European Union.

VOLDEMORT Dare we speak it? Harry Potter's archrival, "he who shall not be named."

VOLTAIRE François-Marie Arouet (1694–1778), French Enlightenment writer, historian, and philosopher who wrote under the pen name Voltaire and was an advocate of civil liberties, freedom of religion, and free trade. A prolific playwright, poet, novelist, essayist, and author of historical and scientific works, he wrote more than twenty thousand letters and, incredibly, two thousand books.

VOODOO A syncretic religion indigenous to Haiti that combines Arawakian religious beliefs and Roman Catholic Christianity. Aspects of voodoo are deeply mystical, secretive, and dark.

VORDEN *See* Dog Names by Category: Breed; Crufts.

VOYAGER A traveler, adventurer, a dog that likes to explore and perhaps dig holes to China.

VUILBAARD Dirty beard (French). Another name for the Bouvier des Flandres.

VULCAN George Washington's American Staghound. *See* History.

VULCI An ancient Greek vase made ca. 500 BC was discovered with an image of a Maltese painted on it

W

WABE The grass plot around a sundial according to Lewis Carroll in *Alice in Wonderland.*

WADDLE Toddle, sway, wobble. Corporal Waddle, character in the kingdom of *The Wonderful Wizard of Oz.* Great name for a dog that waddles, like a Bulldog.

WAFER Thin cookie or cracker. Good name for a Greyhound or an Egyptian Pharaoh Hound.

WAFFLES Pancake batter poured into a waffle iron and when it's done, served piping hot with maple syrup and butter. Mary's dog in the 1979 Woody Allen film *Manhattan.*

WAGHYA A famous dog that personifies loyalty and eternal devotion throughout India. The dog so deeply mourned the death of his master, Chhatrapati Shivaji, a seventeenth-century Maratha aristocrat of the Bhosle clan who founded the Maratha empire, that he jumped upon his master's burning funeral pyre to join him in death. A statue of Waghya stands by the tomb of Shivaji at Raigad Fort.

WAGNER Richard Wagner (1813–1883), German composer noted for his elaborate works, most especially his operas. A soprano must have a great big pair of lungs to sing Wagner. An anti-Semite of Jewish descent, Wagner produced writings and works that deeply influenced Hitler, who ardently called him "the Master." Hitler ordered Wagner's music piped into Dachau and other Nazi death camps.

WAGS Good name for any dog with a tail that wags.

WAIU Milk (Hawaiian).

PUG PUPPY

WAIUPAKA Butter (Hawaiian).

WALDO Ralph Waldo Emerson (1802–1882), New England essayist and poet who led the Transcendentalist movement with his 1836 essay "Nature." Dog in the *Heathcliff* comics.

WALES Country in the northeast corner of the British Isles and inhabited by the Celts. *See* Pwyll.

WALHAM Historical name for a Pug breed. *See* Morrison.

WALKER Thomas Walker of Albemarle County, Virginia, imported foxhounds from England in 1742.

WALLACE Foreign (Celtic) Historical name for a Bloodhound. *See* Sleuth.

WALLY Steve Martin's yellow Labrador Retriever, for whom he named his banjo-strumming song "Wally on the Run." Walter M. "Wally" Schirra, Donn Eisele, and Walter Cunningham, crew of Apollo 7, the first manned launch since the Apollo 1 tragedy. Launched October 11, 1968, Apollo 7's successful eleven-day flight was the first live telecast from a US space mission.

WALTERS Queen Victoria referred to the Clumber Spaniel in her diary entry of October 16, 1840: "Walked out directly after breakfast before Albert went to shoot. We had his seven fine Clumber Spaniels with us and we went into the Slopes, with such a funny old Gamekeeper, Walters, in order that I should see how the dogs found out their game. They are such dear, nice dogs."

WANDA Daughter of King Krak, the legendary founder of Krakow, Poland.

WANG Wang Meng of China won six Olympic medals in short track speed skating in the 2006 and 2010 games.

WAPITI Wapiti is the true elk, which the Norwegian Elkhound would have hunted.

WARBLE A bird's song. If your bird dog brays or barks a lot, then Warble might be just the right name for him.

WARHOL Andy Warhol (1928–1987), American painter and print-maker who spearheaded Pop Art in America.

WARLORD Powerful tyrannical leader of military forces. *See* Dog Names by Category: Breed; Westminster.

WARNER Guard, army (German). From the Norman given name Werner. Good name for a guard dog.

WARREN Preserve (Germanic). *See* Dog Names by Category: Breed; Westminster.

WARRIOR Soldier, brave fighter. One of the great early Scottish Deerhounds, painted by English artist George Earl and in the collection of the American Kennel Club.

WART King Arthur's nickname as a boy in T. H. White's *The Once and Future King* (1958).

WASHI Eagle (Japanese).

WASHINGTON President George Washington received some French Foxhounds from General Lafayette in 1785, who said their cries were "like the bells of Moscow."

WAT One of the dogs in Sir Ector's kennels in T. H. White's *The Once and Future King* (1958).

WATERLOO Waterloo Cup Meet, a famous dog race held since 1836 with the exception of the war years.

WATSON John H. Watson, MD, born 1852 in London, only friend and colleague of Sherlock Holmes, detective, and chronicler of Holmes's amazing cases.

WATTAN From the homeland (Japanese).

WATTEAU *See* Rubens.

WEDNESDAY Daughter of Morticia and Gomez Addams described by cartoonist Charles Addams, as "Child of woe is wane and delicate . . . sensitive and on the quiet side, she loves the picnics and outings in the underground caverns . . . has six toes on one foot." The Addams Family cartoons first appeared in *The New Yorker* in 1938.

WEEJIE President Herbert Hoover's Norwegian Elkhound. *See* Dog Names by Category: History.

WEENIE Dog in the *Eloise* books.

WELLINGTON Mrs. Shear's dog in *The Curious Incident of the Dog in the Night-Time*, by Mark Haddon.

WELLS Historical name for a Boston Terrier. *See* Eph.

WENDESSA Soldier, brave fighter (Germanic).

WHARTON Edith Wharton (1862–1937), American author of *The House of Mirth* (1905) and *The Age of Innocence* (1920), for which she won the Pulitzer Prize, the first woman writer to be awarded that distinction. She married well but unhappily and ultimately left her husband and home, the Mount, which she designed, in Lennox, Massachusetts, for Paris, where she lived until her death. She was a close friend and traveling companion of Henry James.

WHAT-A-MESS The accident-prone Afghan puppy in a series of children's books by Frank Muir.

WHATNOT Ch. Warland Whatnot, foundation sire of the Airedale Terrier breed.

WHEAT A dog's coat the color of wheat is called *wheaton*, an obvious name for a Wheaten Terrier.

WHEELY Paraplegic Chihuahua from Long Beach, California, immortalized in two best-selling children's books by Deborah Turner and Diana Mohler.

WHEY Good name for a Komondor.

WHICH Historical name for a Welsh Terrier. *See* Prescott.

WHINSTONE Term used for a hard, dark-colored rock in mining. Historical name of the Scottish Terrier breed. *See* Glenlyon.

WHISKERS Canine actor that played Fala in MGM's *Princess O'Rourke*.

WHISKEY Distilled alcohol from fermented grain mash made in many countries. Scotland is the preeminent distiller of whisky, called Scotch, and single malt Scotch is considered by devotees to be the nectar of the gods. Indeed, the very name comes from the Scottish-Gaelic *uisge beatha*, which means "water of life." The Scotch malt whiskeys are divided into five regions, Highland, Lowland, Islay, Speyside, and Campbeltown.

WHISPER To speak softly.

WHISPERWIND *See* Dog Names by Category: Breed; Westminster.

WHISTLER American radio mystery drama that aired from 1942–1955, sponsored by the Signal Oil Company. "I am the Whistler, and I know many things, for I walk by night. I know many strange tales, hidden in the hearts of men and women who have stepped into the shadows. Yes . . . I know the nameless terrors of which they dare not speak." Does that make your skin crawl or what?

WHITAKER Whitaker was a writer that described the Toy Manchester Terrier in 1771 as "a short-legged, crooked-legged dog."

WHITE FANG Dog in Jack London's classic adventure novel of the same name.

WHITE TIPS President John F. Kennedy's dog.

WHOOP Shout of enthusiasm or joy.

WHOPPER Yet another one of Tonka's Pound Puppies.

WIDO Wood (Germanic).

WIGGINS Maria's dog in *The Little White Horse*.

WIGGLES Name for an active puppy that won't sit still.

WILBER *See* Dog Names by Category: Breed; Westminster.

WILBUR Wild boar (Middle English).

WILBY Boy cursed by the enchanted ring of the Borgias and turns into a sheepdog in the 1959 Disney Film *The Shaggy Dog*, starring Fred MacMurray.

WILD DOG Dog in *The Jungle Book*, by Rudyard Kipling.

WILDFIRE The Bull Terrier that narrates the 1955 film *It's a Dog's Life*.

WILFRED Desiring peace (Old English).

WILHELMINA Feminine of **William** in German and Dutch.

WILLIAM Protector (Celtic) From *willa* ("desire") and *helm* ("helmet").

WILLIE General George Patton's English Bull Terrier, named after William the Conqueror, who accompanied the dynamic commander of the US Third Army in World War Two until his master's death.

WILLIS Willis A. Lee of the United States won seven Olympic medals in shooting in the 1920 games.

WILLOUGHBY Scoundrel in Jane Austen's 1811 novel *Sense and Sensibility*, who woos Marianne Dashwood, Elinor's sister, then dumps her for the wealthy, arrogant Miss Grey and her fortune of 50,000 pounds.

WILLOW One of Queen Elizabeth II of England's beloved Pembroke Welsh Corgi.

WILLS Affectionate name for the very popular Duke of Cambridge, son of the late Princess Diana and husband of Kate.

WILLUM *See* Dog Names by Category: Breed; Westminster.

WILLY *See* Dog Names by Category: Breed; Crufts.

WILSON Masters of the hunter-bred packs of Harriers from the fourteenth to eighteenth centuries were supplied by Wilsons of Broomhead Hall.

WIMPY *See* Popeye.

WINCHELL *See* Edwin.

WINDSOR Royal house of the British Commonwealth, founded by King George V by royal proclamation in 1917, when it was changed from Saxe-Coburg and Gotha, as it was known in Queen Victoria's reign, to avert anti-German sentiment in the United Kingdom as a result of World War One. HRH Queen Elizabeth II of England has been head of the House of Windsor since 1952. The year 2012 marks her Diamond Jubilee.

WINDY Blustery, breezy.

WINFRED Friend of peace (Old English). **Winifred** is the female version.

WINKIE Wee Willie Winkie, Scottish nursery rhyme by William Miller, published in 1841 in the children's book *Whistle-binkie: Stories of the Fireside*.

WINKIES Character in the kingdom of *The Wonderful Wizard of Oz*, of which there were thirteen sequels written by American author L. Frank Baum.

WINKLE Mr. Winkle, Mr. Pickwick's young friend who perceives himself to be a great sportsman—but proves to be far from it in Charles Dickens's *The Pickwick Papers*.

WINKS President Franklin Delano Roosevelt's Llewellyn (English) Setter.

WINN-DIXIE Scruffy dog in *Because of Winn-Dixie*, the award-winning children's novel by Kate DiCamillo published in 2000 and made into a motion picture in 2005.

WINSTON The English Bulldog was associated with Great Britain's greatest prime minister, Sir Winston Churchill.

WINTER The coldest season of the year and a name to consider for a white-coated or heavy-coated dog, such as an Icelandic Sheepdog or Swedish Vallhund.

WINTHROP Wine's village (Old English).

WISTFUL Another of the many hounds that "were singing" in Frederick Watson's *In the Pink* (1932).

WISHBONE Title character in the award-winning animated children's television series about "the little dog with the big imagination."

WISP Pincurl or slight bang. If your dog has a curly coat, try Wisp on for size.

WISTERIA "Welcome" in the language of flowers.

WIZARD Middle Earth beings with great powers in J. R. R. Tolkien's *The Lord of the Rings*, most notably Gandalf ("elf of the staff"), the great friend and protector of Frodo Baggins and his uncle. The Elves refer to Wizards as Istari, or *Quenya*, which means "wise one."

WIZZER *See* Disney.

WOGGLE Thin ring of leather, portion of a Boy Scout's neckwear.

WOGGS Robert Louis Stevenson's Skye Terrier, of whom he said, "Had he been Shakespeare, he would then have written *Troilus and Cressida* to brand the offending sex; but being only a little dog, he began to bite them" whenever a bitch refused his amorous advances.

WOLF Along with Grip and Fang, three fierce dogs owned by Farmer Maggot that protected his mushroom farm in *The Lord of the Rings*; President John F. Kennedy's Irish Wolfhound–Schnauzer mix.

WOLFGANG Rising wolf (Germanic).

WOLVERHAMPTON Historical name for a Flat-Coated Retriever. *See* Moore.

WOLVEY *See* Dog Names by Category: Breed; Westminster.

WOODSTOCK The little yellow bird that's Snoopy's closest friend in Charles M. Schulz's world of Charlie Brown.

WOODY Woody Allen (b. 1935), prolific Jewish American director who has acted in a number of his own movies. A serious jazz clarinetist and native New Yorker, the man's utterly brilliant.

WOOFER American actress Renée Zellweger's Golden Retriever and constant companion until the dog's death in 2003. "When she died, home didn't exist anymore," mourned the actress.

WOOFIE Little dogs have little barks that go "woofie, woofie."

WOOLLY Describes the undercoat of the Eskimo breed of dog.

WOOZY Four-legged fictitious creature who lives on a diet of honey bees in *The Patchwork Girl of Oz*, a sequel to *The Wonderful Wizard of Oz*, by L. Frank Baum.

WOPSLE Parish clerk in *Great Expectations*, by Charles Dickens.

WORDSWORTH William Wordsworth (1770–1850), English Romantic poet who spearheaded the movement and whose magnum opus, the autobiographical *The Prelude*, published posthumously, is considered one of the great poetical works of the nineteenth century.

WORONZOVA Historical name for a Russian Wolfhound. *See* Balderoff.

WOTAN Supreme god of Norse mythology.

WRAGA Historical name for a Japanese Chin. *See* Commodore.

WRANGLER An individual who handles animals, notably cattle and horses. Swell name for an Australian Shepherd.

WREN Small bird whose name in Old German means "kinglet." Christopher Wren (1632–1723), English architect whose greatest achievement is St. Paul's Cathedral in London. This brilliant man was also an astronomer and a physicist.

WRINKLES Good name for a dog with a wrinkled face or coat, such as a Bulldog. Also try **Creases**, **Crinkles**, **Rumples**, and **Crumples**.

WÜRTTEMBERG The Württemberg Kennels became famous for breeding Schnauzers.

WYATT Wyatt Earp (1848–1929), Old West law enforcement officer known as "the toughest and deadliest gunman of his day," best known for the thirty-second long Gunfight at the O.K. Corral.

WYNDHAM Earliest known Flat-Coated Retriever was introduced at the Birmingham Show by R. Braisford in 1860.

XANADU Palatial summer residence of Kublai Khan in China, built in in AD 1252 Marco Polo visited Xanadu in 1275 and wrote, "There is at this place a very fine marble Palace, the rooms of which are all gilt and painted with figures of men and beasts and birds, and with a variety of trees and flowers, all executed with such exquisite art that you regard them with delight and astonishment." Alas, only the ruins of the foundation walls remain today.

XANTHIPPUS Commander of the Athenian naval forces in the fifth century BC during the decisive Battle of Mycale against the Persians, which ended the invasion of Greece. For a while.

XAVIER The inimitable Xavier Cugat (1900–1990), Cuban-born Spanish American bandleader who brought Latin music to the American scene. His band played at the 1931 opening of the Waldorf-Astoria (he subsequently became the Waldorf's resident bandleader) and from there he went to Hollywood and was featured with his band in five motion pictures, including *You Were Never Lovelier*, with Fred Astaire and Rita Hayworth.

XENA Fictional franchised warrior princess—in books, comics, animated movies, and on television as portrayed by the leather-garbed, breast-plated New Zealand actress Lucy Lawless.

XENOPHON Ancient Greek writer who referred to hounds that may have been the ancestor of the Beagle, ca. 400 BC.

XOLOTL Dog in Aztec mythology.

Y

YACHI Eight thousand (Japanese).

YAHOOEY, YIPPIE, YAPPY Hanna-Barbera's three canine cartoon muskeeters.

YAIR Bold (African).

YALE Ivy League university in New Haven, Connecticut, founded in 1701. Five US presidents, three US Supreme Court justices, actors Paul Newman, Jodie Foster, Meryl Streep, and Vincent Price, composer Cole Porter, and the first American spy to be hanged, Nathan Hale, attended Yale.

YAMA Mountain (Japanese).

YANA Method of the spiritual practice of Buddhism.

YANESEI Historical name for a Samoyed. *See* Sayantsi.

YANKEE Term for a native-born resident of New England. Mark Twain wrote *A Connecticut Yankee in King Arthur's Court*, and Bing Crosby interpreted the role of Hank Morgan, a nineteenth-century New England blacksmith who wakes up in King Arthur's Court and falls hard for Alisande la Carteloise, played by flame-red-haired Rhonda Fleming.

YARO Son (African).

YARROW "Health" in the language of flowers. Terrific name for a dog with white in his coat, such as a Boxer.

YASUO Peaceful one (Japanese).

YEATS William Butler Yeats (1865–1939), Nobel Prize–winning poet, driving force behind the Irish Literary Revival, a founder of the Abbey Theatre in Dublin, his emotional prose mirrored his emotionally charged private life.

YELLOW DOG Yellow Labrador Retriever in *Far From Home: The Adventures of Yellow Dog*, a 1994 family adventure film starring canine actor Dakotah.

YELLOW DOG DINGO Dog in Rudyard Kipling's *Just So Stories*.

YEOMAN Yeomen Warders of Her Majesty's Royal Palace and Fortress of the Tower of London, Members of the Sovereign's Body Guard of the Yeoman of the Guard Extraordinary, "the Beefeaters," have served the British monarchy since 1485.

YEVGENY Yevgeny Grishin of the Soviet Union won five Olympic medals for speed skating in games held between 1956 and 1964.

YO Cultivating (Japanese).

YODA Renowned Jedi Master in the *Star Wars* saga who teaches Luke Skywalker a thing or two.

YODEL One of the Siberian huskies in *Snow Dogs*.

YOGI Lawrence Peter "Yogi" Berra (b. 1925), American Major League Baseball catcher, outfielder, and manager who played for the New York Yankees almost all of his nineteen-year baseball career (1946–1965). One of only four players to be named the Most Valuable Player of the American League three times, and one of only six managers to lead both American and National league teams to the World Series. Yogi played or coached in twenty-one World Series and was elected to the Baseball Hall of Fame in 1972, the greatest catcher in the history of the game.

YOKO Free, sunny, or glorious child (Japanese). Yoko Ono, widow of John Lennon, interprets her name to mean "ocean child."

YORI Reliable (Japanese).

YORK The white rose is the emblem of Great Britain's House of York. Perfect name for a Yorkshire Terrier. The Yorkshire Terrier first competed in an English bench show in 1861.

YOSHE Beauty (Japanese).

YOSHI Quiet (Japanese).

YOSHIKO Good child (Japanese).

YOSHINO Respectful (Japanese).

YOUNG MUSTARD Historical name for the Dandie Dinmont Terrier breed. *See* Auld.

YOYO A toy made up of two disks, a length of string looped around the disks, and endless hours of entertainment for children since the twenties.

YUKI Snow (Japanese).

YUKIO Gets what he wants (Japanese).

YUKON Part malamute, part wolf in Ron D. Lawrence's book *The North Runner*.

YUKON KING Nineteen thirty-eight radio series that spun off a television series about the adventures of Sergeant William Preston of the North-West Mounted Police and his courageous dog, Yukon King, an Alaskan Husky. The program was originally called *Challenge of the Yukon* and later changed to *Sergeant Preston of the Yukon*.

YUKONAN President Herbert Hoover's Eskimo Dog.

YUMA Desert in southwestern United States, part of the Sonoran Desert, and one of the driest places on earth, receiving less than eight inches of rainfall a year.

YUMIKO Beautiful child (Japanese).

YUMMY Strawberry shortcake! Brownies! Sushi! *Yummy!*

YVES Yew (French). *See* Lafayette.

YVONNE Yvonne de Carlo (1922–2007), Canadian-American actress best known for her television role as Lily Munster on the CBS sitcom *The Munsters* with Fred Gwynne. It eclipsed her prodigious dramatic career, which included *For Whom the Bell Tolls* with Gary Cooper and Ingrid Bergman, *The Captain's Paradise* with Alec Guinness, and a cameo in the 1976 film *Won Ton Ton*, a spoof of the craze surrounding Rin Tin Tin.

Z

ZACHARY Zachary Taylor, twelfth president of the United States.

ZAHUR Flower (African).

ZAMPA Son of Satan and Madame, two foundation dogs of the Wire-haired Pointing Griffon.

ZANE Zane Grey (1872–1939), American author of *Riders of the Purple Sage* (1912) and other novels that idealized the Old West. A prolific writer, he was the first millionaire author. Several of his books became movies starring the likes of Gary Cooper, Randolph Scott, Wallace Beery, William Powell, and Shirley Temple. But perhaps his biggest claim to fame was the creation of *The Lone Star Ranger* and *Sergeant Preston of the Yukon,* which blazed a trail from the silver screen to the television screen. Grey was also a dedicated fisherman and wrote several books on sportfishing.

ZAPHARA Exuberant (Old English).

ZAPPA Frank Zappa (1940–1993), prolific, innovative American rock and jazz orchestral composer, singer, electric guitarist, lyricist, and producer of over sixty albums with the band the Mothers of Invention and as an independent artist. Arguably the most intellectual musical artist of his day, he was an advocate of human and religious rights and a great admirer of Russian neoclassic composer Igor Stravinsky and French composer Edgard Varèse, known as "the father of electronic music," who influenced Zappa's work throughout his life. In 1990, Zappa visited Czechoslovakia at the invitation of President Václav Havel, who made him an unofficial cultural attaché. That year he was diagnosed with terminal prostate cancer and died three years later at the age of fifty-three, leaving his wife, their four children, and the world a better place.

ZASU ZaSu Pitts (1894–1963), Kansas-born actress who started her career in silent movies and was one of the few that transitioned successfully to talkies and then television to become one of America's best known comediennes.

ZEB Zebulon, sixth son of Jacob and Leah and founder of the Israelite Tribe of Zebulun.

ZECHARIAH God has remembered (Hebrew). **Zack** is the diminutive form, **Zaccharia** is the female Scottish version.

ZEKE Zeke the Wonder Dog, Labrador Retriever, mascot of Michigan State University. Zeke, another of Auntie Em and Uncle Henry's farmworkers on their Kansas farm becomes the Cowardly Lion in Dorothy's dreamland of Oz. Bert Lahr was one of the best-loved actor-comedians of his day.

ZELDA Zelda Van Gutters, the "roving reporter" dog in *Nickelodeon* magazine. Troubled muse and wife of American write F. Scott Fitzgerald.

ZEN God's gift, religious and spiritual person.

ZEPPELIN Airship pioneered by German Count Ferdinand von Zeppelin in the early twentieth century and operated by Deutsche Luftschiffahrts-AG, used commercially to transport passengers before World War One and, during the Great War, used as bombers and scouting aircraft. The *Hindenburg* disaster over Lakehurst, New Jersey on May 1937 cost the lives of thirty-six people and put an end to the zeppelin. The cause of the fire was never discovered.

ZEPHYR Wind, flying with the wind (Old English).

ZEPHYRANTH Fond caresses.

ZERO American actor Humphrey Bogart's dog. Jack's ghost dog in Tim Burton's *The Nightmare Before Christmas*.

ZEUS Ruler over all the Greek gods. The Roman equivalent is Jupiter, and in the Hindu religion he is known as Indra.

ZHANG Zhang Yuining of China won four gold medals in table tennis in the 2004 and 2008 Olympics.

ZHEMCHUZHNAYA Soviet space dog.

ZHUCKA Dog in Dostoyevsky's *Brothers Karamazov*.

ZHULKA Soviet space dog.

ZIB Soviet space dog.

ZIEGFELD *See* Glinda.

ZIGGY *The Rise and Fall of Ziggy Stardust and the Spiders from Mars* ("Ziggy Stardust") is a 1972 album by innovative English rock musician David Bowie.

ZIMBO Dog that plays Homo the domesticated wolf in the rather bizarre silent film *The Man Who Laughs*, a 1928 Universal picture based on the novel by Victor Hugo and directed by German Expressionist filmmaker Paul Leni.

ZINNIA "Here's to absent friends" in the language of flowers.

ZIP Blue Heeler Australian Cattle Dog that starred in the 1995 film *Last of the Dogmen* with Tom Beringer and Barbara Hershey.

ZITA Little girl (Italian).

ZODIAC Celestial coordinate system composed of twelve divisions that originated in Ancient Babylon around the seventh century BC and used by astronomers to interpret all sorts of things ever since.

Zöe Life (Greek). Among the thirty most popular female dog names.

Zola Early champion Bouvier des Flandres dogs that established the breed were **Nella**, **Picard**, **Zola**, and **Pickzwaurt**.

Zorba English-born English Mastiff registered as Aicama Zorba of La-Susa but affectionately called Zorba, he was recognized by *The Guinness Book of World Records* in 1989 as the heaviest dog in the world, weighing in at over 343 pounds and measuring thirty-seven inches at the shoulder and eight feet, three inches from the tip of his nose to the tip of his tail.

Zorro aka Don Diego de la Vega, fictional Spanish swashbuckling nobleman who has swashed his buckle since 1919 in books, films, magazines, and on the radio.

Zsa Zsa Gabor (b. 1917), flamboyant Hungarian-born actress and sister of Magna and Eva, the nine-times married actress was a familiar face on television.

Zsuzsa Character in the kingdom of *The Wonderful Wizard of Oz*, of which there were thirteen sequels written by American author L. Frank Baum.

Zuberi Strong (African).

Zucker German word for "sugar" and for your sweet puppy.

Zulu Largest South African ethnic group and noted warriors. Their great chief Cetshwayo kaMpande (1826–1884), king of the Zulus during the Anglo-Zulu War of 1879 and the last king of an independent Zulu nation in Natal.

Zurich Historical name for a St. Bernard. *See* Künzli.

Zuriel Spiritual woman (African).

Zvyozdochka Soviet space dog.

Zwergh Zwergh Teckel, a miniature Dachshund.

PART II

DOG NAMES BY CATEGORY

COLOR

BREED

LANGUAGE

DESCRIPTIVE WORDS

HISTORY

MYTHS AND LEGENDS

LITERATURE

THE ARTS

HOLLYWOOD

SPORTS

THE NATURAL WORLD

PART II

COLOR

Here you'll find some wonderful and unusual names that may suggest the color of your dog's coat.

Adobe
Argent
Auburn
Banana
Bay
Beaver
Belton
Bianca
Biscuit
Bisque
Bistre
Blaine
Blanche
Blitter
Blizzard
Brass
Brindle
Bronwen
Brownie
Brun
Bruno
Brunoz
Buff
Burgundy
Burnet
Burnish
Butter
Buttermilk
Butterscotch
Café

Café au Lait
Cappuccino
Caramel
Cary
Castor
Charcoal
Chiaro
Chocolate
Ciaran
Cinnamon
Clorox
Cloud
Cocoa
Coffee
Cordovan
Cranberry
Crimson
Crystal
Davy
Dove
Duff
Dun
Ebony
Ecru
Eggshell
Fawn
Frost
Fulvia
Gamboge
Garnet

Goldie
Harlequin
Indigo
Ink
Isabelline
Ivory
Khaki
Kyra
Lemon
Linen
Magenta
Marigold
Melon
Merle
Midnight, Midna
Milky
Mustard
Nettle
Nutmeg
Ochre
Onyx
Pale
Paloma
Papaya
Patches
Patina
Payne
Piebald
Platinum
Pycombe

Raven

Red, Red Wine

Roan

Ruby

Russet

Sable

Salmon

Sapphire

Seashell

Sepia

Shimmer

Sienna

Silver

Slate

Snow

Snowball

Snowflake

Soot

Sorel

Spade

Spectacles

Straw

Sunny

Taupe

Tawny

Umber

Wheat

BREED

The names listed here are specific to the seven American Kennel Club dog groups. Many have historical connotation, some geographical and others reflect the physical nature of a dog.

NON-SPORTING

Abso
Antwerp
Ban
Black Diamond
Bond
Bouldogue
Boxer
Chesty
Coach
Crib
Critter
Dockleaf
Don Carlos
Don Leon
Frenchie
Gamin
Henriette
Jowls
Leopold
Lhassa
Maison
Mighty
Mouton
Nellcote
Orry
Oxford
Possum
Pub

Skipper
T'ang
Taikoo

HOUNDS

Adolfo
Aibe
Alaunt
Amten
Archibald
Arten
Azor
Audacity
Badger
Balderoff
Bangle
Basque
Beatrice
Beauregard
Belvoir
Bernadette
Birdsong
Blackstone
Boos
Bradley
Brian Boru
Brooke
Buffon
Camel

Canute
Charles
Cnut
Colonsay
Comte
Connacht
Contealx
Cuthbert
Damsel
Dolphus
Drunkard
Edwin
Elfric
English
Essex
Everett
Flavianus
Francquevilli
Galway
Genesee
Gram
Honeywood
Hornet
Jebel
Kernochan
King John
Kurzhaar
Langhaar
Lead

Maida
Master
Matabele
Maupin
McNeill
Melton
Memphis
Mesrodia
Mick the Miller
Midget
Misse
Mobray
Modena
Mons Lane
Nile
Nordic
Norsk
Old Drum
Onslow
Otho
Oxford
Otter
Ovid
Paget
Parson
Penistone
Philip
Picts
Pompeii
Prada
Rauhhaar
Reiver
Rock
Romanoff
Rowett

Royal
Runner
Saddle
Sleuth
Snip Nua
Splash
Sunblush
Sunglow
Swaffham
Symmachus
Tallyho!
Teckel
Tennessee
Tree
Trigg
Twici
Vendee
Virginia
Walker
Wallace
Wapiti
Warrior
Wilson
Winchell
Woronzova
Xenophon
Zwergh

SPORTING
Augot Clariette
Avendale
Banco
Beaufort
Beaumont
Beechgrove

Bhisti
Blade
Bolingbroke
Boughley
Brigadier
Brighton
Buccleuch
Burdett
Caledonia
Calgary
Calvert
Calvin
Canton
Carlisle
Castle
Chessy
Clitheroe
Comforter
Count Noble
Curly
Dan
Dash
Dobri
Douron
Dudda
Dudley
Earl
Elcho
Enaud
Enniskillen
Epagneul
Fairy
Fansome
Faskally
Fermanagh

Five, Four, Three
Flame
Flapper
Flodden
Flute
Francis
Fuller
Galway
Genesee
Gram
Honeywood
Hornet
Jebel
Koni
Korthals
Lady Howe
Lambert
Laverack
Leda
Lillian
Lina
Lloyd
Lomax
Lorna
Mabws
Madame Augot
Mallard
Malmesbury
Mannering
Mansell
Manton
Marjoribanks
McCarthy
Merry
Mimsy

Miss Hud
Monson
Moore
Mop
Mortimer
Mouche
Mr. Buck
Nellie
Noailles
Norwich
Nuggle
Ogo
Old Moll
Phineas
Plumber
Ponto
Poole
Powder
Purcell
Purdey
Quail
Querida
Rake
Randolph
Rhoebe
Roderigo
Ruddy
Sailor
Sally
Sandringham
Scrummy
Shotgun
Skeet
Spatterdock
Spaynel

Sport
Springer
Stiffy
Tracker
Trench
Trouvee
Velox
Venatici
Vesta
Walters
Wolverhampton
Wyndham
Zampa

TERRIER
Allister
Auld Mustard
Auld Pepper
Bailiff
Battleship
Belingham
Bixby
Black Jack
Bolton
Bonnie Belle
Border
Briar
Brigand
Bully
Burnett
Buster
Cadwalder
Caldwell
Cavalier
Chalky

Chandler
Clee
Clonmel
Coral
Courtier
Crompton
Cumberland
Edwin
Elfric
English
Essex
Everett
Flavianus
Francquevilli
Gamekeeper
Gaston
Gerwn
Ghilly, Gillie
Grinchy
Gunmetal
Hans
Hardy
Hastings
Hawker
Hazzard
Henry
Hershey
Hill
Holland
Home
Horsford
Hunter
Huzzar
Janus
Jason

Jocko
Joicey
Joy
Junon
Justin
Keighley
Kerry
Kersurck
Kiltie
Kokomo
Laird
Lawrence
Little Mustard
Little Pepper
Lonsdale
Lorna
Malcome
Meddle
Megargee
Meggie
Messenger
Mina
Mirabelle
Misty Isle
Molly
Monarque
Montravia
Morrison
Mr. Atlas
Naylor
Newcastle
Nina
Old Crab
Old Jock
Old Trap

Otley
Phiz
Phoebe
Pitch
Preacher
Prescot
Red Palm
Romani
Roseneath
Ross
Rothbury
Roxie
Scotty
Shire
Skean
Skipton
Skye
Sluggy
Sprite
Squire
Stevens
Strathbogie
T'Other
Tam Glen
Touberville
Truffles
Whatnot
Which
Whinstone
Whatnot
Whitaker

TOY
Ah Cum
Bibilis

Biche	Goelet	Mitzy
Blenheim	Gordon	Painter
Blinde	Gyp	Pall Mall
Brabancon	Haverfordwest	Peek
Cal	Hawick	Pom
Carolus	Hindlee	Pom-Pom
Chi Chi	Hinks	Publius
Cuba	Hooper	Pudel
Dutch	Huddersfield Ben	Ruffle
Dwarf	Hulme	Salvo
Ewe	Jacket	Sans Souci
Ferret	Jacques	Sassafras, Sassy
Filipponi	Jeannie	Sleeve
Gladitor	Jock	Smythe
Glencoe	Lady	Sparrow
Glenlyon	Loftus	Sun
Glenmere	Malta	Tang
Glynn	Mazatlan	Tea

TOY FOX TERRIER PUPPY

Techichi
Topknot
Topsell
Vulci
Walham
Wraga

HERDING
Berger
Bewick
Bramble
Bronant
Celt
Colley
Colne
Darlington
Dragon de la Lys
Droya
Flag
Kelpie
Keul
Laeken
Louvois
Lyda
Maddy
Malines
Mason
Neckar
Nella
Nic
Nord
Officer
Old Hemp
Oshkosh
Pembroke

Pickzwaurt
Prince D'or
Rustler
Siske
Squirrel
Sterling
Tervueren
Tundra
Vuilbaard
Wrangler
Zola

WORKING
Apolda
Barreges
Bavaria
Bilka
Black Forest
Bodinus
Boot
Bordeaux
Boston Blackie
Bourdet
Cadet
Caesar
Cardigan
Caribou
Cassel
Cato
Ciaburri
Cragsman
Cranach
Dake
Dare-Devil
Darley

Dick Turpin
Dinkie
Dublin
Dusty
Dauphin
Devonshire
Don
Fingal
Fire Chief
Foxy
Fracas
Estramadura
Fallow
Flemish
Gilbert
Greenthorpe
Han
Hebe
Huejotzingo
Inez
Issa
Itsy Bitsy
Kwasz
Keeper
Keller
King
Knight
Kobuk
Kotzebue
Kunzli
Lara
Louis
Lourdes
Lucas
Maintenon

Matin
Matthias
Mechlinburg
Menthon
Mida
Molossus
Monarch
Montagnes
Nansen
Navarre
Nell

Nic
Norah
Plavia
Poacher
Police
Prinz
Protector
Resy Patricia
Rimshot
Sami
Sayantsi

Seppel
Settchen
Sheriff
Sieger
Snowdrift
Talhund
Whey
Wurttemberg
Yanesei

The names below are champions down through the ages of the two most prestigious international purebred dog shows, the Westminster Kennel Club Show, founded in 1876, which is held annually in New York City, and the Crufts Dog Show in England, founded in 1891 by Charles Crufts.

WESTMINSTER

Acclaim
Bang
Bingo
Black Knight
Bobby's Girl
Bootlegger
Bruce
Carmichael
Chidley
Chik
Cinnar
Cob
Command
Conqueror
Crest

Daro
Diamond Jim
Ditto
Dobe
Dragonora
Duc
Faultless
Fearnought
Felicity
Fleetfoot
Frolic
Gaelforce
Giralda
Glee
Good News
Governor

Gretchen
Groenendael
Holly
Innisfree
Just Right
Kippax
Laud
Little Sister
Lonesome Dove
Loteki
Marjetta
Maryscot
Moonhill
Parsifal
Penny
Perfection

Pitter Patter
Postscript
Pouch
Pretzel
Prima Donna
Prince Albert
Promise
Rarebit
Red Baron
Remedy
Rhythm
Rise and Shine
Rocket
River
Sabine
Salilyn
Sensation
Sesto
Signal
Sirrah
Slumber
Stump
Surry
Takya
Talavera
Trick
Tudor
Vic
Warlord
Warren
Whisperwind
Wilber
Willum
Wolvey

CRUFTS
Banchory
Banker
Bells
Blackcap
Blaise
Boots
Bramshaw
Broadwater
Caitland
Callaghan
Canigou Cambrai
Choonam
Choo-tai
Chuckles
Clare
Cobyco
Cockspur
Collarbone
Craknor
Crufts
Debounair
Derry
Dora
Elder
Falcon
Faune
Fenton
Giant George
Graco
Grant
Gray Dawn
Gwynne
Hansa
Hartenstein

Hazelnut
Heather
Helvetia
Hit and Miss
Hitari
Horand
Hung Kwong
Huntsman
Inuit
Jafrak
Kentuckian
Knur
Leader
Luckystar
Merman
Mite
Moonhill
Necessity
Notts
Potter
Pride
Puckshill
Raycrofts
Recruit
Sandstorm
Saxon
Scarf
Sceptre
Shelton
Sunblush
Tracey
Treetops
Tweed
Twynstar
Willy

LANGUAGE

The names in this section are classified by language or country of origin.

FOREIGN WORDS FOR DOG (see Part I for language of origin)

Aso	Runt	Fakih
Cao	Собака (Sobaka)	Farhani
Chien	Suns	Gamba
Cho	Suo	Gazali
Ci	Xolotl	Gazelle
Cabaka		Ghalib
Dogge	**AFRICAN**	Girma
Doggie	Abiola	Gyasi
Gos	Ajani	Haamid
Grech	Anam	Haben
Greg	Bakari	Habib
Hond	Bomani	Hagos
Hund	Cetshwayo	Hamisi
Hundur	Chacha	Hasani
It	Chinwendu	Idi
Koira	Couscous	Idrissa
Kutya	Dakarai	Ipyana
Madra	Dia	Jabari
Mbwa	Diallo	Jabarl
Nac	Din	Jabir
Pas	Dumisani	Jabulani
Paws	Elewa	Jaja
Perro	Elimu	Jamal
Pes	Erasto	Jamar
Pies	Erevu	Jawara
Pinyin	Eze	Jelani
Pooch	Fabumi	Kellan
Qen	Fahim	Kendi

Kibwe
Kirabo
Kofi
Kojo
Koto
Latif
Lesedi
Lobengula
Lutalo
Maalik
Mahari
Mamelo
Merman
Mhina
Minkah
Naasir
Nadia
Nassor
Negasi
Negus
Nuru
Ochi
Obi
Ohin
Omarr
Omorede
Otieno
Paulo
Phomello
Quaashie
Raimi
Ramsea
Rashidi
Reth
Roho

Rudo
Rufaro
Runako
Saad
Said
Saleem
Tahir
Taj
Taji
Talib
Tanishia
Tau
Ubora
Umar
Upendo
Viscount
Vorden
Yair
Yarrow
Suberi
Zulu
Zuriel

ARABIC
Ali
Amala
Amir
Asima
Edelmira
Emir
Topazos

CHINESE
Chopsticks
Chow Mein
Chzi Gou

Confucius
Foo Dog
Ginseng
Jing Jing
Ping
Songshi
Txakurra
Tao
Vbos
Yana
Zen

DUTCH
Anneke

SCOTTISH
Aileen
Ailsa
Alpin
Andrew
Andy
Angus
Argyle
Armstrong
Balmoral
Caledonia
Carlyle
Chieftain
Chivas
Clyde
Cosmo
Douglas
Duncan
Dundee
Ewan

Falkirk
Fiona
Fitzgilbert
Guisachan
Hamilton
Hamish
Hunda
Keith
Leslie
Lindsay
Lochinvar
Mac
MacTavish
Malcolm
Meg
Montieth
Monty
Nessie
Rawdon
Saunders
Scotsman
Spats
Stuart
Veni
Whiskey

IRISH/GAELIC
Cloven
Conan
Dara
Donald
Eldritch
Elodie
Fergus
Ferguson

Flurry
Gaelic
Njal
O'Neil
O'Toole
Paddy
Quinn

ENGLISH
Ainsley
Alan
Alden
Aldrich
Aldys
Alexandra
Allen
Alnwick
Alvin
Annie
Aqualate
Arlene
Ascot
Ashley
Ashton
Atherton
Audley
Avery
Avon
Babs, Barbara
Bailiwick
Barrett
Barton
Benjamin
Bentley
Beth

Beverly
Blackwell
Blake
Blythe
Bourne
Bradford
Brandon
Brayton
Brice
Brinsley
Brodie
Bruton
Burke
Callie
Camden
Carolyn
Carson
Carter
Cassidy
Chatsworth
Cheerio
Chelsea
Chequers
Cheviot
Chin-Chin
Cinder
Clayton
Cleveland
Clifton
Clinton
Clive
Clue
Codger
Constable
Cornwall

Courtney
Crawford
Culverton
Cyneburga
Dale
Dalton
Danforth
Daphne
Darlene
Denholm
Denne
Devon
Dexter
Diana
Dodie
Donner
Drover
Duchy
Ducky
Duffield
Durham
Galump
Gelvira
Gotham
Grady
Graham
Granville
Gyre
Halcyon
Harold
Harris
Hayden
Hayley
Herbert
Humphrey

Jackson
Jub
Kate
Katherine
Kenneth
Kenny
Kimberly
Kingsley
Knox
Lance
Laura
Lillibet
Lizzie
Logan
Lord

Lynk
Majesty
Manxome
Maya
Minke
Mitch
Nibbles
Paige
Paisley
Piccadilly
Pim
Pippa
Pixie
Poltallock
Pryse

SHETLAND SHEEPDOG PUPPY

Quaker
Queen
Spear
Tanner
Tesso
Travis
Turner
Twinkle
Vicar
Wilfred
William
Willow
Wills
Windsor
Winfred
Winthrop
Yeoman
York
Zaphara
Zephyr

IRISH
Arra
Barrington
Basset
Bewley
Blarney
Blemie
Brianna
Bridget
Briton
Cael
Caitlin
Callahan
Colpach

Desmond
Donahue
Donovan
Edmund
Eldric
Edward
Emerson
Emmett
Exeter
Fancy
Fay
Figgy
Fitzgerald
Foxhall
Frolick
Fulton
Eileen
Erin
Finnegan
Flanagan
Guernsey
Guinness
Kennedy
Liam
Moira
Rachel
Reilly
Robbie
Sabre
Salem
Seamus
Shelley
Shirley
Sloane
Smitty

Somerset
Spotted Dick
Susie
Sussex
Terrence
Ulster

WELSH
Andreas
Ceffyl Dwr
Chad
Conway
Corrin
Emrys
Gabriel, Gabby
Gwen
Meredith
Morgan
Mumbles
Owen
Rhosddu
Wales

FRENCH/NORMAN
Aimee
Alano
Alfonse
Algernon
Allaire
Ames
Antoine
Arlette
Babette
Baguette
Beau

Bebe
Belle
Bijou
Brie
Brittany
Cabaret
Cabernet
Carcassone
Cartier
Cerise
C'est Moi
Chablis
Champagne
Chanel
Chantilly
Chardon
Chase, Chasse
Chauffer
Chauffeur
Chauve
Chere
Cherise
Chic
Cognac
Coquette
Courvoisier
Écossais
Elle
Emperor
Esme
Faux Pas
Fave
Fitzgerald
Foie Gras

Fondue
François
Je t'aime
Lacey
Leroy
Les Amis
Madame
Madamoiselle
Marshall
Meeka (Dominique)
Mon Ami
Mon Petite
Monsieur
Montgomery
Natalie
Patou
Pierre
Pontou
Russell
Savoy
Simplon
Veronique

GERMAN
Alberta
Archer
Arnold
Ase
Aubrey
Autobahn
Baldwin
Bertha
Conrad
Derek

Deutsche
Didi
Dieter
Donar
Gerald
Geraldine
Gesundheit
Gunther
Herman
Hexe, Hexen
Hilda
Hildebrand
Hummel
Jaegar
Karl
Liebchen
Linda
Lorelei
Lulu, Luisa
Milicent
Olivia
Panzer
Raymond
Reginald
Reinagle
Roland
Rotweil
Rudolf
Siegfried
Sternchen
Stuttgart
Warner
Wido
Wilhelmina

Wolfgang
Zucker

GHANA
Adeben
Bobo

GREEK
Agnes
Ambrose
Anastasia
Angel
Arfara
Ari
Aristides
Beta
Briony
Calla
Delphi
Europa
Gaius
Jade
Lazarus
Lydia
Miklos
Omega
Plato
Plutarch
Roxanne
Selene
Socrates
Steve, Stephanos
Sybil
Zoe

HAWAIIAN
Akaika
Akama
Alani
Alemana
Aliikai
Aliki
Amoka
Anela
Aneuenue
Apala
Asera
Ealani
Edega
Eneki
Eno
Etana
Halia
Hanai
Hoku
Hula
Kahili
Kai
Kaiya
Kalani
Kale
Kalea
Kalei
Kaloke
Kamin
Kana
Kanin
Kaori
Kaoru

Kapono
Kata
Keanu
Ki
Kopa'a
Kope
La
Laka
Lani
Lau
Lemi
Liko
Lupo
Mahina
Mai'a
Makenna
Malo
Manu
Mauna Kea
Meka
Meli
Mikie
Miliani
Nan
Neolani, Lani
Niu
Noa
Olina
Pua
Ua
Waiu
Waiupaka

HEBREW
Aaron
Abigail
Abraham
Absalom
Adam
Adira
Amos
Anais
Arend
Axel
Beulah
Chen
Cherub
Chutzpah
Daniel, Danny
Elbe
Eli
Elias
Elizabeth, Elsie,
    Elspeth
Elkanah
Emerald
Emmeline
Emory
Ernestina
Epstein
Eve
Ezekiel
Gideon
Gomer
Hannah
Hebel
Ishmael
Jacob

Jemima
Jethro
Jude
Keilah
Leader
Leah
Levi
Maribel
Samson
Saul
Shayna
Susannah
Tamara
Zack
Zeb

ITALIAN
Adamo
Adelina
Adona
Alfonso
Agapeto
Agostina
Alda
Alfredo
Allesandra
Amaretto
Amari
Amato
Amedea
Amore
Anacleto
Anatolio
Andrea
Annalisa

Annunziata
Anselmo
Antonia
Arianna
Armando
Armani
Baci
Baldovino
Bambina, Bambino
Basilio
Belladonna
Benigno
Beppe
Bernardino
Bettina
Biaggio
Bibiana
Bonaventure
Bonfiolio
Calandra
Callisto
Calogera
Calvina
Carla
Casimiro
Caterina
Cecil
Cecilia
Celso
Cesare
Chianti
Christian
Christine
Ciao
Cinzia

Cipriana
Ciro
Clara
Clemente
Cleto
Coger
Colombina
Concetta
Consolata
Corona
Cosima
Costanzo
Crispin
Crispino
Cristiana
Cucina
Damiano
Dario
Davide
Debora
Delfina
Desi
Diamante
Dino
Dolce
Domenica
Dona
Donatella
Dorotea
Drago
Edmonda
Edoardo
Edvige
Elario
Eleonora

Elettra
Elisabetta
Elma
Eloisa
Elpido
Enrica, Enrico
Enzo
Ermina
Ersilia
Espresso
Eufemia
Eula
Fabrizia
Federica
Feliciano
Felicita
Ferdinanda
Ferrari
Ferro
Fiammetta
Filberto
Filipo
Fina
Filomena
Fioralba
Fiore
Fiorella
Fiorenza
Firmino
Fonsie
Francesca
Franco
Gaspare
Gastone
Gemma

Germano
Gianni, Giovanni
Gilda
Gino
Gioconda
Gioffreda
Giorgio
Giovanna
Gisella
Giuliana
Giuseppe
Giustina
Grazia
Guerino
Guiditta
Guido
Ignazio
Ilaria
Ines
Italia
Italo
Jolanda
Lalia
Letizia
Luciana
Lucrezia
Ludovica
Luigi
Mafalda
Manfredo
Manilo
Marcella
Margherita
Maria
Mariella

Marietta

Marta

Maso

Massimo

Matteo

Maura

Melania

Mirella

Modesto

Moe

Natale

Nereza

Nerina

Nerio

Nevio

Nico

Nicola

Nino

Orabella

Orazo

Orlando

Orsina

Panfilo

Paola

Patsy

Pellegrino

Pepe

Petronella

Ponzio

Primo

Raul

Remo

Riccardo

Rinaldo

Roberta

Rocco

Ruffino

Sabato

Samanta

Santa

Santino

Savio

Selvaggia

Silvana

Sofia

Stefano

Strega

Tacito

Taddeo

Tammaso

Tancredo

Teofilo

Terzo

Uberto

Urbano

Valeria

Vanda

Vanni

Verona

Vico

Vincent

COLLIE PUPPY

Vittorio
Zita

JAPANESE
Ai
Aikido
Aiko
Akio
Amaya
Aneko
Ayame
Bushido
Chika
Emiko
Geisha
Gen
Genki
Gin
Goro
Haiku
Haru
Haruki
Haruko
Hide
Hikari
Hiroko
Hiroshi
Hisano
Hoshiko
Ignatius
Inari
Jin
Jiro
Kaeomon
Kagami

Kaida
Kaiko
Keiko
Keitaro
Kendo
Kimi
Kobe
Kohana
Koko
Kujo
Kumiko
Kumu
Kuniko
Kura
Kuri
Kyoko
Leiko
Lencho
Machiko
Maeko
Maemi
Mai
Makoto
Mariko
Marlene
Masako
Matsu
Mea'ono
Michi
Michiko
Midori
Mieko
Miki
Miso
Miya

Miyoko
Mura
Nami
Nariko
Nishi
Oki
Ringo
Rya
Saburau
Sachi
Sada
Salira
Samurai
Shino
Shogun
Suki
Suzuki
Tama
Tamasine
Toshi
Umeko
Uta
Washi
Wattan
Yachi
Yama
Yasuo
Yo
Yoko
Yori
Yoshe
Yoshi
Yoshiko
Yoshino
Yuki

Yukio
Yumiko

MALAY
Anjing

LATIN
Acer
Alida
Aloysius
Amanda
Anna
Dominic
Duke
Dulcie
Eugenia
Felix
Josephine
Justus
Leo
Leonora
Lucinda
Lupin
Mabel
Magnum
Mark
Miles
Noble
Orient
Orsina
Pauline
Regulus
Serena
Silas
Silvia
Simone
Ursula

NIGERIAN
Abayomi
Abeti
Ade
Adebayo
Adeen
Ayo
Azibo
Chidi
Chike
Chimalsi
Chisulo
Ebo
Eko
Uba

NORSE
Asleikr
Baldur
Brunhilda
Bruni
Corey
Dagmar
Dana
Darby
Elof
Elvis
Farmann
Fenris
Fredi
Gerda

Ginnungagap
Gunnar
Heimdall
Helga
Hod
Hundolf
Idun
Kari
Kirby
Loki
Njord
Norseti
Roscoe
Sigmund
Stigandr
Tryg
Tyr
Wotan

RUSSIAN
Anton
Anya
Danica
Ivan
Ivana
Kuma
Ludovik
Mischa
Olga
Sasha
Valdamarr

SPANISH
Alejandro
Alhaja
Allegra
Amable
Amiga
Azura
Belinda
Caramba
Chica
Chiquita, Chiquito
Corazon
Cucaracha
Cuervo
Delora
Desperado
Diablo
Diego

Dip
Dolores
Elvira
Esperanza
Ferdinand
Fiesta
Flan
Jose
Kiki
Libby (Isabel,
   Isabelle)
Matador
Paco
Pino
Rio
Sierra
Uno
Vaquero

Vegas
Vida
Viva

SCANDINAVIAN
Anderson
Barke
Birgitta
Brita
Emilie
Ingrid
Karen
Koira
Konig
Ludvig
Mette
Viking

DESCRIPTIVE WORDS

These names do not fall into any specific category. They are wonderfully descriptive words that may suit the personality of your dog.

Ability
Able
Affinity
Aim
Airborne
All Right
Alpha
Amiable
Anorak
Answer
Aristocrat
Aura
Baby
Baby Doll
Baccarat
Bachelorette
Baldy
Ballerina
Bandanna
Banner
Barbie
Baring
Barnacle
Bashful
Beanie
Beater
Bedlam
Beer
Beggar
Beret

Bishop
Bitsy
Blackjack
Blasé
Blessing
Bloke
Bold
Bonbon
Bones
Bonfire
Bonnet
Booker
Bosco
Boss
Bourbon
Brad
Braveheart
Brawny
Breeze
Brisk
Britches
Bubbles
Buccaneer
Buckaroo
Builder
Bumpkin
Bunting
Caboose
Cadbury
Caddy

Calico
Caper
Caprice
Captain
Cargo
Cartwright
Cashmere
Chalet
Chambray
Charisma
Charity
Charmer
Cheeky
Cheers
Chi
Chiffon
Chip
Chops
Chortle
Chum
Coaster
Cog
Confetti
Cordial
Cowboy
Crash
Crinoline
Cruiser
Crusher
Cuckoo

Curious

Cutie

Dabble

Daddy

Daredevil

Dazzler

Dearest

Debutante

Déjà vu

Derby

Destiny

Detonator

Detour

Digger

Ditzy

Divorcee

Dizzy

Doctor

Dolly

Doodle

Dreamer

Drud

Dude

Dusk

Dynamo

Endeavor

Epic

Faith

Farthingale

Farthingale

Fedora

Feisty

Fellow

Fiddle

Fighter

Firecracker

Firehouse

Fizz

Fortune

Frisbee

Frisky

Gadget

Geezer

Genius

Ghost

Giddy

Giggles

Gimble

Gingham

Girl

Gizmo

Guide

Gumball

Guru

Gusto

Harmony

Heaven

Hermit

Hero

Hope

Hurricane

Ice Tea

Indra

Intrepid

Jake

Joker

Junior

Karma

Kid

Kin

Kisses

Kristall

Lace

Limbo

Lovely

Mana

Manners

Mate

Maverick

Meadow

Mellow

Merchant

Metro

Mini

Miracle

Mohawk, Mohican

Morsel

Moxie

Muffy

Mugsy

News

Noel

Noodle

Outlaw

Partner

Patience

Pep

Pizzazz

Poppet

Pretty

Quibble

Raider

Rascal

Rebel

Rogue

Saber
Satin
Scallywag
Scoundrel
Sekani
Sekayi
Serendipity
Sergeant
Shorty
Silky
Sir
Sissy
Snapshot
Sneakers
Socks
Soldier

Southpaw
Sparkle
Spirit
Spy
Steffi
Stetson
Stony
Suede
Swashbuckler
Sweetie
Trinket
Trip
Trucker
Tuffy
Turbo
Tutu

Tuxedo
Tweet
Tycoon
Vagabond
Warble
Whisper
Whoop
Wiggles
Windy
Wisp
Woofie
Woolly
Wrinkles
Yoyo
Zephyranth

HISTORY

Here you'll find names that have to do with a person, event, or place in history. As with so many of the names you'll find in this book, these have terrific stories to tell.

Abelard	Baroness	Cabot
Abra	Bartholomew	Cadillac
Abruzzi	Batz	Caius
Adams	Beefeater	Calamity Jane
Adelaide	Big Ben	Carnarvon
Adele	Bismarck	Carnegie
Adrian	Blackbeard	Caruso
Aelian	Blackberry	Casanova
Alaric	Blackie, Blacky	Casino
Albemarle	Blaze	Castaway
Alexander	Blitz	Challenger
Alexis	Blitzen	Champion
Ambassador	Blondie	Chang
Anscombe	Bo	Charlemagne
Anthony	Bolik	Checkers
Aristotle	Bolo	Chernushka
Arius	Boodles	Chester
Arrian	Boone	Ching
Asquith	Boris	Churchill
Augustine	Boston Beans	Claudius
Augustus	Boswell	Cleopatra
Aurelius	Brinkley	Clipper
Avanti	Buchanan	Coco Chanel
Averill	Buckingham	Cody
Bacon	Buick	Colonel
Balboa	Busy	Colt
Balthasar	Buzz	Columbia
Balto	Byrd	Columbus
Barnum	Caacie	Commodore

Corbett
Corporal
Corsica
Cortez
Crockett
Cromwell
Crusader
Culloden
Cyrus
Czar, Czarina
D'artagnan
Dalai
Dasher
Dave

Delilah
Descartes
Desoto
Disraeli
Doc
Dorians
Dot
Duffy
Dwight
Eaglehurst Gillette
Edsel
Eisenhower
Eleanor, Ellie
Elgin

Ember
Erasmus
Escapade
Escort
Esther
Eugene
Euripides
Faithful
Fala
Feller
Fiala
Flannel
Flicker
Flirt
Forbes
Franklin
Frederick
Gandhi
Garfield
Gaullie
Gem
General
Genghis
Geronimo
Gladstone
Grim
Grits
Gus
Hadley
Hadrian
Hancock
Harley
Harrison
Harrriman
Harry

ENGLISH TOY SPANIEL PUPPY

Heloise
Hidalgo
Hilary
Houdini
Ike
Jimmy
Johnson
Juno
Kaiser
Kensington
Khafra
King Cole
King Tut
Kit
Kometka
Krasavka
Kudryavka
Lady Jane
Lafayette
Laika
Le Beau
Leif
Liberty
Lincoln
Lindbergh
Linnet
Lisichka
Little Breeze
Livingstone
Lorenzo
Lovell
Lyndon
Machiavelli
MacMillan

Madame de
   Pompadour
Major
Majora
Malyska
Mamie
Marco Polo
Marcus
Marie Antoinette
Marquis
Martin
Mary
McDonald
Mercedes
Mike
Millie
Mimi
Ming
Minister
Miss Beasley
Monroe
Montezuma
Morris
Mushka
Muttnick
Myles
Nebuchadnezzar
Nixon
Obama
Octavia
Oh Boy
Old Fritz
Otvazhnaya
Palo Alto
Pasha

Pat
Patrick
Patriot
Patton
Paul
Pchelka
Pchyolka
Peritas
Perry
Pete
Pharaoh
Pierce
Player
Polk
Prince
Princess
Prudence
Prussia
Pushinka
Quicksilver
Quincy
Raisa
Ramayana
Rani
Reagan
Ritz
Rob Roy
Roi
Rollo
Roman
Rothschild
Ruffian
Rusty
Ryzhik
Sabina

Sachem

Sassy

Saucisse

Scentwell

Schiaparelli

Schmitt

Scotch (and Soda)

Seaman

Seymour

Shackleton

Shannon

Shutka

Smelaya

Snezhinka

Soleil

Solomon

Sonnie

Sphinx

Squire

Standish

Starlet

Steenie

Strelka

Sumarian

Sundance Kid

Susan

Sweet Lips

Taca

Tad

Taster

Tattoo

Telek

Tenochititlan

Trooper

Truman

Tsyganka

Tut

Twiggy

Tyler

Ugolyok

Veterok

Veto

Viceroy

Vicky

Victoria

Victory

Visa

Vladimir

Voodoo

Voyager

Vulcan

Wanda

Washington

Weejie

Wendessa

White Tips

Willie

Winston

Wren

Wyatt

Xanadu

Xanthippus

Yale

Yukonan

Yves

Zeppelin

Zhemchuzhnaya

Zhulka

Zib

Zvyozdochka

MYTHS AND LEGENDS

Here are heroes and heroines of myths and legends from many different cultures and from all over the world. And after that I've listed the names of some very special dogs who are legends themselves.

MYTHOLOGY AND FABLES

Acheron
Achilles
Aesir
Aesop
Agilaz
Agu
Ajax
Aladdin
Ambrosia
Andromeda
Anubis
Aphrodite
Apollo
Ares
Argos
Athena
Atlantis
Atlas
Aurora
Avalon
Bacchus
Bedivere
Biton
Boreas
Bragi
Breunor
Brewer

Bunyan
Caledfwlch
Calypso
Carados
Cassandra, Cassie
Catulla
Cerberus
Charon
Cinderella
Clarance
Cúchulainn
Cupid
Cyclops
Dagonet
Damocles
Danu
Demeter
Dionysus
Du Lac
Eira
Elf
Eos
Eostre
Eros
Eumaeus
Excalibur
Faust
Fido
Flora

Flower
Fra Mauro
Freya
Friflet
Frigg
Fable
Galahad
Gareth
Gavin
Gawain
Gemini
Genie
Gretel
Guinevere
Hades
Hansel
Hecuba
Helen
Helios
Hephaestus
Hera
Hermes
Herodotus
Hest
Homer
Icarus
Ironside
Jupiter
Kay

Kleobis	Neptune	Pwyll
Laelaps	Nixe	Qigirn
Lancelot	Nona	Rheanna
Leprechaun	Odin	Robin (Hood)
Linus	Odysseus	Romulus
Lohengrin	Olaf	Sachem
Lua	Orion	Sagramore
Lucan	Orthrus	Sorcerer
Luna	Owain	Soter
Luxovius	Pandora	Trojan
Marea	Percivale	Ulysses
Merlin	Persephone	Ve
Midas	Perseus	Vidar
Minerva	Phoenix	Vili
Mordred	Pollux	Zeus
Muse	Poseidon	

LEGENDARY DOGS

This is a wonderful group of names. They are names of dogs that have earned a place in canine history—brave, devoted, and determined: all the best in canine, and human, nature.

Adjutant	Beauty	Choo-Choo
Admiral	Belka	Cider
Aliduke	Bluey	Cindy
Antis	Bob the Railway Dog	Colonel Rock
Appollo	Bobbie	Dakota
Asgard	Buddy	Damka
Baekgu	Bugle Ann	Dezikn
Balto	Cafall	Donnie
Bamse	Casey	Dookie
Barry	Cedric	Dubs
Baudwin	Chilla	Elwood
Baxter	Chinook	Endal
Beautiful Joe	Chips	Gander

George Tirebiter
Greyfriars Bobby
Gunner
Hachi, Hachiko
Hale
Handsome
Heidi
Hobo
Horrie
Irma
Jack
Jackie
Jane
Jefferson
Jekyll
Jet
Jiggs
Jo-Fi
Jonathan
Judy
Just Nuisance
King Buck
Klondike
Laddie
Lava
Le Diable
Leao
Legolas
Lex
Lucky
Lyme
Malchik

Malchik
Manchu
Mancs
Master McGrath
McKinley
Mex
Misty
Moustache
Nemo
Nicholas
Nick
Old Drum
Old Shep
Owney
Peers
Peter Piper
Piccolo
Pierce
Piers
Pipsqueak
Pluto and Juno
Pompey
Punch and Judy
Rags
Rajah
Reveille
Ricky
Rico
Rifleman
Rip
Rob
Robot

Rodney
Sabi
Sadie
Saris
Shasta
Sheeba
Sheila
Sherwood
Sinbad
Smokey
Smoky
Snag
Squeak
Streaker
Stubby
Stuka
Suening
Sultan
Swansea Jack
Taffy
Trackr
Treo
Turk
Uga
Velvet
Verdun Belle
Viste
Waghya
Waterloo
Zeke
Zorba

LITERATURE

These names were a blast to gather together. If you love literature, you're sure to be drawn to many of these. There are dedicated sections for some classics: Charles Dickens, Shakespeare, J. R. R. Tolkien, and popularly, J. K. Rowling's Harry Potter, the Oz books. But there are many authors in the general section who are among my very favorites: Daphne du Maurier, John Galsworthy, Lewis Carroll, and Rudyard Kipling, among others. Enjoy!

Agatha	Barrie	Bodkin
Aistem	Baskerville	Boo Radley
Akela	Beamish	Borogove
Aldo	Bean	Bounce
Alfred	Beatrix	Bouncer
Alice	Bella	Bowser
Alisande	Bendico	Bramwell
Almondine	Bennet	Brillig
Appolon	Bernard	Bristle
Archie	Big Red	Brontë
Arlo	Big Sam	Browning
Atticus	Bingley	Bru
Bagheera	Bitty Bit	Brutus
Baker	Black Beauty	Buck
Balcia	Black Shuck	Buckeye
Ball	Blandings	Bulls-eye
Baloo	Blinkie	Bummer
Bandar-log	Blitzee	Burbled
Bandersnatch	Blood	Bushy
Bandit	Bloomsbury	Byron
Banga	Bluff	Carl
Bangalore	Boatswain	Carraway
Baree	Bob	Caspian
Barge	Bob the Retriever Dog	Cavall
Barghest	Bobbin	Ceril

GERMAN WIREHAIRED POINTER puppy

Dingus
Dodo
Doolittle
Doyle
Dr. Watson
Du Maurier
Duchess
Dylan
Eddie
Edythe
Eliza
Emily
Ernest
Estella
Evan
Fang
Fantome Noire
Father Wolf
Faun
Favell
Feather
Fidele
Finn
Fitzwilliam
Flanders
Fleur
Flinder
Flopsy
Flossie
Fluke
Flush
Fly
Forsyte
Frabjous
Freckles

Cesario
Chalk
Charley
Charlotte
Chaucer
Chekhov
Cheney
Chillywalla
Chowder
Chris
Chuchundra
Cimarron
Cinders
Cisco
Clavell
Clumsy
Coleridge
Colle

Colter
Comely
Cosy
Crackerjack
Cranford
Crawley
Crusoe
Cujo
Cummings
Cyrano
Cyril
Dandy
Dante
Darcy
Darling
Darzee
Dashiell
Dingo

Friar	Hutchinson	Lad
Frith	Ibsen	Laska
Galsworthy	Iceman	Lassie
Gargery	Igor	LED
Garyowen	Ikki	Little Ann
Gaspode	Ivanhoe	Little Bear
Gator	Izaak	Loony
Gatsby	Jaberwocky	Lothario
Gelert	Jacksie	Luath
Georgiana	Jasper	Luffra
Gerland	Jeeves	Mackintosh,
Giles	Jennie	McIntosh
Ginger Pye	Jerry	Macnamara
Gnash	Jess	Madgie
Grey Brother	John Joiner	Maeterlinck
Grizzle	Jolly	Mammy
Gulliver	Julyan	Mang
Gunga Din	Kaa	Marie Louise
Gusty	Kafka	Marit
Guy	Karait	Marley
Gypsy	Kashtanka	Marlowe
Haman	Kazak	Marmee
Hampton	Kazakh	Marple
Hank	Kazan	Matilda
Harper	Kep	Max
Harriet	Kiche	Maxim
Hathi	Kilimanjaro	Mehitibel
Hemingway	Kim	Merlyn
Hercule	Kipling	Merriwether
Holmes	Kitty	Mildred
Houdini	Kotick	Millard
Hound	Ku-Klip	Milne
Howard	La Beale	Mirabelle
Hugo	Labumpko	Miss Lemon

Mitchell
Mithe
Moonstone
Mopsy
Mor
Moriarty
Mountain Boy
Mouse
Mowgli
Mrs. Danvers
Mrs. Dingley
Mycroft
Nag
Nagaina
Najib
Nana
Nash
Nello
Neos
Nero
Nietzsche
Nip and Tuck
Noah
Nop
O'Connor
O'Hara
October
Ogier
Old Dan
Old Jolyon
Orson
Orthros
Ouida
Owd Bob

Paddington
Pansy
Parker
Patrasche
Patter
Pecksniff
Penelope
Pepper
Pequod
Peter Pan
Pickles
Pilot
Pippi
Pirate
Pittypat
Poet
Poiret
Poky
Pooh
Porthos
Postboy
President
Prince Terrien
Pugnax
Punch
Pym
Queen Adora
Queenie
Queequeg
Quicksilver
Rab
Raksha
Ralph
Ranger

Rann
Ravisher
Rex
Rhett
Ribsy
Roald
Rontu
Rover
Roy
Rudyard
Ruffle
Rufus
Ruggles
Ryl
Saga
Sam Spade
Sammy
Samur
Sanders
Sandy
Santa Paws
Savage Sam
Sawyer
Scarlett
Scout
Scruffy
Scupper
Sea Catch
Sea Cow
Sea Vitch
Searchlight
Septimus
Seuss
Shangri-la

Shaw
Shere Khan
Sherlock
Shiloh
Sidney
Silver Blaze
Sinclair
Skip
Skylar
Smith
Smither
Snitter
Snowy
Soames
Specs
Spenser
Studs
Stumpy
Swithin
Sylax
Tabaqui
Tailless Tyke
Talbot
Tam-o'Shanter
Tapster
Tara
Tarzan
Tennyson
Terhune
Towzer
Tray
Treve
Trezorka
Tricki Woo

Trixie
Trout
Trowneer
Tuck
Tulgey
Tulip
Turnip
Twain
Val
Valetka
Vanity
Vixen
Voltaire
Wabe
Waldo
Wart
Wat
Watson
Wednesday
Weenie
Wellington
Wharton
What-a-mess
Wheely
White Fang
Wiggins
Wild Dog
Willoughby
Winks
Wistful
Woggs
Woogle
Wordsworth
Yankee

Yeats
Yellow Dog Dingo
Yukon
Zane
Zelda
Zhucka

CHARLES DICKENS
Aged P
Arabella
Artful Dodger
Avenger
Bachelor
Bagman
Bagstock
Barkis
Biddy
Clickett
Copperfield
Cratchit
Crimple
Crisparkle
Crummles
Dickens
Diogenes
Dodger
Dombey
Fagin
Fezziwig
Jaggers
Jingle
Jip
Lion
Magwitch

Micawber

Mr. Jaggers

Mrs. Joe

Nelly

Nickleby

Peggotty

Pelleas

Pickwick

Pip

Pocket

Pumplechook

Trotter

Tupman

Uriah

Winkle

Wopsle

HARRY POTTER

Aberforth

Albus

Animagus

Barty

Bellatrix

Berry

Cho Chang

Dobby

Draco Malfoy

Emma

Filius

Fluffy

Granger

Gryffindor

Hogwarts

Horton

Hufflepuff

Lucius

Mandrake

McGonagall

Neville

Padfoot

Pomona

Poppy

Quidditch

Radcliffe

Ravenclaw

Remus Lupin

Rita Skeeter

Ron

Rubeus Hagrid

Rupert

Sirius Black

Slytherin

Snape

Voldemort

OZ

Almira

Auntie Em

Bamboula

Bastinda

Bell-Snickle

Betsy Bobbin

Billina

Binx

Boglodore

Boq

Bungle

Button-Bright

Cap'n Bill

Cayke

Chalulu

Chang Wang Woe

Chiss

Colonel Crinkle

Coo-ee-oh

Diggs

Dorothy

Dr. Pipt

Eureka

Felina

Fess

Getsom

Gotsom

Gillikins

Guardian

Herby

Hickory

Hunk

Ippty

Jellia Jamb

Jenny Jump

Jinjur

Jinnicky

Kabumpo

Kalidah

Knooks

L. Frank Baum

Lollipop

Maribella

Mombi

Munchkin

Mustard

Nikko
Nimmie Amee
Ojo
Oz
Pastoria
Patchwork
Peggo
Pinny
Princess Ozma
Professor
Pudge
Rak
Rolly
Queen Lurlie
Scarecrow
Scraps
Shaggy Man
Skeezers
Snif
Tandy
Tatters
Tik-Tok
Tin Man
Tinker
Tip Topsy
Tollydiggle
Toto
Trot

Twiffle
Unc Nunkie
Uncle Henry
Vinegar
Waddle
Winkie
Woozy
Zeke
Zsuzsa

SHAKESPEARE

Ariel, Arielle
Bard
Celia
Desdemona
Gertrude
Hamlet
Juliet
Macbeth
Ophelia
Othello
Petruccio
Portia
Prospero
Romeo
Scrooge
Shakespeare
Shrew

Slammer
Snodgrass
Tempest
Trey

TOLKIEN

Aragorn
Arwen
Bilbo Baggins
Frodo Baggins
Galadriel
Gandalf
Garm
Gimli
Grip
Hobbit
Huan
Istari
Meriadoc
Morgorth
Peregrine
Pippin
Precious
Samwise
Sauron
Strider
Wizard
Wolf

THE ARTS

The names of some of the greatest artists in history are listed here.

**PAINTING,
SCULPTURE, AND
OTHER VISUAL ARTS**

Albrecht	Edouard	Mona Lisa
Alphonse	Edvard	Mondrian
Baroque	Fay Ray	Mr. Winkle
Battina	Fragonard	Myrtle and Lassie
Beardsley	Francisco	Pablo
Botticelli	Gainsborough	Picasso
Boucher	Georgia	Rembrandt
Chagall	Goya	Remington
Crooky	Joe	Renoir
Da Vinci	Joshua	Reynolds
Dali	Leonardo	Rubens
Degas	Man Ray	Toulouse
Durer	Mary Cassatt	Van Gogh
	Matisse	Warhol
	Michelangelo	Watteau
	Miro	

MUSIC

This was an enormously fun section to create and includes classical composers and singers in many styles—blues, soul, pop, jazz, swing.

Nat "King" Cole	Bing	Carol
Aida	Bizet	Cello
Allegro	Blue	Chopin
Anthem	Bolero	Clearwater
Arrow	Bono	Clementine
Bach	Bossa Nova	Crosby
Bali	Brava	Dancer
Banjo	Cadence	Diva
Beethoven	Calloway	Dizzie
Billie	Carmen	Domino

Don Giovanni	Laurie	Presley
Drummer	Layla	Rattle
Duet	Lead Belly	Reba
Ella	Lightnin'	Rhapsody
Etta	Ma	Rosa
Fandango	Maestro	Rosemary
Figaro	Magic	Rumba
Fionoula	Mazurka	Sabrina
Gershwin	Melody	Satchmo
Goethe	Mikado	Shubert
Handel	Minstrel	Sinatra
Harmonica	Mozart	Sinfonia
Howlin' Wolf	Muddy	Singer
Hugh	Music	Sonata
Irving	Nipper	T-Bone
Jazz	Ozzy	Troika
Jean	Pavarotti	Verdi
Jelly Roll	Pavlova	Wagner
Jimi	Peetie	Xavier
Kingston	Polonaise	Zappa
Lady Gaga	Pops	Ziggy

HOLLYWOOD

Although this section is called "Hollywood," you'll find quite a variety of names—of actors and characters from films and television shows made in Hollywood but also many made elsewhere, such as England's *Downton Abbey*. You'll also find names from comics, such as *Peanuts*.

Ace	Asta	Barbara Ann
Addison	Attila	Barfy
Afghan Hound	Augie Dog	Barkerville
Agent 11	Aussie	Barkley
Alex	B. Dawg	Barney
Alfie	Baby Cinnamon	Baron
Almira	Baby Face Nelson	Barrymore
Amtrak	Babycakes	Bart
Animal	Bailey	Bascom
Annabelle	Bam Bam	Basil
Arabesque	Bambi	Batman
Argus	Banks	BB

AUSTRALIAN SHEPHERD PUPPY

B-Dawg
Beasley
Beejay
Belvedere
Ben
Benji
Benny
Bert
Bess
Betsey
Betty
Biff Barker
Big Bird
Big Mo
Bill
Bitzer
BJ
Black Bob
Black Tooth
Blacktoe
Blair
Blinky
Bluto
Bob Dog
Bodger
Bogart
Bogie
Bojangles
Bolivar
Bolt
Bonnie
Boomer
Brain
Brando
Brandy

Breezy
Brenda Starr
Brian Griffin
Bronson
Bruiser
Bruno
Buckles
Buckley
Buckshot
Bugs Bunny
Bull
Bullet
Bullwinkle
Burton
Butch
Butler
C.J.
Cagney
Cain
Cairo
Captain Woof
Carface Carruthers
Carson
Casino
Casper
Ceelo Vicious
Chance
Channing
Chaplin
Charade
Charkie
Charlene
Charlie
Charlie Brown
Charlie Dog

Charming
Chasen
Chauncey
Chayka
Cherokee
Cherry
Chewbacca
Chief
Child
Chloe
Cho Cho
Chopper
Chu Chin Chow
Chucho
Chundo
Clarence
Claude
Clifford
Coco
Colleen
Confusion
Cookie
Cooler
Copper
Cora
Corky
Corneil
Costello
Courage
Cranky
Crawley
Cubby
Cubitus
Cynthia
D.J.

Dachsie

Daffy Duck

Dagwood

Darin

Darth Vader

Data

Dawg the Dog

De-Dop-De-Diddly-
   Dog-Bop

Delgado

Delta

Demon

Deputy

Destry

Devil

Dewey

Dickey

Dietrich

Digby

Diggs

Dillinger

Dimples

Dippy Dog

Dipstick

Disney

Dixie-Doo

Dog

Dogbert

Doggie Daddy

Dogmatix

Dogtanian

Dolly Martin

Donald Duck

Dooley

Doonesbury

Doonie

Dougal

Downton

Dr. Doppler

Dr. Strangelove

Dr. Teeth

Dr. Who

Dreyfus

Droopy

Dug

Dukey

Duran

Durante

Duvall

E.T.

Earnest

Edna

Ein

El Diablo

Electra

Elizabeth Taylor

Elmer

Elsa

Elsie

Epcot

Ernie

Errol

Esmeralda

Ewok

Ex

Ezel

Fairbanks

Falcor

Fanny

Fantasia

Faro

Fatima

Fellowes

Fidget

Fifi

Firth

Flealick

Flo

Florenz

Fogey

Fontaine

Fonzie

Fozzie

Frank Sinatra

Frank the Pug

Fred

Freeway

Friday

Froofie

Fu-Fu

Fuzz

Garbo

Garcia

George

Gidget

Gilligan

Gnasher

Gnipper

Go Go Girl

Goddard

Goliath

Gonzo

Goofy

Grantham

Greer

Grifter	Ivy	Little Man
Gromit	January	Lola
Groucho	Jedi	Lolly
Grover	Jeep-Jeep	London
Haley	Jerry Lee	Lou
Ham	Jezebel	Luca
Happy	Jiggy	Lucky and Flo
Harlow	Jiminy	Luis
Harpo	Jinxy	Luke and Duke
Harrod	Johnny	Luther
Harvey	Jones	Ma Barker
Hawkeye	Junkyard	Madison
Hector	K-9	Maggie
Hepburn	Kelly	Maisie
Hercules	Kent	Mandy
Higgins	Kermit	Manfred
Hobbes	Kibbee	Margaret
Holden	Kipper	Marmaduke
Hondo	Kiva	Martha
Honey Tree Evil Eye	Kyle	Matzoball
Hong Kong Phooey	Kyte	Maui
Hooch	Lady Edith	Max Goof
Hotdog	Lady Mary	McBarker
Hotel for Dogs	Lady Sybil	McGruff
Howler	Ladybird	Melanie
Hubble	Lamb Chop	Meryl
Huckleberry Hound	Laurel and Hardy	Mia
Hudson	Lawless	Mickey
Hush Puppy	Lenny	Mignon
Indiana	Lifesaver	Miniver
Indo	Lilac	Minnie
Iron Will	Lili Marleen	Minus
Isabel	Lillipop Kid	Miranda
Isobel	Lionel	Miss Ladyship
Itchy	Little Brother	Miss Piggy

Missis

Missy

Mister

Monte

Montgomery

Moonie

Moose

Moses

Mother Teresa

Mr. Beefy

Mr. Bones

Mr. Magoo

Mr. Peabody

Mr. Smith

Mr. Weenie

Mr. Whiskers

Mudbud

Mushroom

Muttley

Myrna

Nanook

Napoleon

Neal

Nevins

Nevins

New Baby

Nigel

Nikki

Nugent

Nunzio

Odie

Old Jack

Old Yeller

Olive Oyl

Olivier

Oscar

Otis

Otto

Pal

Papi

Pard

Patch

Peanuts

Pebbles

Pedro

Peewee

Peg

Pencil

Penny Dog

Percy

Perdita

Petals

Pete the Pup

Petra

Petula

Pickford

Pidgeon

Piggy

Pluto

Pogo

Policeman

Pongo

Pootzy

Popeye

Preston

Pretty Box

Pudgy

Pup

Pussy Galore

Quigley

Quint

Rafa

Randal

Rattler

Ravenwood

Rawhide

Rebecca

Reckless

Reddy

Reflex

Rene

Rhonda

Riff

Rin Tin Tin

Roberto

Rochester

Rocky

Roger

Ronnie

Roobarb

Rooney

Rose Marie, Rosie

Rosebud

Rowlf

Ruff

Sabu

Sallah

Sam

Sam Sheepdog

Samantha

Satipo

Scamp

Scamper

Scooby-Doo

Scooter

Scud
Sebastian
Sgt. Tibbs
Shadow
Shaggy
Shelby
Shep
Shoestring
Short Round
Shug
Skippy
Skywalker
Slim
Slinky
Sniff
Snippy
Snoopy
Snow White
Snuggles

Soccer
Sophie
Spanky
Sparky
Speck
Spike
Spotty
Spud
Spunky
Star
Statler (and Waldorf)
Storyteller
Strongheart
Sugar
Suger-Pie
Sui
Superman
Sure Grip's Rattler
Swee' Pea

Sweet Polly Purebred
Sweetheart
Sweets
Sykes
Tallulah
Tango
Tank
Tatty
Taz
Teddy
Tennsy
Topper
Toughy
Tracy
Tramp
Tripod
Trusty
Tucker
Two-Tone

COCKER SPANIEL PUPPY

Uggie
Uncle J.R.
Underdog
Verdell
Violet
Vivien
Wally
Whiskers
Whistler
Whooper
Wilby

Wimpy
Winn-Dixie
Wishbone
Wizzer
Woodstock
Woody
Xena
Yahooey
Yellow Dog
Yoda
Yodel

Yukon King
Yvonne
Zachary
ZaSu
Zero
Zimbo
Zip
Zorro
Zsa Zsa

SPORTS

Baseball, Olympic, and other sports legends are listed in this section.

Akinori	Ecaterina	Jeno
Al	Einar	Jesse
Aladár	Elena	Joe Willie
Alberto	Emil	Johann
Alexei	Eric	Jon
Alsgaard	Ermakova	Joseph, Joe
Andre	Evelyn	Katarina
Andretti	Fu	Kathrin
Babe	Galina	Kato
Barbel	Gambler	Katrin
Bass	Gehrig	Kevin
Beamer	Georgeta	Kjetil
Birdshot	Gert	Knave
Bjorn	Gillis	Kornelia
Bungey	Gipper	Kosuke
Button	Gunde	Kristi
Caliber	Gyozo	Kristin
Champ	Hamill	Larisa
Checkmate	Hannes	Leontien
Chess	Heiss	Lewis
Chun	Henri	Li
Clas	Herma	Lidia
Claudia	Hubert	Lucien
Cricket	Ian	Ludger
Dawn	Inge	Ludmilla
Dempsey	Irina	Lyubov
Deng	Ivar	Matt
Deuce	Jager	Matti
Dice	Janet	Mel
Dillard	Janica	Michael
Doina	Jean-Claude	Michele

Mitsuo	Polo	Tamas
Moseley	Popov	Tenley
Mungee	Pulu, Puli	Teresa
Naber	Ramon	Toro
Namath	Ray	Ty
Nedo	Red Sox	Ulrich
Nicole	Reiner	Valentino
Nikolai	Robinson	Venus
Ole	Rodeo	Vera
Olsen	Salnikov	Viktor
Olympia	Shatraj	Ville
Paavo	Sixten	Vitaly
Parcheesi	Sonja	Wang
Peggy	Stanislav	Wildfire
Phelps	Striker	Willis
Philidor	Sven	Yevgeny
Picabo	Swat	Yogi
Pinsent	Tag	Zhang
Polina	Takashi	

THE NATURAL WORLD

These names are derived from nature, to include flowers, trees, and natural phenomena, from geography and—such fun!—to do with food and drink.

Abelie	Bayou	Carnation
Acacia	Beachcomber	Carob
Agaric	Beans	Carrot
Aldrovanus	Bear	Caviar
Alfalfa	Bedouin	Cayenne
Alpine	Begonia	Celeste
Alps	Beluga	Celstina
Amaranth	Bittersweet	Chamois
Amaryllis	Black Pearl	Cheetah
Amber	Blossom	Chestnut
Amethyst	Bluebell	Chiclet
Anemone	Bongo	Chicory
Anise	Bonsai	Chili
Apple	Bouquet	Chipmunk
Apricot	Bracken	Christmas (Rose)
Arbutus	Braeburn	Citron
Artemis	Brink	Citrus
Arthur	Bron	Clove
Ash	Bronco	Clover
Aspen	Bunny	Coconut
Aster	Butterfly	Comet
Autumn	Cajun	Condor
Ava	Caladium	Coors
Avalanche	Camelia	Cornflake
Azalea	Canis Major	Cornflower
Balm	Canis Minor	Cornsilk
Balsam	Capers	Crane
Barbarian	Capricorn	Crème
Barbary	Caraway	Crescent

Cress
Curry
Daffodil
Dahlia
Daiquri
Daisy
Dandelion
Day-Lily
Delphinium
Denim
Dewdrop
Diamond
Dogwood
Duckling
Eagle
Echo
Eclipse
Edelweiss
Eglantine
Endine
Eucalyptus
Euphorbia
Everlasting
Fauna
Fennel
Fern
Filbert
Flax
Florabelle
Forget-Me-Not
Forsythia
Fuchsia
Gardenia
Geranium
Gerbera

Gladiolus
Gloxinia
Goldenrod
Grace
Gracie
Hawk
Hazel
Heliotrope
Hibiscus
Hollyhock
Honeyflower
Honeysuckle
Hyacinth
Hydrangea
Ipomoea
Iris
Japonica
Jasmine
Jewel
Jonquil
Juniper
Ladybug
Lantana
Larkspur
Laurel
Lavender
Lemon Blossom
Lightning
Lily
Linneaus
Lotus
Magnolia
Mako
Mallow
Mango

Maple
Maraschino
Marjoram
Marlin
Mimosa
Monkey
Moonbeam
Moonlight
Moonshadow
Mugwort
Mulberry
Narcissus
Nasturtium
Needles
Nighthawk
Nightingale
Nightshade
Nosegay
Oak
Oleander
Opal
Orchid
Osmunda
Panda
Partridge
Pearl
Periwinkle
Petunia
Phlox
Pliny
Pound Puppies
Precious Baby
Primrose
Prunella
Pua

Puddles	Sprout	Talon
Rain	Squash	Terry
Rainbow	Storm	Tornado
Rhinestone	Strelitzia	Trillium
Rhododendron	Summer	Tumbleweed
Rosabella	Sunbeam	Twilight
Saffron	Sundown	Typhoon
Sandstorm	Sunflower	Vernon
Saphira	Sunrise	Veronica
Savannah	Sunset	Violet
Shambala	Sunshine	Winter
Siouxsie	Swan	Wisteria
Slipper	Sweet Pea	Zahur
Snapdragon	Sweet William	Zinnia
Snowdrop	Tadpole	

SCIENCE, MATH, COMPUTERS, AND ASTROLOGY
Some of the stories behind these names will amaze you!

Ada	Backslash	Galileo
Addie	Bars	Halo
Albert	Carbon	Kilo
Albina	Chet	Kilogram
Alchemy	Cipher	Madame Curie
Alen	Copernicus	May, Mae
Algebra	Count	Minor
Ambriel	Cousteau	Mystic
April	Cuvier	NASA
Aquarius	Cyber	Neon
Archimedes	Cyclone	Newton
Aries	Darwin	Nitro
Arum	Dynamite	Nobel
Astra, Astro	Edison	Nova
Atom	Einstein	Pasteur
August	Freud	Pisces

Pixel

Pulsar

Radar

Scorpio

Spark

Taurus

Zodiac

GEOGRAPHY

Acadia

Acapulco

Aegean

Africa

Alashak

Alaska

Albania

Alyeska

Amazon

America

Anatolia

Andalusia

Apache

Apogee

Arapaho

Arctic

Arizona

Aruba

Asia

Astoria

Austin

Aztec

Bahama

Balaclava

Balkan

Barrin

Beijing

Bengal

Bermuda

Bohemia

Brassy

Broadway

Brooklyn

Budapest

Burma

Calais

California

Carolina

Casbah

Catalina

Changbai

Cheyenne

China

Cholula

Cola

Congo

Crocus

Cruncher

Cypress

Dallas

Dalmatia

Danube

Denver

Desert

Dixie

Durango

Durban

Eskimo

Euphrates

Fargo

Fenway

Formosa

Forrest

Frontier

Gotthard

Havana

Inca

Jamaica

Jericho

Kashmir

Katmandu

Malibu

Mississippi

Mohave

Mont Blanc

Montezuma

Morocco

Nairobi

Napa

Navajo

Nome

Outback

Padua

Panama

Paris

Persia

Rhodes

Sahara

Sand Dune

Sarasota

Siberia

Sonoma

Stream

Tahoe

Tejas

Terra

Vesuvius
Vienna
Yuma

FOOD AND DRINK
Chardonnay
Cheddar
Cheesecake
Chutney
Cocopuff
Confection
Crackers
Cream
Crisco
Croissant
Crouton
Crumb
Crumpet
Cupcake
Doughnut

Drambuie
Dumpling
Enchilada
Fajita
Falafel
Fudge
Garlic
Gazpacho
Gingersnap
Honey
Java
Julia
Kahlua
Kibble
Kirsch
Kiwi
Korbel
Mai Tai
Marmalade
Marshmallow

Martini
Marzipan
Mocha
Muffin
Omelette
Oreo
Panini
Parsley
Peaches
Peppermint
Pinot Grigio
Plum Pudding
Pretzel
Pudding
Raisin
Sauerbraten
Sauerkraut
Schnapps
Schnitzel
Shiitake

PUG PUPPY

Spice

Stilton

Strudel

Sundae

Sushi

Tarragon

Tequila

Tidbit

Vanilla

Verbena

Vinegar

Vodka

Wafer

Waffles

Whiskey

Yummy

AFTERWORD

Before you bring a dog home, you need to do some serious thinking.

FIRST, EVALUATE WHERE YOU LIVE

Can your home accommodate a dog? It's not necessarily how *much* space you have but whether your living space—indoors and outdoors—can meet the needs of a dog. If you live in an apartment, is there a park nearby? Are you willing to clean up after your dog on streets and in public places?

IF THE BREED FITS, WEAR IT

Which breed suits your lifestyle? If you live in a studio apartment, owning a Saint Bernard would be a tight fit. A dog that's bred to run, such as a Saluki, has running in his blood and needs to be able to do so every day; confining him to a small space verges on cruelty. Even terriers, which were bred to kill rats, are genetically engineered to hunt. So many times you hear of a family that has given their Jack Russell Terrier up for adoption because the dog was biting—but that's exactly what the dog was bred to do. First, you must learn about the breed you are considering and understand its traits and temperament—*then* determine whether its disposition and nature corresponds with your lifestyle.

TIME IS OF THE ESSENCE

Does your work schedule and daily routine allow you to give your surplus time freely to a dog? Do you have the time and patience to devote to a dog that has been waiting for you all day long, when you come home exhausted after work? If you travel a great deal, is that really fair to a dog? Are you ready to deal with a commitment that will last the lifetime of your dog?

DAY CARE FOR YOUR DOG

. . . is a desirable but costly solution for people who work. Can you afford it? If not, what are your options? This is a critical question for people who work or are regularly out of the house for long stretches of time. Look for a good pet day care facility that's clean, bright, cheerful, and well-staffed. A dog sitter is another option. At the very least, someone needs to reliably come into your home to take your dog out for a walk at least once every four to six hours—and that's for a healthy, grown dog. A puppy or elderly dog will require more attention.

CREATING A DOG-FRIENDLY ENVIRONMENT

If you have a yard, look into building an outdoor, all-weather kennel and good perimeter fencing. Indoors, your dog must have his own crate. Dogs are pack animals. From the beginning of time, a dog's den has been his shelter and safe haven. The same holds true today. A crate that is big enough to allow him to move around, has plenty of ventilation, is easily cleaned, and is equipped with a dog blanket or rug for him to comfortably lie upon, is essential. Also, there should be a water dish, preferably attached to the grill of the crate, so that he's always got water. Never keep the crate in the sun, or a room that is too hot or too cold. If it's hot, be sure there's a fan blowing into the crate.

WHO ELSE WILL LIVE WITH YOUR DOG?

Make sure your family is on the same page as you about welcoming a puppy or new dog into the household. What do you do if your small child is frightened of dogs? How do you teach her to handle a puppy? What if your spouse has allergies? If an older person is living with you, how do you ensure he will not get knocked down or fall over an energetic puppy? You wouldn't bring a child into the family without consulting your spouse, partner or children—the same holds true for a puppy or new dog.

HOW DO YOU DEAL WITH YOUR OLD DOG WHEN YOU BRING A NEW ONE HOME?

Adding another dog to the family may not be as easy as you think. Your old dog has long staked his claim—this, after all, is *his* house—and he may not welcome an "intruder." Two males (neither of which are neutered), two alpha females, or a breed that does not favor canine company can spell t-r-o-u-b-l-e. On the other hand, a new puppy or an adopted dog may delight an older dog, fulfill the maternal instincts of a spayed female, and happily add to the household. Consult with your veterinarian before making this important decision.

COHABITATING WITH PETS OF A DIFFERENT ILK

Cats and dogs are notorious for not getting along, but more often than not, they can adapt to sharing the same house. Each may stake claim to his "territory," and there may be a scuffle to establish dominance. Whether or not this can work is a decision only you can make, depending on the personalities of your particular pets.

NOTHING IN LIFE IS FREE

The cost of keeping a puppy is not something you pay for with spare change. The cost of a puppy purchased from a reputable breeder is a significant expense; then there are the veterinary bills for healthy dog care (let alone a dog that becomes ill), dog food, day care, and if you go away, a boarding kennel. Think carefully when choosing a dog; remember, a Chihuahua eats less than a St. Bernard and requires a smaller kennel. It all adds up.

PICKING A BREEDER

All right. You've decided that a dog will indeed fit into your life. You've chosen a breed. Now you're ready to embark upon the next, all-important step: finding the right breeder. How do you find a reputable breeder? What questions should you be prepared to ask a breeder? How do you read a dog's pedigree? A great first step is to visit www.akc.org, the comprehensive website of the American Kennel Club, where you'll find all kinds of helpful information—and answers to many of your questions.

CHOOSING A PUPPY

Now it's time to choose your puppy. Many people will tell you that their puppy chose them. Is he the one that trotted across the whelping box to lick your hand or the one that fell asleep in your arms? And if you decide to adopt a rescue dog or a dog from a shelter, spend time with the dog. Believe me, you'll know if he's the one for you—because *he'll* let *you* know that you're the one for him.

COMMUNICATING WITH YOUR DOG

The sound of your voice . . . the touch of your hand . . . The way you communicate with your dog begins the moment you lock eyes for the first time. How you forge your relationship with your dog depends entirely upon how well you communicate with him. Teaching your dog to come to his name is only the first step in building language and understanding that deepens over a lifetime. That's why it's so important to choose the right name. As the ancient knight that protected the Holy Grail said to Indy in *Indiana Jones and the Last Crusade*, "Choose—but choose wisely."

Once you've given your dog his name, you've recognized that he's yours and he'll soon recognize his name. Then one day, in the not-very-distant future, you'll look into his eyes and find yourself amazed at how much he seems to love and understand you, and you'll think, "Why, he's almost human." But your dog, having loved you from the moment he set eyes on you, has always considered you almost canine.

Inscribe his name on his dog tag, his bowl, or his collar—go ahead. But know that once you have given your dog his name, it will be inscribed forevermore on your heart.

PHOTO CREDITS

5 German Shepherd mother and her puppy

28 Australian Shepherd puppy

74 Papillon mother and her puppy

101 Black Labrador Retriever and her litter

146 Corgi puppy

171 English Setter puppies

187 Belgian Sheepdog puppy

216 Cocker Spaniel puppy

279 Two Labrador Retrievers enjoying the outdoors

300 Yorkshire Terrier mother and puppy

356 Golden Retriever puppy

372 Shih Tzu puppy

407 Pug puppy

433 Toy Fox Terrier puppy

440 Shetland Sheepdog puppy

446 Collie puppy

454 English Toy Spaniel puppy

461 German Wirehaired Pointer puppy

469 Australian Shepherd puppy

474 Cocker Spaniel puppy

482 Pug puppy

Photographs Collection of the Author

40 Basil Rathbone

73 Anita Page (from the private collection of Randal Malone)

92 Carole Lombard

239 Elizabeth Taylor (Warner Bros. Studio)

259 Margaret O'Brien (Courtesy of Miss Margaret O'Brien)

324 Captain Smith (Cunard White Star Line)

325 Randal Malone and his dogs (Michael Schwibs)